Oton de Granson

POEMS

The Middle English Texts Series is designed for classroom use. Its goal is to make available to teachers, scholars, and students texts that occupy an important place in the literary and cultural canon but have not been readily available in student editions. The series does not include those authors, such as Chaucer, Langland, or Malory, whose English works are normally in print in good student editions. The focus is, instead, upon Middle English literature adjacent to those authors that teachers need in compiling the syllabuses they wish to teach. The editions maintain the linguistic integrity of the original work but within the parameters of modern reading conventions. The texts are printed in the modern alphabet and follow the practices of modern capitalization, word formation, and punctuation. Manuscript abbreviations are silently expanded, and *u/v* and *j/i* spellings are regularized according to modern orthography. Yogh (ȝ) is transcribed as *g*, *gh*, *y*, or *s*, according to the sound in Modern English spelling to which it corresponds; thorn (þ) and eth (ð) are transcribed as *th*. Distinction between the second person pronoun and the definite article is made by spelling the one *thee* and the other *the*, and final *-e* that receives full syllabic value is accented (e.g., *charitê*). Hard words, difficult phrases, and unusual idioms are glossed either in the right margin or at the foot of the page. Explanatory and textual notes appear at the end of the text, often along with a glossary. The editions include short introductions on the history of the work, its merits and points of topical interest, and brief working bibliographies.

This series is published in association with the University of Rochester.

Medieval Institute Publications is a program of
The Medieval Institute, College of Arts and Sciences

Western Michigan University

Oton de Granson

POEMS

Edited and Translated by

Peter Nicholson and Joan Grenier-Winther

TEAMS • Middle English Texts Series

MEDIEVAL INSTITUTE PUBLICATIONS

Western Michigan University

Kalamazoo

Manufactured in the United States of America

This book is printed on acid-free paper.

Library of Congress Cataloging-in-Publication Data

Granson, Oton de, -1397.
[Poems. English]
Oton de Granson : poems / edited and translated by Peter Nicholson and Joan Grenier-Winther.
pages cm. – (Middle English texts series)
Includes bibliographical references and index.
ISBN 978-1-58044-206-0 (paperbound : alk. paper)
I. Nicholson, Peter, 1948- editor. II. Grenier-Winther, Joan, editor. III. Title.
PQ1476.G4A3 2015
841'.1–dc23

2014046882

ISBN 978-1-58044-206-0

P 5 4 3 2 1

Contents

ACKNOWLEDGMENTS

Our greatest debt is to Russell A. Peck, who first proposed this edition, whose vision gave it its present form, and who patiently oversaw its execution. We also wish to thank all those who worked on its production: at METS, Assistant Editor Martha M. Johnson-Olin and Staff Editors Jenny Boyar, Laura Whitebell, Alison Harper, and Pamela M. Yee; and at Medieval Institute Publications, Patricia Hollahan, Tom Krol, and their staff. We are also grateful to the National Endowment of the Humanities for its support of the series in which this volume appears; and the Bibliothèque cantonale et universitaire in Lausanne, the Bibliothèque nationale in Paris, and the Van Pelt Library at the University of Pennsylvania, and others (see p. 40) for the privilege of consulting their manuscripts.

Introduction

Life and Reputation

Oton de Granson, knight, diplomat, and poet, lived an active, almost storybook life at or near the center of many of the most important events in the last half of the fourteenth century.[1] Born to the highest nobility in his native Savoy, he was well known in the courts of both France and England, and he spent the better part of his career in the service of the English king. He was also well known to the major poets of his time on both sides of the channel, at least two of whom, Eustache Deschamps and Geoffrey Chaucer, were almost certainly his personal friends. At a time when nobles aspired to be cultured and poets sought the company of nobles,[2] he was among the first and most successful of the poets who were also courtiers; and as one who moved in both a French-speaking and an English-speaking world, he occupies a unique place in the literary culture of his time.

Granson was born sometime in the mid 1340s; we infer the date from his first appearance in the official record, with his engagement and marriage in 1365.[3] The town from which his family takes its name is on the shore of Lake Neuchâtel, in the northwest corner of the Vaud, in modern Switzerland, which during his lifetime was part of the County of Savoy. As a young nobleman, he would have spent time in the court of Amadeus VI, Count of Savoy (1334–83), and there he may have received his first apprenticeship as poet. Amadeus was a patron of the arts, and in 1368 he is known to have purchased a manuscript

[1] His name appears in a bewildering variety of forms in the surviving documents. For his personal name, one finds *Oton, Othon, Ode, Othe, Otz, Otte, Hoton, Otonin, Othoz, Octe, Octhe, Ottho*, plus others that we probably missed; and for his family name, *Granson, Gransson, Grandson, Granzon, Granczon, Grantson, Grançon, Graunson, Garanson*, and *Garenson*. One must make a choice. *Oton* is the simplest form that preserves the distinctive *n*, and it is almost universally established in modern usage. *Grandson*, common in the historical records, is also the modern spelling of the city from which his family takes its name, but it has a distracting homograph for English readers. *Graunson*, on the other hand, while it still occurs in scholarly writing in English, is found only in Middle English sources and was probably never used by the poet himself. In the manuscripts in which his poems appear, the two spellings that appear almost exclusively are *Granson* and *Gransson*, and between these, the shorter has become more common.

[2] See, among others, Poirion's chapter on "amateurs, artistes et serviteurs" [connoisseurs, artists and servants] in *Poète et prince*, pp. 145–90. Complete information on the secondary sources and on editions of the primary sources that we cite will be found in the Bibliography.

[3] The most complete and most fully documented account of Granson's life is still that provided by Piaget in Grandson, *Vie et poésies*, ed. Piaget, pp. 11–104, on which much of the following summary is based. For Granson's final years, the best source is Berguerand, *Duel*. See also Braddy, *Chaucer and Graunson*, pp. 22–37; his earlier "Messire Oton de Graunson," pp. 515–31; and Chaubet, "Duel."

of the works of Machaut,[4] who exercised a dominating influence on Granson and all other poets of his generation. No surviving work can be attributed to Granson at so early a date, however, and virtually all of the early records of his life concern his military career instead. In 1368, he was captured and released during an episode in the border dispute between Savoy and Burgundy. The next time we hear of him, he is in England, where members of his family, along with many other Savoyards, had been established at least since the time of Edward I.[5] In 1372, Froissart places him in the company of the Earl of Pembroke in a naval battle against the Spanish at La Rochelle, in which the English were defeated.[6] Granson, together with Pembroke and others, was captured, and he spent two years in a Spanish prison before being ransomed, probably by Edward III, in 1374. Later in 1374, he entered the service of John of Gaunt, Duke of Lancaster, where, though he was of much higher rank, he might first have crossed paths with Chaucer, who was granted an annuity for his and his wife's service to the Duke in the same year.[7]

In 1376 he was back in Savoy, in Neuchâtel, in the company of the Countess Isabel, and he may have remained there until 1378.[8] In the years that followed he seems to have traveled back and forth between Savoy and England several times. Froissart mentions him in the list of those sent to Cherbourg with the English garrison in 1379,[9] but in 1382 he appears with the Countess Isabel again;[10] and in 1384 he was with the English forces in Calais, where Deschamps encountered him in an incident recorded in one of his ballades.[11] Then in 1386, upon the death of his father, Granson returned to Savoy to claim his inheritance and to enter the service of Count Amadeus VII, and surviving documents from the period that follows record both his service to the count and his engagement in a longstanding dispute over property that he had acquired with his marriage.[12]

In 1391, Amadeus VII died, apparently of a tetanus infection that resulted from an injury sustained in a fall from a horse. The count himself believed that he had been poisoned, and within a short time, the treating doctor, an apothecary, the count's mother, and Granson, who was not even present at the onset of the count's illness, all became implicated in his death. The events that followed were driven by old grudges, by a tug-of-war between the count's mother and his widow (each with her powerful protectors) over the

[4] See Earp, *Guillaume de Machaut*, pp. 43, 46, and 97.

[5] Kingsford, "Otho de Grandison," pp. 125–95; also Braddy, *Chaucer*, pp. 23, 38–40.

[6] Froissart, *Œuvres*, 8:121, 123, 128. We wish to express our appreciation to Lianne Ho Pang, Reference Services Librarian at Northwest University, for her help in securing access to this edition.

[7] Crow and Olson, *Chaucer Life Records*, p. 271.

[8] See the document cited by Piaget in Grandson, *Vie et poésies*, ed. Piaget, p. 19n2.

[9] Froissart, *Œuvres*, 9:136.

[10] At our request, the staff of the Office des Archives de l'État de la République et Canton de Neuchâtel examined the document cited by Piaget in Grandson, *Vie et poésies*, ed. Piaget, p. 16n2, and determined that it dated from 1382. We wish to express our appreciation to M. Lionel Bartolini, Archiviste de l'État, for his gracious assistance.

[11] Deschamps, *Œuvres complètes*, 5:79–80, number DCCCXCIII. See Grandson, *Vie et poésies*, ed. Piaget, pp. 167–69; Braddy, *Chaucer and Graunson*, pp. 7–9; Laurie, "Amitiés métriques," pp. 124–27; and Butterfield, *Familiar Enemy*, pp.140–42.

[12] See Grandson, *Vie et poésies*, ed. Piaget, pp. 17–20; and Berguerand, *Duel*, pp. 9–14.

custody of his son and heir, and by the interests of those who had already tried to lay claim to Granson's property; and the case against the accused was fueled by confessions that were later revealed to be extracted under torture. The immediate consequence was that Granson took refuge, first in Burgundy and then in England. He entered the service of Richard II in 1392, and in 1392–93 he accompanied Henry, Earl of Derby, on his second expedition to Prussia and Palestine. Granson's properties in Savoy were confiscated and sold in 1393, but in 1395, the confessions that had implicated him having been repudiated, Charles VI of France intervened to proclaim Granson's innocence, and his properties were restored. Granson returned to Savoy to reclaim his heritage shortly thereafter, but the old accusations were renewed, and he was challenged to a duel by one of those who had profited from the confiscation. After two postponements, the duel took place on August 7, 1397, and Granson, who was almost certainly at least fifty at the time, was slain by his challenger.[13]

It is not surprising that the official records contain no mention of Granson as poet. (The same is true of Chaucer.) Even his fellow poets, however, at least in France, refer to him only as a gentleman and a soldier. Froissart describes him as a "bannerès et riche homme durement [a knight banneret and a very powerful man]" and as a "vaillant chevalier de Savoie [a worthy knight from Savoy],"[14] and Deschamps' ballade describes an encounter between men of arms, not poets. After his death, Christine de Pisan left him two tributes, in *Le Débat des deux amans* (lines 1615–18) and in *L'Epistre au Dieu d'Amours* (lines 233–44),[15] but she praises him only as a knight, "Courtois, gentil, preux, bel et gracieux [courteous, noble, valiant, handsome, and gracious]" (*Epistre*, line 235). The first reference to Granson as poet, and the only one from his own lifetime, comes from Chaucer, who adapted a sequence of Granson's ballades in his "Complaint of Venus" and acknowledges him in the final line as "Graunson, flour of hem that make in Fraunce [the flower of those that write poetry in France]."[16] The next reference comes from an unusual source: in 1401, Queen Isabel of France purchased two gold clasps for one of her books, entitled "Le Livre des ballades messire Othes de Grantson."[17] Following his death, Granson achieved somewhat greater recognition for his verse. Alain Chartier, in his *Debat de reveille matin* (c. 1420), cites Granson in the same line in which he mentions Machaut,[18] and Martin Le Franc, in his *Le champion des dames* (1441–42), refers his reader to the works of Granson for a better understanding of suffering in love.[19]

---

[13] On this period of Granson's life see Berguerand, *Duel*. Berguerand places the birth of Gérard d'Estavayer, Granson's adversary, in 1349 (p. 16), which would make him 48 at the time of the duel, younger than Granson, but not by very much.

[14] Froissart, *Œuvres*, 8:121, 9:136.

[15] Christine de Pisan, *Œuvres poétiques*, 2:8, 97.

[16] *Riverside Chaucer*, p. 649.

[17] Grandson, *Vie et poésies*, ed. Piaget, pp. 110–11.

[18] Chartier, *Poetical Works*, p. 314, line 231.

[19] Le Franc, *Champion des dames*, lines 14125–28.

Granson also acquired both a reputation and a following in Spain, among poets writing in both Castilian and Catalan.[20] By the middle of the fifteenth century, however, he seems largely to have passed from notice. One reason may be that, as an amateur, he did not take the care to preserve his works as the better known poets did. As we shall see, even the earliest manuscripts of his work still leave some doubt about which poems are really his, and in the few later manuscripts and in the early printed books in which his poems appear, they are intermingled with and often confused with the works of Alain Chartier.[21] In England, of course, by this time French poetry was no longer being read as it was before, when French was the language of the court. In France, too, however, new fashions prevailed. Granson's reputation and importance were restored only in modern times, primarily through the efforts of Arthur Piaget, culminating in his edition of 1941. Piaget's work has since been superseded by the critical edition of Joan Grenier-Winther, which contains the full scholarly apparatus that Piaget did not provide. Both editions are destined, of course, for readers of French. The time has come to close the circle, and to make Granson's poetry available again to English readers too.

ESTABLISHING THE CANON

Virtually all of our knowledge of Granson's writing comes from the surviving manuscripts of his work, and unfortunately, the record is simply not as good as it is for the better-known poets such as Machaut and Deschamps. No single manuscript contains all of the works that are now attributed to him. Only one manuscript (and it is neither among the earliest nor the largest) contains only works thought to be Granson's. Only two manuscripts that contain his poems might possibly date from his lifetime, but no poems in either manuscript are attributed to him (or to anyone else) by name. In fact, only a small number of poems (though this includes most of the longer ones) bear his name in any of the copies in which they appear. To complicate matters further, there are some obvious cases of false attribution that necessarily raise some question about the rest. Before we take a look at his verse, therefore, we have to spend some time considering how we know what is his, and that means taking a close look at the manuscripts to see what kind of evidence they offer for his authorship.[22]

There are two manuscripts on which most of our understanding of Granson's work is based:

MANUSCRIPT F: PARIS, BIBLIOTHÈQUE NATIONALE, FR. 2201. 134 leaves; French; early fifteenth century.[23] The contents are:

[20] Pagès, *Poésie française*, pp. 89–93, and "Thème de la tristesse," p. 29; Grandson, *Vie et poésies*, ed. Piaget, pp. 175–76; and Massó i Torrents, "Oto de Granson," pp. 403–10.

[21] See Grandson, *Vie et poésies*, ed. Piaget, pp. 119–26.

[22] For more complete descriptions of these manuscripts and their contents, see Grenier-Winther's edition, pp. 21–50 (whose sigla we have adopted here). See also Jung, "Répertoire," pp. 98–102, and the list of manuscripts, p. 40 below.

[23] Digital images of the entire manuscript are available at the Bibliothèque Nationale's Gallica website: http://gallica.bnf.fr.

1. *Les Cent Ballades*, a collection of poems from the last decade of the fourteenth century to which we will refer again, lacking two leaves at the end (the conclusion to the penultimate poem and all of the final one), fols. 1–70.
2. A collection of poems without title or heading, including several that bear Granson's name, fols. 71–104v.
3. "Le Lay des Dames" of Guillaume de Machaut ("Amis, t'amour me contraint"), fols. 105–09.[24]
4. *L'Histoire de Griselidis*, in prose, fols. 111–36.[25]

It is the second section of this manuscript that interests us the most. It contains thirty-seven poems: twenty-six ballades (including the "Balade de Saint Valentin double"),[26] one virelai, and two rondeaux,[27] plus eight longer poems.[28] Among the longer poems, three are ascribed to Granson, as follows. (Here and below, numbers in boldface italic refer to the poems in this edition, and numbers preceded by "GW" refer to the poems in Grenier-Winther's edition.)

(70) "La Complainte de l'an nouvel que gransson fost pour un chevalier quil escoutait complaindre"
(71) "Le souhait de saint valentin"
(72) "Complainte de saint valentin"
(74) "Le lay de desir en complainte"
(69) "Lestraine du jour de lan:
(74) "Complainte de gransson"
(73) "La pastourelle granson"
(77) (The last 49 lines only, without a title)

F is the manuscript by which Granson's works were first brought to modern attention by Arthur Piaget in 1890. Piaget argued that apart from two ballades more in the style of Deschamps, whose presence he could not explain (GW86 and GW87),[29] the general uniformity

[24] Machaut, *Poésies lyriques*, 2:352–61.

[25] This is the translation by Philippe de Mézières of Petrarch's Latin translation of the last tale in Boccaccio's *Decameron*. It is not the French version used by Chaucer in The Clerk's Tale. See Severs, *Literary Relationships*, pp. 21–25 and 181n4 (where Severs refers to this manuscript).

[26] The count of the number of poems can become confusing because of the *balade double*, which appears as one poem in manuscripts *F, K,* and *E* (and in Piaget's edition, pp. 256–58), and as two in *A* (so in this edition, numbers ***60*** and ***61***, and in Grenier-Winther's, GW24 and GW30). The first of the two ballades that make up the *balade double* also appears separately in manuscripts *G* and *V*.

[27] On these different types, see p. 15–20 of this Introduction, below.

[28] Jung has some brief comments on the organization of this section ("Répertoire," pp. 96–97). He finds less evidence of planning than in manuscript *A*; see note 31 below.

[29] Piaget, "Oton de Granson," p. 431, and also his edition, Grandson, *Vie et poésies*, ed. Piaget, pp. 169–70. In Deschamps' *Œuvres complètes*, the two ballades are found at 8:77–78 (number MCCCCXXIII) and 10:xxi (number XIV). As Jung notes ("Répertoire," p. 97), the first (GW87), which is found in the most authoritative manuscript of Deschamps' collected works (Paris, Bibliothèque Nationale, fr. 840, fols. 431r–431v), is most certainly his; the other (GW86), found only in a later manuscript (Paris, Bibliothèque Nationale, nouv. acq. fr. 6221, fol. 11r), is somewhat less certain. This

of contents in section two of the manuscript indicated a common authorship. Citing the three poems in which Granson is named plus five others that appear in *F* that are ascribed to Granson in other copies, he concluded that Granson was the author of all but the two anomalous ballades as well.[30]

MANUSCRIPT A: LAUSANNE, BIBLIOTHÈQUE CANTONALE ET UNIVERSITAIRE, MS 350. 181 leaves; French, second quarter of the fifteenth century. The contents are:

1. *Les Cent Ballades*, as above, fols. 1–82.
2. A lament on the death of Bonne d'Artois (who died in 1425), fols. 82v–83v.
3. A collection of poems headed "Balades Rondeaux Lais Virelais et autrez dis compilez par noble homme messire Ode de granson chevalier [Ballades, rondeaux, virelais, and other poems compiled by the nobleman Sir Oton de Granson, knight]" and ending "Cy fenist Granson [Here ends Granson]," fols. 84–151.
4. Three poems by Alain Chartier, fols. 152–80.

The third portion of this manuscript contains seventy-seven poems, including one duplicate.[31] The seventy-six separate pieces comprise of fifty-eight ballades, eight rondeaux, one virelai, and nine longer poems (including all eight that appear in whole or in part in *F*), two of which are ascribed to Granson, as follows:

(74) "Lay en complainte"
(72) untitled
(77) "Le songe saint valentin" (complete)
(71) "Souhait"
(73) "La pastourelle gransson"
(69) "Lestrainne de granson"
(75) "Le lay de desir en complainte"
(68) "Le dit de loiaute"
(70) "La complainte de lan nouvel"

In addition, the poet is named in the heading to two of the ballades, ***61*** "Balade granson" and ***41*** "Balade amoureuse granson" (GW31, the duplicate of GW2).

Though the differences both in the order of the poems and in the text (as illustrated by the titles cited above) indicate that there is no direct relationship between *F* and *A*, there is considerable overlap between them: twenty-five of the thirty-five poems in *F* (excluding the two anomalous ballades), or more than eighty per cent of the contents of *F* as measured in number of lines, also appear in *A*.[32] The discovery of this manuscript,[33] with its attribution to

manuscript includes works by Deschamps alongside some by other poets, but no other work known to be by Granson.

[30] Grandson, *Vie et poésies*, ed. Piaget, especially pp. 408, 439.

[31] For an analysis of the contents see Jung, "Répertoire," pp. 93–96. Jung finds some evidence of conscious organization, identifying six sections based on similarities of theme.

[32] One of the most intriguing puzzles in the relation between *F* and *A* is the fact that both begin with the *Cent Ballades*. This is surely a work that would have appealed to Granson, containing poems very much like his by his exact contemporaries, and while it is possible to imagine that he himself is

Granson, certainly seemed to confirm Piaget's conclusion about the authorship of the poems in *F* while it also added considerably to the canon, and in his 1941 edition, Piaget included all of the poems in the relevant sections of both.

As Piaget recognized, however, this section of *A* also contains works that are not Granson's, for among its fifty-eight ballades are ten by Guillaume de Machaut.[34] With regard to these poems at least, the *compilez* of the heading evidently has to be taken literally and not as an indication of authorship, which leaves room for some question about the many other unattributed poems that it contains. That it or its prototype was compiled from different sources is suggested by the presence of the duplicate of the second poem, which contains four slight variants in the text in addition to many orthographic differences. This poem is one of the "Cinq balades ensuivans [Sequence of five ballades]" that Chaucer attributes to Granson in his adaptation in "The Complaint of Venus"; the second version is also one of the poems ascribed to Granson in manuscript *A* by name, "Balade amoureuse Granson." Its authorship thus need not be in question, but if Granson himself were the "compiler," it seems a bit odd that he not have access to a good master copy, that he not recognize that he had already included the poem, and that he ascribe this poem and not any of its neighbors to himself by name. It is also worth noting that if we count the second copy of ***41*** rather than the first, the five ballades appear in the same order as in manuscript *F*, though not in an unbroken sequence, and without the title that they bear in *F*.

Setting aside, however, these mysteries over the origin of *A*, and discarding only the poems that we know to be Machaut's along with the two anomalies in *F*, we are left with a set of seventy-six poems (counting the *balade double* as two) that appear either in *F* or *A* or in both that constitute the core of what we now understand to be Granson's canon.

Three other manuscripts either offer some confirmation of these attributions or are important for the establishment of Granson's text.

MANUSCRIPT K: LAUSANNE, BIBLIOTHÈQUE CANTONALE ET UNIVERSITAIRE, IS 4254. 22 leaves; France, fifteenth century. This is the only surviving manuscript to contain only works thought to be Granson's. It contains six of the eight long poems that appear in both *A* and *F*, plus the "Balade de Saint Valentin double," five of which are ascribed to Granson by name, as follows:

---

responsible for the juxtaposition, it is also easy to think that it would have occurred to others too, and the appearance in both manuscripts might just as likely be a mere coincidence.

[33] Piaget had heard of its existence in 1890; see "Oton de Granson," p. 423 and 423n2. He himself purchased it in 1939 (Grandson, *Vie et poésies*, ed. Piaget, pp. 112–13).

[34] Piaget refers to only nine (Grandson, *Vie et poésies*, ed. Piaget, p. 139); he failed to recognize the ballade that he prints on p. 289 as a version of Machaut's "Hé! gentils cuers, me convient il morir" (*Poésies lyriques*, 1:51, number XXXVII; *Louange des dames*, p. 71, number 83). As Piaget notes (pp. 166–67), these ballades appear in all of the collected manuscripts of Machaut's works, which are believed to have been prepared, if not under the poet's direct supervision, then from an exemplar in his possession, and the earliest of which is dated 1350–56, when Granson (according to a reasonable guess of the date of his birth) was about ten years old. One of these, moreover, is incorporated into Machaut's *Livre dou voir dit*. See Earp, *Guillaume de Machaut*, p. 120 for a list of these ten poems; pp. 247–55 for the manuscripts in which these are contained; and pp. 77–97 for the dates of these manuscripts, particularly p. 78 for the date of manuscript *C*.

(70) "Cy commence la complainte de lan nouvel que granson fist pour un chevalier quil lescoutoit se plaindre pres dun bouquet"
(72) "Cy apres sensuit la complainte Saint Vallentin"
(75) "Le lay de desir en complainte granson"
(69) "Lestrainne du jour de lan granson"
(60–61) "Balade de saint valentin double"
(74) "Complainte de gransson
(73) "La pastourelle granson"

Though differences in the text indicate that neither could have been copied directly from the other, *F* and *K* are otherwise very similar textually, and the order in which these poems appear is the same in both manuscripts. The titles are also very similar, except that *K* adds the ascription to Granson of ***69*** as found in *A* and an ascription to Granson of ***75*** not found in either other copy.

MANUSCRIPT E: BARCELONA, BIBLIOTECA DE CATALUNYA, 8. 376 leaves, Catalan, 1420–30. This manuscript is the second volume of the "Cançoner Vega-Aguiló," a large miscellany containing mostly works in the Catalan language.[35] It also contains on fols. 408–35 a group of twenty-three poems in French, all in an orthography heavily influenced by Catalan.[36] Of these, twelve also appear in *F* or *A*. These include nine ballades (including the *balade double*, treated as one) and three longer poems. Of these twelve, the last six appear together, and each is attributed to Granson by name. These six include three ballades that are not ascribed to him in any other copy (***56***, ***59***, and ***60***). The other three are the three longer poems. Two of these bear titles: ***74*** "Congié que prist Micer Otto de Granson de sa dame [The leave that Sir Oton de Granson's took of his lady]," and ***73*** "La vergiera de Micer Otto de Gransson [The *pastourelle* of Sir Oton de Granson]." In the third, the first six stanzas of ***70*** appear together with six other stanzas in a dialogue or *tençon* in which the names "Granson" and "Lesparra" appear alternately in the margin (GW100).

These six are preceded by another poem attributed to "Garanson" (the same spelling used in the attribution of ***56***), which appears, however, not to be Granson's at all but the work of another French poet, Jean de Garencières (1372–1415).[37]

The other six poems in this manuscript that are also in *F* or *A* but that do not bear Granson's name appear interspersed amongst a sequence of twelve ballades on fols. 408v–415.[38] One of these twelve (the seventh) is ascribed to the Catalan knight Jacme Scrivà.[39] The first contains the puzzling heading "Glen. Balada." Pagès, who first printed these poems, took this as an abbreviation for "Glenson," and he concluded that it and the

---

[35] See the exhaustive study by Jordà, "Cançoner Vega-Aguiló," esp. pp. 184–92.

[36] All 23 poems are printed by Pagès, *Poésie française*, pp. 173–244. On the orthography, see p. 90.

[37] Pagès, *Poésie française*, pp. 206–12; Grandson, *Vie et poésies*, ed. Piaget, p. 117; GW99. The poem, entitled "L'Enseignement du Dieu d'Amours," appears at the head of a collection of poems all attributed to Garencières in Paris, Bibliothèque Nationale, fr. 19139, pp. 412–17. For the text, Garencières, *Poésies complètes*, ed. Neal, pp. 65–71. Neal dates this poem to 1390–1400, p. xxxii.

[38] They are, in order, ***54***, ***41***, ***37***, ***38***, ***39***, and ***40***. The last five make up the "Cinq balades ensuivans," in the same order as they appear in manuscript *A* if one counts the first copy of ***41*** in *A* rather than the second.

[39] Perhaps mistakenly. See Jordà, "Cançoner Vega-Aguiló," p. 192.

other four ballades in this group that are still unattributed are otherwise unknown works of Granson. His suggestion was rejected by Piaget and has not otherwise found support.[40]

MANUSCRIPT P: PHILADELPHIA, UNIVERSITY OF PENNSYLVANIA, VAN PELT LIBRARY MS CODEX 902 (FORMERLY FR. MS 15). 101 leaves, France, 1395–1400. With three hundred and ten poems, *P* is the largest surviving anthology of French lyric poetry of the fourteenth century, but it bears no indication of authorship, and more than half of its contents still remain anonymous.[41] Of the poems that can be attributed on other evidence, Machaut dominates, with one hundred and seven. The works of at least five other poets can be identified. There are, finally, twenty-seven poems that also appear in manuscripts *F* or *A* and that are on that

[40] See Pagès, *Poésie française*, p. 176, who thus attributes nineteen of the twenty-three poems in this collection to Granson, p. 90; and Grandson, *Vie et poésies*, ed. Piaget, p. 119. Grenier-Winther reprints the five ballades in question, GW94–98. *E* has attracted most attention not for what value it might have in establishing Granson's text or canon but because of what it might suggest about the date of composition of its contents. The "Lesparra" who is named in the *tençon* (GW100) is very likely the Florimont de Lesparre who was imprisoned in Spain at the same time as Granson, between 1372 and 1374. See Grandson, *Vie et poésies*, ed. Piaget, pp. 136–37. The supposition that the *tençon* must date from this time, together with the Iberian origin of the entire manuscript, has led some to believe that all of the works of Granson that are contained here also must therefore date from the period of his captivity. See Braddy, *Chaucer and Graunson*, pp. 74–75; Wimsatt, *Poems of "Ch,"* pp. 88–89; and Wimsatt, *French Contemporaries*, pp. 213, 332n13. That conclusion is important for the identification of the "Isabel" who is named in the acrostic in ***74***, which also appears in *E* (Braddy, *Chaucer and Graunson*, p. 75; Wimsatt, *Poems of "Ch,"* p. 132n2); see p. 35 below. It also has some significance for Granson's relation with Chaucer, for the five ballades on which he based his "Complaint of Venus" also appear (without attribution to Granson) in this manuscript. The *tençon*, however, contains no evidence of a real collaboration: Lesparre's verses respond to Granson's, but Granson's appear to be written without any awareness of Lesparre's, and they were probably simply extracted by Lesparre (if he was indeed the author) from a copy of the longer poem to which they belong. The conditions of the English knights' imprisonment, moreover (Pembroke died due to his ill-treatment shortly after his release), do not suggest that there would have been much opportunity for either poet to practice his craft (compare Braddy, *Chaucer and Graunson*, pp. 28–29), and even if Granson and Lesparre exchanged their verse, it is just as reasonable to suppose that they did so after they had been freed; see Bennett, review of Braddy, *Chaucer and Graunson*, pp. 35–37. There are also other reasons to believe that not all of the poems gathered here can date from so early a time. Jean de Garencières was only just born in 1372, and four of the ballades — the one headed "Glen," the one attributed to Jacme Escrivà, one attributed to Granson (***56***), and one that is unattributed (GW97) — all have envoys, which are not thought to have been common before the last quarter of the century. (In the last of these, the envoy appears to have been imported from a different ballade, since the rhymes do not match the preceding stanzas.) See Kelly, *Saint Valentine*, p. 65n6. On the use of the envoy, see Wimsatt, *Poems of "Ch,"* pp. 86, 87n63, and *French Contemporaries*, p. 259; and Laurie, "Amitiés métriques," pp. 130–34. If any of these poems is later, then none of the contents can confidently be placed in the 1370s, and the interest of this manuscript is actually heightened as evidence of the circulation of Granson's work into the Iberian peninsula well after the period of his imprisonment.

[41] See Wimsatt, *Poems of "Ch,"* pp. 2, 54, and the complete list of the contents of the manuscript, pp. 91–146. Mudge, "Pennsylvania," offers a similar catalog (pp. 244–344), and he edits the ninety-five ballades whose authorship he did not know. Piaget (Grandson, *Vie et poésies*), Mudge, and Wimsatt all failed to recognize that the ballade numbered 279 in Mudge and Wimsatt also appears in manuscript *A*. See the note to ***53***, below. High resolution photographs of the entire manuscript are available online at http://www.library.upenn.edu.

basis attributed to Granson, making this the third largest collection of Granson's verse. It is also among the earliest, and one of only two that might possibly date from Granson's lifetime.[42]

These twenty-seven include six of the eight longer poems that appear in both *F* and *A*, omitting only ***72*** "Complainte de Saint Valentin" and ***77*** "Le Songe Saint Valentin," and also ***68*** "Le Dit de loiauté," which appears only in *A*. The other twenty are all ballades, and all also appear in *A*, including fifteen that are in *A* but not in *F*. All but three of the twenty-seven poems appear in two clusters in the manuscript. Using Wimsatt's numbering, they are numbers 18 and 20–34; and then in a slightly looser grouping, numbers 251–54, 256, 258, 261, and 264.[43] (The three more isolated poems are numbers 136, 228, and 279.) These two clusters may have been derived from different sources. The first group contains all of the longer poems. It also contains all of the poems that also appear in *F*. The second group of poems plus the three isolates all appear, among the manuscripts mentioned so far, only in *A*. The first group in *P* is also like *F* in being the only other source to present the five ballades that *F* labels "Les Cinq balades ensuivans" as an unbroken sequence, though without a title or any other indication that they are to be joined. *P* contains none of the poems that occur uniquely in *F*, however, and even the first cluster cannot be derived exclusively from a collection precisely like *F* since it also contains three ballades (Wimsatt's numbers 21, 23, and 24) that do not appear in *F* but that do appear in *A*.

Since none of the contents of *P* bears an author's name, *P* can offer no direct evidence regarding which of these works are Granson's and which are not, but it does provide additional evidence that certain poems found in *A* and *F* circulated together, strengthening the case for their common authorship.[44]

Poems attributed to Granson in other sources. As already mentioned, Chaucer's attribution to Granson of the ballades on which he based his "Complaint of Venus" itself offers important evidence of Granson's authorship, because only the last of these poems is attributed to him by name in any of the manuscripts in which they appear (in *A*). Further evidence from other sources is sparse. In addition to the five manuscripts already mentioned, there are twelve surviving manuscripts, highly varied in contents, that contain one or more of the poems in *F* or *A*.[45] Altogether seventeen of the seventy-six poems in *A* and/or *F* appear in at least one of these books, but only one appears with an ascription to Granson. That is what was evidently the most popular of his works, ***73*** "La Pastourelle Granson," which is found in four

[42] The other is manuscript *R* (Turin, Archivio di Stato MS J.b.IX.10), which contains, without any attribution, five of Granson's ballades plus a fragment of ***75*** dispersed among a large miscellaneous collection. The entire contents are edited by Vitale-Brovarone, "Recueil."

[43] Wimsatt, *Poems of "Ch,"* p. 139, speculates that among the other poems that occur within this cluster, numbers 255 and 257 might also be Granson's. Mudge ("Pennsylvania," p. 7 and n.) identifies a total of thirty-six ballades of which the attribution to Granson is "not entirely implausible."

[44] Wimsatt, *Poems of "Ch,"* pp. 88–90, offers an intriguing suggestion (that does not bear directly on the question of authorship) that Granson himself was responsible for compiling the contents of this manuscript. His argument deserves to be considered in all its detail, though it is impossible to eliminate other explanations for the collection's origin.

[45] See the complete list on p. 40 below. Manuscript sources for each poem are recorded in the Textual Notes.

other manuscripts (in addition to *A*, *E*, *F*, *K*, and *P*), all of which contain principally the works of Alain Chartier.[46] Granson's name is included in the title in all of these except *P*, where one has to imagine that it was deliberately suppressed. With the remaining poems, the appearance of another copy indicates that the poem circulated separately from the others in *F* and *A*, but lacking an independent attribution, it does not help us determine if it was Granson's.

Two of these manuscripts (*D* and *H*) contain another poem not mentioned yet, since it is in neither *F* or *A*. Included as number ***76*** below, it bears the title "Complainte de saint vallentin garenson" in *D* and "la complainte de saint valentin gransson compilee par M. alain ch[artier]" in *H*.[47] There are two other copies, one complete (manuscript *B*),[48] one partial (manuscript *G*), in which the poem appears without attribution. This poem is unusual for Granson: it describes a situation that does not occur in any of his other poems, and it is the only Valentine poem in which the saint actually appears, in the company of the God of Love. If it is Granson's, it must have circulated independently.

A far more doubtful case is found in *C*, one of the four Chartier manuscripts that contains "La Pastourelle Granson." Much earlier in the manuscript occurs a poem that is headed (like the "Pastourelle," in a later hand) "Complainte amoureuse de Sainct Valentin Gransson" (GW101). The first twenty-one lines of this poem are identical to the opening of ***75***, but the rest is in a different rhyme scheme, and in contents too it plainly has nothing to do with this opening. There is no way to determine how these two poems came to be joined, but despite another allusion to Saint Valentine in the final stanza, we cannot be sure that the attribution to Granson (which also appears in the copy of ***75*** in *K*) applies to anything but the first portion.[49]

Two other cases of attribution to Granson are more clearly doubtful. The poem of Garencières that appears in *E* has already been cited. And in manuscript *T*, a compilation by a nineteenth-century collector that contains two ballades from *A* plus the virelai found in *A* and *F*, there is another ballade with the *explicit* "par Odo de Granson" that is actually one of the ballades of Machaut that is also contained in *A* (GW5).[50]

---

[46] These manuscripts are *C*, *D*, *H*, and *M*. In *C* the title is added in a later hand.

[47] *D* is Bibliothèque Nationale fr. 24440. The poem appears on fols. 221r–225r. *H* is Bibliothèque Nationale fr. 833. The poem is on fols. 172r–174r. Digital images of both manuscripts are available at the Gallica website (note 23 above). The poem appears with the same title as in *H* in the 1489 printed edition of Chartier's works, which also includes ***69*** with the title "La Pastourelle Granson faicte par maistre Alain Chartier." Evidently Granson was so little known by the end of the fifteenth century that his name was no longer recognized as that of poet. See Grandson, *Vie et poésies*, ed. Piaget, pp. 124–25.

[48] See note 51 below.

[49] Doubts on its authenticity are also expressed by Wimsatt, *French Contemporaries*, p. 236.

[50] We reserve one final instance for a footnote, since the attribution is purely modern. In 1904, Piaget ("*Belle Dame*," pp. 203–06) suggested that Granson was the author of "La Belle dame qui eut mercy," a dialogue poem of 378 lines that appears in some of the later manuscripts of Granson's works. Piaget evidently recognized the weakness of his case since he makes no mention of the poem in his 1941 edition. The lack of evidence not just for the attribution but for the likelihood that the poem was even composed during Granson's lifetime is summarized by Grenier-Winther, "Authorship," pp. 50–60.

Summing up the evidence. Setting aside ***76*** "Complainte de Saint Vallentin Garenson" and also ***78*** *Le Livre Messire Ode*, which we will consider separately below, the long poems, as a group, are the best attested and the ones that we can most confidently attribute to Granson. There are nine of these poems, five of which are ascribed to Granson in at least one of the copies in which they occur. Three of the other four, curiously enough, are the ones in which Saint Valentine's name appears in the title in at least one copy: ***71*** "Le Souhait de Saint Valentin," ***72*** "Complainte de Saint Valentin," and ***77*** "Le Songe Saint Valentin." The fourth is ***68*** "Le Dit de loiauté," which is also the only of the long poems to survive in a single copy, and the evidence for its attribution thus rests solely on its appearance in *A*. Of the rest, the appearance of all eight in both *F* and *A*, the appearance of six of these in *K*, and the appearance of a different six in *P* (where they are grouped together in the first cluster) reinforce the likelihood of a common authorship.

The shorter poems are somewhat more problematic. Only a handful of ballades are attributed to Granson by name, two in *A* (***41***, ***61***), three in *E* (***56***, ***59***, ***60***), and the five used by Chaucer (***37–41***). With the one overlap, that makes a total of nine. While the instances of false attribution have to make us cautious, there is no need to doubt these ascriptions, particularly Chaucer's, since in all likelihood he was acquainted with Granson and since this is the only attribution that dates from Granson's lifetime. But for all the remaining short poems that we attribute to him, we must rely entirely on indirect evidence: on their appearance in manuscripts where they are grouped together alongside others that bear Granson's name, on whatever we might infer from the heading in *A* that states that its contents were "compiled" by the poet, and on the similarities in form, diction, and theme.

The similarities must necessarily count for less than the evidence from the manuscripts. Piaget's argument on the unity of the poems in *F* is actually an attempt to demonstrate that they create a single coherent narrative, and it is based on the dubious assumption of a direct relation between the poems and the poet's real experience. Piaget also overstated their homogeneity: the tradition from which these poems derive offered a great many different possibilities to develop, as one can see from the variety of poems in *F* and the even greater variety in *A*. If these poems are Granson's, then his palette was simply more varied than Piaget acknowledged. At the same time, there are a small number of poems that are so dissimilar from the rest (the two anomalous ballades in *F*, the second part of the "Complainte amoureuse de Sainct Valentin Gransson" [GW101] in *C*) that we have to doubt that they are by the same author. The dissimilarity in contents thus might give us reason to exclude certain poems, but what consistency there is among the rest is due to their being grounded in the same inherited commonplaces of form and theme and thus offers no reliable evidence on authorship.

What we deduce from the major manuscripts rests for the most part on the inferences that we make about how the collections that they contain came to be compiled. And whether by accident or design, four out of five of these are clearly not the collected works of a single poet. Manuscript *K* is the exception here, but except for the *balade double*, it contains none of the shorter poems. Manuscript *P* is the model that we have to keep in mind, for it demonstrates both the quantity and the diversity of the anonymous vernacular verse that was in circulation and available to be "compiled" as the fourteenth century ended. Manuscripts *A*, *E*, and we have to suppose *F* as well, while each containing poems ascribed to Granson, also contain at least some poems that are not Granson's, and they too are thus "compilations," though whether more like *K* or more like *P* is not immediately evident. The appearance of the same short poems in more than one of these is perhaps the most valuable evidence that we have, for it suggests, as in the case of the longer poems, that these poems circulated together, which in turn suggests a common origin and offers strong though not conclusive evidence of common authorship. It is worth noting in that regard that none of the poems that we know are *not* by Granson appears in more than one of these manuscripts, and that all of the poems that are ascribed to him by name do appear in more than one. The variations in order, in title, and in the text and the evidence that we find in the manuscripts themselves that their collections derived from more than a single source indicate that there was no single master copy upon which each was based. But there are also examples in which the same poems do appear grouped together and sometimes — as in the case of the "Cinq balades ensuivans" — in the same order, which strengthen further the case for a common origin.

In making the selection for this edition, we have steered a conservative middle course. With Piaget, we accept *F* and *A* as the best sources of evidence on Granson's canon, and we have excluded from consideration only the poems in these two copies that we recognize as likely or certainly to be by someone else. We have also admitted ***76*** "Complainte de Saint Vallentin Garenson"and ***78*** *Le Livre Messire Ode* (which we discuss below), but none of the poems in other manuscripts for which Granson's authorship is merely speculative. The surviving manuscripts leave us much that is reasonably sure, but with all of the mysteries on how their contents came to be compiled, the inclusion of poems clearly not by Granson, together with the wide availability of anonymous verse as illustrated by *P*, has to remind us that there will always be some degree of uncertainty about the precise boundaries of his canon, especially with reference to the poems that appear in only one of these copies. At the same time, there is no reason to believe that *F* and *A* together contain every single poem that Granson wrote, and it is fully possible that other of his works appear among the many unattributed poems not just in *P* and *E* but in other manuscripts as well.

Le Livre Messire Ode. Included in Piaget's edition is the long quasi-autobiographical poem that he entitled *Le Livre Messire Ode* which must be treated as a special case. This work appears in whole or in part in five manuscripts, none of which contains any indication of its title or of the author's name. The five copies are:

B: Paris, Bibliothèque Nationale, fr. 1727, mid fifteenth century; the only "complete" text.[51]
G: London, Westminster Abbey, MS 21, mid fifteenth century; lines 702–833.
J: Paris, Bibliothèque Nationale, fr. 1952, sixteenth century; under the heading "Complainte d'amours," lines 1–326, 872–966, 994–1089.
N: Brussels, Bibliothèque Royale Albert 1er, MS 10961–10970, c. 1465; lines 1–1480.
O: Karlsruhe, Badische Landesbibliothek, MS 410, c. 1430; five fragments on separate leaves, lines 1–32, 617–57, 762–815, 917–54, and 1066–1114.

Manuscripts *B* and *G* have already been cited above for they also contain ***76*** "Complainte de Saint Vallentin Garenson." *G* also contains one of the ballades that appears in *F* (***55***) and another found in *A* that is actually by Machaut (GW36). None of the other three contains any poems that might be Granson's, but all five contain works by Alain Chartier.

[51] Digital images are available at the Gallica Website (note 23 above).

In presenting the work as Granson's, Piaget cited three bits of evidence for the attribution:[52]

- In ***69*** "L'Estraine du jour de l'an," lines 37–38, Granson seems to make an allusion to his "livre" with reference to his fidelity in love, in lines that we have translated, "You will know it, if I may live, / More by my deeds than by my writing" ("Mieux par mez fais que par mon livre").
- In Book 3 of Martin Le Franc's *Le Champion des Dames*, lines 14125–28, Franc Vouloir (the "champion" of the title) alludes to Granson in these words, as part of his argument on the consistency of virtue and true love:

  Se le petit livre lisez
  De messire Ode de Granson,
  Vous trouverez de biens assez
  En l'amoureuse cusançon.

  [If you read the little book of Messire Ode de Granson, you will find enough good in the pains of love.]
- And in the *Livre* itself, lines 7–9, there is a passage that Piaget took as a reference to ***76*** "Complainte de Saint Vallentin Garenson" (compare lines 105–06):

  Amours, par vostre bon vouloir
  Vous a pleu moy faire savoir
  Que je choisisse une maistresse.

  [Love, out of your good will / It pleased you to instruct me / To choose a mistress.]

Each of these requires some qualification. While the last statement is consistent with the "Complainte," it makes no allusion to the specific circumstances of that poem, in which the poet's first lady has died and in which he is counseled to choose another, and it might instead refer to any situation in which a man has been incited by the God of Love. In "L'Estraine," the "livre" appears to be no more than a figure of speech for the poet's writing generally, including the very poem in which this reference occurs. And the "petit livre" to which Le Franc refers is not necessarily a specific poem but could be any collection of Granson's writing, which is how Piaget himself understood it before he attached the title to this particular work.[53]

There is in fact nothing in any of the evidence that Piaget cites to indicate that Granson wrote another poem in addition to those contained in *F* and *A* or that if he did, he entitled it *Le Livre Messire Ode*. Nor is there any evidence that the piece to which Piaget gave that title is that work, or that it was thought to be Granson's by anyone at the time, including the scribes who copied it into the manuscripts in which it is preserved. But that is not to say that Piaget was necessarily mistaken, for the attribution, while speculative, is both plausible and appealing. While this certainly would have been a new sort of composition for Granson, with its extended narrative frame and with at least one new lyric type (the "Debate between Heart and Body," lines 1534–1726), it otherwise contains nothing that is inconsistent with his ability or with his style, and the situation of the narrator, despairing of the good graces of his lady, has abundant echoes in the poems that are more firmly attributed to him. The challenge (in the prose letter that follows line 1089) to one of the knights of "the party of the King of England" (identified more specifically as the "Lord of Cornwall" in manuscripts *N* and *O*) suggests that the work was composed by a French-speaking poet with strong

[52] Grandson, *Vie et poésies*, ed. Piaget, pp. 144–45.

[53] Piaget, "Oton de Granson," pp. 440, 445. He suggests, in fact, that Le Franc may have been referring specifically to manuscript *F*.

English connections such as Granson rather than by someone who was confined to France. Evidence that the author had read Chaucer[54] also suggests Granson rather than anyone else writing in French (unless of course the influence works the other way). There are also three references to Saint Valentine, in lines 828, 1246, and 1996. The mixture of awkwardness and ambition that characterizes the work as a whole suggests someone who rises above the level of the many anonymous poets whose works appear in the manuscripts of the time, but also someone who was not as accomplished as the other poets whose names we know, such as Chartier. And its possibly unfinished state (on which we will say more below) might help explain why it is not included alongside Granson's other poems, for it allows us to speculate that he was still working on it at the time of his death and that it only circulated afterwards. We cannot ever be certain, but it is a good fit, and among the poets that we know, at least, we have no better candidate for its author.

FORMS AND THEMES

The body of work that we attribute to Granson on the grounds that we have just described offers a nearly complete cross-section of French poetry at the end of the fourteenth century, both formally and thematically. The seventy-eight separate poems plus the thirty-two lyrics that are contained in the *Livre Messire Ode* include ninety-two in the *formes fixes* — ballade, rondeau, and virelai — which were the recognized types for lyric poetry at the time.[55] (Only the fourth and least common, the *chant royal* or *chanson royal*, is not represented in Granson.) The eighteen longer poems are more diverse, and though most are referable to a conventional type, these types themselves are far less precisely defined. Though for the most part Granson was content to follow the models that were most current in his time, there is some evidence of inventiveness on his part, and the very variety of his verse demonstrates a consciousness of form and a greater willingness to experiment than is found even among some of his professional contemporaries.

The formes fixes. The conventions of the *formes fixes* had largely been established, by practice and example, by the middle of the fourteenth century, particularly under the influence of Guillaume de Machaut, and they were later codified by Eustache Deschamps in his *Art de Dictier* of 1392. But each also evolved from generation to generation, and even in their strictest form they left room for considerable variation.[56] The ballade, rondeau, and virelai all derive from earlier song forms. Machaut and other poets in the first part of the century often provided music for their compositions. By the end of the century music was much less common, but the poems retain some of the formal characteristics of song, particularly in the

---

[54] See Wimsatt, *French Contemporaries*, pp. 227–31.

[55] English readers will recall Chaucer's *Legend of Good Women*, line F423, where among his other works, Alceste cites Chaucer's "balades, roundels, [and] virelayes" (*Riverside Chaucer*, p. 600).

[56] On the *formes fixes*, the basic work is still Poirion, *Poète et prince*. See also Cerquiglini, "Rondeau," and Heger "Ballade et Chant Royal." In English, Earp provides a survey of the development until mid-century in "Lyrics for Reading." There are also a useful introduction and notes in Wilkins, ed., *One Hundred Ballades*.

structural use of repetition.[57] Each of the *formes fixes* is characterized by a fixed number of stanzas that, identical in form, could be sung to the same melody; by a limited number of rhymes in a repeated scheme; and by some element of repetition in the text, in the form of either a shorter or a longer refrain.

In the rondeau and the virelai, the opening stanza is repeated and thus constitutes the refrain. In the earliest examples, the refrain was probably meant to be sung by the public, in response to the soloist, in alternation.[58] At the end of the century, the rondeau was the *forme fixe* that still maintained the closest affiliation with song. Readers of English poetry will remember the *roundel* that is sung by the birds at the close of Chaucer's *Parliament of Fowls* (lines 680–92).[59] Seven of the ten rondeaux in the *Livre Messire Ode* are labeled "chansons," though no music is provided (the others bear no title), and Granson refers to the rondeaux being sung, or not, in lines 330, 582, 1642, and 1710. The rondeau is also the most "musical" form in employing the greatest amount of repetition both of sense and sound. The typical rondeau at the end of the century has four 4-line stanzas: an opening stanza that provides the refrain and also establishes the rhymes; a second stanza that concludes with the first two lines of the refrain; a new third stanza; and then the repetition of the entire refrain.[60] The whole poem uses only two rhymes, which we can represent schematically in this way (using capital letters for the refrain): *ABBA abAB abba ABBA*. Fifteen of Granson's nineteen rondeaux (nine separate poems, ten in *Le Livre Messire Ode*) are in this form. In ***9***, he creates a double rondeau by adding three more stanzas in the same scheme, and in three of the rondeaux in the *Livre Messire Ode* (lines 583–603, 2034–54, and 2449–69) he uses a 5-line stanza rhyming *aabba*, a variation that appears among other poets too at about the same time.[61]

There is only a single example of a virelai in Granson (***10***). Schematically, it can be represented in this way (again with capitals to indicate the refrain): *AABBA ccdccd aabba AABBA*. In the virelai, the refrain (typically either four or five lines) is repeated only in full, after two stanzas of development, and while the third stanza repeats the rhyme scheme (and when sung, the melody) of the refrain, the second stanza has a different rhyme and metrical scheme and uses a different melody. Though in Deschamps and Christine de Pisan, virelais of seven stanzas were still common, by about 1400 the virelai came more and more to resemble the typical rondeau, with only four stanzas and with lines of equal length, as in the example by Granson.[62]

The ballade is by far the most important of the *formes fixes*, not just for Granson but for fourteenth-century French poetry generally. Granson left seventy-two examples, including

---

[57] On the musical qualities of the *formes fixes*, see Wimsatt, *French Contemporaries*, especially chapter 1, "Natural Music in Middle French Verse and Chaucer," pp. 3–42; and "Chaucer and Deschamps," pp. 132–50.

[58] Poirion, *Poète et prince*, pp. 317–18.

[59] *Riverside Chaucer*, p. 394.

[60] On the variations in the scribal presentation of the refrains, see the note to ***1–9*** in the Explanatory Notes, below.

[61] Poirion, *Poète et prince*, pp. 333–34.

[62] Poirion, *Poète et prince*, pp. 343–48.

fifteen in the *Livre Messire Ode*.[63] The ballade is a 3-stanza form, each stanza employing the same rhymes, and the refrain, consisting of one or two lines, appears not at the beginning of the poem, as in the rondeau and virelai, but at the conclusion of each stanza. Within this general frame, there is room for considerable variety. The stanza can range from six to fourteen lines. Among Granson's closest contemporaries, the lines are all normally eight to ten syllables in length, but especially early in the century, the stanza also allows one or more shorter lines, or *vers coupés*. The number of rhymes typically varies between two and five. Granson's ballades illustrate some of this variety, though he tends to use the schemes that usage had made most common during the decades in which he wrote.[64] All but two of his ballades use lines of a uniform length (that is, they do not employ the *vers coupé*; the exceptions are ***18*** and ***32***), and all but six are in decasyllables.[65] For his 7-line stanzas (Machaut's favorite form), he also prefers the rhyme scheme that Machaut favors, *ababbcc* (five of his six examples). (English readers will recognize this as the model for Chaucer's "rhyme royal.") But where Machaut has a strong preference for a closing couplet, in his longer stanzas Granson prefers some version of crossed rhyme instead (as does Deschamps[66]). His favorite form was the 8-line stanza rhyming *ababbcbc* (the model for Chaucer's Monk's Tale stanza), with twenty-four examples. His next two favorites were a 10-line stanza rhyming *ababbccdcd* (with eighteen examples) and a 12-line stanza rhyming *ababbccddede* (with eight). There are unique examples of ten other schemes and two examples of an eleventh, including stanzas of nine, eleven, and fourteen lines, but the only other scheme that he used more than twice is the unusual 8-line stanza rhyming *ababbccb* that he employed exclusively in his "Cinq balades ensuivans."

The ballade is a form that draws attention to its own difficulty, and it is hard to exaggerate the challenges that were posed by these schemes. Granson's favorite 8-line stanza required him to come up with six different *a*-rhymes, four *c*-rhymes (one of which occurs three times, in the refrain), and twelve different *b*-rhymes in a 24-line poem. The longer stanzas employ additional rhymes (except in ***44***, in which the 9-line stanza requires fifteen *b*-rhymes), but they pose no less a challenge in the requirement to maintain exactly the same scheme in each stanza, and they draw no less attention to the sound of the verse in their greater use of internal couplets. This emphasis on sound — on what Deschamps refers to as

[63] This count takes the first three stanzas of the *complainte* at line 2342 as a separate poem, though it is not marked as such in the manuscript. See the note to ***78***.2342–2448.

[64] Poirion (*Poète et prince*, pp. 385–87) provides a helpful table summarizing the distribution of the different stanza forms among the major poets (though his figures for Granson are not always exact). Jung ("Répertoire," p. 103) presents an inventory of Granson's metrical types. His too requires a few corrections: he includes the two ballades in manuscript *F* more likely to be by Deschamps (his numbers 59 and 60), though he himself labels them "doubtful" (p. 97); he misstates the rhyme schemes of the ballades at ***78***.2125 and 2318 (his numbers 22 and 45); and he counts the ballade at ***78***.2342 (his number 49) as decasyllabic when it is actually octosyllabic (as he notes correctly on p. 113). There are other identifiable patterns in the ballades, for instance concerning the use of masculine and feminine rhymes and the placement of the caesura, that we do not discuss here. A full analysis of the metrical form of each of Granson's poems is provided in Grenier-Winther's edition.

[65] For the exceptions see the note to ***53***.

[66] Laurie, "Amitiés métriques," pp. 128–30.

"natural music" as opposed to the artificial music of melody[67] — is an aspect of the structure of the ballade that cannot be reproduced in translation, and it extends beyond merely the repetition of the same syllable at the end of the line. The careful reader will discover not just virtuosity in fitting sense to sound but also calculated effects in the use of sound: for instance, in ***19***, the use of three very similar rhymes, *-aire*, *-iere*, and *-er* (remembering that final *r* was still pronounced in Middle French), as opposed to ***21***, in which *-ours* and *-ort* are set in contrast to the *b*-rhyme *-eille*, but in which they are echoed in the repeated use of the *-r* termination within the line and lead to the concluding *rime riche* on *fort*.

The ballade form allows greater possibility for rhetorical development than either the rondeau or the virelai, especially as both stanzas and lines tend to lengthen as the century progressed. On the one hand, there are whole stanzas that can be punctuated as single sentences (for instance, the initial stanzas of ***55*** and ***66***, or the first two stanzas of ***18***), and the poet displays his skill in his ability to fit his clauses naturally into the rhyme and metrical scheme. On the other hand, compare not just the shorter clauses but also the quick change of tone that mark the lady's spirited rationalization and self-defense in ***50***. On a larger scale, the rhetorical structure of the ballade as a whole is very much determined by the recurrence of the refrain, which in this respect is much more than merely a matter of sound. In the hands of lesser poets, the necessity of ending each stanza in the same place might induce mere repetition, and there are many ballades in which the stanzas could be switched around without much consequence. In more skillful hands, the ballade form opened up the possibilities that were not available in the other *formes fixes*. In both the rondeau and the virelai, the fact that the ending is identical to the opening inhibits any progression in the thought, and while in the rondeau, the partial repetition in the second stanza requires a certain amount of dexterity on the poet's part, and in the virelai, the contrasting second stanza might allow the introduction of a contrasting perspective, both forms tend to simple, uncomplicated statements and to the development of a single idea with little drama or tension (though not necessarily without humor or wit; see ***1*** and ***9***). The ballade, on the other hand, falls naturally into a three-step argument.[68] A typical pattern (e.g. in ***11*** or ***35***) is almost syllogistic in form: a general statement in the first stanza; a more specific description of the particulars of the poet's condition in the second; and then in the third, a conclusion, which might be, among other choices, a reaffirmation, a judgment, or a plea. But the form accommodates a nearly unlimited number of possibilities, and an essential part of the experience of reading the ballades is discovering the unique way in which each is developed. In ***45***, for instance, the three-part structure is ostensibly provided by the poet's eye, ear, and heart, within which is developed a three-part statement of the poet's devotion to his lady, his praise of her virtues, and his promise to continue serving her. In ***66***, the structure is provided by variations on the theme of looking and seeing. And in ***26***, a three-step statement — your grace will give me joy; it will be the appropriate reward for my loyalty; and from it your honor will increase — is set against the counter-current of the lady's persistent refusal to grant what the lover requests, in the refrain.

Within these structures, the refrain itself can vary in function and in its relation to the rest of the stanza. It might offer a summary (***37***, ***40***), an aphorism (***56***), an affirmation (***55***), a reversal (***26***, ***53***), a unifying image (***59***), or a comment on the poem itself (***11***, ***34***),

[67] See Wimsatt, *French Contemporaries*, pp. 12–14.

[68] See Poirion, *Poète et prince*, pp. 374–82.

depending upon the theme and the poet's ingenuity. In other cases the refrain has no heavy semantic burden, or while meaningful in itself, provides no real clue to the content of the rest of the stanza, but the poet displays his dexterity simply in being able to maneuver back to it three successive times (***18***, ***35***, ***39***). In some cases the refrain acquires slightly different shades of meaning as it is placed in different contexts (***20***, ***49***). Within the whole poem the refrain is an essential unifying device, but in almost all cases, the forward movement of the poem assures that it also accumulates force and meaning as the poem proceeds.

Granson was far from the least accomplished of the poets of his time in exploiting the possibilities of the ballade form, and though not particularly venturesome metrically, he gets some credit for popularizing, if not inventing, forms that became more widespread after his death. Jung mentions the 8-line stanza rhyming *ababbcbc* in the ballade and also the 5-line stanza in the rondeau;[69] Laurie suggests that Granson and Deschamps together helped establish the longer stanza forms in the ballade and the use of the envoy.[70] Granson also shows some inventiveness in his experimentation with longer sequences of poems. There are precedents for stringing ballades together. Poirion cites the Prologue that Machaut composed for the manuscripts of his collected works, which begins with a dialogue between the poet and Nature and Love in the form of four ballades.[71] Machaut includes one *balade double* in the *Louange des dames*, consisting of a dialogue between a lover and a lady in alternating stanzas[72] and other *balades doubles* and *triples* — ballades with identical refrains and set to the same melody — can be found among the poems that Machaut set to music.[73] Granson leaves one *balade double* (***60–61***, two poems with the same refrain, one addressed to his lady and one to Love), plus the remarkable exchange of ballades between lover and lady — each using the same refrain, but to opposite purposes — in ***49–50***. The most striking example, however, is the group of poems that is labeled in manuscript *F* "Cinq balades ensuivans [Sequence of five ballades]" (***37–41***), the ballades that Chaucer adapted in his "Complaint of Venus." It is far from certain who provided this title, and it is particularly puzzling because this group is immediately followed in manuscript *F* by another group labeled "Les six balades ensuivans [The sequence of six ballades]" that is by no means as persuasive a unity, either formally, consisting of poems with stanzas of three different lengths and rhyme schemes, or thematically, having no more in common than any other six ballades that one might pick. The "Cinq balades ensuivans," however, were clearly meant to go together.[74] All five poems are of the same length and they employ the same rhyme scheme, which Granson uses nowhere else. Each poem makes a different statement, but

[69] Jung, "Répertoire," p. 97.

[70] Laurie, "Amitiés métriques," pp. 128–30, 134.

[71] Poirion, *Poète et prince*, p. 369.

[72] Machaut, *Poésies lyriques*, 1:41–42, number XXVI; *Louange des dames*, p. 105, number 214.

[73] Machaut, *Poésies lyriques*, 2:543–45, numbers IX–XI, an exchange between a lover and his lady; 2.557–59, numbers XXXII–XXXIV; and 2:560–62, numbers XXXVIII–XXXIX. All three of these groups appear (without music) in manuscript *P*; see Wimsatt, *Poems of "Ch,"* pp. 109–11, numbers 169–71, 174–76, and 178–79. The latter pair is printed with its music by Wilkins, ed., *One Hundred Ballades*, pp. 28–29, 151–55, who notes (p. 125) that the two ballades were sung simultaneously rather than as a "sequence."

[74] On the manuscript presentation of the "Cinq balades ensuivans" see the explanatory note to ***37–41***. On the "Six balades ensuivans" see the explanatory note to ***35***.

none has the rhetorical complexity of Granson's other most mature compositions, and in most of the five, the second and third stanzas could be rearranged without loss (as indeed occurs in ***38***, ***39***, and ***40*** in manuscript *E*). What development there is comes not from stanza to stanza but rather from poem to poem, as the narrator proceeds from his lady's virtues, to her scorn, to her effect upon him, to the pains of love, before concluding with a reaffirmation of his commitment. The group as a whole thus offers the type of argument that is elsewhere presented in single ballades, and thematically as well as formally, it appears that it was planned as a single poem.

Themes. This sequence of ballades illustrates another feature of late fourteenth-century French poetry: the conventionality of form was matched by a conventionality of theme. However great the variety rhetorically or metrically in the best of the ballades, the first impression of any modern reader is likely to be their sameness: with few exceptions, the lyric poetry of this epoque is concerned not just exclusively with love, but with love conceived within very narrow limits. The speaker is almost always male, and he speaks from one of a small number of predetermined roles, as if continuously re-enacting scenes from a previously constructed drama. Most often his love is unreciprocated; his lady, whom he does not cease to praise, is either indifferent or for some other reason inaccessible to him; or as a variation, he is the victim of *mesdisans*, or slanderers, who cause him to be separated from his lady. There are also poems spoken by women, often complaining of unfaithful men, and a set of "wisdom" poems, offering general reflections upon the nature of love, the commitment it requires, and the suffering it inevitably entails. In all these there is a singlemindedness, not just in the lover's devotion to a single woman (or when the speaker is a woman, to a single man), but in the total subjection to *la vie amoureuse* — the life of love — to the exclusion of all other occupations or activities, the dual commitment expressed in the refrain to ***43***:

Que de riens plus ne me souvient, par m'ame, Fors que d'amours et de ma belle dame.	That by my soul, no longer do I recall Anything but love and my beautiful lady. (Lines 26–27)

In the purest of this poetry, such as we find in Granson, the focus on love operates to the exclusion of any reference outside of the narrator's own private world. One finds no allusion to historical or political events. One also finds virtually no reference to the actual details of the poet's own life. The ballade found only in manuscript *A* (***47***), which is not about love and in which Granson appears to protest the false accusations that followed him during his final years, is the one exception, unless we also count the two poems on the pains of growing old (***9*** and ***25***). There are poems on parting and on particular holidays that might have been written for specific occasions. And there are three poems that bear, in acrostic, the name "Isabel" (on which more below), whom we assume is a real person, but they are otherwise so unspecific that there is no agreement on the identity of the designee, and they provide no more help in determining the chronology of composition than any of Granson's other poems.

For even in these poems, there is nothing to distinguish the lady for whom he writes from the ladies of hundreds of earlier lyrics, and nothing to distinguish his experiences with her from those of his many predecessors. The narrator's pose in these lyrics is not without paradox. One, which can be the source of considerable dramatic interest, stems from the lover's full and candid revelation to his overhearing public of what is by definition not just intimate and personal but necessarily secret, sometimes even from the lady herself. But another is that the intimate and personal is not for that reason necessarily individual or unique. And that is the second impression that the modern reader is likely to come away with, the other aspect of these poems' conventionality: their impersonality. Both in diction and in choice of imagery, there is little to distinguish the works of one poet from those of another: their art does not lie in the evocation of a general truth from a specific and unique experience, but rather in giving expression to a shared, communal, formalized, almost ritualized (even if only imagined) set of feelings.

The poet's obliteration of himself in favor of a generic narrator is an essential aspect of the pose that the lyricist assumed. Such a pose was presumably even more necessary for those who composed for patrons who were, as Poirion points out, more interested in their own affairs than in those of a hired poet.[75] Granson, an aristocrat who may have written for an audience but not for a patron, nonetheless adhered to the same conventions. He thus writes less about love than about a Love that can be personified, that grants grace, that can come to the lover's aid, that can be invoked without necessary reference to an emotional attachment to a particular person. Although, inspired by his lady's beauty, he is afflicted with Desire, there is a complete lack of overt sensuality; and though he is filled with admiration for his lady, we learn less about her than about his own seemingly permanent condition of longing and suffering. He deals less with her than with abstractions of his own feelings — Desire that torments him, Hope that sustains him — or with abstractions of hers, which following the model of the *Roman de la Rose* are less the elements of her personality than projections of his own experience with her: *Dangier* (her natural reserve, manifested in her coldness and inaccessibility), *Durté* (her harshness), *Refus* (rejection), or the much anticipated *Merci*. As he burns with desire and languishes for love, he pledges to fear, obey, and serve his lady, and he pleads for her pity or mercy for only she can relieve him of his pain. He both needs and fears to make known his love, but he prefers to endure his suffering with her rather than finding joy with any other lady, and when he is forced to separate from her, he leaves his heart behind as he departs. Each of these motifs is found more than once in Granson, and as a general rule, whenever the same theme recurs in his work, one can be almost certain that it can be found — often innumerable times — in the work of other poets as well.

It is perhaps easier to recognize the artifice inherent in conventions such as these when they are someone else's. As has been pointed out many times before, our own popular music has its own distinctive genres, each with its own stock situations and conventional devices that might well appear no less artificial to someone who is not already familiar with them. Such conventions can of course serve different purposes at different times. As Wimsatt has emphasized most strongly with reference to fourteenth-century poetry, the stability and predictability of the underlying sense is a precondition of the formal virtuosity of these poems, of the privileging of sound over sense and of the preoccupation with forms of expression rather than with content.[76] Both the conventionality of theme and the privileging of form, moreover, are consistent with what some have seen as the social function of this poetry, in providing not just a set of behavioral norms but also a means of self-definition for its aristocratic audience. At a time when the French knightly class had lost much of its effec-

[75] Poirion, *Poète et prince*, p. 197.

[76] Wimsatt, *French Contemporaries*, e.g. pp. 12, 16, 25; "Chaucer and Deschamps," p. 136.

tiveness if not its very *raison d'être*, these poems offered a refuge in a world of artifice deliberately detached from both history and material circumstance, the security of a coded and ritualized behavior exclusive to a particular class that set its practitioners apart from those who were less privileged, however little this differencing may have corresponded to the economic realities of the time. Loving well, Granson proclaims, "c'est droicte franchise / Du cuer gentifz [is the very right / Of a noble heart]" (***58***.9–10). The self-absorption of the lover-narrator in this poetry might stand as a metaphor for the self-absorption of the entire class for whom these lyrics were composed.

But however conventional, however impersonal, however ritualized, and however detached both from individual experience and from the real world these poems might be, their interest as literature is not limited to their technical virtuosity. The situations they describe, for one, are not entirely without dramatic interest. The lover is often placed in a situation of paradox or conflict, and there are few poems (especially among Granson's, and this may mark a distinction from Machaut's) that express a single undifferentiated feeling. Even in the same stock situations, moreover, there is more than one way of imagining the lover's response. Faced with his lady's indifference, for instance (certainly one of the most common scenarios), in ***11*** he complains about the lack of reward for his loyalty; in ***19*** his pain and grief lead to a reaffirmation of his commitment; and in ***49*** he pleads his excuses for what she has perceived as his neglect. In ***26***, perhaps the most interesting of all, he expresses his plea for regard in the face of the apparent finality of his rejection, and the futility of his persistence is embodied in the poignant repetition of the refrain: "Mais vous m'avez tousjours respondu 'non' [But you have always answered me with 'no']." In other cases we seem to be overhearing a dialogue or debate. This is particularly true in the poems in which the narrator imparts advice to lovers, which often seems to take direct issue with poems spoken by the lover himself. ***56***, on the arbitrary fortunes of love, can be seen as a rebuke to the lovers who protest the unfairness of their lot, as for instance in ***54***. ***33*** constitutes a rebuke to the timorous and fearful and by implication to their whining and complaints, a poem that may be intended to engage with other lyricists since it describes a condition not well represented in Granson. These "wisdom" poems are often more colloquial in tone, in contrast to the formality of the lyrics that adhere to the more conventional poses. ***33*** is again an example: the possibility of viewing the lover's condition from without rather than within permits a candor and a bluntness that move beyond, and that offer a different perspective on, his disappointment and self-absorption.

Granson has far fewer poems that are directly concerned with a woman's experience in love, but they cover just as wide a range. He expresses a remarkable sympathy for women in ***58***, a "wisdom" poem affirming that Love has a natural lordship over women as well as men and defending the right of a young woman to experience love, in rebuke of prudishness. One should also cite here the spirited but somewhat elusive shepherdess in ***73*** "La Pastourelle Granson." Of the five poems in which Granson portrays the woman as the only speaker, one (***16***) is about her grief at her separation from her lover; in one she professes her loyalty, against the reports of slanderers (***32***); and in two she expresses her anger at her betrayal by a faithless man (***20*** and ***34***). The most remarkable, however, is ***50***, in which the woman speaks in a different voice entirely, by turns sweet-talking, arguing, refuting, consoling, and rebuking, as she responds directly to her lover's complaint of her infidelity in the immediately preceding ballade, and as she uses the same refrain with which he both proclaims his unending commitment to her and excuses his own apparent neglect in order to justify her abandonment of him for another lover: "I have done nothing that

Love doesn't make me do" — simultaneously deflating all of his expectations of her and all of the idealism of love on which they are based.

42, Granson's condemnation of "disloyalty in the life of love," together with ***68*** "Le Dit de loiauté," constitute contributions to a debate or dialogue of a different sort. Loyalty was certainly not a new theme at the end of the fourteenth century — it figures often in the works of Machaut — but either or both of these poems might well be Granson's response to the invitation in the one-hundredth of the *Cent Ballades* for other poets to offer their view on the choice between *Loiauté* and its opposite that is debated in the ballades that precede. Granson's was not among the thirteen replies that are included in most manuscripts of the collection, but the poets who wrote were all aristocrats like himself, and in other of his poems, *loiauté* — a more active form of commitment than mere fidelity, embracing by implication the notions of service and the desired reward as well — frequently appears as an ideal of conduct.

42 is also one of twelve of Granson's ballades to have (in one of the copies in which it survives) an envoy. The envoy is an additional shorter stanza (of no fixed length) employing the same rhymes as the rest of the ballade in which the poet often turns to address his listeners directly.[77] Most of the envoys in Granson's ballades are directed to the lady who is also addressed in the ballade,[78] but four are addressed to a listening audience instead — ***42*** to the "princesse d'Amours [Princess of Love]," ***56*** to "gens et gentes [ladies and gentlemen]," ***65*** to "Princes" and a ballade in ***78*** *Le Livre Messire Ode*, lines 363–97, to the "Prince amoureux [loving prince or Prince of Love]" — on the model that was sustained, if it was not in fact created, by the guilds or confraternities known as the *puys*. The *puys*, which flourished during Granson's lifetime in northern France, sponsored organized poetry competitions among their members, often on announced themes or to a set refrain. There is no direct evidence that Granson participated in a *puy*.[79] Their membership seems to have been drawn mostly from the mercantile class rather than from the aristocracy, though they also provided a site where those boundaries were not necessarily rigid, and recent scholarship has emphasized how the *puys* were both imitative of and also influential upon courtly practices.[80] Their very existence seems to have constituted an encouragement to amateur poets that carried over to the aristocracy as well. Perhaps even more importantly, the *puys*, like the *Cent Ballades*, make evident in concrete form the other sense in which the lyric poetry of the time was a communal act. Poets were very conscious of each other's work, and each of their poems constitutes a contribution to a long, ongoing conversation on the experience of love.

The poets' reference to one another is manifested not just in their acceptance of the prevailing conventions of form and theme but sometimes in their quotation of each other's

---

[77] On the variations in the form of the envoy see Poirion, *Poète et prince*, pp. 388–89. Envoys appeared on ballades only in the last quarter of the century. (Machaut included an envoy only on his *chants royaux*.) See Wimsatt, *Poems of "Ch,"* pp. 86, 87n63, and *French Contemporaries*, p. 259; and Laurie, "Amitiés métriques," pp. 130–34.

[78] Who is usually addressed as "princesse" (***57***, ***64***, ***66***; ***78***.139, 2027) or "souveraine" (***67***), a common enough designation for the lady in contemporary poetry that we need not take as a literal signifier of royalty. See Cartier, "Oton de Grandson," pp. 12–15.

[79] On Granson's possible participation see Wimsatt, *French Contemporaries*, pp. 346–47n7.

[80] Wimsatt, *French Contemporaries*, pp. 274–81; and Butterfield, *Familiar Enemy*, pp. 234–37.

verse. As Ardis Butterfield puts it, in many instances "poets do not merely use the same genre of learned love language, they also specifically cite one another's phrases and lines in direct riposte."[81] Scholars have only begun to catalogue these citations, and a modern reader can therefore have only a dim appreciation of the web of inter-reference by which this ongoing dialogue was sustained. Butterfield cites the example of one refrain — "Qui bien aime a tart oblie [He who loves well forgets slowly]" — that appears in twenty-five separate poems from the thirteenth to the fifteenth century (though not in Granson); and she cites other clusters of imagery that are shared and evidently interchanged among Machaut, Froissart, Granson, and the English poets Gower (writing in Anglo-French) and Chaucer.[82] Such a literary culture, she observes, renders almost meaningless the question of who came first, and it challenges all of our traditional notions of source, borrowing, and intertextuality.

In broadest terms, the ongoing conversation in which all these poets participate is concerned with the very nature of love, and from the beginning, despite the sharing of imagery, there is a wide range of underlying views. Guillaume de Lorris' courtly idealism is answered by Jean de Meun's more earthy naturalism; Machaut's commitment to the discipline of Hope over Desire is answered by Deschamps' more pragmatic, often cynical realism; the virtues of *loiauté* are answered by the pleasures of playing the field; and in ***49*** and ***50*** Granson juxtaposes two opposing ethics in his use of a single refrain, "I have done nothing that Love doesn't make me do." The woman's use of this refrain in ***50*** is not Granson's most typical stance: there is certainly much less celebration of libertinage in his work than expression of commitment to the service of love. ***58***, his defense of woman's right to love, is also a defense of *bonne amour* (line 13), and in ***23*** he comes very close to echoing the view that Machaut expressed, particularly in his *dits amoureux*, that love, even if unreciprocated, offers its own rewards to the faithful lover. At the same time, Granson exhibits much less confidence than Machaut in the power of Hope, whose consolations in his hands tend to be much more fleeting. There are more expressions of real suffering in Granson (***11***, ***15***, ***35***, ***55***, and much of ***78***) and little reference to the alternatives that are offered by other poets, whether faith in a transcendent love, the consolations of Reason, the virtue of moderation, or the comforts of faith in God. The advice that he offers, particularly in the "wisdom" poems, tends to be more prudent and practical in nature. At the same time, Granson is not unreflective. ***50***, again, demonstrates that he was not unaware of the challenges to his most idealistic view of love, and the alert reader will find other moments too in which Granson betrays his doubts about the reality of the entire courtly ethic and his comprehension of the paradoxes of love that emerge from the complexities and vagaries of the human heart.

In sum, while working within what we might consider a narrow range, Granson never does write the same poem twice. Each is a new exploration of his subject, and while we can see some consistent elements and some repeating themes, he has more than a single statement to make about love, and we can never be quite sure what will come in the next poem, or the next stanza, or even the refrain. The more familiar we become with the conventions, the more alert we can also be to the variations. And for that reason, none of these poems should be seen in isolation, for each is a contribution to an ongoing dialogue. We can see one small portion of that conversation taking place among Granson's own lyrics,

---

[81] Butterfield, *Familiar Enemy*, p. 243.

[82] Butterfield, *Familiar Enemy*, pp. 250–64.

as they respond, sometimes in quite specific terms, to one another. More broadly, these poems take their place against the background of the community of writers, extending over several generations and several languages, of which Granson was a part and to which, because he did not allow himself to become stuck in a single groove, he provides an excellent introduction.

The longer poems. Granson's longer poems are more difficult to categorize than his short lyrics because the formal traditions on which they draw were less fixed, but their very variety is another token of Granson's willingness to stretch his wings, even if his more ambitious efforts sometimes fall short of his aspirations. There are eleven separate poems: three short *dits* in couplets (***68*** "Le Dit de Loiauté," ***69*** "L'Estraine du jour de l'an," and ***71*** "Le Souhait de Saint Valentin"), five poems in stanzas entitled (in at least one copy) "complainte" (***70***, ***72***, ***74***, ***76***, plus ***73***, the poem more commonly known as "Granson's *Pastourelle*"), one *lai* (***75*** "Le Lai de desir en complainte"), plus his longest poems, his two narrative *dits* in couplets, ***77*** "Le Songe Saint Valentin" and ***78*** *Le Livre Messire Ode*. *Le Livre Messire Ode* itself incorporates, in addition to the ballades and rondeaux already mentioned, another *lai* (the "Lai de plour," lines 702–833) and six *complaintes*.

The shorter *dits*, in octosyllabic couplets, have a freshness and accessibility that result from their freedom from the constraints of the stanza form, and each is only as long as it needs to be. Two are attached to holidays and could well have been written for a specific occasion. ***69*** "L'Estraine du jour de l'an" is obviously rooted in lyric tradition but reads more like a personal message than like a public performance. ***71*** "Le Souhait de Saint Valentin" is even more charming, containing a sincerity that derives from the freedom of the form, the apparent authenticity of the wishes, and the artful combination of unexaggerated compliment with the modest hope to become more worthy. ***68*** "Le Dit de loiauté," as we have already noted, may spring from a specific circumstance of a different sort, for it can be read as Granson's contribution to the debate undertaken by the poets of the *Cent Ballades*, a theme that Granson also treats in ballades ***23*** and ***42***.

At the opposite extreme in formal terms are ***75*** "Le Lai de desir en complainte" and ***74*** "Complainte de Gransson," together with the "Lay de plour" in the *Livre Messire Ode*. ***75*** follows the model for a *lai* set by Machaut, Froissart, and Deschamps.[83] It consists of twelve stanzas, each in a different form except for the first and last, varying in length between fourteen and twenty-four lines, but each falling into two identical halves and employing only two rhymes. The technical difficulties that the form imposes are height-ened by the need to find meaningful rhymes in the very short lines that occur in some of the stanzas, particularly the third and the fourth. The demands of the scheme and the constant shift from one stanza form to another inhibit the sort of thematic development found in the ballade. Granson offers twelve variations on the theme of the force of Desire (which is named in every stanza but two) and on the struggle both to conceal it and to make it known to the lady.

"Granson's Complainte" (***74***) and his "Lay de plour" (***78***.702–833) nearly rival the *lai* in formal difficulty, but they use the same stanza form throughout. The "Complainte" is in twelve 16-line stanzas, each with only two rhymes, divided into four quatrains by the 4-syllable *vers coupé*, indicated here by the underscore: *aaab aaab bbba bbba*. This was a stanza

[83] Poirion, *Poète et prince*, p. 401. See his entire discussion, pp. 400–06.

form also used by Machaut, for instance in the *complainte* in his *Remede de Fortune*, lines 905–1450 (with thirty-six 16-lines stanzas). The "Lay de plour" uses a shorter version of the *lai* stanza, with twelve lines instead of sixteen — *aab aab bbc bbc* — and with concatenation, as the *c*-rhyme of each stanza is carried over to become the *a*-rhyme of the next.

Of the ten other poems by Granson that are labeled *complaintes*, none is in the same stanza form as ***74***. The *complainte* was not a fixed genre metrically: most of Machaut's *complaintes* are in rhyming couplets, and of the rest, no two are in the same stanza form.[84] Granson's use of stanzas (of eight, ten, or eleven lines) is identical to one that he also used in his ballades. Thematically, the most conventional *complaintes* were merely extended dramatizations of the lover's misfortunes, not differing greatly from some of the most conventional ballades. Five of the six *complaintes* in *Le Livre Messire Ode* fall into that category, as does ***72***, the "Complainte de Saint Valentin," a poem on the lover's separation from his lady in the form of five ballades without refrain, and ***74***, discussed above. But *complainte* proved to be a flexible term, especially towards the end of the century, and it came to be applied to poems that don't fit neatly into any precise thematic mold.

In *Le Livre Messire Ode*, for instance, the nine stanzas that are labeled "complainte" in lines 1534–1605 make up only the first part of the debate between the Heart and the Body that continues with a passage in couplets that also incorporates three rondeaux. And ***73***, the poem entitled "Complainte de pastour et de de pastourelle amoureuse [The *Complainte* of a Shepherd and a Loving Shepherdess]" in manuscript *P* (from which we have taken it for this edition), is more commonly called simply "La Pastourelle Granson [Granson's *Pastourelle*]" in the other manuscripts in which it occurs. This was Granson's most popular work, if we can judge by the number of surviving copies. It contains nineteen 10-line stanzas with the same rhyme scheme that Granson used for all but one of his 10-line ballades, and it presents a dialogue between an anxious, lovelorn shepherd and his elusive shepherdess. It is difficult to find any good contemporary models for this poem. Granson's is the only known example of so extended a dialogue in a pastoral setting, for by the fourteenth-century the *pastourelle* had almost assumed the status of a *forme fixe*, consisting of five stanzas with a refrain on the model of the *chant royal*. All twenty of Froissart's *pastourelles* are in this form, as are all twelve of the other *pastourelles* included in manuscript *P*.[85] And while the opening, as the narrator reports overhearing the shepherds in conversation, is entirely conventional, in almost every other respect the poem departs from what is most expected of the genre. It wears its pastoral associations very lightly: there is nothing to anchor the dialogue itself in the world of shepherds, and the shepherdess herself is described as both *gentil* [well-mannered, well-bred, noble] (line 1) and *bien saichant* [wise] (56). And rather than the object of male fantasies of domination, she seems rather to be a projection of male anxieties about female subjectivity, for the rural setting evidently allows her far more freedom to speak than is enjoyed by most of her aristocratic sisters. Witty and resourceful, she asserts both her virtue and her loyalty but also her independence, as she never explicitly proclaims her commitment to this shepherd and as she provides an answer to each of his objections to her conduct. If the poem ends in-conclusively, it also ends, to the shepherd's great disappointment, with the perpetual deferral of all his hopes.

---

[84] See the list in Earp, *Guillaume de Machaut*, pp. 265–71.

[85] See the list in Wimsatt, *Poems of "Ch,"* pp. 83–85, and an edition of these poems, together with a very valuable historical survey, in Kibler and Wimsatt, "Development."

Granson's two other poems that are called *complaintes* are notable for taking a large step away from lyric in the direction of the narrative *dit*. The less developed example is ***70*** "La Complainte de l'an nouvel," in which a narrator, himself melancholy, reports overhearing a knight's six-stanza complaint and then, in the final stanza, steps forward to comfort him, recalling details from, among others, Machaut's *Dit de la fonteinne amoureuse*, Chaucer's *Book of the Duchess*, and the anonymous *Le Songe vert*.[86] In ***76*** "Complainte de Saint Vallentin Garenson," it is the narrator's *complainte*, in the first eleven stanzas, that is overheard, as he expresses his grief at his lady's death, and the poem is even more firmly rooted in the "complaint and comfort" tradition of the *dit amoureux*.[87] In the remaining two-thirds of the poem, Saint Valentine and the God of Love appear in order to comfort him, and the God of Love urges him to transfer his love to another lady that the god has already selected for him. Upon seeing the lady, he does as the god advises, and the poem concludes with a prayer that she accept his service.

The last two poems that we include here are even more fully in the manner of a narrative *dit*, and they indicate that Granson had become familiar with a much wider range of models. Written in couplets rather than stanzas, each contains a much more fully developed setting and is centered upon a dream vision. As ***77*** "Le Songe Saint Valentin" begins, the narrator has lain awake all night, suffering from unspecified troubles. When he finally falls asleep, he dreams that he returns to a garden where he has lost two precious rings, and he finds that every species of bird has assembled there on Saint Valentine's Day in order to choose their mates, under the supervision of a presiding eagle. One bird, a melancholy tercel (a male falcon), remains apart from the others, and when asked by the eagle why it does not choose a mate, it explains that it has already chosen a particular falcon, which it describes at length, but believing itself unworthy, it cannot reveal its love. It has thus escaped to the wood in order to seek some comfort, but it is set to return to captivity in order to be closer to the falcon. With that, it flies away, as do the rest of the birds, and the narrator awakens. In his concluding comments, the narrator, who claims not to be a lover himself (lines 391–92), expresses sympathy for human lovers, who suffer so many more pains in love than do the birds, who choose so naturally and so freely.

The elements that Granson assembles here are familiar from other contemporary poems — one thinks first of Machaut's *Dit de l'alerion* and Chaucer's *Parliament of Fowls*[88] — but they do not fully cohere in Granson's handling. While we are invited to infer what troubles Chaucer's narrator from what follows in his vision, we never reach a clear understanding of the problems that beset Granson's, and Granson passes up the opportunity to draw a link between his disturbed feelings, the loss that brings him back to the garden, the tercel's experience, and the concluding passage, which addresses neither the narrator's situation nor the tercel's and where the narrator's claims about the free and natural choice of the birds are hardly consistent with the tercel's story.

Some of the same disconnectedness can be found in Granson's longest and most ambitious work, *Le Livre Messire Ode*. As this poem opens, the lady that the narrator has chosen, under Love's tutelage, is keeping him at a distance because he has dared to reveal

[86] On the sources see Wimsatt, *French Love Poets*, pp. 138–43, and below.

[87] On the poems in this tradition, see Wimsatt, *French Love Poets,* pp. 103–50, especially 143–46 (on Granson and his likely sources).

[88] On Granson's sources, see Wimsatt, *French Contemporaries*, pp. 220–27.

his feelings to her. Danger and Rejection (*Reffuz*) now guard her, while he is inflamed by Memory and Desire and sustained only by Hope, which blames him for his despair, and Loyalty. He summarizes his condition in the first of the many intercalated ballades (lines 103–44), which he notes that he has carefully recorded in his book (line 146), and then after a plea for aid to both Love and his lady, he falls asleep.

The first portion of his dream (up to line 850) recapitulates in semi-narrative form how he arrived at the condition that he describes in the opening. In the garden in which the dream begins, he complains of the anguish of an unreciprocated love, and following the logic that applies only in dreams, he is met by a man whose condition is the opposite of his, who expresses his joy at the fulfillment of his love. The narrator decides to dress in black as an expression of his suffering, and he also decides to write his lady a letter, boldly revealing his love for her, precisely the lapse that has upset him in the opening lines, and asking for the gift of her mercy to preserve him from death. The servant who returns with her response offers some encouragement, but the narrator remains in anguish (which he expresses in the "Lay de plour"), and when he has a chance to approach her, he finds her, as predicted, closely guarded by *Reffuz*.

At this point a new narrative seems to begin, for the narrator learns that his lady has rejected him because he recently parted from her without taking proper leave (854–64). After several ballades expressing his misery, he approaches her again and receives an ambiguous encouragement, which leads him in his despair to issue a challenge to combat to the "Lord of Cornwall" in the hope of securing an honorable death. No response is recorded. The rest of the narrative portion of the poem consists of two unrelated episodes: an encounter with a man who describes — in the form of an allegory involving his pursuit of a sparrowhawk and a falcon — how he lost the love of his lady because of an unsuccessful flirtation with another woman (1137–1523), and the long debate between the narrator's Heart and Body, which ends in their joint commitment to continue suffering for love (1534–1726).

Here the narrator awakens (1729), and he sums up his condition in an address to Love (1735–1876) that neither recalls the opening nor offers a precise recollection of what occurs in his dream, but that concludes with his wish that he might learn what his lady is thinking of him "par vision [in a vision]" (1873). He immediately falls asleep again, and the first thing that he sees in his new dream is Danger, galloping through a willow grove. It appears that he is about to see his wish fulfilled, but here the narrative ends, and it is followed (in the one manuscript that continues this far) by a group of fourteen[89] *complaintes*, ballades, and rondeaux that echo some of the themes of the preceding narrative but that offer no new insight into the lady's thoughts (indeed most are concerned with the narrator's need to make her more aware of his) and that have no bearing on the allegorical narrative involving Danger. There is also evidence of some disruption in the text, as the poem apparently switches from octosyllables to decasyllables and from couplets to a stanza form in mid-sentence. There are different ways of explaining what happened here (we examine the details and the alternatives more closely in the notes to ***78***.1881–91 and 1977–96), but the puzzles in the manuscript record make it very difficult to be certain either of the poet's intentions or of how fully he was able to carry them out, particularly with regard to the relation between the final group of poems and the rest of the text.

[89] Or fifteen, depending on how one treats ***78***.2342–2448. See the explanatory note.

As it comes down to us, the *Livre Messire Ode* presents a number of such puzzles. The closest model for the poem is Machaut's *Livre dou voir dit,* another narrative of a love relationship that also includes many intercalated lyrics and an account of how they came to be composed; but as those who have commented on the poem have observed, there are many important differences as well.[90] Perhaps the most significant is the virtual absence of the lady: in Machaut's work, she has an active part in an exchange of poems with the narrator, and there is something that resembles a real plot. Granson's is much more lyrical in orientation: focused all but exclusively on the narrator, there is little opportunity for development and almost none for closure. The individual episodes in the poem are more successful than the structure as a whole, and it remains a collection of set pieces rather than a persuasive whole. As Granson blurs the distinction between the waking and the dreaming states and between lyric and narrative, it is even difficult to say whether the poem is best viewed as set in the present, with recollections of the past, as Boulton describes it,[91] or as set in the past with quoted, present-tense lyric insertions. It is Granson's most ambitious work, to be sure, but it is not clear that he ever completed it, and one may fairly claim that he has not yet overcome all of the challenges that he created for himself in his effort.

GRANSON, CHAUCER, AND SAINT VALENTINE

One of the most interesting issues posed by Granson's longer poems is their relation to the works of the English poet Geoffrey Chaucer. Granson's long service in England, to Richard II, to Richard's uncle John of Gaunt, and to John's son Henry, Earl of Derby, would have provided abundant opportunity for the two poets to meet. We can only speculate, however, on their personal relationship. Chaucer was of much lower rank, and in his verse he typically adopts a pose of great deference to his social superiors. But he was certainly familiar with Granson's poetry, as demonstrated by the one indisputable example of direct borrowing between the two, Chaucer's adaptation of Granson's "Cinq balades ensuivans" in "The Complaint of Venus."[92] Chaucer pays an extraordinary compliment to Granson in his

[90] For a bibliography and more details on the commentary, see the notes.

[91] Boulton, *Song*, p. 224.

[92] Chaucer's is far from a close translation. His most notable alteration is to place the entire poem in the voice of a woman rather than a man. The three ballades that make up the "Complaint" are based primarily on ***37***, ***40***, and ***41***, with some details from ***38*** and ***39***. For a bibliography of commentary see the note to ***37–41***. Wimsatt (*Poems of "Ch,"* pp. 56–65) argues that of the four surviving copies of Granson's five ballades, manuscript *P* contains the version that is closest to Chaucer's. Manuscript *E*, with its idiosyncratic text, can be dismissed from consideration. In examining the other three, manuscripts *A*, *F*, and *P*, Wimsatt identifies seven variants that "make equally sound sense" and in which the *P* reading is closest to Chaucer's. In two of these (Chaucer's lines 33 and 61), the similarity is too remote to be persuasive. Of the other five, two of the "closer" readings also appear in *F* and one in *A*. *F* and *A* also have the correct first-person verbs for Chaucer's lines 49 and 51 where, as Wimsatt notes, *P* uses second- and third-person forms. If one takes all seven of these variations into account, then *A* is closer to Chaucer in three instances, *F* in four, and *P* in five. Mudge ("Pennsylvania," p. 12) points out that in *P*, the first poem in the sequence was formerly headed "Complainte" rather than "Balade," which has a suggestive similarity to Chaucer's title, "The Complaint of Venus." *F* nonetheless remains the only copy in which the five poems are presented as

envoy, crediting him as the "flour of hem that make in Fraunce," the only time that he names a French contemporary. As Wimsatt notes, Chaucer's use of "flour" may be as much an acknowledgment of Granson's knightly status as it is a tribute to him as poet,[93] but the compliment also indicates that Granson was known as a poet by Chaucer's audience, who in the court at least would have been as comfortable with Granson's French as with Chaucer's English.

Granson would have had the opportunity to learn of Chaucer's poetry too, though we cannot be sure when. We cannot assume that Granson already read or spoke English when he first arrived in England, sometime before 1372, and there would also have been little reason for him to pay notice to Chaucer that early in his life.[94] There would have been ample opportunity later, however,[95] and in the instances in which we find evidence of possible borrowing, the question of priority inevitably arises. The poems of Granson that enter into this discussion are the four that incorporate some sort of narrative setting, on the model of the *dits amoureux*. In ***70*** "La Complainte de l'an nouvel," the melancholy narrator (see line 1) who overhears the complaint of a knight when he walks alone into the woods and then steps forward to comfort him recalls the opening of *The Book of the Duchess*, in which the narrator, also melancholy (line 23), is unable to sleep, and the central episode in his later dream, when he comes upon a solitary knight in the forest and, overhearing the complaint in which he mourns the death of his beloved, offers to do his best to help him (lines 448–556). ***76*** "Complainte de Saint Vallentin Garenson" provides an analogue for Chaucer's knight's complaint, for it begins with the narrator's lament upon the death of his lady. ***77*** "Le Songe Saint Valentin" has a more detailed resemblance to the final episode in Chaucer's *Parliament of Fowls*. In both, a narrator dreams that he enters a garden where he comes upon a great assembly of birds who have gathered in order to choose their mates under the direction of a female authority figure (an eagle in Granson's poem, Nature in Chaucer's) and in which there is one bird that does not take part in the general joy (though for very different reasons: because he has already chosen in one case, and because she does not wish to choose in the other). Wimsatt, who has made the closest study of Chaucer's relation to the French poetry of his time, also finds a close similarity between the pose of one who is unfit for love that Granson's narrator adopts in the concluding lines and the opening of Chaucer's *Troilus*.[96] He also points to what he regards as Granson's borrowings from Chaucer in several passages in ***78*** *Le Livre Messire Ode*. The narrator's decision to dress in black, first of all, and then in the encounter with the man in the orchard, the narrator's

a single work under a single title, "Les cinq balades ensuivans." It is not necessary to presume, of course, that Chaucer could have learned of this work only from one of the surviving copies.

[93] Wimsatt, *French Contemporaries*, p. 211.

[94] Suggestions that Granson and Chaucer might have met as early as 1368 at the wedding of Prince Lionel in Milan or that Granson might have accompanied the party returning to England (see Braddy, *Chaucer and Graunson*, 27) are purely speculative, since there is no record that either poet actually went to Milan, and even if they did, one can only suppose that they might have become acquainted.

[95] That Granson spoke at least some English by 1384 is confirmed by Deschamps' record of his conversation with the guards at Calais in his ballade, and Chaucer's compliment to Granson would of course have meant little if it was not understood.

[96] Wimsatt, *French Contemporaries*, pp. 221–24.

offer of consolation (lines 1153–56) and his inability to understand his companion's complaint (1364–65) all recall *The Book of the Duchess*; and the narrator's defense of his ability to offer help (1177–82) recalls a very similar exchange between Troilus and Pandarus (*Troilus and Criseyde* 1.622–89).[97]

The least persuasive of these analogues is offered by ***76*** "Complainte de Saint Vallentin Garenson." Chaucer would not have needed Granson to suggest to him that one situation in which a lover might need consolation is that his lady has died, especially since *The Book of the Duchess* was occasioned by a real death, that of Blanche of Lancaster, the wife of John of Gaunt. Chaucer's poem contains, moreover, numerous echoes of Machaut's *Le Jugement du roi de Behaingne*, in which the death of a lover is precisely one of the issues.[98] Nor does Granson display any obvious debt to Chaucer. The situation in his poem instead very closely resembles that in the anonymous *Le Songe vert*, in which it is Venus rather than Saint Valentine and the God of Love who provides the poet's consolation. The chronology is not absolutely certain, but Wimsatt argues persuasively for *Le Songe vert* as Granson's likely source.[99] The resemblance to *The Book of the Duchess* in ***70*** "La Complainte de l'an nouvel" is seemingly closer, but in this case too it may not be necessary to suppose that there is any direct link, because the same general situation — a melancholy narrator, a knight's overheard complaint, the narrator's role as comforter — is found in a poem that Chaucer certainly knew and that Granson certainly could have, Machaut's *Dit de la fonteinne amoureuse*. The one detail that is lacking in Machaut is that both Granson's and Chaucer's narrators meet their lamenting companion in a wood, certainly a small hook on which to hang an argument for borrowing, given the outdoor setting of so many *dits amoureux*. If one poet does draw from the other, the evidence of dating is much too uncertain to allow us to determine which came first.[100] Wimsatt suggests that Granson's poem, in which the consolation motif is much less developed and more poorly motivated, should be regarded as derivative, and Chaucer's, in which it is part of a careful and cohesive design, must therefore have been first,[101] and while that is a plausible scenario, it is also possible to imagine that Chaucer simply saw possibilities for development that Granson did not.

77 "Le Songe Saint Valentin" and the *Parliament of Fowls* offer a very different case, for while there are many other poems in which birds have speaking roles and also some in which they act as stand-ins for human lovers, there is no earlier common source for the Saint Valentine's Day assembly at which the birds choose their mates. Again, Chaucer's greater skill at developing the episode and at integrating it into his composition might

[97] Wimsatt, *French Contemporaries*, pp. 227–30.

[98] See Wimsatt, *French Love Poets*, pp. 89–93 and Colin Wilcockson's notes in *Riverside Chaucer*, pp. 966–76.

[99] Wimsatt, *French Love Poets*, pp. 138–43.

[100] As noted above, an excerpt from Granson's poem appears in manuscript *E* with responses in alternating stanzas attributed to "Lesparra." It is possible, but far from certain, that the poem therefore dates from the period of Granson's Spanish captivity in 1372–74; see note 40 above. The Duchess Blanche died in 1368, but there is no way to be sure how long after her death *The Book of the Duchess* was written. See Wilcockson in *Riverside Chaucer*, p. 976.

[101] Wimsatt, *French Love Poets*, pp. 143–46; *French Contemporaries*, p. 220.

suggest that his rather than Granson's was the original.[102] Perhaps even more persuasive in this case is the evident link to *Troilus and Criseyde* in the narrator's concluding remarks in Granson's poem. The pose that he adopts here, as one who is unapt to love but who looks out for the welfare of other lovers, is completely new for Granson but entirely characteristic of Chaucer. The passages that Wimsatt cites from *Le Livre Messire Ode* fall into the same class: they and the equivalent passages in Chaucer have no common source, but their mild, self-mocking humor is distinctively Chaucerian and unlike anything that we find elsewhere in Granson. The evidence of Granson's borrowing from more than one of Chaucer's poems is consistent with the piecemeal construction of both of Granson's and in itself could constitute evidence that Granson was the borrower. And if Granson was indebted to *Troilus and Criseyde* for the episodes in these poems, that helps clarify the chronology, for both must have been written long after *The Book of the Duchess* and *The Parliament of Fowls* as well.

Establishing the relationship between "Le Songe Saint Valentin" and *The Parliament of Fowls* has bearing on another important issue, the two poets' separate invocations of Saint Valentine. Both Granson and Chaucer refer to the saint in other of their works, and they are evidently the first poets to do so. Chaucer has two references apart from the fully developed scene in *The Parliament of Fowls*. In the opening lines of "The Complaint of Mars," the narrator overhears a bird singing to others on Saint Valentine's Day (lines 13–14), urging them either to go out and choose their mates or to renew their service (16–19). And in the Prologue to *The Legend of Good Women*, the birds are overheard singing to one another,

> "Blessed be Seynt Valentyn,
> For on his day I chees yow to be myn,
> Withouten repentyng, myn herte swete!"
> (F 145–47)[103]

Saint Valentine appears in six other poems of Granson. In one, ***50*** "Complainte de Saint Valentin," the saint is named only in the title, and only in manuscript *F* and in the closely related manuscript *K* (which appear to have a special affinity for the saint). ***17*** "Balade de Saint Valentin" also bears this title only in manuscript *F*, where it immediately follows ***72***, and in *F* alone, the narrator affirms his love by Saint Valentine in line 23, where manuscripts *A* and *P* have "Le Dieu d'Amours [the God of Love]" instead. ***60*** and ***61*** are labeled "Balade de Saint Valentin Double" in manuscripts *F* and *K*, and the second of these two poems (which also appears in manuscripts *A* and *P*) is a plea to the saint for his aid in the narrator's quest for his lady's love. In the final line of ***71*** "Le Souhait de Saint Valentin" (again so named only in manuscript *F*), the narrator asks his lady to accept him as her servant on Saint Valentine's Day. In ***76*** "Complainte de Saint Vallentin Garenson," the saint actually appears in the company of the God of Love to urge the narrator to abandon his grief and to move on, and in the final line the narrator commits to loving his new lady

[102] See Wimsatt's entire discussion, *French Contemporaries*, pp. 221–27. An earlier expression of doubt of Granson's priority is offered by Brewer, ed., Chaucer, *Parlement of Foulys*, pp. 131–32.

[103] In the "Complaynt d'Amours," attributed by Skeat to Chaucer, the narrator offers his poem to his lady on Saint Valentine's Day, "Whan every foughel chesen shal his mak [When every bird shall choose its mate]"(86). The attribution has not been generally accepted, and the poem is now more commonly thought to be the work of a fifteenth-century imitator of Chaucer. See Laila Z. Gross's note in *Riverside Chaucer*, p. 1090.

forever "On this Saint Valentine's Day." Finally, there are three brief references in ***78*** *Le Livre Messire Ode*. In lines 828–31, the narrator prays to Saint Valentine for relief from his sorrow. In line 1996, the narrator reports hearing a voice in a dream that lifts him out of his melancholy on Saint Valentine's Day. And in lines 1246–47, in the man's story of his relation with two birds, where the manuscript that we have chosen as base reads ""L'endemain de saint Valentin / Que tous oyseaulx veullent chanter [The day after Saint Valentine's Day, / When all the birds want to sing]," the only other manuscript that contains this passage has "Que tous oyseaulx prennent leur per [When all the birds choose their mates]."

The origins of the association between Saint Valentine and love are lost in time, and neither Chaucer's nor Granson's references do a great deal to clarify them.[104] It is worth noting, however, that neither poet places the day of his feast in February.[105] In *The Parliament of Fowls*, everything suggests a setting in very late spring, and the rondeau that the birds sing before flying off begins,

> "Now welcome, somer, with thy sonne softe,
> That hast thes wintres wedes overshake,
> And driven away the longe nyghtes blake!"
> (680–82)

In the Prologue to *The Legend of Good Women*, the setting is the month of May (lines F 36, F 45), the birds offer their song "For the newe blisful somers sake" (F 142), and later conclude their song, "Welcome, somer, oure governour and lord!" (F 170). Granson's invocations of the saint give him less opportunity to be specific about the season, but in both "Le Songe Saint Valentin" and the episode in *Le Livre Messire Ode*, the accounts of the pleasure that the men took in visiting their respective gardens certainly suggest a May date rather than one in mid-February.[106]

If on that point Granson and Chaucer seem to be in accord, there are also important differences between them. As Wimsatt has pointed out, for Chaucer, Saint Valentine presides over the birds' choice of mates, but except in "Le Songe Saint Valentin" and *Le Livre Messire Ode*, each of which we have other reasons to believe is both late in his career and perhaps based in part on Chaucer, Granson invokes the saint for his aid to human lovers instead, and his feast is a day on which humans express and celebrate their love.[107] Wimsatt also notes that these two images of the saint remain distinct among the poets' immediate successors. In England, Gower and Clanvowe associate Saint Valentine with the

---

[104] Two very different reconstructions of the background to these works are offered by Oruch, "St. Valentine," and Kelly, *Saint Valentine*.

[105] It is only with Charles VI's institution of the *Cour amoureuse* in 1400 that the amatory rites associated with Saint Valentine are first known to have become attached to the feast of Saint Valentine the Martyr on February 14. See Oruch, "St. Valentine," p. 558, and Kelly, *Saint Valentine*, pp. 131–33.

[106] See Kelly, *Saint Valentine*, pp. 68–69. Oruch ("St. Valentine," pp. 549–56) points out that spring is said to begin in February in a number of medieval sources, but he does not provide any convincing link between February and warm weather.

[107] Wimsatt phrases the distinction slightly differently; *French Contemporaries*, p. 234.

pairing up of the birds,[108] while in France, Christine de Pisan and Jean de Garencières do not.[109] Chaucer's appears to be an exclusively literary motif, while Granson seems to refer to an actual practice. A great many pieces in this puzzle are still missing, but in view of the differences between them, priority seems to be a much less important issue. Each poet seems to have had his own understanding of the traditions associated with the saint and to have made his own contribution to their diffusion. And in this case, Granson's turned out to be the more enduring.

GRANSON AND ISABEL

Three of Granson's poems begin with the name "Isabel" in acrostic. In ***71*** "Le Souhait de Saint Valentin" and ***77*** "Le Songe Saint Valentin," the name is formed by the initial letters of the first six lines, and in ***74*** "Complainte de Gransson," it is formed by the initial letters of the first six stanzas. Acrostics were one of several ways in which the poets of the time identified either themselves, their patrons, or the ladies that they addressed. To take only two examples from Machaut, who seems to have had a particular fondness for such devices,[110] in *Le Livre dou voir dit* (lines 6336–43), he uses numbers corresponding to the letters of the alphabet to encode his lady's name, "Peron," and he too has a ballade that begins with an acrostic for "Isebele."[111] The latter has not been identified, but most of the figures that Machaut names are known, and there has been a natural curiosity about the woman named by Granson as well. There are two principal candidates: Isabel, the daughter of Pedro of Castile (c. 1355–92), who married Edmund of Langley, Duke of York, Edward

[108] See *Cinkante Balades*, numbers 34 and 35, in Gower, *French Balades*, ed. Yeager, pp. 106–09; and *The Boke of Cupide*, lines 79–80, in Clanvowe, *Works*, ed. Scattergood, p. 39. Yeager (pp. 52–53) dates the *Cinkante Balades* to the very early 1390s, arguing that it was written in imitation of *Les Cent Ballades*. *The Boke of Cupide* is clearly written in imitation of Chaucer, and Scattergood dates it between 1386 and 1391 (p. 14). Gower's two ballades are not specific about the time of year, but as Kelly notes (*Saint Valentine*, pp. 72–74), the adjacent ballades strongly suggest a May setting, and Gower places the birds' choice of mates more firmly in May in his *Confessio Amantis* 1.100–03 and 1.2081–90. Clanvowe, on the other hand places Saint Valentine's Day in March (line 80), which does indicate, at least, that the feast of this Saint Valentine had not yet been fixed. Manuscript *E* also contains a Valentine's Day poem in Catalan that refers to the mating of the birds. Jordà, "Cançoner Vega-Aguiló," pp. 331–37 identifies the poet as Pere Pardo de la Casta, whose date of birth (approximately 1366; see Jordà, p. 333) indicates that the poem must have been written after *The Parliament of Fowls*. Its relation to Chaucer's and to these other poems is otherwise entirely uncertain. For an earlier identification of the author see Riquer, "Canción de san Valentín," pp. 338–44; and see Kelly, *Saint Valentine*, pp. 66, 70.

[109] Christine de Pisan, *Œuvres poétiques*, 1:111–12, 2:29–48, 3:281 (see Oruch, "St. Valentine," pp. 558–59, 564, and Kelly, *Saint Valentine*, pp. 134–39); Garencières, *Poésies complètes*, part 2, p. 18, Ballade number 15. Garencières does not actually name the saint, but as Oruch notes ("St. Valentine," p. 559), his use of "Je vous choisy" in four successive lines appears to echo Granson's ballade ***17***, which does, in the version that appears in manuscript *F*.

[110] Some of which have not yet been solved; see Earp, *Guillaume de Machaut*, the index references under "anagrams, cryptograms, acrostics, or number riddles," p. 627.

[111] Machaut, *Poésie lyriques*, 1:85, number LXXIV; *Louange des dames*, p. 75, number 99.

III's fourth son, in 1372;[112] and Isabel (or Isabeau) of Bavaria (1370–1415), who in 1385 married Charles VI of France.[113] John Shirley, a fifteenth-century copyist of the works of Chaucer, reports that "hit is sayde" that Granson composed the last of the ballades that Chaucer translated in "The Complaint of Venus" for Isabel of York, but his source is not known, and the comment is more appropriate for Chaucer's version, in which a woman is the speaker, than it is for Granson's.[114] The strongest argument for Isabel of York is a negative one: it rests on the belief that all of the poems in manuscript *E*, which includes a copy of ***74***, must have been written before 1374, when the second Isabel was only four years old. This argument, however, requires that we accept the conjectural dating of one poem in that book as a firm date for all the rest.[115] The case for the second Isabel is strengthened by the fact that she is known to have owned a manuscript of Granson's work, for which she ordered new clasps in 1401.[116] The link is suggestive, to be sure, but Granson is not known to have spent any time at the court in France between this Isabel's marriage in 1385 and his death in 1397, the period of his life for which we have the fullest record of his movements.[117]

The arguments for both Isabels, moreover, have been marked by the assumption not just that Granson's poetry records a real relationship but that all of his surviving poems were written for the same woman.[118] Thus the search has been limited to royal families because of Granson's references elsewhere to his lady as a "princesse,"[119] and the argument for the second Isabel has depended in large part on the references to "la non pareille de France" and "la non per de France" in *Le Livre Messire Ode*,[120] which contains no reference, however, to "Isabel." As Cartier has noted, *princesse* is a common complimentary epithet in the poetry of the time, and it does not necessarily indicate a lady's actual rank. Cartier is also able to show that there are many passages in Granson's poetry that would have been entirely inappropriate for a royal princess.[121] Even if the "princesse" that Granson addresses in one or more poems was real, there is no reason to assume, especially with so peripatetic a poet, that every one of his poems was written for her, and thus none of his poems can be used to determine who might have been addressed in any other. And none of the three poems in which "Isabel" is named contains any suggestion either that she is royal or that she is French.

---

[112] Braddy, *Chaucer and Graunson*, pp. 71–82.

[113] Grandson, *Vie et poésies*, ed. Piaget, pp. 156–64.

[114] For Shirley's note see Braddy, *Chaucer and Graunson*, p. 78. See also Laila Z. Gross in *Riverside Chaucer*, pp. 1078–79 and 1081, on the dating of both "The Complaint of Mars" and "The Complaint of Venus."

[115] See footnote 40 above.

[116] Grandson, *Vie et poésies*, ed. Piaget, pp. 110–11.

[117] Cartier, "Oton de Grandson," p. 5.

[118] As noted by Kelly, *Saint Valentine*, p. 134n12. That assumption is particularly visible in Galway, "Isabel of France." Galway argues, on the basis of references to the lady's youth in ***52***.29, and elsewhere, that Granson's Isabel was the daughter of Charles VI, who became the bride of Richard II, but who was only seven years old when Granson died.

[119] ***42***.25, ***57***.31, ***64***.37, ***66***.38, ***76***.172; and in ***78*** *Le Livre Messire Ode*, lines 139, 375, 990, etc.

[120] ***78***.1594, 1946, 2091, 2297, and 2384.

[121] Cartier, "Oton de Grandson," pp. 5–7, 12–15.

The three poems together also do not give us much insight into the poet's relation with his Isabel. In ***71*** the narrator has high praise for his lady's accomplishments, and he wants only to be accepted as her servant. In ***74*** he describes his lady as very young, and he grieves at having to part from her. And in ***77*** the narrator himself claims to have no experience in love; if the lady appears at all, it is in the form of the falcon who is very good at hunting. Only the tercel's comment that though he is low in rank, he is nonetheless noble (137–38) suggests a real human parallel, but it does not tell us how much higher in rank his "falcon" might be. Given the nature of the compliments involved, there is no reason to exclude either Isabel of York or Isabel of Bavaria as possible designees, and the parting that Granson describes could have taken place at almost any time in his much-traveled life. If we limit ourselves to these three poems, however, there is also another candidate who is neither royal nor French but whom Granson certainly knew, and that is Isabelle, the Countess of Neuchâtel (c. 1335–95).[122] This Isabel's life was of the type that might encourage such speculation. She was married at the age of four to Rodolphe IV of nearby Nidau, at the northern end of Lake Biel, also in modern Switzerland. They had no children, and when Rodolphe was killed in 1375, he left his property to a nephew rather than to his wife.[123] She became countess in 1373 on the death of her father, who had no male heirs, and during the rest of her life she acted energetically to preserve and enlarge her patrimony.[124] Granson was in her service in 1376 according to the documents cited by Piaget,[125] shortly after her husband's death, and though he parted from her soon after to return to England, he was evidently in her company again in 1382, and they would have had another chance to become reacquainted upon his return to Savoy in 1386, following the death of his father.

The dates and the facts fit well, much better than for either of the other Isabels, but that is really all that we can say. We do not know what other Isabels Granson might have known. The story that the poet creates, moreover, might be no more than an artful compliment to a distinguished lady. Whatever real relationship the poet might have had remains concealed beneath the poetry, and that, no doubt, is exactly what he would have intended.

THE PRESENT EDITION

We present here the seventy-eight poems that can be ascribed to Granson with the greatest degree of certainty, as we describe in this Introduction. Since none of the surviving manuscripts contains all of these poems, our edition cannot be based on any single copy. We have therefore drawn from all three of the major collections, manuscripts *A*, *F*, and *P*. When the same poem appears in more than one of these, the variations in most cases rule out the possibility of establishing a single authoritative text. Each manuscript is imperfect, containing lapses in meter, rhyme, spelling, grammar, and sense, some of which are possible to correct from the other manuscripts when these are available or, more cautiously, from the editor's judgment when only a single copy exists. There are more substantive differences, however, even between the two copies of the same poem in manuscript *A*, that in some cases

[122] As suggested by Cartier, "Oton de Grandson," p. 15. See also Wimsatt, *French Contemporaries*, pp. 333n14 and 335n36.

[123] Bartolini, "Neuchâtel, Isabelle de," and Niederhäuser, "Nidau, Rodolphe IV de."

[124] Courvoisier, *Panorama*, pp. 46–48.

[125] Grandson, *Vie et poésies*, ed. Piaget, pp. 16–17.

appear to stem from an uncertainty in the prototype from which all derive and in other cases might well represent equally authoritative alternatives. Given the nature of the variants, the most reasonable procedure in presenting each poem appears to be to choose one manuscript and to follow it except in case of obvious error. But for the same reason, in many individual instances, the choice of which manuscript to follow is very difficult to make.

What earlier editors have done is to give priority to one of the manuscripts for all of the poems that it contains. Piaget gave priority to *F* and used *A* only for the poems that are not in *F*. Grenier-Winther and Cunningham chose *A* instead and used *F* only for the poems that were not in *A*. We have chosen to give priority to *P* for the twenty-seven poems that it contains. It has the fewest of Granson's poems of the three collections, but it is also the earliest, by as much as three decades. It lacks a small number of passages that appear in other copies, but otherwise it contains a very clean text, requiring no more emendations than *A* and fewer than *F*. For the poems that appear in all three manuscripts, moreover, it contains significantly fewer unique readings than either *A* or *F*, suggesting that it has been subject to less scribal tampering than the other two.[126] And it allows us to provide a version of these poems that is not available in the existing editions.

For the poems that are in both *A* and *F* but not in *P*, there is not an easy choice. *F* may be slightly earlier than *A*, but not enough to make a clear difference. *F* is the only manuscript to give a title to the "Cinq balades ensuivans," which it presents together as in *P*. (The sequence is broken up in manuscript *A*.) *F* also preserves the unity of the *balade double* (as in *E* and *K*) which *A* presents as two separate poems, and it gives it a title (the same as in *K*). But *F* is also manifestly defective in five poems, giving only the last forty-nine lines (out of 450) of ***73*** and lacking whole stanzas in ***38***, ***50***, ***66***, and ***67***. It is also missing individual lines in ***73***, ***74***, and ***75***. Manuscript *A* also lacks some individual lines (in ***58*** and ***75***), and it also lacks the envoy to ***53*** (see the note) and ***56***, but otherwise it is clearly based on more complete exemplars. And with the notable exception of ***74*** and ***75***, which appear to have the most complicated textual history among Granson's works (and which we present here from *P*), *A* has fewer unique readings than *F* in the poems that these two manuscripts share with *P*. Not only does *A* appear to be generally closer to the assumed prototype from which all three copies derive, it also offers a cleaner text than *F* and requires fewer emendations. We have therefore given it priority and used it as the base for the poems that do not appear in *P*.

For the poems that appear only in *F* or *A*, of course, there was no choice to make. For ***78*** *Le Livre Messire Ode* there is an equally easy decision for only manuscript *B* contains the last one thousand lines of the surviving text. The most difficult choice is posed by ***76*** "Complainte de Saint Vallentin Garenson," for which there are two complete medieval copies, in *B* and *D*,[127] which contain very substantial differences, particularly in the last seven

[126] The one exception is ***73*** "La Pastourelle Granson," in which *P* records more unique readings than either *A* or *F*, but most of these are very minor and being equally plausible, require no emendation. The fact that there is an exception is a useful reminder of the complicated history that must lie behind all three of these manuscripts and of the fact that each poem that circulated independently, as "La Pastourelle" clearly did, had a unique textual history of its own. See also the note to ***53***.

[127] There is also a fragment in *G* plus a sixteenth-century copy in *H* which is nearly identical to that in *D*.

stanzas. We have exercised our judgment here to present the version that we believe on the basis of sense and grammar to be likely to be least corrupt, in *D*.

The base manuscript that we have chosen for each poem is identified in the notes. We have followed this manuscript with these exceptions: (1) For ease of reference, both in this introduction and in the text, we have adopted the titles by which Granson's longer poems have become known in modern scholarship (which are based on Piaget's edition, and thus mostly on manuscript *F*). When the title in the base manuscript differs, it is recorded in the notes. We have also supplied titles, drawn from the first line of the rondeaux and the virelai and from the refrain of the ballades, for the poems that are labeled only with the name of the appropriate *forme fixe* in the manuscripts. (2) In accordance with the editorial practice of this series, we have silently expanded all abbreviations, and we have used modern word division, capitalization, and punctuation, including an apostrophe to indicate a contraction. We have also spelled out numbers written in roman numerals, and we have expanded the refrains that are indicated with an "&c" or some similar abbreviation.[128] (3) We have marked passages of dialogue with quotation marks, and in ***76*** and ***78***, we have used a paragraph indentation to mark the break between the present-tense lyrical passages and the past tense narrative passages where quotation marks would have been intrusive. (4) We have distinguished *i/j* and *u/v* in accordance with Modern French orthography. The letter combinations *sf/ff* and *ct/tt* that are difficult to distinguish in the manuscripts have been regularized to *sf* and *ct*. (5) We have inserted a cedilla (*ç*) when appropriate, and we have made a limited use of accent marks to distinguish homographs and other words that might be confused.[129] (6) We have emended the text when we found the base manuscript to be deficient in rhyme, sense, or grammar. We have adopted readings from other copies when these were available; when there was no manuscript support, our corrections are limited to undoing scribal errors of the most easily recognizable sorts. Our practice has necessarily varied somewhat depending upon the quality of the base text and on the number of other copies. Thus, for example, while manuscripts *A*, *F*, and *P* generally require very little emendation, in ***73*** there is a strong manuscript tradition against several of the readings in our base manuscript *P*; and in ***78*** *Le Livre Messire Ode*, the generally poorer quality of our base manuscript *B* has made us turn rather more frequently to the other surviving copies as equally valid witnesses.[130] We have resisted the temptation to emend on metrical grounds alone, even when encouraged by other manuscripts. There are too many instances of metrically deficient lines that cannot easily be repaired — some supported by independent copies — to allow confidence that the poet always adhered to a strict syllable count, and thus when another manuscript seems to offer a better reading, it is impossible to say whether the difference is due to one scribe's lapse or another's unauthorized improvement. And while some lines seem to require only a simple change of spelling, others could be "fixed" in more than a single way. Not knowing where to draw the line, we have chosen to preserve the scribal record unless there is justification either in sense or in grammar for the emendation. All

---

[128] See the notes to ***1–9*** and ***10***.

[129] In Middle French, *qui* and *que* are often used interchangeably, as are *si* and *se*, and *ce* and *se*. All such spellings are left as they appear in the manuscript. Other interchangeable words and letters that have been left untouched include *car/que*, *comme/comment*, *par/pour*, *en/a*, *que/quand*, *et/ne*, *ai/oi*, and *s/z*.

[130] In some cases the manuscripts provide no completely acceptable reading. See our notes to ***59***.21, ***73***.79, ***76***.163–66, and for a very different case, ***78***.1763–64.

emendations and their sources are recorded in the textual notes. We make no effort, however, to provide a complete list of variants, for which one may consult Grenier-Winther's edition.

The manuscripts vary in order far more than they do in text. With the possible exception of sequences such as the "Cinq balades ensuivans," there is clearly no authoritative arrangement, and the underlying collections in all three appear to have been assembled almost randomly, perhaps as individual pieces came to hand.[131] We felt that there was nothing to be gained by preserving the order in the manuscripts from which we derived the texts. There is also no basis for ordering most of the poems chronologically. We have, therefore, chosen to imitate the practice of the contemporary collections of the works of poets such as Machaut, which typically group together the poems in the same *forme fixe*. We have gone one step further and ordered the poems by length, from short to long, and among the ballades, by length of stanza. The arrangement not only facilitates the comparison of the poems in the same form but also reveals how the forms differed, including, for instance, how the longer stanzas imposed greater demands and resulted in a greater sophistication of language.

THE TRANSLATION

Like all translators, we present our work with a deep realization of its inadequacy. Our intent here has been to lead the reader back to the original rather than to replace it, and we have therefore tried to be as literal as one can in going from one language to another. At the same time, when we saw that we had a choice, we have tried to offer a smooth line rather than a rough one, an interesting line instead of a dull one, and a metrical line instead of an unmetrical one. We have also tried to preserve the aphoristic quality of some of Granson's refrains. The reader will find many places in which the literal ruled, however, especially in the longer poems, and then, we hope, he or she will follow our first intent and listen to Granson's language rather than ours.

One difficulty susceptible to no completely satisfactory solution concerns the treatment of abstractions and personifications: whether to capitalize these, first of all, since the distinction is so often blurred, and then whether to designate those that are capitalized as "he" and "she" or as "it," a choice that does not arise in French. We have been liberal in our use of capitals, but we have given preference to "it" except in the case of full personifications, as when "Love" clearly designates the God of Love. The reader may feel free to substitute a different pronoun whenever he or she prefers.

[131] But compare Jung's analysis of the contents of manuscript *A* ("Répertoire," pp. 93–96).

List of Manuscripts

A Lausanne, Bibliothèque cantonale et universitaire, MS 350, second quarter fifteenth century
B Paris, Bibliothèque nationale, f. fr. 1727, mid fifteenth century
C Paris, Bibliothèque nationale, f. fr. 1131, mid fifteenth century
D Paris, Bibliothèque nationale, f. fr. 24440, fifteenth century
E Barcelona, Biblioteca de Catalunya, MS 8, Catalan, 1420–30.
F Paris, Bibliothèque nationale, f. fr. 2201, early fifteenth century
G London, Westminster Abbey Library, MS 21, mid fifteenth century
H Paris, Bibliothèque nationale, f. fr. 833, c. 1600
J Paris, Bibliothèque nationale, f. fr. 1952, sixteenth century
K Lausanne, Bibliothèque cantonale et universitaire, IS 4254, fifteenth century.
L Paris, Bibliothèque nationale, Rothschild MS I.I.9, mid fifteenth century
M Carpentras, Bibliothèque Inguimbertine, MS fr. 390, fifteenth century
N Brussels, Bibliothèque royale Albert 1er, MS 10961–10970, c. 1465
O Karlsruhe, Badische Landesbibliothek, MS 410, c. 1430
P Philadelphia, University of Pennsylvania, Van Pelt Library, MS Codex 902 (formerly Fr. MS 15), 1395–1400
Q Berne, Burgerbibliothek da la Bourgeoisie, MS 473, 1400–40
R Turin, Archivio di Stato, MS J. b. IX. 10, fifteenth century
S Paris, Bibliothèque nationale, f. fr. 24404, thirteenth century (sixteenth century addition)
T Besançon, Bibliothèque municipale, MS 556, 1826
V Carpentras, Bibliothèque Inguimbertine, MS fr. 411, fifteenth century
W Brussels, Bibliothèque royale Albert 1er, MS IV 541, 1564–81
Y Turin, Biblioteca nazionale e universitaria, MS L.II.12, mid sixteenth century

Poems

1. Rondeau: «Se Dieu eust oblié 'non'»

Se Dieu eust oblié «non»
Quant il faisoit le langaige,
Je tien qu'il eust fait que saige
Et que gracieux et bon.

Des dames pas ne fusson
En si dangereux servaige,
Se Dieu eust oblié «non»
Quant il faisoit le langaige.

Certes, a m'entencion,
Ce ne fust point de dommaige.
Mais eust esté avantaige
Tresgrant a maint compaignom.

Se Dieu eust oblié «non»
Quant il faisoit le langaige,
Je tien qu'il eust fait que saige
Et que gracieux et bon.

2. Rondel: «Avril, qui vest de verdure»

Avril, qui vest de verdure
Le monde pour esjoir,
A mains ne me puit tolir
La grant douleur que j'endure.

Oster ne puit la pointure
Que me fait plaindre et gemir
Avril, qui vest de verdure
Le monde pour esjoir.

Sans que je voie la figure
Qui d'amours m'a fait ferir,

Poems

1. Rondeau: "If God had just forgotten 'no'"

If God had just forgotten "no"
When he created language,
I hold he would have proven wise
And gracious and good.

To the ladies we would not be
In so painful a servitude
If God had just forgotten "no"
When he created language.

Certainly, it seems to me,
This wouldn't have been any harm,
But would have been great benefit
To many a companion.

If God had just forgotten "no"
When he created language,
I hold he would have proven wise
And gracious and good.

2. Rondeau: "April, which decks with greenery"

April, which decks with greenery
The world in order to bring joy,
Cannot in the least remove from me
The great sorrow that I endure.

It cannot take away the wound
That makes me lament and sigh —
April, which decks with greenery
The world in order to bring joy.

Unless I see the one
Who caused me to be struck by love,

Je ne puis avoir plaisir
De riens qui soit pour ma cure.

Avril, qui vest de verdure
Le monde pour esjoir,
A mains ne me puit tolir
La grant douleur que j'endure.

3. Rondel: «Je ne voy riens qui me doie suffire»

Je ne voy riens qui me doie suffire,
Ce jour d'avril qui est si bel et gay.
De mon regart ja ne m'esjoiray
Se je ne voy celle que je desire.

Puisq'ainsy est c'on ne pourroit eslire
Dame qui soit se belle com je l'ay.
Je ne voy riens qui me doie suffire,
Ce jour d'avril qui est si bel et gay.

Riens qui soit bel a mon cuer ne puit luire,
Tout ce qui puit gecter mon cuer d'esmay,
Pour ce je doy par tout haultement dire:
«Par vous me vient tretout le mal que j'ay.»

Je ne voy riens qui me doie suffire,
Ce jour d'avril qui est si bel et gay.
De mon regart ja ne m'esjoiray
Se je ne voy celle que je desire.

4. Rondel: «S'il ne vous plaist que j'aye mieulx»

S'il ne vous plaist que j'aye mieulx,
Je prendré en gré ma destresse.
Mais par Dieu, ma plaisant maistresse,
J'aymasse mieulx estre joieux.

De vous suis si fort amoureulx
Que mon cuer de crier ne sesse.
S'il ne vous plaist que j'aye mieulx,
Je prendré en gré ma destresse.

Belle, tournez vers moy voz yeux,
Et veés en quele tristesse

I cannot take any pleasure
In anything at all for my cure.

April, which decks with greenery
The world in order to bring joy,
Cannot in the least remove from me
The great sorrow that I endure.

3. Rondeau: "I don't see anything that should satisfy me"

I don't see anything that should satisfy me
This April day that is so fair and gay.
I will never take any joy in my sight
If I do not see her whom I desire.

Since it is so, that one could not choose
A lady who is as beautiful as mine,
I don't see anything that should satisfy me
This April day that is so fair and gay.

Nothing that is beautiful can brighten my heart,
Anything that can cast my heart from dismay.
Therefore I must say loudly, everywhere:
"From you comes all the pain that I bear."

I don't see anything that should satisfy me
This April day that is so fair and gay.
I will never take any joy in my sight
If I do not see her whom I desire.

4. Rondeau: "If it please you not that I have better"

If it please you not that I have better,
I will willingly accept my pain.
But by God, my charming mistress,
I would much prefer to be in joy.

I am so deeply in love with you
That my heart does not cease to cry out.
If it please you not that I have better,
I will willingly accept my pain.

Beauty, turn your eyes towards me
And see in what great sadness

Je use mon temps et ma jeunesse,
Et puis faitez de moy voz jeux.

S'il ne vous plaist que j'aye mieulx,
Je prendré en gré ma destresse.
Mais par Dieu, ma plaisant maistresse,
J'aymasse mieulx estre joieux.

5. Rondel: «Bien appert, Belle, a vo bonté»

Bien appert, Belle, a vo bonté
Et a vostre maintenement
Que vous aimez tresloiaument
La ou vostre cuer c'est donné.

Pour ce est cil tresbien euré
Qui vous aime non faintement.
Bien appert, Belle, a vo bonté
Et a vostre maintenement.

S'en doit mieulx faire vostre gré
De cuer et plus songneusement,
Car pour vivre amoureusement,
Il ne est nul mieulx assené.

Bien appert, Belle, a vo bonté
Et a vostre maintenement
Que vous aimez tresloiaument
La ou vostre cuer c'est donné.

6. Rondel: «Comment seroit que je fusse joieulx?»

Comment seroit que je fusse joieulx
Quant je ne voy ma tresbelle maistresse
De qui me vient quanque j'ay de leesse,
Par le regart de sez beaulx rians yeux?

Puis que j'en suy sy tresfort amoureux
Que d'y penser a toute heure ne cesse,
Comment seroit que je fusse joieulx
Quant je ne voy ma tresbelle maistresse.

S'elle feust cy, je feusse bien eureux,
Et en mon cuer n'eusse plus de tristesse.

I spend my time and pass my youth,
And then play your games with me.

If it please you not that I have better,
I will willingly accept my pain.
But by God, my charming mistress,
I would much prefer to be in joy.

5. *Rondeau*: "Well does it seem, my beautiful lady"

Well does it seem, my beautiful lady,
From your goodness and from your manner,
That you love very loyally
There where you have given your heart.

Therefore is he very fortunate,
The one who loves you devotedly.
Well does it seem, my beautiful lady,
From your goodness and from your manner.

Thus he ought better to do your will
With all his heart, and more attentively,
For to live a life of love,
There is no one who is better placed.

Well does it seem, my beautiful lady,
From your goodness and from your manner,
That you love very loyally
There where you have given your heart.

6. *Rondeau*: "How could it be that I be joyful?"

How could it be that I be joyful
When I do not see my beautiful mistress
From whom comes whatever happiness I have
By way of the look from her fair laughing eyes?

Since I am so deeply in love with her
That I don't cease to think of her at any time,
How could it be that I be joyful
When I do not see my beautiful mistress?

If she were here, I would be very happy
And there would be no more sadness in my heart.

Mais puis qu'il fault qu'aprez moy je la lesse
Avec Danger qui tant est envieux,

Comment seroit que je fusse joieulx
Quant je ne voy ma tresbelle maistresse
De qui me vient quanque j'ay de leesse,
Par le regart de sez beaulx rians yeux?

7. *Rondel*: «Belle, pour hair faulceté»

Belle, pour hair faulceté
Et vous servir de cuer d'amy,
M'out Amours mis en tel party
Que je pers plaisance et senté.

Car savoir ne puis ce vo gré
Est qu'ayez ja de moy mercy,
Belle, pour hair faulceté
Et vous servir de cuer d'amy.

Mais, s'il vous plaisoit qu'asseuré
En feusse par ung doulx octry,
De tous poins seroye gary
Du gré mal qui tant m'a duré.

Belle, pour hair faulceté
Et vous servir de cuer d'amy,
M'out Amours mis en tel party
Que je pers plaisance et senté.

8. *Rondel*: «Ce premier jour que l'an se renouvelle»

Ce premier jour que l'an se renouvelle,
Joieusement et de loial penser
Vous doins mon cuer a tousjourz sans faulser,
Bonne, saige, gracieuse et tresbelle.

Car, par ma foy, vous estez seule celle
Sans qui ne puis leesse recouvrer,
Ce premier jour que l'an se renouvelle,
Joieusement et de loial penser.

Si pry Amours que pour moy se melle,
Qu'a mercy puit vostre doulx cuer tourner,

But since I am forced to leave her behind
With Danger, who is so envious,

How could it be that I be joyful
When I do not see my beautiful mistress
From whom comes whatever happiness I have
By way of the look from her beautiful laughing eyes?

7. *Rondeau*: "Fair one, in order to hate falsehood"

Fair one, in order to hate falsehood
And to serve you with a lover's heart,
Love has put me in such a state
That I lose both pleasure and health.

For I cannot know if it is your will
Ever to have mercy on me,
Fair one, in order to hate falsehood
And to serve you with a lover's heart.

But if it pleased you that reassured
I might be with a sweet gift,
In every respect I would be cured
Of the sorrow that has lasted me so long.

Fair one, in order to hate falsehood
And to serve you with a lover's heart,
Love has put me in such a state
That I lose both pleasure and health.

8. *Rondeau*: "This first day when the year begins anew"

This first day when the year begins anew,
Joyously and with loyal thought
I give you my heart forever without deceit,
My good, wise, gracious, and beautiful lady.

For by my faith, you alone are the one
Without whom I could not gain happiness,
This first day when the year begins anew,
Joyously and with loyal thought.

Thus I pray to Love that he intercede for me,
For he can turn your gentle heart towards mercy,

Et que Regart atire Bel Parler,
Ou l'un sans plus m'an doint bonne nouvelle.

Ce premier jour que l'an se renouvelle,
Joieusement et de loial penser
Vous doins mon cuer a tousjourz sans faulser,
Bonne, saige, gracieuse et tresbelle.

9. Rondel: «Adieu, Jeunesse, m'amie»

Adieu, Jeunesse, m'amie,
De vous me fault departir.
Plus ne vous puis retenir
Car le temps ne le vuelt mie.

Et sanz vostre compaignie
Ne doit nulz amour servir.
Adieu, Jeunesse, m'amie,
De vous me fault departir.

Helas! tant de bonne vie
Et de gracieux plaisir
Faites a voz genz sentir,
Que c'est bien droit que je die:

Adieu, Jeunesse, m'amie,
De vous me fault departir.
Plus ne vous puis retenir
Car le temps ne le vuelt mie.

Desoremais Merancolie
Me vendra fort assaillir.
Adieu, Jeunesse, m'amie,
De vous me fault departir.

Mais, de vostre druerie
Me lerez le souvenir
En mon cuer pour reverdir
Un joli rains de folie.

Adieu, Jeunesse, m'amie,
De vous me fault departir.
Plus ne vous puis retenir
Car le temps ne le vuelt mie.

And that Looking attract Fair Speech,
Or that just one of these bring me good tidings.

This first day when the year begins anew,
Joyously and with loyal thought
I give you my heart forever without deceit,
My good, wise, gracious, and beautiful lady.

9. Rondeau: "Farewell Youth, my friend"

Farewell Youth, my friend,
From you I must depart.
I can no longer hold onto you,
For Time wishes it not.

And without your company,
No one ought to serve love.
Farewell Youth, my friend,
From you I must depart.

Alas, you make your servants feel
So much good life
And gracious pleasure
That it is fitting that I say:

Farewell Youth, my friend,
From you I must depart,
I can no longer hold onto you
For Time wishes it not.

From now on, Melancholy
Will inflict its harsh attacks.
Farewell Youth, my friend,
From you I must depart.

But you will leave within my heart
The memory of your gallantry
In order to keep fresh and green
A pretty sprig of foolishness.

Farewell Youth, my friend,
From you I must depart.
I can no longer hold onto you,
For Time wishes it not.

10. Vyrelay: «Je vous aime, je vous desir»

Je vous aime, je vous desir,
Je vous vueil doubter et servir,
Je suis vostre ou que je soye,
Je ne puis sans vous avoir joye.
Je puis par vous vivre et mourir.

Oncques si fort ne vous aymay,
Onques tant ne vous desiray,
De tout entier le cuer de moy.
Vostre servant suy et seray.
Jamais aultre ne serviray,
Je le vous jure, par ma foy.

Loial Amour me fait sentir
En penser et en souvenir
Vostre beaulté, que je verroye
Moult voluntiers, se je savoye
Que se fust bien vostre plaisir.

Je vous aime, je vous desir,
Je vous vueil doubter et servir,
Je suis vostre ou que je soye,
Je ne puis sans vous avoir joye.
Je puis par vous vivre et mourir.

11. Balade: «Se je m'en dueil, nul ne m'en doit blasmer»

Or n'ay je mais que dolour et tristesce,
Paine, ennuy, soussy, et desconfort.
Joye me fuit, et Doulx Penser me lesse.
En plains, en plours sont trestuit mi deport.
Autre bien n'ay. Regardez a quel port
Sui arrive pour loiaument amer.
Se je m'en dueil, nul ne m'en doit blasmer.

Las! je languis nuit et jour en destresce
Comme celui qui n'a nul reconfort,
Car je voy bien que ma dame et maistresse
Ne tient compte des grief maulx que je port.
Et si l'aime, se dieu me doint confort,
De bonne amour, sans nul vilain penser.
Se je m'en dueil, nul ne m'en doit blasmer.

10. Virelai: "I love you, I desire you"

I love you, I desire you,
I want to fear and serve you,
I am yours wherever I am.
Without you, I can have no joy.
Through you, I can live and die.

Never have I loved you so strongly,
Never have I desired you so much,
Completely with my entire heart.
I am and I will be your servant.
Never will I serve another,
I swear to you, by my faith.

Loyal love makes me feel
In thought and in memory
Your beauty, which I would see
Most willingly, if I knew
That it were truly to your pleasure.

I love you, I desire you,
I want to fear and serve you,
I am yours wherever I am.
Without you, I can have no joy.
Through you, I can live and die.

11. Ballade: "If I am grieving, no one ought to blame me"

Now all I have is grief and sadness,
Pain, affliction, worry, and distress.
Joy flees from me; Sweet Thought abandons me.
My only pleasures are in plaints and tears.
I have no other good. See at what port
I have arrived for loving loyally.
If I am grieving, no one ought to blame me.

Alas! I languish night and day in woe
Like someone who can find no consolation,
For I see clearly that my lady and mistress
Takes no account of the grievous pains I bear.
And yet I love her, may God give me comfort,
With a good love, with no base thought at all.
If I am grieving, no one ought to blame me.

Qu'en puis je mais? Dont se je me courresce,
Il m'est avis que je n'ay mie tort.
Servir l'ay loyaument sans paresce,
Tout mon vivant, humblement, sans descort.
En guerredon me vueil donner la mort.
C'est un loier aspre, dur et amer.
Se je m'en dueil, nul ne m'en doit blasmer.

12. Balade: «J'ay tout perdu; le festu est rompu»

Un souvenir d'amor asavouré,
Chiere dame, avez en mon cuer mis,
Par quoy Espoir est en moy demouré
Sans recevoir le don de «fins amis».
Aresté suis pour obeir toudiz
A bonne fin. Si en dy con irascu:
«J'ay tout perdu; le festu est rompu.»

Dame d'onneur ou Dieu a estouré
Beaulté, bonté, sens, honneur et advis,
Se le mien corps n'est de vous honnoré,
A tousjours mais, tant com je seray vis,
En maudiray Desir qui m'a surpris,
Quant Doulx Espoir m'a son arc destendu.
J'ay tout perdu; le festu est rompu.

Onquez Tristam ne fut si couloré
D'ardant desir pour Yseult au cler vifz
Comme je suis, combien que labouré
Sens je griefs maulx et muablez delis.
Soppirs et plours qui en moy sont assis
Me font souvent chanter con irascu:
«J'ay tout perdu; le festu est rompu.»

13. Balade: «A ce plaisant premier jour de l'annee»

Belle, que j'aim plus qu'autre ne que moy
De loial cuer tresamoureusement,
Pour le maintien gracieux qu'en vous voy,
Je vous supply, de bon cuer, humblement,
Qu'il vous plaise, dame de tous amee,
Moy retenir vostre povre servant,
A ce plaisant premier jour de l'annee.

What more can I do? If I get angry,
It seems to me that I am not wrong.
I have served her loyally without neglect,
My whole life, humbly, without complaint.
In recompense, she wishes to give me death.
It is a harsh payment, cruel and bitter.
If I am grieving, no one ought to blame me.

12. Ballade: "I have lost everything; the straw is broken"

A delicious memory of love,
Dear lady, you have placed within my heart,
By which Hope has resided in me
Without receiving the gift of "true lover."
I am always ready to obey
For a good purpose. Yet I say like a bitter one,
"I have lost everything; the straw is broken."

Lady of honor, in whom God has placed
Beauty, goodness, sense, honor, and wisdom,
If my person is not esteemed by you,
Forever more, as long as I am alive,
I will curse Desire, which overtook me
When Sweet Hope bent its bow towards me.
I have lost everything; the straw is broken.

Never was Tristam so tinged
With burning desire for Iseult of the bright face
As I am, such that, agonized,
I experience grievous pain and fleeting delights.
Sighs and tears, which are set in me,
Make me often sing like a bitter one,
"I have lost everything; the straw is broken."

13. Ballade: "On this pleasant first day of the year"

Fair one, whom I love better than anyone or than myself
With loyal heart, very lovingly,
For the gracious conduct that I see in you,
I beg you, with good heart, humbly,
That it please you, lady beloved by all,
To retain me as your poor servant
On this pleasant first day of the year.

Laissez pene et douleur et ennoy;
Prenez en vous joye et esbatement.
Laissez le noir. Mettez vous en requoy
Pour mieulx penser a loisir doulcement.
S'ainsy faictez, plus en serez louee
Que d'endurer et vivre tristrement
A ce plaisant premier jour de l'annee.

Et c'il vous playt a moy donner l'octroy
De vostre amour que je desire tant,
Vous me ferez de tous biens mondains roy,
Plus eureux que nul qu'il soit vivant.
C'est mon espoir, c'est toute ma pansee.
C'est ce qui me tendra joyeusement
A ce plaisant premier jour de l'annee.

14. Balade: «En grant desduit et en doulce plaisance»

Ung vrais amans puet tant de biens trouver
En bien amer, que creature humaine
Ne le pourroit nullement esperer.
Car c'est ainsy que la droite fontainne
Qui tousjours cour et tousjours si est plainne
Puet tous amans mectre, sans variance,
En grant desduit et en doulce plaisance.

Qu'esse de bien et loiaulment amer?
C'est tous solas pour cuerz oster de painne.
Qu'esse a dame foy et honneur porter?
C'est tous deduis en la vie mondainne,
C'est pour venir a joye souverainne,
C'est pour tousjours vivre, sans variance,
En grant deduit et en doulce plaisance.

Dame plaisant, ou il n'a qu'amender,
Belle sans per, de mon cuer chastellaine,
A vous me rens sans moy desordener.
Dame, a vous suis sans pensee vilainne,
Car tant vous aim de bonne amour certainne
Que par vous vis d'amoureuse substance
En grant deduit et en doulce plaisance.

Set aside pain and sorrow and vexation;
Devote yourself to joy and to amusement.
Set aside black. Put yourself at rest
In order better to think sweetly of leisure.
If you do so, more will you be praised
Than if you persist and live in sadness
On this pleasant first day of the year.

And if it pleases you to give me the gift
Of your love, which I desire so much,
You will make me king of all worldly goods,
Happier than anyone who is alive.
That is my hope, that is all my thought.
That is what will sustain me joyously
On this pleasant first day of the year.

14. Ballade: "In great delight and in so sweet a pleasure"

A true lover can find so many rewards
In loving well, that no human being
Could ever hope for it in any way.
For thus it is that the true fountain
That always runs and yet is always full
Can place all lovers, without exception,
In great delight and in so sweet a pleasure.

What is it to love well and loyally?
It is every solace to lift hearts from pain.
What is it to bear faith and honor to a lady?
It is all the delights of life in this world.
It is to come unto the sovereign joy.
It is to live always, without exception,
In great delight and in so sweet a pleasure.

Charming lady, in whom there is nothing to improve,
Beauty without equal, the keeper of my heart,
I surrender to you without degrading myself.
Lady, I am yours, without base thought,
For I love you so much with a good, sure love
That through you I live, sustained by love,
In great delight and in so sweet a pleasure.

15. Balade: «Car j'ay perdu ma jeunesse, ma joye»

Fouir m'en fault a chace d'esperon,
Loing de tous biens, ou Deser de Tristour,
Et y feray lever une maison
Pour moy mucier, en ung petit destour.
La vueil languir, sans faire autre labour,
A celle fin, que plaisance ne voye,
Car j'ay perdu ma jeunesse, ma joye.

Mais diverse en sera la cloyson
De ce pourpris ou feray mon sejour.
Courroux, Soussy, Despit et Marrison
Feront le mur et yront entour,
Et Desespoir sera donjon et tour.
C'est le retrait ou il fault que je soye,
Car j'ay perdu ma jeunesse, ma joye.

Il y aura, car c'est tresbien raison,
Ung jardinnet de merveilleux atour
Qui, en tous temps, sera en sa saison
D'estre chargé d'Ennuy et de Doulour.
Et ou milieu, ung grant fleuve de plour.
De m'esnoyer seray souvent en voye,
Car j'ay perdu ma jeunesse, ma joye.

16. Balade: «Or vueille Dieux que brefment le revoye»

De moy se part mon tresloial ami,
Et sy s'en va en estrange contree,
Dont j'ay le cuer courrocié et marry.
Hé! que feray? Lasse, desconfortee,
Je demourray dolente et esploree,
Sans reconfort avoir, soulas ne joye.
Or vueille Dieux que brefment le revoye.

S'estre peust, je feusse avecquez luy
Sans departir, mais trop me desagree
Qu'estre ne puit; ce poise my.
Mieulx amasse faire ma destinee
Avecques luy tousdiz, sans dessevree,
Que loing de moy feust, par quelquonquez voye.
Or vueille Dieux que briefment le revoye.

Se je desir qu'il soit pres d'ycy,
Ou qu'envers moy face tost retournee,

15. Ballade: "For I have lost my youth and my joy"

Flee I must, as fast as I can spur,
Far from all good into the Desert of Sadness,
And I will have a house constructed there
In which to hide, in an isolated corner.
There I wish to languish, without further labor,
To this end, that I see no pleasure.
For I have lost my youth and my joy.

But diverse will be the enclosure
Of the dwelling in which I'll make my stay.
Anger, Worry, Scorn, and Sadness
Will make up the walls that run around it,
And Despair will be the keep and tower.
That is the retreat in which I must reside,
For I have lost my youth and my joy.

There will be, since it is very fitting,
A little garden of wondrous character,
That will be in season throughout the year
And overgrown with Sorrow and Affliction.
And in the middle, a great river of tears.
I will often be found there, drowning myself,
For I have lost my youth and my joy.

16. Ballade: "Now would to God that I see him again soon"

My most loyal friend is leaving me
And going away into a foreign land,
For which my heart is vexed and saddened.
Oh, what will I do? Weary, distressed,
I will remain sorrowful and drained of tears,
Without any consolation, solace, or joy.
Now would to God that I see him again soon.

If it were possible, I would be with him
Without separating, but it is very painful for me
That it cannot be; this troubles me.
I would rather make my destiny
With him always, without separation,
Than for him to be far from me, by whatever path.
Now would to God that I see him again soon.

If I desire that he be nearby
Or that to me he soon make his return,

C'est a bon droit, car bon jour ne demy
N'auray, certez, jusquez a la journee
Que le verray. C'est toute ma pensee,
Car adonquez tresjoieuse seroie.
Or vueille Dieux que briefment le revoye.

17. Balade: «Que nulle autre jamais ne choisiray»

Je vous choisy, noble loyal amour;
Je vous choisi, souveraine plaisance;
Je vous choisi, gracieuse doulçour;
Je vous choisi, tresdoulce souffisance.
Je vous choisi de toute ma puissance;
Je vous choisi de cuer entier et vray.
Je vous choisi par telle convenance
Que nulle autre jamais ne choisiray.

Je vous choisi, des bonnes la meillour;
Je vous choisi sans penser decevance.
Je vous choisi, des plus belles la flour;
Je vous choisi sans faire variance.
Je vous choisi, ma droite soustenance;
Je vous choisi tant com je puis ne sçay.
Je vous choisi et si vous affiance
Que nulle autre jamais ne choisiray.

Je vous choisi, confort de ma langour;
Je vous choisi pour avoir alegance.
Je vous choisi pour guerir ma doulour.
Je vous choisi pour saner ma grevance.
Je vous choisi sans fin en perseverance.
Je vous choisi et choisie vous ay.
Le Dieu d'Amours en prens en tesmongnance
Que nulle autre jamais ne choisiray.

18. Balade: «A Dalida, Jhezabel, et Thays»

Se Lucresce, la tresvaillant Rommaine,
Ou la bonne Troyenne, Hecuba,
Ou Hilie, qui fu de tel bien plaine
Qu'en voulenté chastement se garda,
Revenoient or en vie,
Au jour d'ui est tant de mal et d'envie
Qu'on les compareroit, ce m'est avis,
A Dalida, Jhezabel, et Thays.

It is with reason, for a good day or a half
I surely will not have until the day
I see him. That is all I think about,
For then I would be very joyous.
Now would to God that I see him again soon.

17. Ballade: "That never will I choose any other"

I choose you, noble, loyal love;
I choose you, sovereign pleasure;
I choose you, gracious gentleness;
I choose you, most sweet satisfaction.
I choose you with all my power;
I choose you with full and loyal heart.
I choose you with this affirmation,
That never will I choose any other.

I choose you, the best of the good;
I choose you without thinking of deceit.
I choose you, the flower of all beauties;
I choose you without inconstancy.
I choose you, my very sustenance;
I choose you as much as I know how.
I choose you, and I also pledge to you
That never will I choose any other.

I choose you, the comfort of my languor;
I choose you in order to have relief.
I choose you to remedy my sorrow.
I choose you to relieve my pain.
I choose you with unfailing perseverance.
I choose you and I have chosen you.
I take the God of Love as my witness
That never will I choose any other.

18. Ballade: "To Delilah, Jezebel, and Thaïs"

If Lucrece, the very worthy Roman,
Or the virtuous Trojan, Hecuba,
Or Elie, who was of such quality
That willingly did she keep herself chaste,
Were now to come back to life again,
Today there is so much malice and envy
That one would compare them, it seems to me,
To Delilah, Jezebel, and Thaïs.

Si seroit ce comparoison vilaine
Et contre droit, mais le monde ainsi va,
Car au jour d'ui, li plusieurs mestent paine
De controuver ce que ja ne sera
Sur ceulx qui ne pensent mie
Fors qu'a honnour et bien et courtoisie,
Et leur donnent le los que fu jadis
A Dalida, Jhezabel, et Thays.

Le doulce Yseut, qui fu a la fontaine,
Ne tu Tristan, Jason, et Medea,
Ne tu, Paris, avec ta belle Helaine:
Ne venez plus pour amer par de ça.
Ce seroit trop grant folie.
L'en vous diroit autant de vilonnie
Comme on fist onques, en nul pays,
A Dalida, Jhezabel, et Thays.

19. Balade: «Plus m'escondit, plus la vueil tenir chiere»

Or ne sçay je tant de service faire
A ma dame qu'elle me vueille amer,
Et si me voit pour s'amour grans maulx traire.
Mais envers moy est son cuer si amer
Que je n'y puis point de doulçour trouver.
Plus la depry doulcement, plus m'est fiere.
Et si n'en quier pourtant mon cuer oster.
Plus m'escondit, plus la vueil tenir chiere.

Elle scet bien que ce qui li doit plaire,
Sans atendre deux fois le commander
Songneusement je le fois, sans contraire,
De cuer joieux. Bien y deust regarder,
Mes complaintes aussi considerer
Sans me geter de s'amour si arriere.
Toutes voies, de ce n'estuet doubter,
Plus m'escondit, plus la vueil tenir chiere.

Car pour paine, meschief, durté, ne haire
Qu'en desirant s'amour puisse endurer,
Ne me vouldray de la servir retraire.
Mais plus qu'onques le feray, sans fausser,
Car j'ay espoir que d'elle, au pis aler,
Auray grace amoureuse et plainiere.
Et pour ce dy pour mon fait miex prover,
Plus m'escondit, plus la vueil tenir chiere.

This would be a villainous comparison
And against what's right, but so goes the world,
For today, many make an effort
To make up things that will never be
About those who never think at all
About anything but honor, good, and courtesy,
And they give them the praise that once was given
To Delilah, Jezebel, and Thaïs.

Oh sweet Isolde, who was at the fountain,
And you, Tristan, Jason, and Medea,
And you, Paris, with your beautiful Helen:
Do not pass this way again in order to love.
That would be too great a folly.
They would say to you as much villainy
As they did once, in whatever country,
To Delilah, Jezebel, and Thaïs.

19. Ballade: "The more she rejects me, the more I hold her dear"

I do not know how to do such service
For my lady that she might wish to love me,
And yet she sees me suffer great pains for her love.
But towards me her heart is so sour
That I can find no sweetness there at all.
The more sweetly I beseech her, the haughtier she is.
And yet I do not want to remove my heart from her.
The more she rejects me, the more I hold her dear.

She knows well that whatever ought to please her,
Without waiting to be asked twice
I do attentively, without objection,
With joyful heart. Well ought she take notice,
And also pay attention to my complaints
Without casting me so far from her love.
Nonetheless, of this one must not doubt,
The more she rejects me, the more I hold her dear.

For whatever pain, hardship, harshness, or hate
I might endure in desiring her love,
I will not want to withdraw from serving her.
But more than ever I will do it, without deceit,
For I have hope that from her, at the worst,
I will obtain complete and loving grace.
And therefore I say, to better make my case,
The more she rejects me, the more I hold her dear.

20. Balade: «Ainsi le fait cuer plain de fausseté»

A Medee me puis bien comparer,
Qui a grant tort fu de Jason traie.
Il lui promist, par decevant parler,
Foy, loyaulté porter toute sa vie.
Mais tost lui fust sa promesse mentie.
Quant de lui ot faite sa voulenté,
Il la laissa, par sa grant tricherie.
Ainsi le fait cuer plain de fausseté.

Pourtant le dy qu'ainsi m'est pour amer,
Car je me voy de celui deguerpie
Qui me souloit a tout heure clamer
Sa maistresse, sa dame, et s'amie.
Or m'aperçoy que s'amour departie
Est autrepart par sa desloiauté.
Lasse, dolente, ne le cuidasse mie.
Ainsi le fait cuer plain de fausseté.

Je l'ay amé loyaument, sans fausser,
Et encor fais, non obstant sa folie,
Car je ne vueil ne ne quier regarder
A son errour. Ma foy li ay plevie.
Je li tenray, certes, quoy que nul die,
Et s'il est tel qu'il ne tourne a bonté,
Dire porray, a plaine voix banie,
«Ainsi le fait cuer plain de fausseté.»

21. Balade: «Pour miex garder de ma dame le fort»

Se mon cuer font en larmes et en plours
Par desconfort, ce n'est mie merveille,
Car je ne puis de celle avoir secours
Pour qui Desir si griefment me traveille.
Helas, Pitié si me fait sourde oreille
Quant je requier avoir son reconfort
Contre Dangier, qui a toute heure veille,
Pour miex garder de ma dame le fort.

Sans remede voy definer mes jours
Se Franchise briefment ne s'apareille
A mon secours venir plus que le cours,
Qui par doulçour Dame Pitié resveille.
A Doulx Espoir humblement pri qu'il veille
Moy aidier et me donner confort

20. Ballade: "Thus does a heart that is full of falsity"

To Medea I can easily compare myself,
Who was very wrongly betrayed by Jason.
He promised her, with deceitful speech,
To maintain faith and loyalty all his life.
But soon was his promise to her broken.
Once he had had his way with her,
He left her, out of his great treachery.
Thus does a heart that is full of falsity.

Thus I say, so it is for me in love,
For I see myself abandoned by the one
Who used to call me constantly
His mistress, his lady, and his love.
Now I see that his love has departed
Elsewhere out of his disloyalty.
Weary, sad, I would not have believed it.
Thus does a heart that is full of falsity.

I loved him loyally, without deceit,
And I still do, despite his foolishness,
For I neither want nor seek to heed
His straying. I pledged my faith to him.
I will uphold it, truly, whatever anyone says,
And if he is such that he doesn't return to goodness,
I'll be able to say, loudly and publicly,
"Thus does a heart that is full of falsity."

21. Ballade: "Better to guard the fortress of my lady"

If my heart melts in tears and weeping
Out of distress, it is no wonder,
For I cannot get any help from her
For whom Desire so grievously torments me.
Alas, Pity turns me a deaf ear
When I seek to have her comfort
Against Danger, which keeps watch at every hour,
Better to guard the fortress of my lady.

Without relief I am going to end my days
If Generosity does not soon prepare
To come to my aid at more than a gallop,
Which out of gentleness awakens Lady Pity.
I humbly pray to Sweet Hope that it wish
To aid me and to give me comfort

Contre Dangier, qui a toute heure veille,
Pour miex garder de ma dame le fort.

Courtoisie, sy depriez Amours
Qu'a ma dame, qui d'onnour n'a pareille,
Face savoir les paines, les doulours
Que pour lui sent, et qu'il la conseille
Qu'a son servant humblement me recueille.
Si en seray plus viguereux et fort
Contre Dangier, qui a toute heure veille,
Pour miex garder de ma dame le fort.

22. Balade: «S'a ma cause perdoit sa bonne fame»

Ne doy je bien Male Bouche hair?
Par foy oil, quant par son faulx parler
M'estuet laissier l'aler et le venir
Vers ma dame, que je doy tant amer.
Mais j'ay plus chier, pour son honneur garder,
A m'en tenir que pour moy ait diffame.
On m'en porroit par raison bien blasmer
S'a ma cause perdoit sa bonne fame.

Combien, certes, s'elle ne veult mentir
Mauvaisement, elle n'en puet parler
Que tout honnour; mais pour anientir
Son langage et le faire cesser,
D'elle me vueil un petit eslongier.
Non pas du cuer: il est tout sien, par m'ame.
Bien devroie de tresgrant dueil crever
S'a ma cause perdoit sa bonne fame.

On ne s'en scet si gaitier n'ecapir
Que prest ne soit son arc pour descochier
Fleches teles que qui s'en sent ferir
A grans paine puet garison trouver.
Tel trait doit tout vray amant redouter.
Doubter le vueil pour le bien de ma dame.
Trop aroie le cuer dur et amer
S'a ma cause perdoit sa bonne fame.

23. Balade: «Vous n'en povez tousdiz que miex valoir»

Amis, pensez de loyaument amer
Se vous voulez mener joieuse vie.

Against Danger, which keeps watch at every hour,
Better to guard the fortress of my lady.

Courtesy, you too, beseech Love
That to my lady, who has no equal in honor,
He make known the pains, the sorrows
That I feel for her, and that he counsel her
That she accept me humbly as her servant.
Then I will be more vigorous and strong
Against Danger, which keeps watch at every hour,
Better to guard the fortress of my lady.

22. Ballade: "If because of me she lost her good name"

Shouldn't I really hate Evil Tongue?
In faith, yes, when because of its false speech
I am forced to give up the coming and going
To my lady, whom I must love so much.
But I would rather, in order to guard her honor,
Hold myself apart than for me she be defamed.
One could very rightly blame me for it
If because of me she lost her good name.

How much, indeed, unless it wishes to lie
Maliciously, it cannot say anything about her
Except all honor; but to in order to suppress
Its speech and to make it cease,
I want to distance myself a bit from her.
Not in my heart: it is all hers, by my soul.
I should well perish of great grief
If because of me she lost her good name.

One cannot be on watch, nor prevent
Its bow from being ready to shoot
Arrows such that whoever feels them strike
Can find a cure only with great pain.
Such a shot should every true lover dread.
I want to be on guard for the good of my lady.
I would have a heart too hard and bitter
If because of me she lost her good name.

23. Ballade: "From this you can only come to greater worth"

Friend, consider loving loyally
If you want to lead a joyous life.

Soiez secret, atrempé en parler.
Ne vous praigne de mesdire Envie.
Fuiez orgueil et amez courtoisie.
Amez honneur de tout vostre povoir.
Prisiez les bons, suivez leur compaignie.
Vous n'en povez tousdiz que miex valoir.

Encor vous vueil d'aucuns poins enorter,
Et je vous pry, ne les oubliez mie.
C'est, foy porter, apres honnour garder
De la dame ou vostre cuer s'otrie.
Ce doit faire qui tent avoir amie.
Autre ne doit desirer ne vouloir.
S'ainsi faites, je vous acertefie,
Vous n'en povez tousdiz que miex valoir.

A voir dire et droit considerer,
Qui autrement le fait, c'est grant folie.
Point ne dessert qu'on li doie donner
Des biens d'amours ne petit ne partie.
Aux vrais amans est grace departie.
Or en faites si bien vostre devoir
Que Bonne Amour avecques vous s'alie.
Vous n'en povez tousdiz que miex valoir.

24. Balade: «Car je languis en trop dure tristour»

A doulx pais que je n'ose nommer,
Ou maint mon cuer et toute ma fiance,
Et riens ne scet celle qui demourer
Luy fait toudiz, dont si dure grevance
M'en fault souffrir, que se n'ay allegence
Aucunement luy dire ma doulour,
Jamais n'atens en moy avoir plaisance,
Car je languis en trop dure tristour.

Et s'il advient que lui puisse compter
Comment je l'aims de toute ma puissance,
En ung seul mot me pourra bien donner
Ou bien ou mal, l'un des deux sans doubtance.
Mais tant me doubt d'avoir l'ung sans faillance,
Que je ne cesse de crier nuit et jour,
«Mercy, m'amour, ma doulce bienvaillance,»
Car je languis en trop dure tristour.

Be discreet and moderate in speech.
Let not Envy cause you to speak ill.
Flee pride and love courtesy.
Love honor with all your might.
Esteem the good, pursue their company.
From this you can only come to greater worth.

I wish to advise you further on several points,
And I beseech you, do not ever forget them.
That is, to bear faith, after protecting the honor
Of the lady to whom your heart is given.
This must he do who aspires to have a lover.
He must not desire or wish for any other.
If you do as I say, I guarantee you,
From this you can only come to greater worth.

To tell the truth and consider what is right,
Whoever does otherwise, it is great folly.
He does not deserve that one should give to him
Either a bit or a share of the rewards of love.
Grace is bestowed upon true lovers.
So do your duty there so well
That Good Love attach itself to you.
From this you can only come to greater worth.

24. Ballade: "For I languish in too harsh a sadness"

In a sweet country that I dare not name
Where remains my heart and all of my commitment —
And nothing does she know who causes it
To dwell there always, for which so harsh a pain
I am forced to suffer that if I don't have relief
To tell her in some way of my sorrow,
I never expect to experience any pleasure,
For I languish in too harsh a sadness.

And if it happens that I could describe to her
How I love her with all of my power,
With just one word she could well give to me
Either good or evil, one of the two, no doubt,
But so much do I fear to have only the one,
That I do not cease to cry out night and day,
"Mercy, my love, my sweet benevolence,"
For I languish in too harsh a sadness.

Tant suis dolent, ne sçay quel part tourner,
Si que je pers maniere et contenance.
Quant je pence qu'il me fault eslongner
Sa grant beaulté qui est ma soustenance,
Si tristres suis que je n'ay esperance
De recouvrer ne joye ne baudour.
Desespoir fait en moy sa demourance,
Car je languis en trop dure tristour.

25. Balade: «Car de presant, je veul tout le contraire»

Je filz rondeaux, baladez, virelais,
Ou temps passé que j'amay par amours,
Et me tenoie liéz, jolis et gais,
Car bien cuidoie ainsy faire tousjours.
Festes queroie, dance, joustez, bouhors,
Ne voulsisse lors autre chose faire.
Or m'est ly temps bien tourné au rebours,
Car de presant, je veul tout le contraire.

Las! je voy bien que ne feray jamais
Fors enviellir, dont j'ay assez doulours.
De maint grant mal m'estuet porter le faiz,
Et cy ne treux qui me face secours.
Povre de bien, Fortune, de sez tours
M'a bien monstré, que trouvay debonnaire,
Quant perdoie le mien con folz et lours.
Car de present, je veul tout le contraire.

D'or en avant, veul prier pour la paix
Et Dieu servir, car s'est mon droit recours,
Et savoir veul ou sera mes retrais,
Quant court fauldra, pour demourer ailleurs,
Non pas toudis porter chapeaus de flours,
N'avoir ainsy robez plus de vingt paire.
Ainsy le fis, de quoy ce fut foulours,
Car de present, je veul tout le contraire.

26. Balade: «Mais vous m'avez tousjours respondu 'non'»

Mon treshault bien, ma chierté souveraine,
Mon seul desir, ma joieuse pensee,
Ma vraie amour, de tous biens la fontainne,
Belle par qui la joie m'est donnee,
Qui me sera cent mille fois doublee,

So sad am I, I know not where to turn,
So that I lose my bearing and composure.
When I think that I am forced to separate
From her great beauty, which is my sustenance,
I am so sad that I have no hope
Of recovering either joy or gaiety.
Despair takes up its residence in me,
For I languish in too harsh a sadness.

25. Ballade: "For at present, I want exactly the opposite"

I made rondeaux, ballades, and virelais
In former times, when I was in love,
And I considered myself happy, jolly, and gay,
For I believed that I would be so always.
I sought out parties, dances, jousts, tourneys,
Nor did I did want to do anything else.
Now has time turned upside down for me,
For at present, I want exactly the opposite.

Alas, I see clearly that all that's left for me
Is to grow old, for which I have great grief.
I must carry the burden of many a great pain,
And here I don't find anyone who can help.
Poor of goods, Fortune, whom I used to find gracious,
Has well shown me some of her tricks
When I lost what was mine like a fool and imbecile.
For at present, I want exactly the opposite.

From now on, I want to pray for peace
And to serve God, for that's my proper refuge,
And I want to know where my retreat will be
When soon, in order to dwell elsewhere,
I'll have to give up wearing a chaplet of flowers
And also having more than twenty robes.
So I used to do, which was a folly,
For at present, I want exactly the opposite.

26. Ballade: "But you have always answered me with 'no'"

My supreme good, my sovereign treasure,
My sole desire, and my joyous thought,
My true love, the fountain of all good,
The beauty by whom I have been given joy,
Which will be multiplied one hundred thousand times

Quant vous plaira qu'aye le guerdon
Dont je vous ay par pluseurs fois priee.
Mais vous m'avez tousjours respondu «non».

En bonne foy, ce m'a esté grant pene
Et touteffois je l'ay en gré pourtee,
Car je vous tien de si grant doulceur plainne
Que vostre amour me sera octroyee,
Quant vous aurez bien adroit esprouvee
Ma loiaulté, et m'en ferez le don.
Par maintez fois la vous ay demendee,
Mais vous m'avés tousjours repondu «non».

Pour ce plaise vous, plus belle que Helene,
Qu'a ceste fois ne me soit reffusee
Si en croistra vo louange mondainne,
Car riens ne sçay, dame de moy amee,
Dont vous peussez de nul estre blasmee
Fors de reffus. Pour Dieu, laissez le, don!
Beaucop de fois vous en ay advisee,
Mais vous m'avez tousjours respondu «non».

27. Balade amoreuse: «Car vrayement ce martelé me tue»

En mon cuer a une enclume plantee
Qu'Amours y fit doulcement y entrer.
La vient Desir, sans nulle demouree,
Qui tient en mains le mail de souspirer,
Et Doulx Espoir y vyent avec Panser.
Ferant, maillant, chascun fort s'esvertue.
Languir me fault ou a la mort aler,
Car vrayement ce martelé me tue.

Celle enclume qu'en mon cuer est entee,
C'est le cler vis de ma dame honnorer;
Et sez doulx yeulx, toute jour ajournee,
Soufflent le feu pour le fort eschauffer.
Et puis Beaulté vient avec marteler,
Et Doulz Plaisir, qui trestous lez esmue.
Languir me fault ou a la mort aler,
Car vrayement ce martelé me tue.

J'ay veu ouvriers qui, depuis la vespree
Jusque au matin, guerpissoient leur ouvrer,
Mais trestousjours Souvenir et Pensee,
Martelent fort; n'ont cure d'arrester.

When it pleases you that I have the favor
For which I have beseeched you many times.
But you have always answered me with "no."

In good faith, this has caused me great pain,
And nonetheless I have borne it willingly,
For I consider you full of such great gentleness
That your love will be granted to me
When you have fully put to the test
My loyalty, and you will give me that gift.
Many times I have asked you for it,
But you have always answered me with "no."

Therefore may it please you, lady fairer than Helen,
That this time I not be refused.
Thus will increase your praise in this world,
For I know nothing, my beloved lady,
For which you can be blamed by anyone
Except rejection. For God's sake, give it up.
I have advised you plenty of times to do so,
But you have always answered me with "no."

27. Love Ballade: "For honestly, this hammering's killing me"

Within my heart there is an anvil placed
Which Love caused softly to enter there.
There comes Desire, without any delay,
Which holds in its hand the hammer of sighing,
And then Sweet Hope comes, along with Thought.
Pounding, hammering, each one labors strongly.
I must languish or go to my death,
For honestly, this hammering's killing me.

This anvil that is placed within my heart,
It is to honor the bright face of my lady.
And her sweet eyes, all day every day,
Fan the flame in order to make it hotter.
And then Beauty comes with its hammer,
And Sweet Pleasure, which excites them all.
I must languish or go to my death,
For honestly, this hammering's killing me.

I have seen workers who, from evening
Until morning, set aside their work,
But constantly do Memory and Thought
Pound strongly; they have no wish to stop.

Et se Pitié ne leur vient dire a cler:
«Leissez l'ouvrer, car la feste est venue»,
Languir me fault ou a la mort aler,
Car vrayement ce martelé me tue.

28. Balade: «Car loin de vous vivre je ne pourroye»

Adieu, m'amour et ma doulce plaisance,
Adieu, ma joye et tout mon seul desir,
Adieu, adieu, toute mon esperance.
Helas! adieu, mon joieux souvenir,
Adieu, celle qui tant me fait languir.
Adieu, ma belle et souveraine joye.
Helas! Adieu. Pansés de revenir,
Car loin de vous vivre je ne pourroye.

Tant vous aime que j'en pers contenance,
Tant vous aime que j'en pers le dormir,
Tant vous aime que ailleurs je ne pance.
Tant vous aime qu'autre ne quier veir.
Tant vous aime qu'autre ne veul cherir.
Tant vous aime que rien tant ne sauroie,
Tant vous aime que j'en crains a morir,
Car loin de vous vivre je ne pourroie.

Helas! tant ay fait de vous souvenance,
Helas! tant suis lié de vous veir,
Helas! tant vueil vostre doulce presence,
Helas! tant vueil entre voz bras dormir,
Helas! tant vueil vostre bouche sentir,
Helas! tant suis desirant qu'o vous soye.
Se ce n'estoit, il me fauldroit finir,
Car loing de vous vivre je ne pourroye.

29. Balade: «En languissant defineront my jour»

La grant beaulté de vo viaire cler
Et la doulseur dont vous estez paree
Me fait de vous si fort enamourer,
Chiere dame, qu'avoir ne puis duree.
A toute heure est en vous ma pensee.
Desir m'asault durement par rigour.
Et se par vous ne m'est grace donnee,
En languissant defineront my jour.

And if Pity doesn't come to tell them clearly
"Leave off work, for the holiday is here,"
I must languish or go to my death,
For honestly, this hammering's killing me.

28. Ballade: "For far from you I wouldn't be able to live"

Farewell, my love and my sweet pleasure;
Farewell, my joy and all my only desire.
Farewell, farewell, all of my hope.
Alas! Farewell, my joyous memory.
Farewell, she who makes me languish so.
Farewell, my beautiful and sovereign joy.
Alas, farewell. Think about returning,
For far from you I wouldn't be able to live.

I love you so much that I lose composure.
I love you so much that I lose sleep.
I love you so much that I think of nothing else.
I love you so much that I don't wish to see another.
I love you so much that I don't want to cherish another.
I love you so much that I couldn't do anything as much.
I love you so much that I fear of dying,
For far from you I wouldn't be able to live.

Alas, so much have I thought about you,
Alas, so happy am I to see you,
Alas, so much do I want your sweet presence,
Alas, so much do I want to sleep in your arms,
Alas, so much do I want to feel your mouth,
Alas, so much do I desire to be with you,
If this didn't happen, I would be forced to perish,
For far from you I wouldn't be able to live.

29. Ballade: "In languishing my days will come to an end"

The great beauty of your bright face
And the sweetness with which you are adorned
Make me so deeply in love with you,
Dear lady, that I cannot resist.
My thought is upon you at every hour.
Desire assails me harshly and severely,
And if by you I am not given grace,
In languishing my days will come to an end.

Allegement ne pourroye trouver
Du mal que j'ay par creature nee
Se par vous non, en qui veul affermer
Entierement mon cuer, sans dessevree.
Il est vostre. Longtemps vous ay amee
Celeement, sans en faire clamour,
Et se l'amour de vous m'est reffusee,
En languissant defineront my jour.

Si vous suppli humblement que passer
Ma requeste vueillez, s'il vous agree.
Assez povez congnoistre mon penser
Par ma chanson, qui balade est nommee.
Plus ne vous dy, belle tresdesiree.
Demonstrez moy, s'il vous plaist, vo doulsour,
Car autrement, soiez acertainnee,
En languissant defineront my jour.

30. Balade: «Quant je pense a vo doulce figure»

Vostre gent corps, vostre plaisant viayre,
Et le regart de voz rians yeux,
Vostre parler courtois et debonnaire,
Vo bel maintien, jolis et gracieux,
Contraint mon cuer que je soye amoureux
De vous, dame, par qui sans la pointure
Amoureuse qui me fait tresjoyeux,
Quant je pense a vo doulce figure.

Se mon cuer mets en vous, je le doy faire.
Par droit souhait ne pourroit estre mieulx.
S'en loe Amours qui la l'a voulu traire,
Et sy m'en tien assez plus eureux.
Or vueil estre desormais songneux
De vous amer de vraye amour pure
Car, par ma foy, j'en suis tresdesireux,
Quant je pense a vo doulce figure.

Pour quoy vous pry humblement que desplaire
Ne vous doye, se de cuer tres piteux
Je vous requiers ce qu'il me doit tant plaire.
C'est vostre amour dont je suis famillieux.
Sy ne me soit vo franc cuer rigoreux,
Belle et bonne ou j'ay mise ma cure.
Des dons d'amours ne suis pas souffreteux
Quant je pense a vo doulce figure.

I would not be able to find relief
From the pain that I have from any creature born
If not from you, on whom I wish to fix
Entirely my heart, without separation.
It is yours. I have loved you for a long time
Secretly, without making complaint,
And if your love is refused to me,
In languishing my days will come to an end.

Thus I beseech you humbly that you please
Accept my request, if it pleases you.
You can understand well enough my thoughts
From my song, which is called a ballade.
I say no more, deeply desired beauty.
Show me, please, your gentleness,
For otherwise, be assured,
In languishing my days will come to an end.

30. Ballade: "When I think upon your gentle person"

Your graceful body, your charming face,
And the look from your laughing eyes,
Your speech, courteous and well-bred,
Your fair demeanor, pretty and gracious,
Constrain my heart so that I am in love
With you, lady, from whom I feel the wound
Of love, which makes me very joyful
When I think upon your gentle person.

If I place my heart on you, I ought to do so.
By proper wish, it could not be better.
Thus I praise Love, who wished to draw it there,
And thus I consider myself rather more fortunate.
I wish to be attentive from now on
To love you with a true, pure love,
For by my faith, I very much desire it,
When I think upon your gentle person.

For which I pray you humbly that
I not displease you, if with very piteous heart
I ask of you that which must please me so.
It is your love that I am hungry for.
Thus let not your generous heart be harsh towards me,
Fair and good one in whom I have placed my care.
I am not in want of the gifts of love
When I think upon your gentle person.

31. Balade: «Vous vueil servir tresamoureusement»

D'amoureux mal suis doulcement apris
De vous, dame, que Dieu gart de dommaige.
Par vo regart m'avez doulcement pris.
A vous me rens, sy vous vueil faire hommaige.
D'umble vouloir me met en vo servaige.
Recevez moy, Belle, courtoysement,
Car, par ma foy, de vray et bon couraige
Vous vueil servir tresamoureusement.

D'amer servir dame de sy hault pris,
Com vous estez, bonne, plaisant et saige,
Je ne seroye de personne repris
Qui maintiengne de bien amer l'usaige,
Car en vous maint et prent son hostellage
Honneur, Valour, Humble Contenenment.
Pour ce, de cuer enterin non volage,
Vous vueil servir tresamoureusement.

Or vueille Amours, dont je suis entrepris,
Qui lez griefz maulx amoureux assouage,
Heur me donner d'estre sy bien apris
Que je fasse vo plaisir sans folage,
Et qu'envers moy vous ne soyez sauvage,
Sy que l'amour de vous begninement
Puisse acquerir, car le cours de mon aage
Vous vueil servir tresamoureusement.

32. Balade: «Foy, loiaulté, sans faulcer, vous tendray»

Tresdoulz amis, que j'aim parfaitement
Et aimeray tout le cours de ma vie,
Ne vueillez pas croire legerement
Les mesdisans qui, par tresfaulce envie
Et par tresmauvais rapport,
Mectent souvent vrais amans en descort.
Car, par ma foy, tant comme je vivray,
Foy, loiaulté, sans faulcer, vous tendray.

Pour quoy vous pry affectueusement
Que en vostre cuer telle meslencolie
Vous ne mectez, car tenez vrayement
A tort seroit, de ce ne doubtez mie.
Ja, ce Dieu plaist, le remort
De faulceté n'aura en moy effort.

31. Ballade: "I wish to serve you very lovingly"

I am taught sweetly about the pains of love
By you, lady, whom God protect from harm.
By your look you have gently captured me.
I surrender to you, and I want to pay you homage.
With humble will I place myself in your service.
Accept me, beautiful lady, courteously,
For by my faith, with a true, good heart,
I wish to serve you very lovingly.

For loving to serve a lady of such great worth
As you are, good, charming, and wise,
I would not be blamed by anyone
Who upholds the custom of loving well,
For in you dwell and take their lodging
Honor, Worth, Humble Behavior.
Therefore, with my whole and constant heart,
I wish to serve you very lovingly.

Now may Love, by whom I am overtaken,
Who relieves the grievous pains of love,
Give me the good fortune to be so well taught
That I do your pleasure without folly,
And that you not be hostile towards me,
So that I might obtain your love
Benevolently, since for the rest of my life
I wish to serve you very lovingly.

32. Ballade: "I will offer you faith and loyalty, without falsehood"

Dear friend, whom I love perfectly
And whom I will love for my entire life,
Please do not believe lightly
The slanderers who, out of false envy
And by telling evil tales,
Often put true lovers in discord.
For by my faith, as long as I shall live,
I will offer you faith and loyalty, without falsehood.

For which I beseech you affectionately
That you not put such melancholy
Into your heart, for believe truly
It would be wrong, of this have no doubt.
Never, may it please God, will remorse
For falsehood have any sway in me.

Je suis vostre; n'en soiés en esmoy.
Foy, loiaulté, sens faulcer, vous tendray.

Sy ne doubtez point qu'il soit autrement
Pour parole que personne vous die,
Car je vous ay donné oultreement
Mon cuer, m'amour, sens nulle departie,
Et Dieu m'envoye la mort,
L'eure et le jour que je vous feray tort.
Soiés certain que, de fin cuer et vray,
Foy, loiaulté, sens faulcer, vous tendray.

33. Balade: «Don de mercy ainçois que on le deprie»

Amant qui est cornart et paoureux
De descouvrir ou dire son penser
A celle dont il est fort amoureux,
Pert bien son sens. Cuide il, sans demender,
Avoir se dont il a grant desirier?
Certez, nennil, ne s'y actende mie.
Point n'appartient a dame d'octroyer
Don de mercy ainçois que on le deprie.

Car son honneur n'en vauldroit de riens mieulx,
Mais en pourroit durement abaissier.
Pour ce dy je qu'a blasmer sont tous ceulx
Qui se penent n'entremettent d'amer.
Quant sy cornars sont de grace rover.
Ne mettent point en amer estudie.
Ilz sont musars et nissez d'esperer
Don de mercy ainsois que on la deprie.

Estre ne puet en amours eureux
Qui, a la fois, ne s'ose aventurer
Par doulx parler, courtois et gracieux,
Requerir ce qui le puet alegier.
Ne, pour reffus oyr, ne doit cesser
De poursuir ce qui ly puit faire aye.
On n'a pas sy de dame de legier
Don de mercy ainsois que on la deprie.

34. Balade: «Se je m'en plains, ce ne fait a blasmer»

Hé! doulx amis, qu'avez vous en pensé?
Ou est la foy que vous m'avez promise?

I am yours; of this have no worry.
I will offer you faith and loyalty, without falsehood.

Thus do not fear that it be otherwise
For anything that anyone might say,
For I have given you entirely
My heart, my love, undividedly,
And may God send to me my death
The hour and the day that I do you wrong.
Be certain that, with true and noble heart,
I will offer you faith and loyalty, without falsehood.

33. Ballade: "The gift of mercy before it is requested"

A lover who is stupid and cowardly
About making known or telling his thoughts
To the one with whom he is deeply in love
Has lost his mind. Does he think he'll have
That which he greatly desires without asking?
Certainly not; let him not expect it.
It is just not fitting for a lady to grant
The gift of mercy before it is requested.

For her honor would not increase in worth
But could greatly diminish because of it.
Therefore I say that they are all to blame
Who take pains and undertake to love
When they are so stupid about asking for grace.
They don't apply themselves to loving at all.
They are foolish and silly to hope
For the gift of mercy before it is requested.

Fortunate in love can he never be
Who at the same time does not also dare,
With gentle speech, courteous and gracious,
To ask for that which can relieve him.
Nor on hearing a refusal should he cease
To pursue that which can give him aid.
One does not get from a lady easily
The gift of mercy before it is requested.

34. Ballade: "If I complain, I should not be blamed"

Alas, sweet friend, what were you thinking?
Where is the faith that you promised me?

Je vous voy tout le couraige mué.
Ailleurs, je croy, avez entente mise.
Lasse, dolent, je vous ain sans faintise.
Or me laissiez et pour une autre amer.
Ce n'est pas de bienfait ne de franchise.
Se je m'en plains, ce ne fait a blasmer.

Je vous tiens foy et bonne loiaulté
Et vueil tenir, ne quiers estre reprise
En mon vivant de tour de faulceté,
Car, en droit moy, je la hé et desprise.
Si doit faire chascun qui honneur prise.
Mais ne vous chault guerez de la priser.
Honte n'avez de vostre fole emprise.
Se je m'en plaing, se ne fait a blasmer.

Vous avés bien le cuer plain de durté
De me mener, sans raison, tel service.
Et sy savez que c'est desloiaulté
De maintenir en amours telle guise.
Retraiés vous, que meffait ne vous nuise,
Car, se autrement ne vous voy demener,
Au Dieu d'Amours en requerray justice.
Se je m'en plaing, ce ne fait a blasmer.

35. Balade: «Prouchaine mort en lieu de garison»

La grant douleur qui si fort me destraint
Que, nuit et jour, me convient souspirer,
Et le grief mal de quoy mon cuer se plaint
Et qui me fait toute joye oublier,
Ne puis je plus souffrir ne endurer.
Si me convient, a tresbonne achoison
Et de bon cuer, requerre et demander
Prouchaine mort en lieu de garison.

Ne du meschief qui me palit et taint
Ne puis jamais garison recouvrer
Se non par mort, car mon cuer est attaint
Du mortel cop, de quoy souvent plaier,
Des mesdisans de que le faulx parler
A mains bons cuers honniz par traison.
Le mien se plaint qui me fait desirer
Prouchaine mort en lieu de garison.

I see you with your heart completely altered.
Elsewhere, I believe, you have set your intent.
Weary, sad, I love you without feigning.
But you abandon me, and in order to love another.
This is neither a kind act nor a noble one.
If I complain, I should not be blamed.

I keep my faith and loyalty towards you
And wish to keep it, and don't seek to be blamed
For a trick of falsehood while I am alive.
For as for me, I hate and scorn it.
So should everyone who values honor.
But it hardly matters to you to value it.
You aren't ashamed of your foolish undertaking.
If I complain, I should not be blamed.

You have a heart chock full of hardness
To proffer me such service without reason.
And yet you know it is disloyalty
To maintain such conduct in love.
Quit it, so that the wrong not harm you,
For if I don't see you act otherwise,
I will seek justice from the God of Love.
If I complain, I should not be blamed.

35. Ballade: "A quick death instead of any cure"

The great sorrow that grips me so strongly
That I am forced to sigh both night and day
And the grievous pain of which my heart complains
And that makes me forget every joy
I can no longer suffer or endure.
Therefore I must, with very good reason
And with good heart, seek and demand
A quick death instead of any cure.

Nor from the hurt that makes me both grow pale
And redden can I ever find a cure
If not from death, for my heart has been struck
With a mortal blow, which often wounds,
By slanderers, whose false speech treacherously
Has brought shame on many a good heart.
Mine complains, and it makes me desire
A quick death instead of any cure.

Ma vie hé et ma douleur contraint
Mon povre cuer de ma mort souhaidier,
Et Desespoir, qui dedens moy remaint,
Fait mon grant mal si fort multiplier
Que plus ne puis la destresse porter
Et le meschief dont j'ay si grant foison.
Pour ce humblement a jointes mains requier
Prouchaine mort en lieu de garison.

36. Balade: «Par vo douceur, tresbelle et bonne nee»

C'est a trestous que vous semblez si belle
Qu'on ne pourroit vo pareille trouver.
C'est a trestous que vous ressemblez celle
Par qui amours se doivent gouverner.
Pour ce chascun se vuelt a vous donner
Et vous servir d'amoureuse pensee.
Nul ne vous voit qui ne vous vueille amer
Par vo douceur, tresbelle et bonne nee.

Et quant vo face, clere et nouvelle,
Vuelt de ses yeulx aucun pou regarder,
Son doulz regart trespasse et estinceller
Si que les cuers fait de chascun fermer.
En vostre amour nul ne se puet garder.
Et quant vous estes ainsy de tous amee,
On vous doit bien servir et honnourer
Par vo doulceur, tresbelle et bonne nee.

Quant est de moy, je suiz cilz qui s'appelle
Vostre du tout. Vous me povez mander,
Non obstant que si grande querelle
Ne deusse pas emprendre a demander,
Car je ne suis digne de le penser,
Se vostre grace ne m'en estoit donnee
Et qu'il vous pleust mon fait recommander,
Par vo doulceur, tresbelle et bonne nee.

37–41. Cinq balades ensuivans

37. Balade: «Car chascun a joye de li loer»

Il n'est confort qui tant de bien me face
Quant je ne puis a ma dame parler
Comme d'avoir temps, loizir, et espace

I hate my life, and my sorrow compels
My poor heart to wish for my death,
And Despair, which dwells within me,
Makes my great pain multiply so much
That no longer can I bear the distress
And hardship of which I have so much.
Therefore I humbly request, with joined hands,
A quick death instead of any cure.

36. Ballade: "Because of your gentleness, lady born fair and good"

To everyone, you seem so beautiful
That one could never find your equal.
To everyone, you resemble her
By whom all loves ought to be ruled.
Thus everyone wants to give himself to you
And to serve you with loving thought.
No one sees you who doesn't want to love you
Because of your gentleness, lady born fair and good.

And when your face, bright and fresh,
Wishes to look around a bit with its eyes,
Its sweet regard passes about and sparkles
In such a way that it makes everyone's heart resolved.
No one can keep himself from loving you.
And when you are thus beloved by everyone,
One ought well to serve and honor you
Because of your gentleness, lady born fair and good.

As for me, I am the one who calls himself
Yours completely. You can command me,
Despite the fact that so great a matter
I should not undertake to request,
For I am not worthy to consider it
If your grace were not given to me
And that it pleased you to advance my cause
Because of your gentleness, lady born fair and good.

37–41. The Sequence of Five Ballades

37. Ballade: "For everyone takes joy in praising her"

There is no comfort that does me as much good
When I cannot speak to my lady
As to have the time, leisure, and space

De longuement en sa valour penser
Et ses doulz fais femenins recorder
Dedens mon cuer. C'est ma vie, par m'ame!
Ne je ne truis nul homme qui me blasme,
Car chascun a joye de li loer.

Il a en lui beauté, bonté, et grace
Plus que nulz homs ne saroit deviser.
C'est grant eur quant en si po d'espace
Dieu a voulu tous les biens assambler.
Honneur la veult sur toutes honnorer.
Onques ne vy si plaisant jeune dame
De toutes gens avoir si noble fame,
Car chascun a joye de li loer.

Ou qu'elle soit, bien fait et mal efface.
Moult bien li siet le rire et le jouer.
Son cuer esbat et les autres solace
Si liement qu'on ne le doit blasmer.
De li veoir ne se puet nulz lasser.
Son regart vault tous les biens d'un royaume.
Il samble bien qu'elle est tresnoble femme,
Car chascun a joye de li loer.

38. Balade: «Car trop par est son cuer plain de reffus»

A mon advis, Dieu, Raison, et Nature
En li former se sont bien entendus,
Car faite l'ont de tous les vices pure
Et paree de toutes les vertus.
Ne je ne croy qu'au jour d'ui vive nulz
Qui onques veist dame miex assevie,
Se n'est pour tant que d'amer na envie,
Car trop par est son cuer plain de reffus.

Le vis a bel, fassonné a droiture,
Le plus doulcet qui onques fust veus.
Col, main, et bras, couleur et cheveleure
De tous les beaux sont les plus beaux tenus.
Corps gracieux, mignotement vestus,
Chantant, dansant, et de maniere lie.
Mais son temps pert qui d'amours la prie,
Car trop par est son cuer plain de reffus.

Loyauté, sens, honneur, et nourreture,
Et doulz maintien sont d'elle congneus.

To think at length upon her great worth
And to recall her sweet feminine qualities
Within my heart. She is my life, by my soul!
Nor do I find any man who blames me,
For everyone takes joy in praising her.

In her there is beauty, goodness, and grace
More than any man could ever describe.
It is great fortune that in so small a space
God wished to assemble every good.
Honor wishes to honor her above all others.
I never saw so charming a young lady
Have so noble a reputation among all people,
For everyone takes joy in praising her.

Wherever she is, she does good and effaces evil.
Laughter and play suit her very well.
Her heart amuses and entertains others
So happily that it should not be blamed.
No one can grow tired of seeing her.
Her look is worth all the riches of a kingdom.
It truly appears that she is a most noble woman,
For everyone take joy in praising her.

38. Ballade: "Because her heart is much too full of scorn"

In my opinion, God, Reason, and Nature
Were all in accord in forming her,
For they created her pure of every vice
And adorned with all of the virtues.
And I do not believe that anyone lives today
Who ever saw a more perfect woman,
Except that she has no desire to love,
Because her heart is much too full of scorn.

Her face is beautiful, fashioned to perfection,
The sweetest one that was ever seen.
Neck, hands, and arms, complexion and hair
Are considered the most beautiful of all.
A graceful body, daintily attired,
Singing, dancing, and of joyous manner.
But he wastes his time who asks her for love,
Because her heart is much too full of scorn.

Loyalty, sense, honor, and good upbringing,
And gentle conduct are all well known to her.

Tresbien entent et respont par mesure.
De tous les biens est son cuer pourveux.
Le Dieu d'Amours ne devroit querir plus
Si li prenoit talent d'avoir amie.
Et si croy je que ceste n'aroit mie,
Car trop par est son cuer plain de reffus.

39. Balade: «Priez pour moy, tous les loyaulx amans»

Or est ainsi que pour la bonne et belle,
Gracieuse ou tous biens sont manans,
Je sui ferus ou cuer soulz la mamelle
Du dart d'Amours, dont le fer est tranchans.
Et si vous dy qu'il a passé sept ans,
Mais encor n'est la playe refermee,
Car sans mercy ne peust estre sanee.
Priez pour moy, tous les loyaulx amans.

Helas! Pitié, tresdoulce damoiselle,
Je vous en prie que me soiez aidans.
Contre Dangier soustenez ma querelle,
Car il est fort et ses amis sont grans.
Durté me hait e Paour m'est nuisans.
Se par vous n'est ma santé recouvree,
Pour bien amer yert ma vie finee.
Priez pour moy, tous les loyaulx amans.

De bien amer tous les jours renouvelle
Le cuer de moy, qui est obeissans
En actendant le bon plaisir de celle
A qui je sui et vueil estre servans.
Las! Je ne sui que simples et souffrans,
Et me soustien sur ma loyal pensee
Jusques Mercy m'ait sa grace monstree.
Priez pour moy, tous les loyaulx amans.

40. Balade: «Tout a rebours de ce qu'on vuelt trouver»

Certes, Amour, c'est chose convenable
Que vos grans bien faciez chier comparer:
Veillier ou lit et jeuner a la table,
Rire en plorant et en plaignant chanter,
Baissier les yeulx quant on doit regarder,
Souvent changier couleur et contenance,

She listens well and answers prudently.
Her heart is provided with every good.
The God of Love would need to seek no further
If the desire to have a lover took hold of him.
And yet I believe that she would not have him,
Because her heart is much too full of scorn.

39. Ballade: "Pray for me, all you loyal lovers"

Thus it is that for the good and fair one,
The gracious one in whom all virtues dwell,
I am struck in the heart beneath the breast
By the dart of Love, of which the point is sharp.
And thus I tell you that seven years have passed,
But still the wound is not yet closed,
For without mercy it cannot be healed.
Pray for me, all you loyal lovers.

Alas! Pity, most sweet damsel,
I beseech you to come to my aid.
Support me in my quarrel against Danger,
For he is strong and his friends are great.
Harshness hates me and Fear does me harm.
If through you my health is not restored,
For loving well my life will come to an end.
Pray for me, all you loyal lovers.

In loving well is each day renewed
My heart, which is obedient
While awaiting the pleasure of her
Of whom I am and wish to be the servant.
Alas! I am but simple and suffering,
And I sustain myself with loyal thought
Until Mercy has shown her grace to me.
Pray for me, all you loyal lovers.

40. Ballade: "Exactly the opposite of what one wants"

Surely, Love, it is a fitting thing
That you exact a high price for your goods:
Lying awake in bed and fasting at table,
Laughing while crying and singing while lamenting,
Lowering the eyes when one ought to look,
Often changing color and expression,

Plaindre en dormant et songier a la dance,
Tout a rebours de ce qu'on vuelt trouver.

Jalousie, c'est la mere du deable.
Elle veult tout veoir et escouter,
Ne nulz ne fait chose si raisonnable
Que tout a mal ne le veult tourner.
Amours, ainsi fault voz dons acheter,
Et vous donnez souvant sans ordonnance
Assez doulour et petit de plaisance,
Tout a rebours de ce quon vuelt trouver.

Pour un court temps, le geu est aggreable,
Mais trop par est encombreux a user,
Et ja soit il a dames honnorable,
A leurs servans est trop grief a porter.
Tousdiz convient souffrir et endurer,
Sans nul certain languir en esperance,
Et recevoir mainte male meschance,
Tout a rebours de ce quon vuelt trouver.

41. Balade: «De li servir ne seray jamais las»

Amours, sachiez que pas ne le veulz dire
Pour moy getter hors des amoureux las,
Car j'ay porté si long temps mon martire
Qu'a mon vivant, ne le guerpiray pas.
Il me souffit d'avoir tant de soulas
Que veoir puisse la belle gracieuse.
Combien q'elle est envers moy dangereuse,
De li servir ne seray jamais las.

Certes, Amours, quant bien a droit remire
Les hauls estas, les moiens, et les bas,
Vous m'avez fait de tous les liex eslire,
A mon adviz, le meilleur en tous cas.
Or ayme, Cuer, si fort com tu porras,
Car ja n'auras paine si doloureuse
Pour ma dame qui ne me soit joieuse.
De li servir ne seray jamais las.

Cuer, il te doit assez plus que souffire
D'avoir choisi si bien que choisi as,
Ne querir plus royaume n'empire.
Car si bonne jamais ne trouveras,
Ne si belle, par mes yeulx, ne verras.

Lamenting while sleeping and dreaming at the dance,
Exactly the opposite of what one wants.

Jealousy is the mother of the devil.
She wants to see and listen to everything,
Nor does anyone do anything so reasonable
That she doesn't want to turn it into evil.
Love, that's how we have to pay for your gifts,
And you often give out arbitrarily
Grief enough and very little pleasure,
Exactly the opposite of what one wants.

For a short time, the game is agreeable,
But it is much too hard to keep it up,
And though to ladies it is honorable,
It is too painful for their servants to bear.
One must constantly suffer and endure,
Languish in hope without any certainty,
And receive many a harsh misfortune,
Exactly the opposite of what one wants.

41. Ballade: "I will never grow tired of serving her"

Love, know that I don't want to say it
In order to free myself from the snares of love,
For I have endured my suffering for so long
That while I live, I will not give it up.
It is enough for me to have so much solace
As to be able to see the fair gracious one.
However disdainful she is with regard to me,
I will never grow tired of serving her.

Certainly, Love, when I consider rightly
The high estates, the middle, and the low,
Among all places, you have made me choose,
It seems to me, the best in every way.
So love, Heart, as strongly as you can,
For you will never have a pain so grievous
For my lady's sake that it is not joy to me.
I will never grow tired of serving her.

Heart, it ought to more than satisfy you
To have chosen as well as you have
And no longer to seek a kingdom or an empire.
For you will never find anyone as good,
Nor will you ever see one as beautiful, by my eyes.

C'est jeunesse sachant et savoureuse.
Ja soit elle de m'amour desdaigneuse,
De li servir ne seray jamais las.

42. Balade: «Desloiaulté en l'amoureuse vie»

Vous qui voulez l'oppinion contraire
De loyaulté en amours maintenir,
Bien vous povez tous d'une part retraire.
Point ne devez soubz le pagnon venir
Du Dieu d'Amours. On vous en doit banir
Et debouter comme gent deffaillie,
Qui soustenez ce qu'on doit plus hair:
Desloiaulté en l'amoureuse vie.

C'est un renom tres noble, qui doit plaire
A un chascun, que loiaulté tenir.
Tout cuer gentil y doit prendre exemplaire
Et la raison aidier et soustenir
Des vrais amans, et l'autre anientir.
Quant endroit moy, je tien de la partie
De trestous ceulx qui veulent deguerpir
Desloiaulté en l'amoureuse vie.

Et me samble – de ce ne me quier taire –
Qu'on puet assez plus d'onneur acquerir
En loyaument amer, sans lui meffaire,
Qu'estre tenu vilotier ne querir
Son fol vouloir, s'il ne la a complir.
Car la est foy souventesfois mentie.
C'est deshonnour; pour ce doit on fuir
Desloiaulté en l'amoureuse vie.

Princesse d'Amours, ne vueillez consentir
Que loiauté soit pour eux amoindrie
Qui soustiennent, par largement mentir,
Desloiaulté en l'amoureuse vie.

43. Balade: «Fors que d'amours et de ma belle dame»

Loyal amour, ardant et desireuse,
Ferme, sans fin, entierement donnee,
Et ma dame, plaisant et gracieuse,
Plaine d'amour, de tout bien renommee,
N'ont en mon cuer laissié nulle pensee

She is a wise and delectable youth.
Although she is disdainful of my love,
I will never grow tired of serving her.

42. Ballade: "Disloyalty in the life of love"

You who wish to hold the view
Opposed to loyalty in love,
You can all step to one side.
You aren't allowed to come beneath the banner
Of the God of Love. You should be banished
And thrown out as unworthy followers,
You who uphold what one ought most to hate:
Disloyalty in the life of love.

It is a most noble quality, remaining loyal,
That ought to please each and every one.
Every courteous heart should heed the example
And ought to help and sustain the cause
Of true lovers, and destroy the opposite.
As for me, I hold with the party
Of all those who wish to reject
Disloyalty in the life of love.

And it seems to me — on this I won't be silent —
That one can acquire much more honor
In loving loyally, without doing wrong,
Than in being held a knave or in pursuing
A foolish wish, if he doesn't have to.
For there faith is oftentimes belied.
It's a dishonor; therefore one should flee
Disloyalty in the life of love.

Princess of Love, please do not consent
That loyalty be reduced because of those
Who maintain, by lying abundantly,
Disloyalty in the life of love.

43. Ballade: "Anything but love and my beautiful lady"

Loyal love, burning and desirous,
Constant, endless, given entirely,
And my lady, charming and gracious,
Full of love, renowned for every virtue,
Have not left in my heart a single thought

Fors que celle qui d'eulz deux me vient,
Et en celle tant penser me convient
Que de riens plus ne me souvient, par m'ame,
Fors que d'amours et de ma belle dame.

Je sens amour, puissant et oultrageuse,
De trop amer fort et desmesuree,
Et je congnois ma dame dangereuse,
Froide d'amer, sachant, bien avisee,
Pour sa bonté de plusieurs desiree.
Tousdiz meilleur et plus belle devient,
Et penser cilz si pres de moy se tient
Que de riens plus ne me souvient, par m'ame,
Fors que d'amours et de ma belle dame.

Mais trop seroit amour plus savoureuse,
Mieulx avenant et plus aise portee,
Se ma dame, jeune, gente, joieuse,
Belle sans per, bonne, bien euree,
Vouloit savoir comment elle est amee
En tous les poins que loyal cuer maintient,
Car loyaulté de si pres m'apartient
Que de riens plus ne me souvient, par m'ame,
Fors que d'amours et de ma belle dame.

44. Balade: «Ainsi puet il don d'amours desservir»

Qui veult entrer en l'amoureux servage
Ne si mette s'il ne veult maintenir
Ce qui s'ensuit, selon le droit usage,
De vray amant qui tant a aquerir
Grace d'amours et a honneur venir.
Premierement, c'est d'amer loyaument,
Estre secret, pour son fait miex couvrir.
Soit doulx, courtois, de gent contenement.
Ainsi puet il don d'amours desservir.

De soy vanter ne tiengne point langage;
Sur toute riens s'en doit bien abstenir.
De trop parler se gart, car c'est oultrage,
Et s'en voit on souvent mesavenir.
De son povoir doit sa dame servir,
Honneur porter sur toutes bonnement,
Craindre, doubter, amer, et obeir,
Souvent prier tresamoureusement.
Ainsi puet il don d'amours desservir.

Except for that which comes to me from those two,
And on this I am forced to think so much
That by my soul, no longer do I recall
Anything but love and my beautiful lady.

I feel love, powerful and excessive,
Strong and uncontrolled in loving greatly,
And I know my lady to be disdainful,
Cool to love, wise and very prudent,
Desired by very many for her goodness.
She constantly gets better and more beautiful,
And this thought adheres to me so closely
That by my soul, no longer do I recall
Anything but love and my beautiful lady.

But love would be much more delightful,
More pleasant and more easily borne,
If my lady, young, gracious, joyful,
Beautiful without equal, good and fortunate,
Wished to know how much she is loved
In all the ways that a loyal heart maintains,
For loyalty is so much a part of me
That by my soul, no longer do I recall
Anything but love and my beautiful lady.

44. Ballade: "That's how he can earn the gifts of love"

Let him who wants to enter love's servitude
Not do it if he does not want to observe
What follows, according to proper custom,
For a true lover who tries to acquire
Grace in love and to come to honor.
First of all, it is to love loyally,
To be discreet, to better hide his state.
Let him be gentle, courteous, of noble bearing.
That's how he can earn the gifts of love.

Let him not use speech in order to boast;
Above all else, from that he must refrain.
Let him keep from talking too much, for that's an offense,
And one often sees misfortune follow.
As best he can, he ought to serve his lady,
To do honor to all women humbly,
To fear, to dread, to love, and to obey,
To pray often in a deeply loving way.
That's how he can earn the gifts of love.

A Doulx Espoir face tousdiz hommage.
Pour mal qu'il ait, ne le vueil guerpir.
Et ne soit pas a largesse sauvage:
Son fait, son bien en pourroit amenrir.
Par largesce puet on bien adoulcir
Et amolir un dur cuer grandement.
A tous face et a toutes plaisir.
S'en aura pris, loz, et avancement.
Ainsi puet il don d'amours desservir.

45. Balade: «Que mon cuer voit tousdiz, ou que je soye»

J'ay en mon cuer un oeil qui toudiz veille
Ne riens ne fait fors que vous regarder.
Et quant des yeulx de ma teste sommeille,
L'ueil de mon cuer, belle, vous voit tout cler.
Celui regart ne me peust nulz oster.
Je l'ay repris d'Amours en droit hommage,
Et par cest oeil ay je grant avantage,
Car autrement trop pou souvent verroye
Vostre bel, doulz, gent et jeune visage,
Que mon cuer voit tousdiz, ou que je soye.

Il a aussi en mon cuer une oreille
Qui veult tousdiz de vous oir parler.
En bonne foy, ce n'est mie merveille,
Que moult en peust de grans biens escouter.
Vostre bonté vous fait des bons louer,
Et vous amez honneur de droit usage.
Le Dieu d'Amours escript en mon courage
Voz loyaulx fais, pour ce que servir doye
Plus humblement vostre noble corsage,
Que mon cuer voit tousdiz ou que je soye.

Je sçay de vray que vous n'avez pareille
De loyauté, de sa ne de la mer.
C'est la chose qui plus fort me conseille
Qu'en vous servant doye mes jours finer.
Si feray je, de ce ne faut doubter.
Vous en tenez le cuer de moy en plaige.
Bien tient le corps qui a le cuer en gage.
Pour nul dangier oublier ne porroye
La grant beauté de vostre doulz aage,
Que mon cuer voit tousdiz ou que je soye.

Let him always pay homage to Sweet Hope.
Whatever pain he has, let him not give up.
And let him not be a stranger to largesse:
His state and his well-being could be reduced.
By largesse one can very easily sweeten
And soften a hard heart to a great extent.
Let him be pleasing to every man and woman.
Then he will have esteem, praise, and advancement.
That's how he can earn the gifts of love.

45. Ballade: "Which my heart sees constantly, wherever I am"

I have in my heart an eye that always wakes
And it does nothing else but look at you.
And when the eyes in my head are asleep,
The eye in my heart, my fair one, sees you clearly.
No one can take away from me this sight.
I received it from Love as his vassal,
And from this eye I have great benefit,
For otherwise too rarely would I see
Your fair, sweet, gracious, and youthful face,
Which my heart sees constantly, wherever I am.

There is also in my heart an ear
That wishes constantly to hear talk of you.
In good faith, this is certainly no wonder,
For it can hear of many great virtues this way.
Your goodness makes you praised by all good people,
And you love honor out of good custom.
The God of Love has inscribed within my heart
Your loyal nature, so that I be obliged to serve
More humbly your noble person,
Which my heart sees constantly, wherever I am.

I know for truth you haven't any equal
In loyalty, here or beyond the sea.
That is the thing that counsels me most strongly
That I should end my days in serving you.
So will I do, of that one must not doubt.
Of that you hold my very heart in pledge.
She owns the body who has the heart as gage.
For no disdain would I be able to forget
The great beauty of your sweet youthfulness,
Which my heart sees constantly, wherever I am.

46. Balade: «Ma belle dame et ma loyal amie»

Je vous mercy, des belles la plus belle;
Je vous mercy, de bonnes la meillour;
Je vous mercy, jeune, fresche, nouvelle;
Je vous mercy, trop plus blanche que flour.
Je vous mercy quant, par vo grant doulçour,
Il vous a pleu recevoir en bon gré
Le petit don que vous ay envoyé
Par mon ami en qui du tout me fie.
Et me vueilliez tenir pour excusé,
Ma belle dame et ma loyal amie,

Se plus souvent n'oyez de moy nouvelle.
Car par ma foy j'en ay mainte dolour
En mon las cuer, combien que je le celle,
Par plusieurs fois, et de nuit et de jour,
Ne je ne quier fors a trouver le tour
Que veoir puisse vostre belle beaulté,
Car il m'en vient une telle santé
Que gary sui de toute maladie
Quant de vos yeulx puis estre regardé,
Ma belle dame et ma loyal amie.

Pour ce, Pitié, tresdoulce damoiselle,
Vueilliez tantost venir a mon secour,
Car a toute heure contre moy renouvelle
Dangier le fel un moult cruel estour,
Et avec lui sont Reffus et Paour,
Qui desja mont tresdurement navré.
Mais s'il vous plaist que soye conforté
Du nom d'ami, vous sauveriez ma vie.
Or en soit a vostre voulenté,
Ma belle dame et ma loyal amie.

47. Balade: «Car je languis par deffault de raison»

Froit estomac et pommon eschauffé,
Sang esmeu et le servel boillant –
En tel estat m'a ung mire esprouvé.
Mais il n'est pas de mon mal congnoissant,
Car j'ay au cuer unne douleur plus grant
Dont je seuffre dangier, peril et peine.
Le maistre dit que ce n'est que ciertaine,
Pour ce que j'ay ung jour bon, l'autre non.

46. Ballade: "My beautiful lady and my loyal love"

I thank you, the fairest of the fair;
I thank you, the best of the good;
I thank you, who are young, fresh, new;
I thank you, who are much whiter than flour.
I thank you when, out of your great gentleness,
It pleased you to accept in good will
The little gift that I sent to you
By way of my friend in whom I fully trust.
And please hold me excused,
My beautiful lady and my loyal love,

If you don't hear tidings of me more often.
For by my faith, I have many a sorrow
In my weary heart, however much I hide it,
Oftentimes, by both night and day,
And all I seek is to find a way
That I might look upon your fair beauty,
For from it comes to me such well-being
That I am healed of every malady
When I can be beheld by your eyes,
My beautiful lady and my loyal love.

Therefore, Pity, my sweet damsel,
Please come quickly to my aid,
For at every hour, the felon Danger
Renews a cruel battle against me,
And with it are Rejection and Fear,
Which have already hurt me very badly.
But if it pleases you that I be comforted
With the name of lover, you will save my life.
Now may it be according to your will,
My beautiful lady and my loyal love.

47. Ballade: "For I am languishing from a lack of justice"

A cold stomach and a heated lung,
Excited blood and a seething brain —
In such a state did a doctor find me.
But he doesn't understand my illness,
For I have a greater grief within my heart
From which I suffer danger, peril, and pain.
The doctor says that this is just a fever
Because one day I'm fine and the next I'm not,

Mais je seuffre doleur cothidiainne,
Car je languis par deffault de raison.

Jeune seigneur, conceil de volunté,
Gens ennuyeux et commun trop puissant
M'ont eforcé du mien et desherité,
Et vont toudiz mon honneur chalangant.
Mais, se Dieu plaist, j'en seray deffendant,
Prest de venir a l'espreuve certainne.
Le juge fault que ne lez y amainne.
Pouvre me fait sa grant dilacion.
Pour ce n'est pas ma complection sainne,
Car je languis par deffault de raison.

Dieu qui est juge de toute loiaulté,
Juste, piteux et par tout cler voyant,
En vueille tost monstrer la verité.
C'est la santé que je vais demendant
Et le mire ou je me fie tant,
Et qui congnoist toute creature humaine
Et du monde, qui ainsi me demainne.
Se brief ne ay autre conclusion,
Je m'en plaindray a sa court souveraine,
Car je languis par deffault de raison.

48. Balade: «C'est mon talant, belle dame sans per»

Pour avoir plus de plaisir et de joye
Et pour estre du tout a mon vouloir,
En ce monde mieulx choisyr ne saroye
Que vous, ma dame, car a dire le voir,
Riche beaulté est en vostre pouoir,
Et d'autres biens avez si grant partie
Qui nuit et jour vous tienent compaignie,
Que Dieu a dame n'en devroit plus donner.
Si veul user en vous servant ma vye.
C'est mon talant, belle dame sans per.

Et s'il vous plaist que vostre servant soie,
Je renonce richesse et avoir;
Ne d'aultre bienz, en quelque lieu que soye,
Se non par vous, jamais ne quiers avoir.
Ains vueil mectre tout autre a nonchaloir,
Et puis serez seulle de moy servie.
Car d'autre amer, certez, je n'ay envie.
Et me vueillez, sy vous plaist, pardonner

But I suffer from a daily sorrow,
For I am languishing from a lack of justice.

A young lord, a willing council,
Malicious people and too powerful a commons
Have forced me from what is mine and disinherited me,
And they are constantly challenging my honor.
But if it pleases God, I will defend it,
Ready to come to the final test.
The judge who doesn't lead them there is lacking.
His great delay is making me poor.
That's why my constitution is not healthy,
For I am languishing from a lack of justice.

May God, who is judge of all loyalty,
Just, piteous, and omniscient,
Wish to reveal the truth of this matter soon.
That is the health that I am requesting
And the physician in whom I trust so much,
And the one who knows every human being
And all worldly creatures, who thus governs me.
If I don't have some other conclusion quickly,
I will lodge a complaint in his sovereign court,
For I am languishing from a lack of justice.

48. Ballade: "That is my wish, fair lady without peer"

In order to have more pleasure and joy
And to be entirely as I desire,
In this world I could not choose better
Than you, my lady, for to tell the truth,
Rich beauty is in your possession,
And you have so great a share of other virtues
Which night and day keep you company
That God should not give any lady more.
Thus I want to spend my life in serving you.
That is my wish, fair lady without peer.

And if it please you that I be your servant,
I renounce riches and possessions;
And other goods, wherever I might be,
Shall I never seek to have if not from you.
Rather I wish to set everything else aside,
And then you alone will be served by me.
For I certainly have no desire to love another.
And may you wish, if it please you, to pardon me

Se j'en dy trop. Pour Dieu, ne vous annuie.
C'est mon talant, belle dame sans per.

Or est ainsy, combien que ne vous voie,
Ma volenté povez apersevoir,
Car estre aimé de vous mieulx aimeroye
Que de nule autre en bien, sans decevoir.
Mez penseez sont en vous main et soir
Par le vouloir d'Amours, qui me doctrine.
Espoir me dit qu'aray dame et amie
Et, par pitié, s'il vous plaist, le serez
Qui sur les cuers a toute seignorie.
C'est mon talant, belle dame sans per.

49. Balade: «Je n'ay riens fait qu'Amours ne m'ait fait faire»

Ay my! quel mal, quel ennuy, quel doleur,
Quel grant meschief, quel soussy ne quel pene,
Seuffre et fera dosreenavant mon cuer
Pour vous que j'ay, sans pensee villainne,
Plus amé que autre chose mondainne,
Et loiaument servie main et soir
Selon mon sens. Et se par non savoir
J'ay fait pourquoy vous pensez le contraire,
Ce me poise, mais, pour vous dire le voir,
Je n'ay riens fait qu'Amours ne m'ait fait faire.

Vous me blasmez que j'ay fait grant longueur
D'aler vers vous, et m'estiez cy prouchainne,
Mais se me fist Amours, que la rigueur
Des mesdisans, qui ont trop grant alainne,
Craingnoie trop fort. Sy ay bien dure estrainne,
Quant pour si pou je me voy decevoir,
Et a autrui lez doulz biens recevoir
C'om m'a tolus, dont je ne me puis taire.
Car puis le temps que ma dame en fut hoir,
Je n'ay riens fait qu'Amours ne m'ait fait faire.

Qu'en puis je mais, se je me plains et plour
Que j'ay ainsy sans achoison certainne
Perdus lez biens, le plaisir, la doulssour
Que je cuidoye avoir comme demainne?
Or estez vous de bien grant durté plainne
Qui me laissez pour autre amy avoir
Et jurez que voz beaulx yeux veoir
Ne pourroient riens sans moy qui vous puet plaire.

If I say too much. By God, may it not trouble you.
That is my wish, fair lady without peer.

Now it is such that, though I do not see you,
You are able to perceive my wish,
For I would much prefer to be loved by you
Than by any other in comfort, without a lie.
My thoughts are upon you both morning and night
By the wish of Love, who instructs me.
Hope tells me that I will have a lady and friend
And out of pity, if you please, it will be you
Who has complete lordship over hearts.
That is my wish, fair lady without peer.

49. Ballade: "I have done nothing that Love didn't make me do"

Alas! What hurt, what trouble, and what sorrow,
What great hardship, what care, and what pain
My heart endures, and will from now on
For you, whom I, without base thought,
Have loved more than anything else in this world
And loyally served, both morning and evening,
As best I knew how. And if unknowingly
I have done anything for which you think the opposite,
This troubles me, but to tell the truth,
I have done nothing that Love didn't make me do.

You blame me that it took me a long time
To come to you, and you were close nearby,
But Love made me do this, for I feared too greatly
The harshness of slanderers, who draw too deep a breath.
Thus I have quite hard luck
When for so little I see myself deceived,
And I see another receive the sweet rewards
That were taken from me, on which I cannot be silent,
For since the time that my lady was their heir,
I have done nothing that Love didn't make me do.

What more can I do, if I complain and weep
That I have thus, without any real reason,
Lost the rewards, the pleasure, and the sweetness
That I believed to have as my own?
But you are full of great harshness,
Who abandon me to take another lover
And swear that your fair eyes could not see
Anything other than me that can please you.

Et sy n'est pas pour moy, qu'a mon pouoir,
Je n'ay riens fait qu'Amours ne me fait faire.

50. Balade: «Je n'ay riens fait qu'Amours ne me fait faire»

Dea, doulx amiz, vous vous desconfortez
Trop durement a petit d'achoison.
Vous regretez lez biens que vous avez
Envers Amours par moult longue saison.
Et puis dictez que je fais trayson
Quant autrement de vous ne me souvient.
Mais se, par force, autre amer me convient,
En devez vous crier sur moy ne brayre?
Prenez en gré le temps tel comme il vient:
Je n'ay riens fait qu'Amours ne me fait faire.

Amours me fist, ou temps dont vo parlés,
Donner a vous entierement en don.
Maintenant veult c'un autre en soit doués
Que j'ayme autant que ou temps dont parlons
Faisoye vous, quar il est bel et bon.
A mon advis, aussy il apartient
Qu'au gré d'Amours le face, et c'il avient
Q'on en dye riens qui me puet desplaire,
Je respondray que droit a droit revient.
Je n'ay riens fait qu'Amours ne me fait faire.

Apaisiez vous et Amours merciez
Quant de sez biens avez eu foyson.
S'il lez reprent, humblement l'endurez.
Car sez jeux sont de tel condicion.
Quant il se joue aux gens de sa maison,
L'un corrocié, l'autre liel en devient,
L'un bouté hors, l'autre avec lui retient.
Or suis a luy, s'il lui plaist, sans retraire.
Et pour ce dy je a qui fausse me tient:
«Je n'ay riens fait qu'Amours ne me fait faire.»

51. Balade: «Dame, de moy plus que nulle autre amee»

Comment qu'il soit, mon cuer vous aimera,
Belle, plaisant, jeune, fresche et nouvelle.
Jamais autre que vous ne servira,
Car en ce monde ne pourroit servir telle
Comme vous estez, sy bonne ne sy belle,

And yet it is not my doing, for within my power,
I have done nothing that Love doesn't make me do.

50. Ballade: "I have done nothing that Love doesn't make me do"

Really, sweet friend, you are distressed
Too greatly for very little reason.
You miss the rewards that you have had
From Love for quite a long time,
And then you say that I commit treason
When I remember someone other than you.
But if I must necessarily love another,
Should you be screaming and shouting about me for it?
Accept willingly the time such as it comes:
I have done nothing that Love doesn't make me do.

Love, at the time of which you are speaking,
Caused me to be given to you fully, as a gift.
Now he wants that another be so given,
Whom I love just as much as, at that time,
I did you, for he is handsome and good.
It seems to me that it follows that, by Love's will,
I should do so, and if it happens
That anyone says anything that can displease me,
I will reply that right returns to right.
I have done nothing that Love doesn't make me do.

Calm down, and give thanks to Love
Since you have had an abundance of his rewards.
If he takes them back, humbly endure it.
For his games are of just such a kind.
When he plays with those in his retinue,
One becomes angry, another becomes gay;
One gets booted, the other he retains.
Now I am his, if it please him, without repeal.
And thus I say to anyone who calls me false:
"I have done nothing that Love doesn't make me do."

51. Ballade: "My lady, loved by me more than any other woman"

However it may be, my heart will love you,
Oh Beauty, charming, young, fresh, and new.
Never will it serve any other,
For in this world it could not serve a woman
Such as you, as good and as beautiful,

Ne qui tant soit plaisant a regarder,
Ne qui tant face de tous biens a louer.
Et par cela, de cuer et de pensee,
Serez et estez, a tousjours sans muer,
Dame, de moy plus que nulle autre amee.

Ne, par ma foy, jamais ne me vendra
Autre vouloir pour nesune nouvelle
Que oir puisse, n'Amours le pouoir n'a,
Ne ja n'aura, pour chose tant s'en mesle,
Que puist faire, car tousjours renouvelle
L'ardeur en moy de plus fort vous amer.
Ne je ne puis en autre rien penser,
Car tant me plaist se penser et agree
Qu'en joye en fault mez griefz douleurz tourner,
Dame, de moy plus que nulle autre amee.

Pour ce doy je trop plus c'onquez n'ama
Homme qui fut vous amer, car par celle
Amour je puis, quant vo doulsour plaira,
Doulce plaisant que ma maistresse appelle,
Avoir dez biens, combien que je le celle,
Si largement qu'en cent ans deviser
Ne lez pourroit nul homme ne compter,
Et fust ung jour aussy long c'une annee.
Or en vueillés tout vo gré ordonner,
Dame, de moy plus que nulle autre amee.

52. Balade: **«Il m'est advis que vostre beauté voye»**

Si durement me destraint la pensee
Qui m'est venue, Belle, pour vous amer
Que nullement en nesune journee
Mon cuer ne puit tant soit pou reposer.
Car, en veillant, par force de penser,
Veoir vous cuide, sans heure desfaillir,
Dez yeux du cuer, et quant ung pou dormir
Il me convient, ainsy con je veilloye,
Pour la tristesse qu'Amours me fait sentir,
Il m'est advis que vostre beauté voye.

Ne je ne sçay lequel plus fort m'agree,
Pour la doulour qui me vient conforter,
Ne dont ma pene puit mieulx estre alegee,
Ou par dormir ou par tousjours voillier.
Car quant je dors, tout ainsy sans seser

Nor one who is as pleasing to behold,
Nor one who does so much of all that is to praise.
And for that reason, in heart and in thought,
You will be and are, forever without change,
My lady, loved by me more than any other woman.

Nor, by my faith, will ever come to me
Any other wish, for any tidings
That I might hear, nor does Love have the power,
Nor will it ever, however much it tries,
To bring it about, for constantly renews in me
The burning desire to love you more strongly.
Nor can I think of anything else,
For so much does this thought please and satisfy me
That my grievous sorrows must turn into joy,
My lady, loved by me more than any other woman.

Therefore I must love you much much more
Than any man who was has ever loved, for by this love
I can, when it pleases your gentleness,
Sweet charming one whom I call my mistress,
Obtain rewards, however much I hide it,
So generously that in a hundred years
No man could describe or count them,
Even if a day were as long as a year.
Now please command your every pleasure,
My lady, loved by me more than any other woman.

52. Ballade: "It seems to me that I see your beauty"

So thoroughly does the thought of loving you
That has come to me constrain me, my fair lady,
That not at all on any day
Can my heart rest, however little.
For when awake, by force of thought,
I think I see you, without missing an hour,
With the eyes of my heart; and when I am compelled
To sleep a bit, just as when I'm awake,
Because of the sadness that Love makes me feel,
It seems to me that I see your beauty.

Nor do I know which pleases me more,
Because of the sadness that comes to comfort me,
Nor by which my pain can better be relieved,
Whether by sleeping or by remaining awake.
For when I sleep, just as much without cease

Com quant je veille, il me fault soustenir
Lez maulx d'amours. Pour ce dis, sens mentir,
Ce n'est poinct songe, car tousjours ou que soye,
Ou veille ou dorme, soit mon mal ou plaisir,
Il m'est advis que votre beauté voye.

Mais ce les yeulx, par quoy vous fuz donnee
L'amour de moy, vous peussent regarder
Aussy souvent, ma plaisance celee,
Comme font ceulx de mon cuer, ja doubter
Ne me faulssist de joye recouvrer.
Car tant en eusse com peust resjoir
Cent cuers doulens. Mais quant a ce venir,
Pour riens ne puis je demourer sans joye,
Tant que je dy, pour vray et sans faillir,
Il m'est advis que vostre beaulté voye.

53. Balade: **«Puis qu'il lui plaist, il me souffist»**

Pourquoy virent onques mes yeulx
Vostre beauté, belle sans per?
Pourquoy fu je si oultrageux
De vous vouloir onques amer?
Pourquoy me mis je en tele mer,
Ne mon cuer pourquoy y pensa?
Car onques puis d'un an an sa,
Ses pensees ailleurs ne mist,
Et dist qu'en vous servant mourra.
Puis qu'il lui plaist, il me souffist.

Combien que j'amasse trop mieulx,
S'il se peust faire, l'en garder,
Car il n'en a ne ris ne jeux,
Ne riens for doulour a porter.
S'il ne vous plaist le conforter,
Je croy que bien brief finera.
Car onques mais nul cuer n'ama
Qui en tele doulour languist.
Or languisse tant qu'il vouldra.
Puis qu'il lui plaist, il me souffist.

Et non obstant ce, je m'en deulx,
Ne vous en vueilliez merveillier,
Car je vous jure, se m'aist Dieux,
Il ne puet dormir ne veillier
Qu'il ne lui faille traveillier

As when I'm awake, I am forced to endure
The pains of love. Therefore I say, without lying,
This isn't a dream, for constantly, wherever I am,
Whether I wake or sleep, be it pain or pleasure,
It seems to me that I see your beauty.

But if the eyes by which you were given
My love were able to look at you
As often, my pleasure being concealed,
As do those of my heart,
I would never have to doubt recovering joy.
For I would have as much as could rejoice
A hundred sorrowing hearts. But as for that,
I cannot remain without joy for anything
As long as I say, in truth and without failing,
It seems to me that I see your beauty.

53. Ballade: "Since it pleases my heart, that's enough for me"

Why did my eyes ever see
Your beauty, fair lady without peer?
Why was I ever so foolishly bold
As ever to want to love you?
Why did I put myself on such a sea,
And why did my heart consider it?
For ever since a year ago,
It directed its thoughts nowhere else
And said that it will die in serving you.
Since it pleases my heart, that's enough for me.

How much I would have preferred
If it were possible, to prevent it,
For it has neither laughter nor play,
Nor anything but sorrow to bear.
Unless it please you to comfort it,
I believe that very shortly it will die.
For never did any heart ever love
That languished in such sorrow.
But let it languish as much as it wants.
Since it pleases my heart, that's enough for me.

And nonetheless, I am in sorrow.
Please do not be amazed,
For I swear to you, so help me God,
It can neither sleep nor remain awake
That it is not compelled to struggle

A penser comment il pourra
Guerir des maulx qu'il en a.
Mais il n'a gueres qu'il me dist
Que vostre bon gré atandra.
Puis qu'il lui plaist, il me souffist.

54. Balade: «Un seul confort de ma tresbelle dame»

Amours, je voy des autres amoureux
Que vous tenez en vostre gouvernement,
Que maintes foiz vous les faites joyeux
Et leur donnez de voz biens largement.
Ceulx vous doivent servir songneusement
De cuer, de corps, sanz rien y espargnier.
Maiz moi qui suiz et seray sanz fausser
Vo serviteur a tousjours maiz, par m'ame,
Onques nul jour ne me voultes donner
Un seul confort de ma tresbelle dame.

Amours, Amours, se je suiz doulereux,
Triste, pensiz, sanz nul esbatement,
Nulz m'en doit blasmer, se m'aist Dieux.
Car il y a trois ans entierement
Que j'entrepris de servir loyaument
Celle du monde que on doit plus prisier.
Sa grant beauté fist en mon cuer entrer
Feu mortel qui art, bruit et enflame,
Ne onques mais si n'en peuz recouvrer
Un seul confort de ma tresbelle dame.

Amours, Amours, je suis sy envieux,
Puis que fere ne se puet autrement,
De nulle rien pour garir mes douleurs,
Fors que sanz plus de la mort seulement.
Se je me plains de voz fais trop souvent,
Helas! Amours, vueilliez moy pardonner.
Ce que j'en dy, c'est par force d'amer.
Onques mais, las! je ne me plains, par m'ame.
Ce sont mes maulx qui me font demander
Un seul confort de ma tresbelle dame

55. Balade: «De mieulx en mieulx serviray ma maistresse»

Amours, Amours, puisque c'est vo plaisance
Du tout en tout moy ainsy deserter

Thinking about how it will be able
To recover from the pains it bears.
But it wasn't long ago that it told me
That it would await your good will.
Since it pleases my heart, that's enough for me.

54. Ballade: "A single comfort from my most beautiful lady"

Love, I see, with regard to other lovers
That you have in your governance,
That many times you make them joyous
And give them generously of your rewards.
These ought to serve you attentively
In heart, in body, without ever sparing.
But to me, who am and will be, without deceit,
Your servant forever more, by my soul,
Never on any day have you wanted to give me
A single comfort from my most beautiful lady.

Love, Love, if I am sorrowful,
Sad, pensive, without any mirth,
No one ought to blame me, so help me God,
For it has been three whole years now
Since I undertook to serve loyally
Her whom one must most esteem in the world.
Her great beauty made enter into my heart
A mortal fire which burns, roars, and inflames.
Yet never am I able to obtain thereby
A single comfort from my most beautiful lady.

Love, Love, I am so envious
Because it cannot turn out otherwise
In any way in order to heal my sorrows,
Except for death alone and nothing else.
If I complain about your nature too often,
Alas, Love, please pardon me.
What I say is under the force of loving.
Never more, alas, do I complain, by my soul.
These are my pains that make me request
A single comfort from my most beautiful lady.

55. Ballade: "Better and better will I serve my mistress"

Love, Love, since it is your pleasure
Completely to desert me in this way

Et forbanir de toute esperance,
A tousjours maiz, sanz mercy recouvrer,
Dont la grieﬅé me convient endurer,
De par moy je vous faiz assavoir,
Se jamais bien je n'en devoye avoir,
Que, se mourir devoye de tristesse,
De cuer, de corps, a mon loyal pouoir,
De mieulx en mieulx serviray ma maistresse.

Amours, de vous un jour ay alegence,
Autresfoiz je suiz a commancier.
Quant de vous cuide avoir l'acointance
Lors m'y faites devenir estrangier.
A grant paine me dangniez regarder.
Quant je me mis du tout en vo pouoir,
Pas ne cuidoye si dur guerredon avoir.
Maiz puis qu'ainsy vo vouloir s'adresse,
Tresloyaument, tousdiz en bon espoir,
De mieulx en mieulx serviray ma maistresse.

Amours, je croy vous feistes ordonnance,
Quant je me volz en vostre court bouter,
Que avoir devoye a ma gouvernance
Trestouz les maulx que vous povez donner.
Mieulx m'eust valu avoir esté bergier
Et demourer es champs en un manoir,
Boire de l'eaue et mengier du pain noir,
Que de souffrir la douleur qui me blesse.
Mais nonpourquant, sanz changier mon vouloir,
De mieulx en mieulx serviray ma maistresse.

56. Balade: «Car le couroux n'y vault pas une maille»

Salus assez par bonne entencion,
A tous amans qui le vouldront avoir,
Et aus dames recommendation
De par celui qui vous fait asavoir
Que nul ne doit chalengier par devoir
Les biens d'amours et de graces donnés.
Aidiez vous en tant com vous les tenez.
Quant cil lez veult ravoir qui les vous baille,
Du temps passé mercier le devez,
Car le couroux n'y vault pas une maille.

Le Dieu d'Amours a fait une maison
Comme chastel pres de son grant manoir,

And to banish me from every hope
Forever more, without obtaining mercy,
For which I am forced to endure the grief,
For my part, I wish to have you know,
If I am never to have any reward,
That, if I am obliged to die of sadness,
In heart, in body, with all my loyal power,
Better and better will I serve my mistress.

Love, one day from you I have relief,
And then I am back again where I began.
When I think that I have your friendship,
Then you make me become a stranger again.
Hardly do you deign to look at me.
When I put myself fully in your power,
I didn't expect to have so harsh a reward.
But since that is where your will is directed,
Most loyally, and always in good hope,
Better and better will I serve my mistress.

Love, I believe that you gave the order,
When I wished to place myself in your court,
That I was always to have at my disposition
All the pains that you are able to give.
It would have been better for me to be a shepherd
And to live in a dwelling in the fields,
Drinking water and eating black bread,
Than to endure the sorrow that afflicts me.
But nonetheless, without changing my wish,
Better and better will I serve my mistress.

56. Ballade: "For anger just isn't worth a stitch"

Abundant greetings, with good will,
To every lover who wishes to receive them,
And commendations to the ladies
On the part of him who wishes to have you know
That no one ought to claim as something owed
The goods that are bestowed by love and grace.
Enjoy them for as long as you have them.
When he who grants them wants to have them back,
You ought to thank him for the time that has passed,
For anger just isn't worth a stitch.

The God of Love has built a house
Like a fortress near his own great dwelling,

Et si a mis deux huis en son donjon,
Dont l'un a nom Joye, l'autre Dolloir.
Et bien vous dy, se la l'alez veoir,
Par Joye faut que devers ly entrez,
Et par Doulour faut que vous en sailliez.
Nul n'y entre que par la ne s'en saille.
Prenez en gré quant vous en revenrez,
Car le couroux n'y vault pas une maille.

Or me dites, n'est ce pas bien raison
Que li sires face son bon vouloir
En son pays et en sa nacion
Et de ses gens sur qui il a pouoir?
Amours depart ses biens et son avoir,
Dont a aucuns est trop abandonnez,
Aux autres pou, et aux autres assez,
Aux autres riens, pour ce que plus leur faille.
Soit droit ou tort, il faut que vous souffrez,
Car le couroux n'y vault pas une maille

Gens et gentes, se vous me demandez
Comme je sçay les amoureux secréz,
Je n'en dy rien fors que par devinaille
Pour resjoir les cuers desconfortéz,
Car le couroux n'y vault pas une maille.

57. Le Desert (**«Fors que la mort prouchainement»**)

Las! je voy bien qu'il me fault eslongnier
Desoremaiz le pays gracieux
Ou je souloye tant de joye trouver,
Tant de douceur et de bien amoureux,
Qu'en ce monde ne vouldroye mieulx.
Et puis qu'ainsy me convient estrangier,
De tout en tout, sanz y plus revenir,
Et que souffrir il m'en convient a tant,
Je ne requier pour mes maulx alegier
Fors que la mort prouchainement.

Car jamais riens ne me puet conforter,
Et pour ce j'ameroye trop mieulx
Plus tost ennuit que demain trespasser
Pour brief garir de mes dolours.
Et se je suy de ma mort envieux,
Nulz ne m'en doit que saige tenir,
Car trop mieulx vault a un cop mourir

And he has placed two doors there in its tower,
One of which is called Joy, the other Sorrow.
And I assure you, if you go to see it,
You have to enter it by way of Joy,
And you have to leave by way of Sorrow.
No one goes in who doesn't leave that way.
Accept it willingly when you return,
For anger just isn't worth a stitch.

Now tell me, doesn't it stand to reason
That the lord do whatever he wish
In his country and in his nation
And with the people over whom he rules?
Love distributes his goods and his possessions,
Of which to some he allots too much,
To others little, and to others just enough,
To others nothing, so they lack even more.
Whether right or wrong, you have to accept it,
For anger just isn't worth a stitch.

Ladies and gentlemen, if you ask me
How I know the secrets of love,
I don't say anything except by supposition
In order to bring joy to troubled hearts,
For anger just isn't worth a stitch.

57. The Destitute One **("Except for death, immediately")**

Alas, I see well that from now on
I must take my leave of the gracious country
Where I was accustomed to find so much joy,
So much sweetness and so much good in love
That in this world I would not wish for better.
And since it is so, that I must depart
Completely, without ever returning,
And that I am compelled to suffer so much,
I don't seek anything to relieve my pain
Except for death, immediately.

For never can anything comfort me,
And therefore I would much prefer
To die tonight rather than tomorrow
In order to quickly recover from my sorrows.
And if I am desirous of my death,
No one should consider me anything but wise,
For it is much better to die in one stroke

Que de languir en dueil et en torment.
Pour ce ne vueil autre bien requerir
Fors que la mort prouchainement.

Adieu, adieu, Belle qu'on doit loer,
Qui tant de foiz m'avez fait joyeux.
Doresenavant, pour vo bon los garder,
Mon cuer fondra en larmes et en pleurs,
Pour ce que plus ne vous verront mes yeulz
Dont me souloit ma grant joye venir.
Car quant je voy qu'il me convient fuir
De coste vous par paour du mesdisant,
En ce monde, par ma foy, ne desir,
Fors que la mort prouchainement.

Princesse des belles, jeune sanz per,
Vous qui povez desur moy ordonner
Et commander tousjours vo bon plaisir,
Savoir vous fait vostre loyal martir
Qu'il a pour vous des maulx largement,
Que riens ne vuelt pour son cuer resjoir
Fors que la mort prouchainement.

58. Balade: «D'un tel amer que faire tous honnis»

Se une dame, jeune, gente et jolie,
Belle et bonne et paree d'onnour,
Met son penser, son cuer, son estudye
En bien amer, loiaulment, sans folour,
Bel, bon et gent, plain de toute valour,
Saige, courtois, secret, vray amoureux,
De maintien honneste et gracieulx.
Doit elle dont pour tant estre reprise?
Je dy que non, que c'est droicte franchise
Du cuer gentifz. Si fait mieulx, si m'est vis,
D'un tel amer que faire tous honnis.

N'est ce pas dont tresgracieuse vie
Et joieuse que amer de bonne amour,
Sans mal penser? Sy est, quoy que nul die.
La n'y a point blasme ne deshonneur.
Telle amour est nourrie de doulçour.
Si me dy je: «Com lait de estre songneux!»
De Dieu amer et servir, c'est le mieulx.
Mais non obstant, celle point ne desprise
Qui s'amour a ainsy qu'ay dit assise.

Than to languish in grief and in torment.
Thus I don't want to seek any other good
Except for death, immediately.

Farewell, farewell, Beauty whom one must praise,
Who has made me joyful so many times.
From now on, to safeguard your good name,
My heart will melt in tears and in weeping,
Because my eyes will no longer see you
From whom my great joy used to come.
For when I see that I am forced to flee
From your side for fear of the slanderer,
In this world, by my faith, I desire nothing
Except for death, immediately.

Princess of beauties, youth without peer,
You who can rule over me
And always command your good pleasure,
Your loyal sufferer wishes you to know
That for you he bears pains abundantly,
That he wants nothing to rejoice his heart
Except for death, immediately.

58. Ballade: "To love in such a way rather than causing shame"

If a lady, young, gracious, and pretty,
Beautiful and good and adorned with honor,
Directs her thought, her heart, and her effort
Towards loving well, loyally, without folly,
One who is fair, good and noble, full of great worth,
Wise, courteous, discreet, sincere in love,
Honest and gracious in his conduct,
Should she then be blamed for this?
I say no, that it is the very right
Of a noble heart. She does better, it seems to me,
To love in such a way rather than causing shame.

Isn't it then a most gracious life
And a joyous one, to love with a good love,
Without evil thought? It is, whatever anyone says.
There is neither blame nor dishonor there.
Such a love is nourished with gentleness.
Thus I say to myself, "How ugly to be prudish."
To love and serve God, that is best,
But nonetheless, I do not blame at all
The one who has placed her love as I have said.

Ainsois son fait assez plus los et pris
D'un tel amer que faire tous honnis.

Point ne doubte qu'Amours n'ait seignorie
Sur dame qui est en sa droite flour
De jeunesse, qui la tient et guerrie.
Si en convient que elle en sente l'odour
D'amourettes et la doulce savour.
Pas ne sera son cuer sy oultrageux
Que d'un amant vray ne soit desireux.
Amours le veult qui du cuer a la prise,
La saisine, et le duit a sa guise,
Et le contraint que plus soit ententiz
D'un tel amer que faire tous honnis.

59. Balade: «Qui fondre peust et lui renouveller»

Je congnois bien les tourmens amoureux,
Mais je ne sçay mon cuer vers eulz deffendre,
Car quant je puis eschaper a l'un d'eulz,
Soudainement m'en vient un plus fort prendre.
En mon bon droit, me fault coulpable rendre,
Crier mercy et dire que j'ay tort.
Ma vie vault un po plus que la mort,
Car chascun jour j'ay un nouvel martire,
Et de mes mauls le derrain m'est le pire.
Se longuement doy languir sans finer,
Il me fauldroit avoir un corps de cire
Qui fondre peust et lui renouveller.

Car tieulx tourmens sont si fort angoisseux
Que bonnement je ne porroye attendre
Les grans meschiez et les fais perilleux
Qui de doulour me font souvent estandre.
Trop cherement scet Amours ses dons vendre,
Qui travaillent l'esperit quant il dort,
Et en veillant n'a point de resconfort.
L'un fait plourer pour l'autre faire rire.
Si fais assez ne pie peuent souffire,
Et se mon cuer s'i vouloit accorder,
Il me fauldroit avoir un corps de cire
Qui fondre peust et lui renouveller.

Je truis Dangier hautain et oultrageux,
Qui nulle fois ne m'est souef ne tendre,
Ne de mes maulz ne veult estre piteux.

Instead I praise and esteem her conduct more
To love in such a way rather than causing shame.

I have no doubt that Love has lordship
Over a lady who is in the very flower
Of youth, and that he keeps and protects her.
Thus she is compelled to smell the fragrance
And to taste the sweetness of love affairs.
Her heart will not be so unrestrained
That she not desire a true lover.
Love wishes it, who captures the heart,
Possesses it, and leads it in his own way,
And compels it to be more intent
To love in such a way rather than causing shame.

59. Ballade: "That was able to melt and then be made again"

I know well the harsh torments of love,
But I don't know how to protect my heart from them,
For whenever I can escape from one of them,
Suddenly another stronger comes to seize me.
In all fairness, I have to surrender, guilty,
Cry out for mercy and say that I am wrong.
My life is worth little more than death,
For each day I endure new suffering,
And of my pains the last one is the worst.
If I must languish long without an end,
I would have to have a body of wax
That was able to melt and then be made again.

For such torments are so very painful
That I couldn't easily support
The great hardships and the perilous attacks
That often cause me to collapse in sorrow.
At too high a price Love sells its gifts,
Which torment the mind when it is sleeping,
And when awake has no comfort at all.
Love makes one cry to make another laugh.
[The text is corrupt. See the note.]
And if my heart wished to go along,
I would have to have a body of wax
That was able to melt and then be made again.

I find Danger haughty and excessive,
And that it is never soft or tender towards me,
Nor does it wish to have pity on my pains.

Quant de dueil voit mon cuer partir et fondre,
A paines veult mes complaintes entendre.
Je suis par lui arrivez a mal port.
Jamaiz n'auray joye, bien, ne deport
Puis que Pitié ne le peut desconfire.
Bien doy mon temps et ma vie maudire
Quant de durté me veult ainsi grever.
Il me fauldroit avoir un corps de cire
Qui fondre peust et lui renouveller.

60. Balade amoreuse: **«Pardonnés moy, besoing le me fait faire» (1)**

Il a passé des ans sept et demy
Que je vous ay pour ma dame choisie,
Et au jour d'ui derrechief vous choisi
Pour une fois et pour toute ma vie.
Et si sçay bien que de vous ne doy mie
Estre choisy comme pour vostre per,
Ne je ne l'ose souhaidier ne penser,
Mais s'il vous plaist, belle, bonne et plesent,
Choissicés moy comme vostre servant,
Qui loiaulment vous veult servir et plaire.
Et si marcy vous requier trop avant,
Pardonnés moy, besoing le me fait faire.

Besoing me fait querir vostre mercy
Mais de l'avoir humblement je vous prie,
Car je say bien, plusieurs y ont failly
Qui mieulx de moy l'avoient desservie.
Et non pour tant, belle, quoy que je die,
Chascuns homs doit son meilleur desirer.
De l'autrui fait n'ay je riens a parler,
Fors que du mien, qui m'est le plus pesant.
Pour ce vien je devers vous a garant
Quar autre part ne me vueil ne doy traire.
Et se je dy trop en moy complaignant,
Pardonnés moy, besoing le me fait faire.

Vostre beaulté trespace si parmy
Le cuer de moy, belle, je vous affie,
Qu'il ne lui chault ne de moy ne de lui
Fors que de vous, ou yl a s'estudie.
Tout ce qu'il voit devant mez ieulx oblie,
Mais nuit et jour lui fault ymaginer
De vous servir, obeir et doubter
Plus que celles toutes qui sont vivant.

When it sees my heart break apart and split with grief,
Hardly does it wish to hear my complaints.
Because of it, I have come to an evil port.
Never will I have joy, good, or pleasure
Because Pity is unable to overcome it.
Well should I curse my time and my life
When out of harshness it wishes to hurt me thus.
I would have to have a body of wax
That was able to melt and then be made again.

60. Love Ballade: "Please pardon me; need makes me do it" (1)

Seven and a half years have gone by
Since I first chose you as my lady,
And today I choose you once again
For once and for all, for my entire life.
And yet I know well that I ought not
Be chosen by you as your equal,
Nor do I dare to wish it or to think it,
But if you please, fair, good, and charming one,
Choose me as your servant
Who wishes loyally to serve and please you.
And if I ask you too soon for your mercy,
Please pardon me; need makes me do it.

Need makes me ask you for your mercy,
But I pray you for it humbly,
For I know well, many have there failed
Who had deserved it more than I.
And nonetheless, fair one, whatever I say,
Each man must desire what is best for him.
Of another's condition I have nothing to say,
Except of my own, which for me is most pressing.
Therefore I come before you in safety,
For elsewhere I neither want nor ought to go.
And if I say too much in presenting my plaint,
Please pardon me; need makes me do it.

Your beauty so pervades my heart,
Oh beautiful one, I promise you,
That it doesn't care about me or itself
But only about you, on whom it is fixed.
All that it sees before my eyes it forgets,
But night and day it is compelled to imagine
Serving you, obeying and fearing you,
More than all other women who are alive.

Se mercy n'ay dont je suis desirant,
Tant le desir que je ne m'en puis taire.
C'est maulgré moy que je vous en dy tant;
Pardonnés moy, besoing le me fait faire.

61. Balade Granson: «Pardonnez moy, besoing le me fait faire» (2)

Saint Valentin, humblement vous supply
Qu'a vostre jour me soiés en aye,
Et me faitez avoir le doulx octry
Ou il n'a rien que bien et courtoisie
Et bonne foy; c'est jeu sans villenie.
Bien y povés voz myracles monstrer,
Car de plusieurs vous ferez aourer
Et requerir de maint loyal amant,
Se en ce cas m'estez bien aidant.
Or m'y aydez, tresdoulz saint debonnaire.
Et se rien dy qui vous soit desplaisant,
Pardonnez moy, besoing le me fait faire.

J'ay de longtemps et de bon cuer choisy
Le noble corps pour qui Amours me lye,
Greslet, grasset, gracieux et joly,
Jeune, gentis et de maniere lie.
Sa grant blancheur et sa pel tresdelie,
Ses mains, son col et son visaige cler,
Ses biaux doulx yeulx, plaisans a regarder,
Et sa petite bouche bien parlant
M'ont sy ravy que je vif en mourant.
Helas! Amours, ne me soiez contraire,
Et se je suis trop hastif en priant,
Pardonnez moy, besoing le me fait faire.

Car je congnois Danger, mon ennemy,
Et sa Durté, ma mortel ennemie.
Et se ne fust Espoir, mon bon amy,
Et Loiaulté, qui tousjours m'est amye,
Ma jounesse feust de long temps finie,
En desirant la convendroit finer.
Ne je ne sçay si bon juge trouver,
Comme le cuer de ma dame saichant
Qui est loial, sagez et congnoissant.
A son vouloir me tiens tout sans retraire.
Se je desir avoir son doulx semblent,
Pardonnez moy, besoing le me fait faire.

If I don't have the mercy that I desire,
So greatly do I desire it that I cannot be silent.
It is despite myself that I tell you as much.
Please pardon me; need makes me do it.

61. Ballade of Granson: "Please pardon me; need makes me do it" (2)

Saint Valentine, humbly I beseech you
That on your feast day you come to my aid,
And that you make me have the sweet gift
In which there is only good and courtesy
And good faith; it is a game without wickedness.
Well can you demonstrate your miracles there,
For you will make yourself adored by many
And sought out by many a loyal lover
If you are helpful to me in this case.
So help me, gentle gracious saint,
And if I say anything that displeases you,
Please pardon me; need makes me do it.

Long ago and with good heart I chose
The noble one for whom Love binds me,
Slender, well-formed, gracious, and pretty,
Young, courteous, and of happy manner.
Her great whiteness and her delicate skin,
Her hands, her neck, and her bright face,
Her beautiful sweet eyes, pleasing to behold,
And her little mouth that speaks well,
So delighted me that I live while dying.
Alas, Love, do not oppose me,
And if I am too eager in beseeching,
Please pardon me; need makes me do it.

For I know Danger, my enemy,
And its Harshness, my mortal enemy,
And were it not for Hope, my good friend,
And Loyalty, which is always my friend,
My young self would have perished long ago.
It would have been forced to die of desire.
And I do not know how to find as good a judge
As the heart of my knowledgable lady,
Who is loyal, wise, and understanding.
I submit myself to her will without repeal.
If I desire from her a gentle look,
Please pardon me; need makes me do it.

62. Balade: «Trop plus de biens que penser ne sauroye»

Puisqu'Amours veult et lui plaist et agree
Que vostre soient du tout entierement
M'amour, m'espoir, mon plaisir, ma pensee,
Mon cur, ma joye, tout mon esbatement,
Je l'en mercy, quar je sçay fermement
Que plus grans biens ne me pourroit donner
Que de vous faire par moy cherir, doubter,
Obeir, craindre, honnorer et servir.
Car, en ce faire, je prens plus de plaisir
Cent mille fois que se d'une autre avoye,
Sans mal avoir, a prendre et a choysir
Trop plus de biens que penser ne sauroye.

Car la beaulté, l'onneur, la renommee,
Le los, le pris, le bel maintenement,
Le bien, la grace dont vous estez louee,
A mis en moy amour si ardenment
Dont je vous ayme, que certez nulement
Ne vous ne autre ne le pourroit penser.
N'onquez Amours ne me fist endurer,
Jusquez a orez, son effort ne souffrir.
Mais maintenent bien le m'a fait sentir,
Dont j'ay main mal, maiz je le prens en joye
Quant c'est pour vous en qui sont, sans mentir,
Trop plus de biens que penser ne sauroye.

Ne pour douleur qui ja me soit donnee
Ne me vendra voulenté ne talant
D'autre servir, car mon cuer la devee,
Qui tant vous aime, craint et sert loiaulment.
Que sy falloit que douloureusement
Pour vous servir deust ma vie finer
Prouchainnement, ou par une autre amer
Eusse lez biens dont l'en puet resjoir
Ung cuer dolent, cent mille fois mourir
Mieulx me plairoit, s'en ce party estoye.
Car seulement me puet par vous venir
Trop plus de biens que penser ne sauroye.

63. Balade: «Ma seule dame, plus que nulle autre amee»

Vostre beauté, ma belle douce dame,
A mon cuer mis en si tresdur party
Que par desir il art tout et enflame

62. Ballade: "Far more good than I could ever imagine"

Since Love wishes it, and it pleases him
That they be completely yours in every way
— My love, my hope, my pleasure, my thought,
My heart, my joy, all of my enjoyment —
I thank him, for I firmly know
That he could not give me any greater reward
Than to make you cherished, dreaded,
Obeyed, feared, honored, and served by me.
For in doing so, I take more pleasure
One hundred thousand times than if I had from another,
Without any pain, to take and choose
Far more good than I could ever imagine.

For the beauty, the honor, the renown,
The praise, the worth, the beautiful comportment,
The good, the grace, for which you are praised
Have set love in me so ardently
By which I love you that surely in no way
Could you or anyone else imagine it.
Nor did love make me ever endure,
Till now, or suffer its effects.
But now it has made me feel them strongly,
For which I have much pain, but I take it in joy
When it is for you in whom is, without lying,
Far more good than I could ever imagine.

Nor for any sorrow that might ever be given me
Will come to me the wish or the desire
To serve another, for my heart forbids it,
Which loves you, fears you, and serves you loyally,
So much that if it were necessary that, sadly,
My life were to come to an end at once
In order to serve you, or that by loving another
I might have the rewards with which one can rejoice
A sorrowful heart, to die one hundred thousand times
Would please me more, if I were in that state.
For only from you can come to me
Far more good than I could ever imagine.

63. Ballade: "My only lady, beloved more than any other"

Your beauty, my beautiful gentle lady,
Placed my heart in so difficult a state
That out of desire it burns and is inflamed

Si asprement que, pour certain, mal vy,
Se bien prochaine ne m'est vostre mercy,
L'eure et le jour que premier vous amay.
Car je sçay bien que pour celle morray,
S'il ne vous plaist a moy reconforter
Prouchainement et ma douleur muer
En la leesse que tant ay desiree.
Et s'ainsy n'est, brief me fauldra finer,
Ma seule dame, plus que nulle autre amee.

Car la douleur qui me point et entamer
Me fait avoir si doulereux soussi
Que pluseurs fois du mal mon cuer se pasme,
En vous priant que par vous resjoy
De la tristesse qui l'a taint et noircy
Soit, s'il vous plaist. Ou autrement bien sçay
Que bien briefment ma vie fineray,
Car en ce point ne pourroit durer
Mon dolent cuer. Et se brief alegier
Ne m'en voulez, la mort me soit donnee,
Si que fauldront les maulx qu'ay a porter,
Ma seule dame, plus que nulle autre amee.

Et s'il vous plaist que je muire, par m'ame,
Trop bien le vueil, car de ce monde cy
Suy ennuié, car je le hé et blasme,
Jusques a tant que par vous adoucy
Soit mon grief mal et mon cuer enrichi
De vostre amour que tant vueil et vouldray
Que saichiez bien, Belle, se je ne l'ay,
Que tout le monde ne me pourroit garder
Qu'il ne me faille la mort brief endurer.
Maiz bien me plaist, s'a vo doulz cuer agree.
Or m'en vueilliez vo vouloir commander,
Ma seule dame, plus que nulle autre amee.

64. Balade: «Faitez de moy tout ce qu'il vous plaira»

Il me convient estre mal de mez yeux;
Mon cuer le veult et vers moy le pourchace,
Et leur met sur tant de cas et de tieulx
Que je ne sçay bonnement que j'en face.
Maiz toutesfoiz ilz m'ont demendé grace,
Et m'ont prié par bonne entencion
De recevoir leur excusacion.
Et je n'ay pas de ce faire pouoir.

So sharply that, for certain, I fare poorly
If very soon your mercy is not mine,
On the hour and day that I loved you first.
For I know well that I shall die of this
If it doesn't please you to comfort me
At once, and to change my sorrow
Into the happiness that I have desired so much.
And if it is not so, soon I must die,
My only lady, beloved more than any other.

For the sorrow that pierces and consumes me
Causes me to have such sorrowful care
That many times my heart faints from the pain
In praying you that it be brought to joy
From the sadness than has colored and darkened it,
If it pleases you. Or otherwise, I know
That very shortly my life will end,
For in this state cannot endure
My grieving heart. And if you do not wish
To relieve me quickly, may death be given to me,
So that the pains that I must bear will cease,
My only lady, beloved more than any other.

And if it please you that I die, by my soul,
I want it very much, for of this world
I am tired, for I hate it and reproach it,
Until by you is softened
My grievous pain, and my heart is enriched
By your love, which I want and will want so much
That, know well, fair one, if I do not have it,
That all the world could not prevent
My being forced soon to suffer death.
But it pleases me well if it pleases your gentle heart.
Now please command of me what you wish,
My only lady, beloved more than any other.

64. Ballade: "Do with me anything you please"

I am forced to be hurt by my eyes;
My heart wishes it and seeks it for me,
And places them in so many such situations
That I don't really know what to do.
But they have constantly asked me for grace,
And they have begged me with good intent
To accept their apology.
And I don't have the power to do so.

Si en vueillez ordonner voz vouloir,
Belle plaisant, qui a jugier lez a,
Et puis aprez, tost et tart, main et soir,
Faitez de moy tout ce qu'il vous plaira.

Mon cuer me dit que me vaulsist trop mieulx
N'en avoir nulz et que plus endurasse,
Car ilz ne sont de rien sy tres joyeulx
Que de souvent me mener en la place
La ou mon cuer devient plus froit que glace,
Et autre fois plus chault que ung tison.
Et non pourtant c'est mon oppinion
Qu'il me vault mieulx beaucop de maulx avoir
En vous servant que d'autre recevoir
Trestous lez biens que jamais homme aura.
Pour ce, Belle, quant vous iré veoir,
Faitez de moy tout ce qu'il vous plaira.

Car, par ma foy, maulgré lez envieux,
Il ne pourroit que je ne vous aimasse,
Combien que j'ay grans annemis mortieulx
Vers vous, comme Danger, qui me menasse.
Durté aussy me veut mal. Mais quant a ce,
Je ne lez crains ne ne prise ung bouton,
Car vous avés Courtoisie et Raison
Qui vous conceillent a faire vo devoir,
Et j'ay tousjours avec moy Bon Espoir,
Qui mainte fois vo doulceur ditte m'a.
C'est quanque j'ay de bien, a dire voir.
Faitez de moy tout ce qu'il vous plaira.

Princesse belle, je puis trop mieulx valoir
Pour vostre amour, quant donnee me sera.
Je ne le dy que pour ramentevoir.
Faitez de moy tout ce qu'il vous plaira.

65. Balade: «Je n'en congnoiz nulle si belle»

Tous les biens que l'en sauroit
Deviser ne de bouche dire
Sont en celle pour qui reçoit
Mon cuer maint martire.
Ou royaume ne en l'empire,
N'en a nulle de tele façon.
Car je croy que Pymalion
Ne l'eust sceu si bien tailler,

Therefore please command your will,
Charming beauty, who has the power to judge them,
And then afterwards, early and late, morning and eve,
Do with me anything you please.

My heart tells me that I would be better off
Not to have any eyes, and that I would last longer,
For they are not so joyous of anything
As of often leading me to the place
Where my heart becomes colder than ice
And another time hotter than a burning log.
And nonetheless it is my opinion
That it's better for me to have a great deal of pain
In serving you than to receive from another
All the rewards that a man will ever have.
Therefore, fair one, when I come to see you,
Do with me anything you please.

For by my faith, despite the envious,
It could not be that I do not love you,
However many great mortal enemies I have
Around you, such as Danger, who threatens me.
Harshness also wishes me ill. But as for that,
I do not fear or care about them a bit,
For you have Courtesy and Reason
Who counsel you to perform your duty,
And I always have Good Hope with me,
Who has told me many times of your gentleness.
That's all the reward I have, to tell the truth.
Do with me anything you please.

Beautiful princess, I can be worth much more
Because of your love, when it is given to me.
I don't say so except as a reminder.
Do with me anything you please.

65. Ballade: "I don't know any woman as beautiful"

All the virtues that one was able
To imagine or to describe by mouth
Reside in the one for whom my heart
Receives much suffering.
In the kingdom and in the empire
There is no woman of such a kind.
For I believe that Pygmalion
Could not have fashioned her as well,

Ne l'en pourroit recouvrer
Une si douce damoiselle.
Par Dieu! sanz les autres blasmer,
Je n'en congnoiz nulle si belle.

Car il n'est homme, s'il la voit
De ces tresbeaux yeux rire,
Qu'il ne faille que sien soit
A tousjours maiz sanz contredire,
Pour ce qu'elle a plus qu'a suffire
De senz, d'onneur et de raison,
Et sa noble condicion
Attrairoit de cuers un millier.
De bel acueil, de doulz parler,
Ne s'i compare nulle a elle.
Pour ce vous di qu'a tout compter
Je n'en congnoiz nulle si belle.

Et se le Dieu d'Amours vouloit
Amer, mieulx ne pourroit eslire.
Mais je croy que point ne l'auroit,
Car trop est preste d'escondire.
Je n'y sçay plus rien a redire
Qu'elle n'ait tout le bon renom
Qu'en dame trouver pourroit on.
Dont c'est merveilles a penser,
Quant en si jeune aage trouver
On puet les biens qui sont en celle
Qui ne fait qu'en .xvi. ans entrer.
Je n'en congnois nulle si belle.

Princes, toute m'entencion
Sera de bien tost retourner
Pour veoir son viaire clerr
Et sa beauté fresche et nouvelle.
Car, a tout bien considerer,
Je n'en congnoiz nulle si belle.

66. Balade: «Car quanque voy ne me fait que desplaire»

Dolent de cuer et triste de pensee,
Plain de soucy, d'ennuy et de tourment,
Sans riens veoir qui me plaise n'agree,
Et sans avoir joye n'esbatement,
Et sans espoir avoir n'allegement
Suy et seray sans faillir, main et soir,

Nor would one be able to find
Any maiden as gentle as she.
By God, without disparaging the others,
I don't know any woman as beautiful.

For there is no man, if he sees her
Laughing with her beautiful eyes,
Who is not compelled to be hers
Forever after, without denial,
For she possesses more than enough
Of sense, of honor, and of reason,
And her noble quality
Would attract a thousand hearts.
In fair welcome, in gentle speech,
No other woman compares to her.
Therefore I tell you that, everything considered,
I don't know any woman as beautiful.

And if the God of Love desired
To love, he could not choose better.
But I believe that she wouldn't have him,
For she is too ready to say no.
I don't know what else to say
But that she has all the good renown
That one could find in a lady.
Thus it is a marvel to think,
When in so young an age one can find
The virtues that are found in her,
Who has just reached sixteen years.
I don't know any woman as beautiful.

Princes, all of my intention
Will be very quickly to return
To see her bright face
And her beauty, fresh and young.
For when all is taken into account,
I don't know any woman as beautiful.

66. Ballade: "For whatever I see only displeases me"

Sorrowful in heart and sad in thought,
Full of care, of difficulty, and of torment,
Without seeing anything that pleases or satisfies me,
And without having any joy or mirth,
And without having any hope or relief
I am and will be without cease, at morn and eve,

Jusquez a tant que j'aye le pouoir
Que vo beaulté je puisse regarder,
Ma belle dame, a qui mez yeux donner
Ont fait Amours et mon cuer sans retraire,
Et se brief n'est, il me fauldra finer,
Car quanque voy ne me fait que desplaire.

Ne il n'est heure qui soit en la journee
Qui ne me dure assez plus longuement
Qu'en vous veant ne feroit une annee.
Or regardez se je vis lielment;
Certez, nennil! n'Amours si durement
Oncquez ne fist a nul homme savoir
Que c'est d'amer et d'estre sans avoir
Celle c'on aime, dont me fault deporter.
Mez crueux maulx m'en fault mains endurer.
En gré le vueil, puis qu'il le me fault faire,
Sans bien avoir, ne veoir n'en parler,
Car quanque voy ne me fait que desplaire.

Ne jamais joye ne me sera donnee
Jusquez a tant que par vous doulcement
Soit ma doleur en pitié regardee,
Et que je voye ce qui si asprement
Donne a mon cuer le mal qu'i porte et sent
Et qui me fait en toute heure douloir.
C'est vo beauté, car sen sez biens avoir
Nulle leesse je ne puis recouvrer,
Pour tous lez biens c'on pourroit deviser.
Car nulle rien ne me pourroit tant plaire
Sans vous veoir, qui me peust conforter,
Car quanque voy ne me fait que desplaire.

Belle princesse, en qui maint mon espoir,
Par qui mon cuer est mat, pensiz et noir,
Moy qui suis voostre, vous prie et vueil prier
Qu'il vous plaise moy vouloir envoier,
Pour adoulcir le mal qu'il me fault traire,
De vo doulx cuer ung gracieux penser,
Car quanque voy ne me fait que desplaire.

67. Balade: «Ma seule amour, en quelque lieu que je soye»

Mes yeulx sont plains d'ennuy et de tristesse
Et de souspirs qui font mon cuer doloir.
Ne si ne sçay se jamais ma maistresse

Until the time that I have the power
That I might look upon your beauty,
My beautiful lady, to whom Love and my heart
Have caused my eyes to be given, without repeal,
And if it is not soon, I will be forced to die,
For whatever I see only displeases me.

Nor is there any hour in the day
That does not last for me considerably longer
Than, in seeing you, would last a year.
Now behold if I live happily:
Surely not at all. Nor did Love so harshly
Ever cause any man to know
What it is to love and to be without possessing
The one he loves, which I must do without.
I must endure my many cruel pains.
I wish it willingly, for I am forced to do so
Without having, seeing, or speaking of any reward,
For whatever I see only displeases me.

Never will any joy be given to me
Until the time my sadness is beheld
By you, gently and with pity,
And until the time I see that which so sharply
Gives to my heart the pain it bears and feels
And which causes me to grieve at every hour.
That is your beauty, for without its benefit,
I cannot recover any happiness
For all the good that one could imagine.
For nothing at all could please me so much
That it could comfort me without my seeing you,
For whatever I see only displeases me.

Beautiful princess, in whom rests my hope,
For whom my heart is sad, pensive, and dark,
I who am yours beseech you and wish to pray
That it please you to want to send to me,
In order to soften the pain that I must bear,
A gracious thought from your gentle heart.
For whatever I see only displeases me.

67. Ballade: "My only love, in whatever place I be"

My eyes are full of distress and sadness
And of sighs that cause my heart to grieve.
And yet I do not know if my mistress

Par sa doulçour tournera son vouloir
A m'alegier le mal que, main et soir,
Me destraint si qu'il n'est un seul plaisir
Qui soit en moy, fors qu'a mon dormir,
Je cuidoye veir des yeux de ma pensee
Son beau corps gent. Dont ma paine est doublee
A resveillier, quant il n'en est neant,
Dont je reçoy, certes, de douleur tant.
Car il n'est riens qui me peust donner joye,
Quant ne vous voy assez plus que souvent,
Ma seule amour, en quelque lieu que je soye.

Si sçay je bien que ma dure destresse
Ne me laira un seul bien recevoir
Jusques alors que verray a largesse
Voz tresbeaux yeulx, car je sçay de voir
Que sanz cela je ne puis joye avoir.
Savez pourquoy? C'est mon joyeux desir,
C'est tout mon bien, mon plaisant souvenir,
C'est mon confort, c'est ma joye celee,
C'est mon espoir par qui sera cessee
Ma dure paine, qui dure longuement
Si ne vous plaist que bien prouchainement
Fine le dueil qui en larmes me noye,
Car mon mal fault qui ne croit tant ne quant,
Ma seule amour, en quelque lieu que je soye.

Ma souveraine, qui toutes autres passe,
Avant mouroye que jamais amasse
Autre que vous, journee ne demie.
Car mieulx vouldroye par vous perdre la vie
Que recevoir de tous biens a monjoye,
En esperance que ne m'oubliez mie,
Ma seule amour, en quelque lieu que je soye.

68. Le Dit de Loiauté

Loiaulté d'amour, necte et pure,
Clere, sans tache et sans laidure,
N'a en luy fait ne demonstrance,
Parler, regart ne contenance,
Atrait, acueil ne couverture,
Atour, devise ne brodure,
Prise, don, signe ne semblance
Pour donner a nullui esperance,
Fors ung tout seul d'autre nature.

Will ever, out of gentleness, turn her will
To relieving the pain that, morning and night,
Constrains me such that there is not a single pleasure
That remains in me, except that, in my sleep,
I would think that I saw with the eyes of my mind
Her fair sweet self. Then my pain is doubled
On awakening, when there is nothing to it,
For which I receive, surely, so much sorrow.
For there is nothing that can give me joy
When I do not see you much more than often,
My only love, in whatever place I be.

Thus I know well that my harsh distress
Will not allow me to receive a single good
Until I see abundantly
Your beautiful eyes, for I know in truth
That without that, I can have no joy.
Do you know why? It is my joyous desire;
It is all my good, my pleasing memory;
It is my comfort; it is my hidden joy;
It is my hope, by which will be brought to an end
My harsh pain, which lasts a long time
If it doesn't please you that very soon
Ends the grief that drowns me in tears.
For my pain lacks that does not grow and grow,
My only love, in whatever place I be.

My sovereign, who surpasses all other women,
I would die before I would ever love
Anyone but you, for a day or a half,
For I would rather lose my life through you
Than to receive an abundance of all goods,
In the hope that you do not forget me ever,
My only love, in whatever place I be.

68. The Poem about Loyalty

Loyalty in love, clean and pure,
Bright, without stain and without blemish,
Has not within it act or outward sign,
Speech, look, or countenance,
Attraction, welcome, or pretense,
Ornament, emblem, or embroidery,
Prize, gift, sign, or appearance
In order to give hope to anyone,
But just one thing of a different nature.

La prent confort et nourriture,
Joye, soulas et souffisance,
Et toute mondaine plaisance.
C'est celle par qui Amour dure.
C'est Loiaulté qui, par droicture,
Deffent Amour de varience
Et la tient en sa grant puissance
Fine, fort, ferme et seure,
Et lui fait peser par mesure
Tous sez fais en juste balance.
Car Amours, qui a congnoissance,
Sent et entent de sa nature
Qu'est faucеté et mespriseure,
Et puet mettre par sa science
Sez faiz en loyal ordonnance,
Si que aigait ne aventure
Ne nul engin de creature
Ne font a Loiauté nuysance,
Tant soit de soubtil percevance.
Et se la chose a faire est dure,
Amours tresloiaument l'endure
Pour monstrer foy et afiance,
Mais non d'Amours est decepvance.
C'est une tresfause pointure.
Amour ne veult autre pasture
Que droicte, loial gouvernance.
C'est sa paix, c'est sa soustenance,
C'est tout son bien, je le vous jure.

69. L'Estraine du jour de l'an

Joye, santé, paix, et honneur,
Bon an, bonne nuit, et bon jour,
Bonne aventure et bonne estraine,
Ma belle dame souveraine,
Et en tout parfaite plaisance
Vous doint Dieu, qui en a puissance,
Et vous ottroit, ma doulce dame,
Aise de corps et salut d'ame,
Joyeux cuer et lie pensee,
Grace et bonne renommee,
Et vous gart ce que vous avez,
Et vous doint ce que vous voulez,
Tousdiz acroissant en plaisir
Au souhait de vostre desir.
Et je, de trestout mon pouoir,

There it takes comfort and sustenance,
Joy, solace, and satisfaction
And every worldly pleasure.
It is that by which Love endures.
It is Loyalty that, out of right,
Protects Love from inconstancy
And keeps it, in its great power,
Pure, strong, firm, and secure,
And causes all it actions to be weighed
By measure in a true balance.
For Love, which has understanding,
Feels and understands by nature
What is falsity and wrong,
And with its knowledge, it can put
Its deeds in loyal arrangement,
So that neither ruse nor chance
Nor any device of any creature
Does any harm to Loyalty,
So subtle is its perception.
And if the thing is hard to do,
Love very loyally endures it
In order to demonstrate faith and commitment,
But deceit does not belong to Love.
It is a most false wound.
Love does not want any other nurturing
But proper, loyal governance.
That is its peace; that is its sustenance,
That is all its good, I swear to you.

69. The New Year's Gift

Joy, health, peace, and honor,
A good year, good night, and good day,
Good luck and good fortune,
My beautiful sovereign lady,
And complete pleasure in every way
May God, who has the power, give you,
And may he grant you, my gentle lady,
Ease of body and salvation of soul,
Joyous heart and happy thought,
Grace and good reputation,
And may he protect what you have,
And may he give you what you want,
Constantly increasing in pleasure
According to the wish of your desire.
And I, with all my power,

Loyalement et de bon vouloir,
Pour ce que je n'ay don meillour,
Vous donne mon cuer et m'amour,
Mon corps, et tous les biens que j'ay.
Et quanque faire puis ne sçay.
Et se mieulx peusse finer,
De mieulx vous vouldroye estrener,
Non pas pour nouvel don donner,
Mais pour le viel renouveler,
Et sur telle condicion,
Que jamais a m'entencion
Par mon advis ne de mon sens,
A mon vivant ne a mon temps,
Ne vueil penser, dire, ne faire
Chose qui vous doye desplaire.
Mais ay propos et voulanté
De vous servir tousdiz a gré,
Et de vous amer et doubter,
Et obeir et dezirer,
Plus fort de ce jour en avant
Que je ne fis onques devant.
Vous le sarez, se je puis vivre,
Mieulx par mes fais que par mon livre.
Or vous doint Dieu vouloir aussi
Que vous ayez de moy mercy,
Et lors seray bien estrenez
Ce jour de l'an qui est entrez.

70. La Complainte de l'an nouvel

Jadis m'avint que par merancolie,
De toutes gens me pris a eslongnier.
Pour estre seul, laissay la compaignie.
Au bois alay jouer et soulacier,
La nuit devant que l'an doit commencier.
Mais je n'eus pas alé moult longuement
Que j'escoutay la voix d'un chevalier
Qui se plaignoit d'amours trop durement.

Le chevalier disoit en sa complainte:
«Certes, Amours, de vous plaindre me doy,
Et si sçay bien que po me vault ma plainte.
Car vous n'avez nulle pitie de moy.
Helas, Amour, or me dites de quoy
Je doy mon cuer au matin estrener,

Loyally and with good will,
Because I have no better gift,
Give you my heart and my love,
My body, and all the goods I have.
And what to do next I do not know.
And if I could conclude better,
I would want to offer you a better gift,
Not in order to give you a new one,
But in order to renew the old,
And upon this condition,
That never intentionally
By my decision or my conscious thought,
While I am alive or in my time,
Do I wish to think, say, or do
Anything that might displease you.
But it is my purpose and my will
To serve you constantly and willingly,
And to love and fear you,
And obey and desire you,
More strongly from this day forward
Than I ever did before.
You will know it, if I may live,
More by my deeds than by my writing.
And may God also give you the wish
To have mercy upon me,
And then will I be well provided with a gift
On this New Year's Day.

70. The New Year's Complaint

Once it happened that, out of melancholy,
I chose to be apart from everyone else.
To be alone, I left all company.
I went to the wood to play and to seek comfort,
The night before the year was to begin.
But I hadn't gotten very far
When I heard the voice of a certain knight
Who was complaining very strongly about love.

The knight was saying in his complaint:
"Surely, Love, I must complain about you,
And yet I know well that little avails my plaint.
For you have no pity upon me.
Alas, Love, then tell me the reason why
I ought to offer my heart as a gift in the morning,

Puis qu'ainsi est que ma dame ne voy
Au jour de l'an qui demain doit entrer.

«Demain aront pluseurs la bonne estraine
Qui la prendront en leurs dames veir,
Et je n'aray fors que douleur et paine.
Bien suis usez a tel don recevoir.
Amour, Amour, nulz homs ne peust savoir
L'estat de vous s'il ne l'a esprouvé.
Et quant chascun en dira son voloir,
Je me plaindray de ce que j'ay trouvé.

«Je me plaindray d'Amours et de ma dame,
Qui sont cause de tout mon desconfort.
Mais je ne veil a nul donner le blasme
Fors a mon cuer, qui amer me fait si fort.
Et si voy bien que tuit trois sont d'accort
De moy mener a fin prochainement.
Amour me hait, ma dame veult ma mort,
Et je voy bien que mon cuer le consent.

«Mez yeulx en ont aussi tort, ce me samble,
Car il n'est cuer qui peust tenir d'amer
Puis qu'il veist tant de beautez ensamble
Comme l'en peust en ma dame trouver.
Et quant le cuer fait les yeulx regarder
Et leur regart font le cuer amoureux,
L'un ne porroit par droit l'autre blasmer,
Mais de ma part, je me plaing de tous deux.

«De eulz me plaing, et si me doy bien plaindre,
Car je les truis mes mortelx anemis.
Nulz d'eulz n'y a qui poy se veille faindre
Pour moy geter dez bas ou ilz m'ont mis.
Chascun d'eulz deux deust estre mes amis
Et moy garder ainsi comme leur corps.
Et ce sont ceulz qui tousdiz me font pis.
En eulz ne tient que pieça ne sui mors.

«C'est le guerdon que j'ay de mon servise.
Certes, Amours, bien m'avez guerdonné!
Sur moy avez toute la paine mise,
Ne nul confort ne m'en avez donné.
Jadis estoit le plus de ma santé
En regarder celle qui tant me plaist.
Or sui par vous en tel lieu arrivé
Ou ne la voy, dont trop fort me desplaist.»

Since it is thus, that I do not see my lady
This New Year's Day which is to come tomorrow.

"Tomorrow many will have good fortune,
Who will receive it just in seeing their ladies,
And I will have nothing but grief and pain.
Well am I used to receiving such a gift.
Love, Love, no one can understand
Your nature unless he has experienced it.
And when everyone reveals his wish,
I will complain about what I have found.

"I will complain of Love and of my lady,
Who are the cause of all of my distress.
But I don't want to put blame on anyone
Except my heart, which makes me love so strongly.
And yet I see that all three are in accord
To lead me imminently to my end.
Love hates me, my lady wishes my death,
And I see clearly that my heart consents.

"My eyes are also wrong, it seems to me,
For there is no heart that can refrain from loving
When it sees so much beauty joined together
As one can discover in my lady.
And when the heart makes the eyes look,
And their looking makes the heart fall in love,
One could not rightly blame the other,
But for my part, I complain of both.

"I complain about them, and well should I complain,
For I consider them my mortal enemies.
Neither of them is only slightly reluctant
To raise me up after having thrown me down.
Each of these two ought to be my friend
And protect me just as they would themselves.
And it is they who constantly make me worse.
They are not to thank that I'm not long dead.

"That is the reward that I have for my service.
Truly, Love, you have well rewarded me!
On me you have placed all the pain,
And you haven't given me any consolation.
Formerly the best part of my well-being
Was to look upon her who pleases me so much.
Now through you I have come to such a place
That I do not see her, which greatly troubles me."

Le chevalier qui menoit tele vie
De cuer parfont bien souvent souspiroit.
Il sambloit bien qu'il eust grant envie
De retourner la ou son cuer estoit.
Et quant son plaint recommencier vouloit,
Je vins avant pour le reconforter,
Et le getay du penser qu'il avoit.
Aussi li fis sa complainte cesser.

71. Le Souhait de Saint Valentin

Il me convient par souhait conforter.
Sans souhaidier, ne porroye porter
Au long aler les griefs mauls que je port.
Bon est souhait qui fait au cuers deport.
En souhaidant, se puet uns homs deduire,
Lui soulacier, et sans nul autre nuire.
Et puisque j'ay des souhais habondance
Et mon souhait ne fait a nul nuisance,
Et j'ay si po des autres biens d'amour,
Souhaidier veil sans fere long demour.
Tout le premier souhait que je veil faire,
S'il ne devoit a ma dame desplaire,
Je vouldroye que je fusse, par m'ame,
Pour homme, tel come elle est pour femme,
Pareille a li de tout amendement,
Et mon cuer fust aussi entierement
En dieu servir et faire bonnes euvres
Comme le sien est, a toute les heures;
Et sceusse mon honneur tant amer
Et moy garder qu'on ne me deust blasmer.
Et vouldroye que j'eusse la grace
D'estre tenus en toute bonne place
Pour aussi bon entremy de gens d'armes
Comme on la tient pour belle entre les dames,
Et fusse plain de voulenté hardie
Tant comme elle est plaine de couardie;
Ne nul travail que je deusse souffrir
Ne me grevast plus que le dormir;
Et mon corps fust si fort et si poissant
Comme le sien est foibles et souffrant;
Et me veint de jouster le mestier
Tout aussi bien comme a elle le dancier;
Et me plaisit si bien mon honneur querre
Comme a li plest estre loing de la guerre,
Et amasse les chevalereux fais

The knight who led such a life
Often sighed from deep within his heart.
Well did it seem that he desired greatly
To return there where his heart remained.
And when he wanted to resume his plaint,
I came forward in order to comfort him,
And I freed him from the thought he had.
I also made him cease his complaint.

71. The Saint Valentine's Wish

I am forced to comfort myself with wishes.
Without wishing, I wouldn't be able to bear
For very long the grievous pains I bear.
Good is the wish that gives pleasure to the heart.
In wishing, a man can entertain himself,
Comfort himself, and not hurt any other.
And since I have wishes in abundance
And my wish does no harm to anyone,
And I have so few of the other rewards of Love,
I want to make my wish without delay.
The very first wish that I want to make,
If it did not displease my lady,
I would wish that I were, by my soul,
For a man, such as she is for a woman,
Equal to her in each good quality,
And that my heart were just as completely
Engaged in serving God and doing good deeds
As is hers, at every hour;
And that I knew how to love my honor as much,
And to guard lest anyone should blame me.
And I would wish that I had the grace
To be considered in every respectable place
As good among men of arms
As she is considered beautiful among women,
And that I were as full of courageous will
As she is full of timidity;
And that no task that I should endure
Would grieve me any more than sleep;
And that my body were as strong and powerful
As hers is weak and passive;
And that skill in jousting came to me
As easily as dancing does to her;
And that it pleased me to seek my honor
As much as it pleases her to be far from the war,
And that I should love chivalric deeds

Tant comme elle ame repos et paix.
Et vouldroye que je fusse touzdis
En cuer, en fait, en pensé, et en dis,
Si gracieux comme elle est gracieuse
Et si courtois comme elle est dangereuse,
Si bel pour homme, si plaisant et si gens,
Et tant amez de toutes bonnes gens,
Et fusse nez en si grant gentillesse,
Et en mon cuer eust tant de noblesce,
Que tous mes fais fussent d'omme si fins
Comme les siens sont parfais femenins;
Et feusse tout a la plaisance d'elle,
Si bon et bel comme elle est bonne et belle.
Et quant cilz biens me seroit avenus,
Que bons et beaux seroye devenuz
Et souffisant en tous cas pour li plaire,
Je vouldroye que mi quatre contraire,
Dangier, Reffus, Paour, avec Durté
(Je l'ay longtemps en devise porté,
Et ont souvent mon cuer taint et noircy)
Fussent tournez en Doulceur et Mercy,
Et de Mercy en Grace et Pitié.
Si tourneroit ma dolour en santé,
Et mueroit ma grief dolour en joye.
Et en la fin de mon souhait, vouldroye
Que je fusse de ma dame choisi
Pour son servant, non mie pour ami,
Mais que ce fust ce samedi matin,
Pour ce qu'il est le jour saint Valentin.

72. Complainte de Saint Valentin

Je vous vueil plus tousdis servir
Sans jamais guardon recevoir
Que par autre tout mon plaisir
A souhait en guerdon avoir.
Faictes de moy vostre vouloir,
Je prens bien en gré ma doulour,
Car vous estez, a dire voir,
Des bonnes toute la meilleur.

Vostre grace sans plus desir.
Autre ne me puist riens valoir.
Je vueil bien grant peinne souffrir
Pour monstrer mon loial devoir.
Nulle durté n'a le pouoir

As much as she loves repose and peace.
And I would wish that I were always
In heart, in deed, in thought, and in speech,
As gracious as she is gracious
And as courteous as she is reserved,
As good-looking for a man, as charming and well-bred,
And just as well beloved by all good people,
And that I were born to such great gentility,
And that in my heart there were as much nobility,
That all my deeds were as fine for a man
As hers are accomplishments for a woman;
And that I were entirely to her liking,
As good and handsome as she is good and fair.
And when this good fortune happened to me,
That I became handsome and good
And sufficient in every way to please her,
I would wish that my four adversaries,
Danger, Refusal, Fear, along with Harshness
(I have long borne this as my motto,
And they have often colored and darkened my heart)
Were turned into Gentleness and Mercy,
And from Mercy into Grace and Pity.
Then my pain would turn into well-being,
And my grievous sorrow would change into joy.
And in conclusion to my wish, I would wish
That I might be chosen by my lady
As her servant, not at all as her lover,
But that this would take place this Saturday morning,
Because it is Saint Valentine's Day.

72. Saint Valentine's Complaint

I would rather serve you always
Without ever receiving a reward
Than to have every pleasure from another
According to my wish as my reward.
Do with me just as you wish,
I willingly accept my grief.
For to tell the truth, you are
Of all good women the very best.

I desire your grace and nothing more.
Nothing else can have any worth for me.
I am very willing to suffer great pain
In order to demonstrate my loyal duty.
No harshness has the power

Pour esloingnier de vous m'amour.
Mes fais le vous feront sçavoir
En la fin de mon derrenier jour.

Humblement vous vueil requerir
Que panser vueilliez et veoir
En quel doubte cuer doit languir
Qui bien aime sans desepvoir;
Et lors pourrez aparcevoir
Que mes plaintez et ma clamour
Me fait bien aimer esmouvoir
Qui ne puit estre sans paour.

Hors du pais me fault aler;
Et quoy qu'il soit du revenir,
Il convient mon cuer demourer
A vous, sans jamais departir;
Ce n'est vie que pour languir,
Car jamais ne sera joieux
Tant que je puisse reveir
Vostre plaisant corps gracieux.

Le cuer de vous ne puit penser,
Croire, deviser ne sentir
Comme le mien le scet aimer
Tousdis plus fort sans repantir.
Pour mez souhais tous acomplir
Je ne demenderoie mieulx
Que vostre doulce vois oyr
Et le regart de voz beaulx ieulx.

Or me fauldra mon dueil celer
Et mon mal mucier et couvrir,
Et pour mez souspirs mieulx embler,
Plains de lermez mez ieulx ouvrir.
Se pour estre d'Amours martir
Doit nulz aimans avoir le mieulx,
J'ay esperance de venir
Ou paradis des amoureux.

Certez, ma tresfine clarté,
Le jour que je ne vous verray
Mes ieulx seront en obscurté,
Et en tenebres languiray.
Helas! jamais joie n'auray
Se je fais de vous loing demour;

To separate my love from you.
My actions will make it known to you
At the end of my very last day.

Humbly do I wish to ask you
That you please consider and see
In what fear a heart must languish
That loves well without deceit;
And then will you be able to see
That loving well makes me arouse
All my plaints and my crying,
And that it cannot be without fear.

I am obliged to leave the country;
And whatever may happen with my return,
My heart is compelled to remain
With you, without ever leaving;
Languishing is its only life,
For never will it be joyful
Until I am able to see again
Your charming gracious self.

Your heart cannot think,
Believe, imagine, or feel
How mine is able to love it
Always more strongly, without regret.
In order to fulfill all my wishes,
I would not ask for more
Than to hear your sweet voice
And a glance from your beautiful eyes.

But I will have to hide my grief
And conceal and cover up my pain,
And in order better to hide my sighs,
To open my eyes full of tears.
If in order to be Love's martyr
No lover must have any better,
Then I have hope of coming
Into the paradise of lovers.

Truly, my fine brightness,
The day that I do not see you
My eyes will be in darkness
And I will languish in the shadows.
Alas, I will never have joy
If I stay away from you long,

Et pour ce mon cuer vous larray,
Qui fera haster le retour.

La façon de vostre beaulté
Pour souvenir enporteray,
Et les fais de vostre bonté
En mon penser tousdiz auray.
Ja pour doubtance n'obliray
Le bien de vous et la valour,
Mais loing et prés vous en feray
Service, plaisir et honnour.

Belle qui amez loiaulté
Trop plus fort que dire ne sçay,
Aiés d'un loial cuer pitié
Que loiaulment donné vous ay,
Et pour loial le maintiendray;
Et si monstrez vostre doulçour,
Car le corps est en tel esmay
Que vivre ne scet a nul tour.

Bonne, belle, doulce, plaisant,
Gracieuse en faiz et en dis,
Je suis vostre loial servant,
Et loial vous seray toudiz.
Ne me vueillez vouloir le pis
Se mon cuer vous aime trop fort,
Car Amours l'a en vous assis
Pour aimer jusques a la mort.

Et se je ne suis cognoissant,
Saige, courtois et bien apris,
Je me repens, et suis doulant
Se j'ay de riens vers vous mespris.
Mon cuer qui est d'amour souspris
Juige souvent du droit le tort,
Et puit faillir sur son advis
Aucune fois quant raison dort.

Le Dieu d'Amours me soit garant,
Qui m'a de sa livree mis.
C'est un seigneur si tres puissant
Qu'il veult estre des sien serviz
En pleurs, en plains, en jeux, en ris,
En desespoir et en confort,
Des cuers joieulx, dez cuers marris,
Et de chascun prent son deport.

And therefore I will leave you my heart,
Which will hasten my return.

I will carry away as a memory
The image of your beauty,
And the features of your goodness
I will always have in my thought.
Never out of uncertainty will I forget
Your virtue and your worth,
But far and near I will do for you
Service, pleasure, and honor.

Beautiful lady, who loves loyalty
Much more strongly than I can say,
Have pity on a loyal heart
Which I have given to you loyally,
And I will keep it loyal.
And also show it your gentleness,
For the body is in such distress
That it cannot live in any way.

Good lady, beautiful, gentle, charming,
Gracious in deeds and words,
I am your loyal servant,
And I will be loyal to you always.
Please do not wish the worst for me
If my heart loves you too strongly,
For love has fixed it upon you
To love until its death.

And if I am not perceptive,
Wise, courteous, and well taught,
I am sorry, and I am sad
If I have wronged you in any way.
My heart, which is overcome by love,
Often judges the wrong to be right,
And it can err in its counsel
On occasion, when reason sleeps.

May the God of Love be my pledge,
Who has placed me in his livery.
He is so very powerful a lord
That he wishes to be served by his followers
In tears, in laments, in play, in laughter,
In despair and in comfort,
By joyous hearts, by sorrowful hearts,
And he takes pleasure in each one.

Je ne plaindroie nullement
Les maulx que j'ay a endurer
Se je vous veisse souvent.
Plus ne voulsisse demander
Que seullement le regarder.
Vostre doulx visaige bien fait
Me fait mes peinnes oblier,
Tant l'aime et si bien me plaist.

Mes or me va trop malement
Quant il me convient deporter
Maulgré mes deus si longuement
De vous veoir n'a vous parler.
Le dur temps que j'ay a passer
Me semble sy noir et sy lait
Que de paour me fait trambler
Mon cuer que toute joie lait.

Et non obstant tout ce tourment
En un propoux vueil demourer:
C'est de vous servir loiaulment
Et moy en vous bien affier,
Et vous aimer et desirer
De plain vouloir non contrefait,
Et vostre grace demender
En tout ce qui ne vous desplait.

73. La Pastourelle Granson

Une jeune, gentil bergiere
Et un simple loyal bergier
Vy jadis sur une riviere
Entre les autres soulacier,
Tost apres ouy comencier
Au bergier demandes et plaintes,
De joye poy, de doulours maintes.
Car il disoit en sa clamour
Et en juroit et sains et saintes
Que trop le tourmentoit Amour.

LA BERGIERE

La bergiere, plaisant et belle,
Qui de tous biens savoit assez,
Lui respondoit: «Certes, fait elle,
De trop grant tort Amours blasmez.
Puisqu'a li vous estes donnez

I would not complain at all
About the pains I must endure
If I were to see you often.
I would not ask for anything else
Except only to look at you.
Your sweet well-formed face
Makes me forget all my pains,
I love it so, and so much does it please me.

But now it goes very badly for me,
When I am forced to refrain,
Despite my sorrows, for such a long time,
From seeing you and speaking to you.
The harsh times that I must endure
Seem to me so dark and ugly
That my heart, which leaves behind all joy,
Makes me tremble in fear.

And despite all of this torment,
I wish to adhere to one purpose:
It is to serve you loyally
And to place my trust in you,
And to love you and desire you
With complete and unfeigned will,
And to ask for your grace
In everything that does not displease you.

73. Granson's Pastourelle

A young, well-mannered shepherdess
And a simple, loyal shepherd
I once saw on a riverbank
Amusing themselves among the others.
Soon afterwards I heard the shepherd
Begin to make demands and complaints
With little joy, with many sorrows.
For in his outcry he proclaimed
And swore by the male and female saints
That Love tormented him too greatly.

THE SHEPHERDESS

The shepherdess, charming and fair,
Who knew enough of every good,
Answered him: "Surely," she said,
"You blame Love very wrongly.
Since you have been given to him

Et mis tout en sa gouvernance,
Vostre cuer doit prendre plaisance
En tout ce qui est son vouloir
Et recevoir en souffissance
Le bien que vous povez avoir.»

LE BERGIER

«Belle, s'il vous plaisoit a dire,
Dist le bergier en complaignant,
Quelle chose me doit souffire
Et quelle ne m'est souffissant,
Le dieu dAmours prens a garant
Que voulentiers content seroye.
Mais Amours veult que doubteux soye
Quant a plusieurs voy desirer
Ce que tout seul avoir vouldroye
Et je ne l'ay pas a garder.»

LA BERGIERE

«Dont, dit celle, nul n'a puissance
De tollir a gens le penser.
Soit de monstrer leur contenance,
De rire ou de regarder,
De ce ne les puet nulz garder.
Mais qui en Loyauté se fie,
Je croy Amours ne s'en plaint mie.
Ainçois lui plaist que honneur face,
Soulas et bonne compaignie,
Pour acquerre bon non et grace.»

LE BERGIER

«Cuer gracieux, ne vous desplaise.
Ce dit le bergier doulereux.
Cuidiez vous que mon cuer soit aise
Quant de vous sui fort amoureux
Et j'en puis veir un ou deux
Ou cinq ou dix ou vingt ou trente,
Que chascun dez leur met s'entente
A moy vers vous desavancier?
Certes Amours veult que je sente
Ce qui me nuit et puet aidier.»

LA BERGIERE

«Et quant Amours n'y a pensee,
Intencion ne voulenté,
Pourquoy est elle donc blasmee
Se les nices font niceté?

And placed entirely under his rule,
Your heart ought to take pleasure
In everything that is his wish,
And receive with satisfaction
Whatever good that you can have."

The Shepherd

"Fair one, if it pleased you to say,"
The shepherd said complainingly,
"What thing ought to satisfy me
And what is not sufficient,
I take the God of Love as warrant
That I would willingly be content.
But Love wishes me to be fearful
When I see that many desire
That which I would like to have for myself
And that I do not fully possess."

The Shepherdess

"Well," she said, "No one has the power
To prevent people from thinking.
Whether just to show their face
Or to laugh or to look,
No one can keep them from doing so.
But whoever trusts in Loyalty,
I believe that Love does not complain.
Rather is he pleased that one acts honorably,
Entertains, and keeps good company
In order to acquire a good name and earn grace."

The Shepherd

"Gracious heart, may it not displease you,"
The sorrowful shepherd said.
"Do you believe that my heart is at ease
When I am so deeply in love with you
And I can see one or two
Or five or ten or twenty or thirty,
And that each of them is trying his hardest
To get ahead of me in your regard?
Surely Love wishes me to feel
That which hurts me, and can help."

The Shepherdess

"And when Love gives no thought to it
And has neither the intention nor the will,
Why is it then blamed
If fools act foolishly?

Quant Honneur garde Loyaulté,
Ce dit la bien sachant pastoure,
Amours aroit vie trop dure
Se jeunesce ne se jouoit.
Autant vauldroit tort que droiture
Se nulz en bien ne se fioit.»

LE BERGIER

«Belle, voirs est ce que vous dites,
Que jeunesce se doit jouer,
Et de tous biens doit estre quittes
Cilz qui ne s'i ose fier.
Mais s'il vous plaisoit aviser
A qui se doit jouer jeunesce
Fors a Honneur et Gentillesce
Et la ou ses jus sont bien pris,
Car foleur, cuidier, et rudesse
Donnent souvant blasme pour pris.»

LA BERGIERE

«Dont vouldroy je bien apprendre,
Dist elle, et moy acointier
Par quel tour me doye deffendre
De celle gent acompaignier.
Se un fol me dit son cuidier,
J'ay ma response toute preste
Devant tous loyal et honneste.
Mais puisque nul ne parle riens,
On doit d'onneur suyr la feste
Et laissier a monstrer ses biens.»

LE BERGIER

«Ha, se respondre vous osoye
Selon ce que je sens et sçay,
Certes, belle, je vous diroye
Que Loyaulté en fait l'esay.
Car qui aime de fin cuer vray,
Il y faut monstrer sa maniere
Selon son cuer, forte ou legiere,
Et quant Amours regne bien fort,
Bel Acuel s'en tient si arriere
Que nul cuidier n'y prent confort.»

LA BERGIERE

«Si Bel Acuel ne venoit mie
Fors en un lieu tant seulement,
Ce dit la bergiere jolie,

When Honor protects Loyalty,"
The wise shepherdess said,
"Love would have too hard a life
If youth did not amuse itself.
Wrong would be worth as much as right
If no one ever trusted in good."

The Shepherd

"Fair one, what you say is true,
That youth ought to amuse itself,
And that he who does not dare to trust
Must be excluded from all good.
But if you please, advise me
With whom youth ought to seek amusement
Except with Honor and Courtesy
And there where its games are well conducted.
For folly, presumption, and ignorance
Often give blame as the prize."

The Shepherdess

"Then I would like very much to learn,"
She said, "and to get to know
By what means I should prevent myself
From keeping company with these people.
If a fool tells me his thoughts,
I have my response all ready
In front of all who are loyal and honest.
But since no one says anything,
One ought to frequent the party honorably
And allow one's virtues to be shown."

The Shepherd

"Oh, if I dared to reply to you
According to what I feel and know,
Truly, fair one, I would say to you
That Loyalty conducts a test.
For whoever loves with a true noble heart,
It is necessary to show one's manner
According to one's heart, whether heavy or light,
And when Love reigns very strongly,
Fair Welcome holds itself so far back
That no presumption takes comfort there."

The Shepherdess

"If Fair Welcome didn't come at all
Except in one place exclusively,"
The pretty shepherdess said,

Chascun verroit appartement
La ou amour de cuer entent,
Dont honneur porroit avoir blasme
Et encontre raison diffame.
Et se amour se doit celer,
Il convient donques une femme
A plus d'un veir et parler.

LE BERGIER

«Je ne dy mie le contraire,
Mais tel parler et tel voir
Ne doivent conforter ne plaire
Nulz de ceulz qui font leur povoir
De vostre grace recevoir.
Puis que vous savez leur courage
Par leur dit ou par leur message,
Se plus fort ne les estranges,
Ilz cuident bien que leur langage
Vous soit plaisant, dont ilz sont liez.»

LA BERGIERE

«Je fais souvent grant abstinence
De vivre ainsi que je me veil,
Mais dessoubz autruy gouvernance
Me faut departir mon acueil
Sans espargnier joye ne dueil.
Et puis que loyal sui trouvee
Et je seray loyal prouvee,
Cuide chascun ce qu'il vouldra.
Car ou que bonté soit celee,
Touzdis le bon la trouvera.»

LE BERGIER

«Belle, des bons n'avez vous doubte,
Car les bons dient bien et font,
Mais les nices ne voient goute
Quant ou cuidier sont bien parfont.
Par folie le bien deffont
Et prennent sur eulz voz samblances,
Vos regars, et vos contenances,
Et tout ce qui leur puet valoir,
Et apres en font leurs vantances
Et si n'en dient rien de voir.»

LA BERGIERE

«Ilz peuent prendre par folie
En eulz mes regars et mes yeux,

"Everyone would see openly
Where the heart's love was tending,
For which honor could have blame
And, contrary to reason, slander.
And if love is supposed to be hidden,
Then it is necessary for a woman
To see and speak to more than one."

The Shepherd
"I don't say the opposite at all,
But such speech and such sight
Should neither comfort nor please
Any of those who do their best
To obtain your grace.
Since you know their innermost heart
From their speech or their messages,
If you don't more strongly hold them off,
They truly believe that their words
Are pleasing to you, for which they're happy."

The Shepherdess
"I often strongly abstain
From living just as I wish.
But under the governance of another
I am obliged to share my welcome
Without sparing joy or grief.
And since I am found to be loyal
And loyal will I be proven to be,
Let everyone think what he wishes,
For wherever goodness is hidden,
The good one will always find it out."

The Shepherd
"Fair one, have no fear of the good,
For the good say and do what is right,
But the foolish don't see at all
When they are deep in presumption.
Out of folly they undo what is good,
And they believe intended for them,
Your appearance, your looks, and your expression,
And everything that can be of worth to them,
And afterwards they boast about them,
Though they don't say anything that's true."

The Shepherdess
"Out of folly, they can take
My looks and my eyes as their own,

Mais riens que je face ne dye
A mon propos n'est pas pour eulz.
Soient dolens, soient joyeux,
Il ne m'en chault, je n'en ay cure.
Franche sui, loyal, nette, et pure.
Je met les mesdisans au pis.
Les venteurs ont leur droiture,
Car les maistres en sont honnis.»

LE BERGIER

«Je maintien d'Amours la parole,
Mais les fais sont maistres de moy.
Quant Loyaulté tendra escole,
Chascun estudie pour soy.
J'ay grant desir en bonne foy
De lire ou Livre de Joye,
Et plus volentiers le saroye
Par cuer pour mes mauls allegier.
Mais se par vous ne le luisoie,
Autre ne m'en porroit aidier.»

LA BERGIERE

«Nul ne puet en ce livre lire
Si n'est souffrant et pacient.
Amours le fait de grace escripre
Invisible pour mainte gent
Qui y regardent tout leur temps
Et si n'y congnoistront ja lettre.
Car qui a lire se veult mettre,
Il n'y doit pas si cler veoir
Que vueille tout ce qui puet estre
Encontre lui appercevoir.»

LE BERGIER

«Comme puet cuer loyal ce faire
Quant Amour gouverne ses sens,
Voir son mal et puis se taire
Et faindre qu'il soit bien contens?
Certes, selon ce que je sens,
Comme la mort la souffreroye
Malgre mien, quant mieulx ne porroye.
Mais la ou sens l'amour fauldroit,
De celui cuer je jugeroye
Que sans douleur le soufferroit.»

But nothing that I do or say
Is meant for them in my intent.
Whether they are mournful or joyful,
It doesn't matter, I don't care.
I am free, loyal, clean, and pure.
I defy the slanderers.
Braggarts get what they deserve,
For the masters are ashamed of them."

The Shepherd

"I uphold the word of Love,
But the facts are my masters.
When Loyalty holds school,
Everyone studies for himself.
I greatly desire, in good faith,
To read from the Book of Joy,
And more willingly would I know it by heart
In order to relieve my pain,
But if I didn't read it because of you,
No one else would be able to help me."

The Shepherdess

"No one can read from this book
If he isn't resigned and patient.
Love in his goodness has it written
Invisibly for many people
Who look at it all the time
And never recognize a single letter.
For whoever sets himself to read,
He should not see so clearly there
That he might want to perceive
Everything that can be before him."

The Shepherd

"How can a loyal heart do this
When Love governs his feeling —
To see his pain and then be silent
And pretend that he is content?
Truly, based on what I feel,
I would suffer it like death
Despite myself, when I could do no better.
But there where sense is lacking love,
Of that heart I would judge
That it could bear it without sorrow."

LA BERGIERE

«Et puis que c'est dont la maniere
Que servant veulent chalongier,
Amour se doit tenir si fiere
Que tousdis soient en dangier
De requerir et de prier
Pitié, mercy, misericorde.
Quant Amours les tient en sa corde,
Faire son gré en puet et doit,
Car ce grace ne si accorde,
Sur lui n'ont chalenge ne droit.»

LE BERGIER

«Chalengier ne sçay ne porroye.
Crier mercy est mon mestier.
Mais se trop fort ne vous amoye,
Mieulz saroye mon cuer aisier
Sans lui grever ne ennuier
Par rage ne par jalousie,
Par doubtance ne par envie.
Et qui tel chalonge querroit
La ou amour est refroidie,
Ja un tout seul n'en trouveroit.»

74. Complainte de Gransson

Je souloye de mes yeulx avoir joie.
En mon parler souvent me deduisoye,
Et voulentiers les autres escoutoye.
Mais en presant
Je ne sui liez de chose que je voye
Ne conforté de nouvelle que j'oye,
Et le parler de riens ne me resjoye,
Car vrayement,
Mes paroles et mon entendement
Et mes regars sont de tel sentement
Que se vivre vouloye liement,
Je ne porroye.
Mais suis si long de tout esbatement
Que point n'en ay, ne mon cuer ne s'entent
Fors en penser. C'est mon soustenement,
Ou que je soye.

Se Doulz Penser ne m'estoit en aye
Sur la voye que j'ay encommencie,
Je seroye mort de merancolie

The Shepherdess

"And since it is then the fashion
That servants wish to challenge him,
Love must conduct himself so proudly
That they are constantly compelled
To beseech and to pray
For pity, mercy, and compassion.
When Love holds them on his leash,
He can and should do as he wishes,
For if he doesn't grant them grace,
They have no right or claim against him."

The Shepherd

"I neither could nor know how to make a claim.
My need is to cry for mercy.
But if I didn't love you so much,
I would know better how to ease my heart
Without irritating or angering him
With anger and with jealousy,
With fearfulness and with envy.
And whoever pursued such a claim,
There where love has cooled off,
He wouldn't ever obtain a single one."

74. Granson's Complaint

I used to have joy from my eyes.
Speaking often used to give me pleasure,
And willingly would I listen to others.
But now
I am not happy with anything I see
Nor comforted by any news I hear,
And conversation doesn't cheer me up,
For truly,
My words and my understanding
And my looks are of such sentiment
That if I wished to live happily,
I couldn't.
But I am so far from every pleasure
That I have none, nor is my heart inclined
Except to thought. That is my sustenance,
Wherever I am.

If Sweet Thought were not a help to me
On the course that I have undertaken,
I would be dead of melancholy

Doresenavant.
Car Plaisance demourra endormie
Et Leesce s'en estoit ja fouye
Quant je lessay la belle, jeune, lie
Que j'aime tant.
La se parti de moy mon cuer, plourant,
Et me laissa pour ma dame plaisant,
Car il est sien et sera son servant
Toute ma vie.
Je pris congie de ce tresdoulz enfant
Les yeulx moilliez et la bouche riant,
Par semblant liez et de cuer bien doulant,
Ce vous affie.

Au departir de ma dame sens per,
Convient mon cuer tendrement souspirer,
Le corps fremir, et les membres trambler,
Et de doulour,
Perdy souvent ma bouche le parler,
Et mes jambes ne savoient aler.
Il n'est nul homme qui peust endurer
Telle languour,
Se ce n'estoit par grant fors d'amour,
Car je senti, plus de cent fois le jour,
Mon corps tout froit, sans sang et sans vigour,
Par trop amer.
Puis me prenoit une si grant chalour
Que tout le corps m'embrasoit de l'ardour.
Je ne cuiday de ce mal par nul tour
Vif eschaper.

Bien sçay que mort feusse, sans doubtance,
Se n'eust esté la droite soustenance
De mon penser, qui me fist alegance.
Car sans mentir,
Mon cuer, mon bien, ma joye, ma plaisance,
Tout mon confort et toute m'esperance
N'orent depuis voulenté ne puissance
De moy servir.
Mais les senti de mon cuer departir
Quant je me vouls de ma dame partir.
Onques n'en peus un tout seul retenir,
Et par samblance
Ne leur chaloit de moy veoir languir.
Ainsi me fault, jusques au revenir,
Ma grief dolour porter et soustenir
Et ma grevance.

From the start.
For Pleasure remained asleep
And Happiness had already fled
When I left the beautiful, young, happy lady
Whom I love so much.
There my heart departed from me, weeping,
And left me for my charming lady,
For it is hers and will remain her servant
All my life.
I took my leave of this very sweet child
With eyes wet and with laughing mouth,
Happy in appearance but deeply grieved in heart,
I swear to you.

On departing from my lady without peer,
My heart was forced to sigh tenderly,
My body to shake, and my limbs to tremble,
And out of grief,
My mouth often lost its speech,
And my legs were unable to walk.
There is no man who could endure
Such sorrow,
If it weren't for the great power of love,
For I felt, more than a hundred times a day,
My body completely cold, without blood and strength,
For loving greatly.
Then so great a heat took hold of me
That it burned my entire body with its flame.
I didn't expect from this pain by any means
To escape alive.

I know well that I'd be dead, without a doubt,
If it had not been for the direct support
Of my thought, which gave me relief.
For without lying,
My heart, my well-being, my joy, my pleasure,
All my comfort and all my hope
Have not since had the will or power
To serve me.
Rather I felt them leave my heart
When I wished to depart from my lady.
I could not retain a single one of them,
And it appeared
It didn't matter to them to see me languish.
Thus until my return, I must
Bear and endure my grievous sorrow
And my pain.

En grant plaisance vit qui est bien aise
Et qui souvent voit chose qui lui plaise.
Mais se ne suis je pas, qui mon cuer lesse
Darriere moy,
Et si m'en vois, commant qu'il me desplaise,
Ne ne voy riens qui ma doulour apaise;
Ainçois convient que de mon mal me taise.
Savez pourquoy?
Car les autres qui sont en esbanoy
N'acontent riens en trestout mon annoy,
Et leur deduit le mal que je resçoy
De riens n'abaise.
Ainçois me croist par leur joyeux arroy
Quant je suis la ou ma dame ne voy,
Et m'est advis que riens avoir ne doy
Fors que desaise.

Lointain de moy, en estrange contree,
Laisse mon cuer, ma joye, et ma pensee,
Ou service de la plus belle nee,
A droit jugier,
De la meilleur et la mieulx renommee
Qui soit entre ciel et rousee,
Et je m'en vois, blasmant ma destinee,
Quant eslongnier
Me fault son corps qui a mon cuer entier.
Ne je ne puis vivre sens son dangier.
Dont me doit bien tendrement ennuyer
La dessevree.
Si fait il voir, se riens m'y puet aidier,
Bien deveroye le retour souhaidier,
Car a mon cuer fauldra comparer chier
Ma demouree.

En mon dormant n'ay que traveil et paine,
Et a mengier ne treuve viande saine,
Et puis les nuys m'est la teste si vaine
Qu'il m'est advis,
Par mes songes, comme chose certaine,
Que je voye ma dame souveraine.
Elas, non fais; elle m'est trop lointaine,
Dont je vauls pis.
Je n'en congnois ne mes fais ne mes dis,
Car mes pensers sont en elle tousdis,
Et la beauté de son gracieux vis
A ce me maine:
Que quant je doy eslongnier le pais,

He lives in great pleasure who is well at ease
And who often sees the thing that pleases him.
But this is not I, who leave my heart
        Behind me,
And yet I go, however it displease me,
Nor do I see anything to appease my sorrow;
Instead I must remain silent about my pain.
        Do you know why?
For the others who are in joy
Take no account at all of all my torment,
And their amusement does not lessen at all
        The pain I feel.
Instead it increases because of their joyous conduct
When I am where I do not see my lady,
And it seems to me that I am to have nothing
        Except distress.

Far from me, in a foreign country,
I leave my heart, my joy, and my thought,
In the service of the most beautiful one ever born,
        To judge rightly,
The best and the one of the highest repute
Who now is between heaven and the dew,
And I depart, blaming my destiny,
        When I must
Depart from the one who possesses my entire heart.
Nor can I live without being in her power.
Therefore well ought to pain me tenderly
        The separation.
Thus it is true, if nothing can help me,
Well should I wish for my return,
Because my heart will have to pay dearly
        My absence.

In sleeping, all I have is torment and pain,
And at meals I don't find the food healthy,
And then at night my head is so weak
        That it seems to me,
In my dreams, as if it were real,
That I see my sovereign lady.
Alas, I don't; she is too far from me,
        Thus I fare worse.
I don't know my own actions or my words,
For my thoughts are constantly upon her,
And the beauty of her gracious face
        Leads me to this:
That when I must depart the country,

Mon corps se part et mon cuer revient, pris.
Ce fait Amours, qui de tous poins m'a mis
En son demaine.

Nulle chose ne me puet a droit plaire
Quant je ne voy le gracieux viaire
De la belle plaisant et debonnaire
Que chascun prise.
C'est ma dame, ou tout honneur repaire,
A qui bien siet tout ce qu'elle veult faire,
Et tous ces fais fait a bonne fin traire,
La bien aprise.
En son cuer n'a que bonté, franchise,
Et Dieu y a si haulte grace mise
Que loyauté a en son cuer assise
Pour tout parfaire.
De bel atour fait de nouvelle guise,
Bien paraissant, et de bonne devise.
Ne s'est nulle des autres a lui prise,
Sans contrefaire.

Tant est plaisant a veoir sa jeunesse
Et en ses fais a tant de gentillesse
Qu'il n'est nul cuer si chargé de tristesse,
Se il congnoist
Sa grant valour et sa haulte noblesse,
Sa grant bonté et sa tresgrant humblesse,
Que tost ne soit tournee en leesse
Quant il la voit.
Nulz homs assez prisier ne la porroit,
Ne sa beaulté deviser ne saroit,
Ne nul des siens jamais plaindre ne doit
Riens qui le blesse.
Car c'est celle qui tout scet et congnoist
Et tous ses fais clerement apperçoit.
Quant riens y a qui bien seant n'y soit,
Tantost l'adresse.

Onques ne vy certes, a dire voir,
D'un foible corps yssir si grant povoir,
Ne d'un jouvent monstrer si grant savoir,
Comme fait celle
A qui mercy je desir main et soir,
Car seulement pour ses beaulx yeulx movoir,
Fait son doulz cuer paour au mien avoir,
Et doubte d'elle,
Et non pas pour force qui soit en elle.

My body leaves and my heart returns, captured.
Love does this, who in every way has put me
In his power.

Nothing can truly please me
When I do not see the gracious face
Of the charming and courteous beauty
Whom all admire.
That is my lady, in whom all honor resides,
To whom is well suited all that she wishes to do,
And she makes all that she does result in good,
The accomplished one.
In her heart there is only goodness, nobility,
And God has placed there so high a grace
That he has set Loyalty in her heart
To make all perfect.
She decks herself out according to fashion,
Judging well, and with good discernment.
No other woman is admired as much as she,
Without pretending.

Her youthfulness is so pleasing to see
And in her deeds there is so much graciousness
That there is no heart so burdened with sadness,
If it knows
Her great worth and her great nobility,
Her great goodness and her great humility,
That it is not soon restored to joy
When it sees her.
No man could admire her enough,
Nor could he describe her beauty,
Nor should any of her followers ever complain
Of any harm.
For she is the one who knows and understands all
And who clearly discerns all of her own actions.
Whenever there is something that is not fitting,
She immediately addresses it.

Certainly I never saw, to tell the truth,
So great a power come from a feeble body,
Nor such great wisdom shown by a youth,
As does she
Whose mercy I desire morning and evening,
For only by moving her fair eyes,
Her gentle heart causes mine to fear,
And I dread her,
And not by any strength that is in her.

Mais je la say si plaisant et si belle
Que chascun doit doubter et amer telle
D'umble vouloir.
Et je le fais. En tesmoing en appelle
Le Dieu d'Amours, qui bien scet ma querelle
Et qui tousdiz mon desir renouvelle
De lui veoir.

Voire, pardieu, a veoir la desire
Tant que souffrir me convient grief martire,
Et par souffrir cuide je desconfire
Les mauls que j'ay.
Mais mon pouoir ne puet a ce souffire,
Car quant je voy les gens juer et rire,
Mon cuer s'en plaint et mon corps en souspire.
Certes bien sçay
Que par nul tour jamais joye n'aray
Jusques a tant que ma dame verray.
Le departir m'a mis en tel esmay
Et tant m'empire,
Que nul confort en ma vie ne sçay
Fors de penser comment tost revendray,
Et entre deux, ne sçay que je porray
Faire ne dire.

Tout le dangier et toute la durté
Que j'ay au cuer de ma dame trouvé
Ne le reffus qu'elle ma monstré,
Ce sache dieux,
Ne m'ont tant fait d'annuy et de grief té
Ne tant mon corps empiré ne grevé
Comme le temps depuis que j'ay esté
Loing de ses yeulx,
Car de veoir son gent corps gracieux,
Maugre Dangier, devenoye joyeux,
Et tous mes maulz en passoye trop mieulx
Pour sa beauté.
Or la gart dieux du mal Saint Encombreux
Et du dengier des jeunes et des vieux,
Et de tous cuers qui seront envieux
Sur sa bonté.

75. Le Lay de desir en complainte

Belle, tournez vers moy vos yeulx
Et congnoissiez mon grief martire,

But I know her to be so charming and so beautiful
That everyone ought to fear and love such a one
With humble will.
And so I do. As witness to which, I call upon
The God of Love, who well knows my case
And who constantly renews my desire
To see her.

Truly, by God, I desire to see her
So much that I must endure harsh suffering,
And by suffering I expect to overcome
My pains.
But my power cannot suffice for this,
For when I see the people play and laugh,
My heart complains and my body sighs.
Surely I know well
That in no way will I ever have joy
Until the time that I see my lady.
The separation has put me in such distress
And hurts me so much
That I don't know any comfort in my life
Except to think how I will soon return,
And in the meantime, I don't know what I will be able
To do or say.

All the disdain and all the harshness
That I have found in my lady's heart
And the rejection that she has offered me,
May God know,
Have not caused me as much pain and grief
Nor harmed or injured me as much
As has the time since I have been
Far from her eyes,
For to see her noble gracious self,
Despite Danger, I used to become joyful,
And I would endure much better all my pains
Because of her beauty.
Now may God protect her from the evil Saint Vexation
And from the oppression of both young and old,
And from all hearts who will be envious
Of her goodness.

75. The Lai of desire in complaint

Fair lady, turn your eyes towards me
And recognize my grievous suffering,

Car pour riens ne vous ose dire
Le mien desir; ainçois veil mieux
En vous servant devenir vieux.
Ce qui vous plaist me doit souffire,
Et me souffist, sans contredire,
Combien que mon cuer soit tieux
Que pluseurs fois et en mains lieux
De la bouche me convient rire
Quant le cuer ou corps me souspire.
Mais pas ne veult d'Amours li Dieux
Que trop vous face l'ennuieux
Pour vous monstrer a quoy je tire.
Ains me fait doubter l'escondire
De vostre gent corps gracieux.

Si vous suppli que le regart
De vos beaux doulz yeulx, que Dieu gart,
Veilliez adrecier ceste part,
Tant que bien clerement voiez
Comment le mien cuer, main et tart,
De vous amer esprent et art,
Sans engin et sans mauvais art,
Ja soit ce que moult est bleciez
Et ferus d'un amoureux dart
Qui tout parmi le fent et part.
Mais penser ne peut autrepart.
Tant est de loyaulté loyez
Que de mourir suis en regart.
Vie n'ay pas, au tiers n'a quart,
Se de vos plaisans yeulx l'espart
Doulcement vers moy n'envoyez

Pour congnoistre le dezir,
        Et plaisir
        Qui gesir
        Sans joir
Me fait tousdiz, et bruir
Dedens l'amoureuse flame
Ou je ne fais que languir
        Et gemir.
        Mais couvrir
        Sans gehir
Me convient sans descouvrir
Le mal qui mon cuer entame.
Et vous ne voulez oir
        Ne veir,
        Consentir

For I do not dare at all to tell you
Of my desire; instead I prefer
To grow old in serving you.
What pleases you should suffice for me,
And it does suffice, without denial,
However much my heart is such
That oftentimes and in many places
I am compelled to laugh with my mouth
When the heart in my body sighs.
But the God of Love does not wish
That I be too annoying to you
In order to show you what I'm aiming at.
Instead he makes me fear refusal
From your noble gracious self.

Thus I beseech you that you please
Turn the gaze of your fair sweet eyes,
Which God preserve, in this direction,
In such a way that you clearly see
How my heart, both early and late,
Takes fire and burns from loving you,
Without trickery or evil design,
Even though it is greatly hurt
And struck with a dart of love
That splits and divides it down the middle.
But it cannot think otherwise.
To loyalty it is so tightly bound
That I am in fear of dying.
I have no life, not even a fraction,
If the brilliance of your charming eyes
You do not gently send my way

In order to know the desire,
        And the pleasure
        Which makes me lie down
        Without joy
Constantly, and makes me burn
Within the flame of love
Where I can only languish
        And moan.
        But I must hide
        Without declaring
And without revealing
The pain that consumes my heart.
And you don't want to hear
        Or see,
        To consent

Ne assentir
Entendre ne retenir
Mon dezir, tresdoulce dame.
Se ainsi me fault mourir
Et fenir
Pour servir
Sans merir,
Je seray d'amours martir,
Et Dieux ait mercy de l'ame.

Helas, je fais
En tous mes fais
Chançons et lays
Et virelais
Seulement pour vous adviser.
Mes diz sont lais
Car homs suis lais,
Mais je les trais
Et les attrais
Du plus parfont de mon penser
Pour vous monstrer,
Soit par chanter
Ou par rimer,
Que sans fausser,
De vous sui fins amoureux vrais,
Et vueil amer
Et bien celer
Sans plus rouver
Ne demander
Fors que mon cuer soit mis en paix.

Certes, mon desir ne me laisse
Avoir paix, santé, ne repos.
S'il ne fust, je fusse bien aise,
Mais il me deront tous de cops.
Il se muce dedens mes os,
Plus embrasé q'une fournaise.
Toudiz le treuve sur mon dos,
Et me soit bel ou me desplaise.
Et quant dezir est grant et gros,
Et il convient que je m'en taise,
De tant ay je plus de mesaise
Et de tourment, bien dire l'os,
Qu'a paine dure les galos
Un fort cheval qui trop le faise,
Et le mien cuer pas ne delaise
Pour trop endurer son propos.

            Or agree
To listen to or to remember
My desire, most gentle lady.
If thus I must die
            And end
            For serving
            Without deserving it,
I will be a martyr of love,
And may God have mercy on my soul.

            Alas, I make
            In all my works
            Songs and lais
            And virelais
Solely in order to address you.
            My poems are rough
            For I am a layman,
            But I draw them forth
            And I recite them
From the deepest part of my thought
            In order to show you,
            Either by singing
            Or by rhyming,
            That without lying,
I am your true and noble lover,
            And I wish to love
            And keep it secret
            Without asking more
            Or requesting
Except that my heart be set at peace.

Truly, my desire does not let me
Have peace, health, or repose.
If it didn't exist, I would be at ease,
But it consumes me constantly.
It hides itself within my bones,
Blazing hotter than any flame.
I constantly find it upon my back,
And whether I like it or not.
And when desire is great and huge,
And I am forced to remain silent,
Then I have so much more distress
And torment, I dare well say,
Than he who whips too much
Endures the gallops of a horse,
And my heart does not desist
In order to better endure its condition.

Et pour ce, ma souveraine,
Vous devez bien en ma paine
Piteusement regarder,
Et penser,
Que quant je n'ose parler
Du mal qui a mort me maine,
Du cuer me tramble la vaine,
Et se je dois reschafer
Mon trambler,
Couvrir me faut pour suer
D'autre chouse que de laine.
Car dezir ad ce me maine,
Qui de chault me fait bruler
Et grailer
Quant je dois aterminer.
Mon mal vault pis que tiersaine,
A tout bien considerer.

Le fort dezir que j'endure
Dont l'ardure est si dure,
Nuit et jour, tousdiz me dure,
Sans aucun delay avoir,
Ne rien ne m'y puet valoir
Si non Amour et Nature
Et vous, doulce creature,
Qui le pouoir et savoir
Avez bien, d'apercevoir
En quel lieu j'ay l'enclaure
Dont je me dueil main et soir.
Car certes, a dire voir,
Vo beauté fist la pointure
Qui si fort me fait douloir.

Pas ne m'avez point de retraite,
Car cilz poins n'yert jamais retrais.
Desir me point, qui tousdiz traite
Que plus parfont soit mon cuer trais
De vous amer d'amour parfaite,
Dont je seray martir parfais,
Se Pitié, qui telz poins afaite,
Ne se met sur moy tout a fais.
Pour ce je tiens ma fin pour faite;
En vous dezirant la parfais
Sans contenance contrefaite,
Ne l'amant pas ne contrefais.
Car du desir qui me deshaite
N'ay plus de bien que beaux souhais,

And for this reason, my sovereign lady,
You ought well upon my pain
To look with pity,
          And to think,
That when I do not dare to speak
Of the pain that leads me to my death,
The vein of my heart is trembling,
And if I am to warm up
          My shivering,
I must cover myself in order to sweat
With something other than wool.
For desire leads me to this,
That makes me burn with heat
          And fry
When I ought to cease.
My pain is worse than a fever,
When all is taken into account.

The strong desire that I endure
Of which the burning is so strong
Continues constantly, night and day,
Without having any respite,
Nor can anything avail me
If not Love and Nature
And you, gentle creature,
Who the power and knowledge
Certainly have, to recognize
In what place I have the hardship
Of which I grieve morning and evening.
For certainly, to tell the truth,
Your beauty made the wound
Which makes me sorrow so greatly.

You have left me absolutely no retreat,
For this point will never be withdrawn.
Desire pricks me, which constantly incites
My heart to be drawn to love you
More deeply, with a perfect love,
Of which I will end up a martyr,
If Pity, which treats such wounds,
Doesn't turn my way immediately.
Thus I consider my end to be decided;
I bring it about in desiring you
Without counterfeit appearance,
Nor do I pretend to be a lover.
For of the desire that afflicts me
My only reward is pretty wishes,

Et non pour quant, tousdiz agaite
Que mon maintien soit liez et gais.

Est ce donc esbatement
D'amer telement
Et si ardanment
Qu'amer est tourment
Sans alegement?
Le tenez vous a solas,
Par Saint Nicolas,
Hors mis tous debas?
Je ne li tien pas.
Le beuf, pas a pas,
Ce dit l'en, le lievre prent.
Ainsi faitement,
Se Dezir en prent
Mon destrivement, *(see note)*
Tousdiz entre jeux et gas
Seront my esbas
Du tout mis au bas.
Lors diray «Elas,
Amours, trahy m'as.»
Veez la bel revengement.

Maistre Guillaume de Machaut
Dit bien que revengier n'y vault.
Envers Dezir rendre se faut.
Mort est qui oeuvre de rigour.
Et Guillaume de Saint Amour
Montre comment le Dieu d'Amour
Le cuer des amoureux assault
Par un dezir cuisant et chault,
Si chault que de riens ne leur chault
Fors que de bien amer toujour.
Cuer desireux n'a nul sejour.
Pour ce, ma dame de valour,
Ne me trovez pas en deffaut
Se maniere souvent me fault.
Car le mien dezir est mout hault,
Et a besoing de grant doulçour,
Sans vouloir mal ne deshonnour.
Mais le reffus me fait paour
Tant que tout le cuer me tressault
Et li corps de parler m'est chault.
Et quant le hardement y fault,
Adont est double ma doulour.

And nonetheless, I am always on guard
That my behavior be happy and gay.

Is this then enjoyable
To love this way
And so ardently
That love is a torment
Without relief?
Do you think it a pleasure,
By Saint Nicholas,
Beyond all debate?
I don't think it so.
The cow, step by step,
They say, overtakes the hare.
In that same way,
If Desire undertakes
A struggle with me, *(see note)*
Always between games and jests
Will my pleasures
Be completely brought low.
Then will I say, "Alas,
Love, you have betrayed me."
See its sweet revenge.

Master Guillaume de Machaut
Says well that vengeance isn't worth it.
One must surrender to Desire.
He is dead who struggles without bending.
And Guillaume de Saint Amour
Shows how the God of Love
Assails the hearts of lovers
With a hot and burning desire,
So hot that nothing matters to them
Except to love well forever.
A desirous heart has no relief.
For that reason, my worthy lady,
Do not find me at fault
If my manners are often lacking.
For my desire is very great,
And it needs great gentleness,
Without wishing pain or dishonor.
But refusal makes me afraid
So greatly that my whole heart trembles
And my body is eager to speak.
And when courage is lacking,
Then my sorrow is doubled.

Et li bons maistres qui parfist
La fin du *Romant de la Rose*
Il m'est advis qu'il ait escript,
Je ne sçay en texte ou en glose,
Que dezir est moult ardant chose,
Et a paine se refroidit.
Et je voy bien qu'il a voir dit
Par le mien, qui pas ne repose,
Ne d'ardoir ne prent nul respit.
C'est un amoureux esperit
Qui en mon cuer a fait sa fosse,
Et paour m'a la bouche close
Pour ce que nul mot n'en yssit.
Ainsy dezir mon cuer noircit,
Qui mon destruisement propose.
Ne descouvrir pas ne vous ose,
Dame, pour quoy mon cuer languist.

Ne doy je bien estre joyeux
Quant chascun jour mon mal empire?
Il n'a usurier en l'empire
Qui soit d'avoir si convoiteux
Comme je sui tresangoisseux
De vous ma pensee descripre.
Mais a tel mal ne me vault mire,
Tant par soit sage ne soucieux,
Se vo cuer n'est du mien piteux.
Autre confort n'y sçay eslire.
Ce fait dezir, qui me martire.
Belle dont je sui envieux,
Entendez mon lay desireux,
Et voyez qu'il me fait deffrire,
Et pour mieulx appercevoir l'ire
Dont je sui merancolieux,
Belle, tournez vers moy vos yeulx.

76. Complainte de Saint Vallentin Garenson

Je voy que chascun amoureux
Ce veult ce jour apparier.
Je voy chascun estre joieulx.
Je voy le temps renouveller.
Je voy chanter, rire et dancer,
Mais je me voy seul en tristesse,
Pour ce que j'ay perdu mon per —
Non pas per, mais dame et maistresse.

And the good master who brought to an end
The *Romance of the Rose*,
It seems to me that he wrote,
I don't know whether in text or gloss,
That desire is a very burning thing,
And that it hardly ever cools down.
And I see well that he told the truth
From my own, which does not rest,
Nor does it take any respite from burning.
It is a loving spirit
That has buried itself within my heart,
And fear has closed my mouth
So that no word escapes.
Thus does desire blacken my heart,
Which is planning my destruction.
And I do not dare to reveal to you,
Lady, why my heart languishes.

And should I really be joyous
When every day my pain grows worse?
There is no usurer in the empire
Who is as covetous to possess
As I am anxious to describe
To you my thought.
But for such a pain no doctor avails,
However wise or caring he is,
If your heart has no pity on mine.
I cannot choose any other comfort.
Desire does this, which makes me suffer.
Beautiful lady whom I desire,
Listen to my lai of desire,
And see that it makes me burn,
And to better perceive the sorrow
Of which I am melancholy,
Fair lady, turn your eyes towards me.

76. Granson's Saint Valentine's Complaint

I see that everyone in love
Wants to be with his partner today.
I see everyone being joyous.
I see that springtime has arrived.
I see singing, laughter, and dancing,
But I see myself alone in sadness,
For I have lost my companion —
Not companion, but my lady and mistress.

J'en ay perdu ma contenance.
J'en ay perdu toute ma joye.
J'en suis deserté de plaisance,
Trop plus que dire ne pourroie.
J'en suis quelque part que je soye
Triste, dolent, oultre mesure.
J'en suis tel que mourir vouldroie
Quant je voy ma douleur si dure.

Mourir, voire, certainement,
Car j'ay perdu ma plaisant vie,
Mon espoir, mon advancement,
De tout bien ma droicte partie.
J'é tant perdu que j'entroublie
Tout plaisir et toute liesce,
Et toute plaisant compaignie
Me tourne souvent a destresse.

Jamais ne feray que languir.
Plourer sera mon reconfort
Quant je pourray estre a loisir.
Je ne requerray que la mort.
Mon cuer et moy sommes d'acort
De vivre ainsi piteusement.
Je ne quier que haster bien fort
La mort pour mon alegement.

Plourés pour moy, je vous en pri,
Tous cueurs qui aymez loyaument.
Mais assez plus, je vous suppli,
Plourés tres douloureusement
Ma dame et son tres beau corps gent
Que la mort a fait definer
Par son dart oultrageusement,
Que mon cuer mauldit sans cesser.

Helas! il n'estoit pas saison
Si tost de son department.
S'a bien esté contre raison.
Mais il ne peut estre autrement,
Car, quant a moy tant seulement,
C'estoit tout mon bien en ce monde
Que de la servir humblement,
Seule sans nulle autre seconde.

Sans plus, telle doulce pensee
Me tenoit en ris et en jeux.

Because of this, I have lost my composure.
Because of this, I have lost all my joy.
Because of this, I am bereft of pleasure
Much more than I could ever say.
Because of this, wherever I am,
I am sad, grieving, beyond measure.
I'm in such a state that I would like to die
When I see my grief so harsh.

To die, indeed, certainly,
For I have lost my pleasing life,
My hope, everything I've gained,
My proper share of every good.
I have lost so much that I forget
Every pleasure and happiness,
And all pleasant company
Often turns into distress for me.

All I will ever do is languish.
Crying will be my consolation
When I am able to be at leisure.
I will seek nothing except death.
My heart and I are in agreement
To live thus piteously.
All that I seek is quickly to hasten
Death, in order to bring relief.

Weep for me, I beg you,
All hearts that love loyally,
But even more, I beseech you,
Weep very sorrowfully
For my lady and her beautiful gracious self
Whom death has brought to an end
With its dart, unconscionably,
Which my heart curses without cease.

Alas, it was not the time
So soon for her departure.
It was totally contrary to reason.
But it cannot be otherwise.
For, as for me and me alone,
My only good in this world
Was to serve her humbly,
Her alone, without any other.

All by itself, so sweet a thought
Kept me in laughter and in play.

Toute grace m'estoit donnee
D'en estre bien fort amoureux.
Je m'en tenoie plus eureux
Cent fois que dire ne sauroye
Quant de ses doulz beaux rians yeulx
Ung doulx regart sans plus avoye.

Plus me valoit l'amer ainsi,
En aucune bonne esperance
D'avoir en aucun temps merci,
Que d'estre roy de toute France.
C'estoit la seule soustenance
De tout le bien de ma jeunesce.
Pour la servir dés mon enfance
Print mon cuer l'amoureuse adresce.

Or voy bien que j'ay tout perdu
Et si ne se peut amender,
Dont je me vy si esperdu
Que nul ne le pourroit penser
De dire que je peuse amer
Aprés elle parfaictement.
Mon ceur ne se peut acorder
A le desirer nullement.

Aussi croy je bien, par ma foy,
Qu'ame ne le prendroit en gré,
Car mon cuer vouldroit, a par soy,
Choisir selon le temps passé,
Et jamais ne seroit amé
De nullc qui approuchast d'elle
Se trop grant debonnaireté
Ne se mesloit de la querelle.

Ainsi seul et plain de douleur
Demourrai je, le voy trop bien.
Jamais ne plaisir ne doulceur
N'aprouchera a moy de rien.
Je serai de simple maintien
Comme tout dolent et honteux.
Ne nulle ne me vouldra bien
De qui je puisse valoir mieulx.

Ainsi que je me complaingnoie,
Je voy Saint Valentin venir,
Venant a moy la droicte voye.
Aussi que pour moy resjouir

Every grace was given to me
To be greatly in love with her.
I considered myself more fortunate
A hundred times more than I could say
When from her fair sweet laughing eyes
I had a sweet look and nothing more.

It was worth more for me to love her thus,
In no great hope at all
Of ever having mercy from her,
Than to be the king of all of France.
These were the only grounds
For all the good in my youth.
In order to serve her since my childhood
My heart took the course of love.

Now I see I have lost everything
And that it cannot be restored,
For which I see myself so lost
That no one could ever think
Of saying that I could ever love
Anyone completely after her.
My heart cannot consent
To desire it in any way.

I also believe, by my faith,
That a soul would not accept it willingly,
For my heart would want, for itself,
To choose according to time past,
And it would never be loved
By any woman who came close to her
If too great graciousness
Were not involved in the case.

Thus alone and full of grief
I will remain, I see it too well.
Never will pleasure or gentleness
Come near to me at all.
I will be of plain demeanor
Like one who is grieving and ashamed.
Never will any woman want me
From whom I could be better off.

While I was lamenting thus,
I saw Saint Valentine approach,
Coming directly towards me.
Also in order to cheer me up

Mais pour mieulx son fait acomplir,
Le dieu amoureux admena,
Qui par la main me vint saisir
Et doulcement me raisonna

En moy disant, «Loyaulx amis,
Te veulx tu de tous poins deffaire.
Tu scez que pieça t'es submis
Soubz ma puissance debonnaire,
Mais celle qui te fist faire
Ne te peut plus reconforter.
Pour ce te vueil a moy attraire
Et te vueil bon conseil donner.

«C'est que choisissés de nouvel
Une dame gente et jolie.
Et a ce faire je t'appel
Et Saint Valentin te deprie.
Aussi Loyaulté le t'octrie,
Car tu as loyaulment servi
Jusqu'en fin ta dame et amie
A qui je t'avoye asservi.»

«Helas! comme se peut il faire,
Se lui dis je piteusement,
Qu'a nulle autre ne puisse plaire
Pour servir amoureusement?»
Mais Amours, qui si puissamment
Si garist mon cuer en jeunesce,
Respont qu'i ne veult nullement
Que je demeure sans maistresse.

«Et comment te veulx tu deffendre,
Dist il, contre ma voulenté?
Ne le fay plus, mais vien toy rendre
En tresgrant debonnaireté
A la non pareille beaulté
Qu'on peut en ce monde choisir,
A qui tu seras presenté
De moy pour l'amer et servir.»

«Helas! sire, pardonnez moy,
Et me laissez souffrir ma peine.
Je ne quier qu'estre en requoy
Pour regretter ma souveraine,
De qui ma plaisance mondaine
M'estoit venue entierement,

But to better accomplish his goal,
He brought along the God of Love,
Who came and seized me by the hand
And he addressed me gently,

Saying to me, "Loyal friend,
Do you want to completely destroy yourself?
You know that you submitted long ago
To my gracious power,
But she who made you do so
Can no longer comfort you.
Therefore I wish to draw you close
And I want to give you some good advice.

"That is, that you choose anew
A lady gracious and pretty.
And I call upon you to do this,
And Saint Valentine begs it of you.
Loyalty also grants it to you,
For you served loyally,
Until the end, your lady and love
To whom I had made you subject."

"Alas, how can it be,"
I said to him piteously,
"That I might please any other woman
In order to serve in love?"
But Love, which so powerfully
Watched over my heart in my youth,
Replies that it does not wish at all
That I remain without a mistress.

"And how do you wish to defend yourself,"
He said, "Against my will?
Do so no more, but come surrender
In great graciousness
To the beauty without peer
That one can find in this world,
To whom you will be presented
By me, in order to love and serve her."

"Alas, lord, pardon me,
And allow me to suffer my pain.
All that I seek is to remain secluded
In order to mourn my sovereign lady,
From whom my worldly pleasure
Came to me in its entirety,

Car jamais liesse certaine
Ne puis avoir aucunement.

«Plus me plaist plaindre et souspirer
Et regretter mon grant dommage
Que d'ouir rire et chanter
Ne veoir gens de joieux couraige.
Je ne quier autre avantaige
Qu'en ce point attendre la mort,
Puis que la belle, bonne et sage,
J'ai perdu qu'amoye si fort,

«Et que je vueil tousjours amer
Aussi bien morte comme vive.
Ne ja ne la quier oublier
Pour nulle assemblee ou j'arrive,
Et pour ce ainsi vers vous estrive.
Si vous pri qu'il ne vous desplaise
Se par vous ma douleur n'eschive,
Mais me souffrez en ma mesaise.

«Car achoison ne puis avoir
Que de languir en desconfort,
Ne je ne puis apparcevoir
Que mon cuer en soit en discord.
Certes ce seroit a grant tort
Qu'il fust jamais nul jour actains
De plaisir ne de joieulx port
Quant j'ay perdu tout ce que j'aims.»

«Au moins seuffre que te conseille,
Puis dy ce qu'il te plaira.
Viens vers celle dont la merveille
Volle tousjours et volera;
En fait par tout les lieux tresra
Ou on congnoist sa renommee.
Car ta mort se abregera,
Ou grace t'en sera donnee.

«Car en voyant son doulx acueil,
Son regart de doulce simplesce,
Il te souvendra du sercueil
Que tient ta premiere princesse.
Ainsi acroistra ta destresse
Du mal qu'i te convient porter,
Ou tu choisiras la richesse
De mon service recouvrer.

For never assured happiness
Can I have in any way.

"It pleases me more to lament and sigh
And to mourn for my great loss
Than to hear laughter and singing
And to see people with joyous hearts.
I don't seek any other benefit
Than in this state to await death,
Since I have lost the fair, good, and wise one
Whom I loved so strongly,

"And whom I want always to love
Just as well dead as alive.
I do not seek to forget her
For any acquaintance that I might make,
And that's why I struggle against you thus.
I beg you that it not displease you
If through you I do not escape my grief,
But allow me to remain in my distress.

"For I can have no reason
Except to languish in distress,
Nor can I see that my heart
Is in any way opposed.
Surely this would be very wrong
That it were ever overtaken
By pleasure or by joyous conduct
When I have lost all that I love."

"At least allow me to advise you,
Then say whatever you please.
Come to the one of whom the wonder
Flies constantly, and will in the future;
Indeed, it will go in every place
Where one knows her reputation.
For either your death will be hastened,
Or you will be granted grace.

"For upon seeing her gentle welcome,
Her look of sweet simplicity,
You will remember the coffin
That holds your first princess.
Thus will increase your distress
From the pain that you are forced to bear,
Or you will choose to receive
The rich gifts of my service.

«Accorde moy pour mon plaisir
Ceste requeste a tout le moins.
Acomplis en ce mon desir,
Je le te pri a jointes mains.
Et pour te faire plus contrains
Te commande a ainsi le faire
Sur peine d'en estre ratains
De ma seigneurie contraire.»

«Sire, je ne sçay plus que dire.
Soit pour esjouir ou pour douloir,
Ou pour souffrir mort ou martire,
Je feray vers vous mon devoir,
D'aler tout a vostre vouloir
Vers celle dont faictes devis,
Qu'a plain ce peut apparcevoir
De beaulté le droit paradis.»

Adonc me vins Amours monstrer
Une dame tant belle et gente
Comme l'en pourroit deviser
A y mettre toute s'entente.
Et lors m'a dit que je m'assente
A la servir tant seulement
Comme le feu de toute rente
Et que mieulx ne puis nullement.

Et quant je la vy si tres belle,
Si jeune et si bien renommee,
Et que chascun bonne nouvelle
Disoit de sa beaulté louee,
J'en fu en trop forte pensee,
Car aucunement ressembloit
A la belle qu'avoye amee,
Pour quoy mon cuer tant se douloit.

Car tant avoit belle maniere
Et le regart doulx et riant,
Si doulce et si joieuse chiere
Et tant par estoit bien duisant
Que chascun estoit desirant
En son pouoir de bien en dire.
Adonc congneu tout maintenant
Qu'elle faisoit trop a eslire.

Au devant de toutes les belles
Qui sont humaines a present,

"Grant me, for my pleasure,
This request at very least.
Accomplish my desire in this,
I beseech you with joined hands.
And in order to make you more obliged,
I command you to do so
On pain of being held
A rebel to my rule."

"Lord, I no longer know what to say.
Whether to rejoice or to grieve,
Or to endure death or suffering,
I will do my duty to you,
To go according to your wish
To her of whom you make mention,
So that plainly can be seen
The very paradise of beauty."

Then Love came and showed to me
A lady as beautiful and gracious
As anyone could ever describe
In giving it all of his effort.
And then he told me to agree
To serve her exclusively
Like the fief from which comes all wealth,
And that I can do no better in any way.

And when I saw her, so very beautiful,
So young and of such good renown,
And that everyone had good to say
About her highly praised beauty,
I thought very deeply about it,
Because she somewhat resembled
The beautiful one that I had loved
For whom my heart was in such grief.

For she had such a beautiful manner
And so gentle and laughing a look,
So sweet and joyous a countenance,
And she was so well brought up
That everyone was desirous
To say good of her, as best he could.
Thus I knew at once
That she was very worthy to be chosen.

Before all the beautiful women
Who are alive at present,

Entre dames et demoiselles,
La prisoit on tout oultrement.
Chascun disoit communement
«Ceste est de tous biens acomplie,»
Ne nul ne la voit vivement,
Se croy je, qu'Amours ne le lie.

A peine l'eusse je peu croire.
C'est la merveille de ce monde.
Nulluy ne se pourroit retraire
D'amer sa beaulté blanche et blonde.
Le bien d'elle par tout suronde.
C'est le tresor d'amour mondaine.
Qui n'auroit guere que une onde,
Si l'en feroit il souveraine.

Adoncques ne peus je contredire
D'Amour la treshaulte puissance.
De grant piece ne peuz mot dire.
De pasmer fus en grant doubtance
Pour cause de la grant muance
Que je trouvay soubdainement.
Au fort je reprins contenance
Et m'affermay aucunement.

Je devins aussi amoureux
Comme parfaictement contraint
De ses tresgrans biens gracieux
Qui m'ont tout droit au cuer ataint.
Et pour ce sans nul penser faint
Le serviray toute ma vie,
Priant pour celle dont j'ay plaint
Si longuement la departie.

Or vueille Amours sa grace estandre
Vers moy par son aide piteuse
Tant qu'il lui face bien entendre
Ma voulenté tresamoureuse
Qui n'eust esté jamais joieuse
Se ne fust par la doulceur d'elle,
Que tous temps est tant amoureuse
Qu'en acroissant se renouvelle.

Et qu'il plaise a son doulx vouloir
Recueillir en gré mon service,
Car par autre ne puis avoir
Grace qui tout bien acomplisse.

Among the ladies and the damsels,
One valued her by far the most.
Everyone said in common,
"She is provided with every good."
Nor is there anyone who sees her in person,
I think, whom Love does not bind.

Hardly could I have believed it.
She is the wonder of this world.
No one would be able to refrain
From loving her beauty, pale and blond.
Her goodness extends everywhere.
It is the treasure of earthly love.
Whoever would have only a bit of it,
Yet it would make her a sovereign.

Therefore I could not oppose
The very great power of Love.
For a long time I could say no word.
I was in great fear of fainting
Because of the great change
That I suddenly experienced.
Finally I regained composure
And steadied myself to some degree.

I fell so deeply in love with her
As one who was totally compelled
By her great gracious virtues
Which struck me directly in the heart.
And therefore, without any hesitation,
I will serve her all my life,
Praying for her whose departure
I have so long lamented.

Now may Love please extend his grace
Towards me, by means of his piteous aid,
Until he make her understand
My very loving will,
Which would never have been joyous
If it were not through her gentleness,
Which is always so loving
That in increasing it is renewed.

And may it please her gentle wish
To willingly accept my service,
For from another I cannot get
The grace that bestows every good.

De tout ennuy oultre je ysse
Seulement par son reconfort.
Par telle fault que je guerisse
Ou que je reçoive la mort.

Amours l'a ainsi commandé
A qui vueil et doy obeir,
Et sa non pareille beaulté
M'i a fait du tout consentir.
Pour ce suis sien sans departir
Entierement jusqu'a la fin,
Ainsi lui prometz sans mentir
Ce jour de la Saint Valentin.

77. Le Songe Saint Valentin

Il est grant aise de panser,
Se ce n'estoit que pour passer
Aucune fois l'eure d'un jour.
Bien met le corps en grant sejour,
En grant repoux et en grant aise
Le panser, qui le cuer apaise.
Panser puit homme jour et nuit
Ce qui lui plaist ou qui lui nuist.
Que ja nul ne pourra sçavoir
C'il panse fouleur ou sçavoir
Tant qu'il meisme le descouvre
Ou par parole ou par euvre.
Et si fait au cuer grant soulas,
Quant ungs homs est pesans ou las
Et il veult prandre son repoux.
Il puit panser sur tel propoux
Qu'en son propoux s'endormira.
Et, en dormant, il songera
Aucune chose merveilleuse,
Bonne pour lui ou dangereuse,
Aussi com je feis, au matin,
Le jour de la saint Valentin.
Celle nuit avoie voillié,
Car mon cuer m'avoit travaillé
Pour plusieurs diverses pansees,
Qui ne sont pas toutez passees.
Si m'avint que je m'endormis
Sur un lit ou je m'estoie mis.
Et me sembloit en mon dormant
Q'un rubis et un diamant,

I escape from every annoyance
Only by her comfort.
By such a one I must be healed
Or I must receive my death.

Love has so commanded it,
Whom I wish to and must obey,
And her beauty without equal
Has made me fully agree.
Therefore I am hers, without exception,
Entirely until the end.
So I promise her without lying,
On this day of the feast of Saint Valentine.

77. The Saint Valentine's Dream

It is very comforting to think,
Even if it is only to pass
Occasionally the time of day.
It puts the body in great rest,
In great repose and at great ease —
Thinking, which calms the heart.
A man may think, day and night,
What pleases him or what does him harm.
For no one will ever be able to know
If he thinks folly or wisdom
Until he himself makes it known
Either by speech or by action.
And yet to the heart it does great solace
When a man is depressed or tired
And he wishes to take his rest.
He can think about such things
That in his thoughts he will fall asleep,
And while sleeping, he will dream
Some marvelous thing,
Good or difficult for him,
Just as I did, in the morning,
The day of the feast of Saint Valentine.
That night I had lain awake,
For my heart had troubled me
With many different thoughts
Which haven't entirely gone away.
Yet it happened that I fell asleep
Upon a bed on which I lay,
And while I slept, it seemed to me
That the day before I had left behind

Le jour devant, leissié avoie
En un vergier, et lez devoye,
Ad ce matin, aler cherchier.
Mais quant je vins prés du vergier
Ou cuiday trouver mez anyaux,
Je vy dedens pluseurs oyseaulx,
Blans et noirs, privés et sauvages,
Sors, muéz, nyais et ramaiges,
De bois, de champs et de riviers,
De maisons et de colommiers.
Petiz et grans, tous y estoient,
Et devers la mer y venoient
Oyseaulx de diverses fassons.
Illec faisoient leurs parssons.
Chascun y choisissoit son per
Qui veist l'un l'autre apper,
Bec et bec, masles et femelles,
Ilz se embrassoient dez elles
Et alignoyent leur plumectez.
Lez doulcez avec lez doulcetes,
L'un prés de l'autre se jognoyent
Et au souleil se pourrygnoient.
Et seulz qui savoient chanter
Vouloient leur mestier hanter.
Le roussinol et la maulvis
Se taisoient moult envis,
Dessus tous ouyr se faisoient.
Et les columbeaux se baisoyent.
Chascun faisoit en sa maniere
Ce qui lui sembloit que bon yere.
Et bien se sçavoient aisier,
Fust de regard ou de baisier,
Ou de tout se que l'un sçavoit
Qui a l'autre plaire devoit.
A leur samblant apparoit bien
Que chascun estoit liéz du sien,
Car ilz avoient souffisance
Et de tieulx biens grant habondance.
Entre eulx tous estoit assise
L'aigle, qui tenoit sa justice
Et faisoit a chascun raison,
Selon le jour et la saison.
L'aigle tenoit son per prez d'elle.
Celle parsson estoit moult belle,
Car tous estoient deux et deux.
Moult me plaisoit la vie d'eux
Et leur desduit que je veoye,

A ruby and a diamond
In a garden, and I had to go
That morning to look for them.
But when I came near to the garden
Where I thought to find my rings,
I saw within a great many birds,
White and black, tame and wild,
Fledgling, molted, nestlings, tree dwelling,
From the woods, the fields, and the rivers,
From houses and from dovecotes.
Small and large, all were there,
And from the sea there came
Birds of many different sorts.
There they were forming into pairs.
Each one there chose its mate
As they saw each other in the open.
Beak to beak, male and female,
They embraced each other with their wings
And they aligned their feathers.
The gentle with the gentle,
They joined, one next to the other,
And they stretched out to the sun.
And those who knew how to sing
Wanted to display their skill.
The nightingale and the redwing
Kept silent much against their will;
They made themselves heard above the rest.
And the doves kissed one another.
Each one did in its own way
What it found to be good.
And well did they know how to please,
Whether by a look or by a kiss,
Or by anything that one knew
That would give pleasure to the other.
By their appearance it certainly seemed
That each was happy with his own,
For they had just what they wished
And a great abundance of such good.
Among them all there was seated
The eagle, who dispensed justice
And gave each one what was right
According to the day and season.
The eagle had her mate beside her.
The pairing up was very beautiful,
For all were arranged two by two.
Their way of life greatly pleased me,
And their joy which I saw,

Et de ce grant soulas avoie
Qu'il me sembloit, en mon couraige,
Que j'entendoye leur langaige,
Dont j'estoie moult confortéz.
Et si estoit mon confort telz
Que j'oubliay mes anelés
Pour escouter les oyselés
Et pour ouyr ce qu'ilz disoient.
Si entendy bien qu'ilz usoient,
Trestous lez ans, a celle feste,
Que chascun d'eulx, teste pour teste,
Choisist a per en son degré
Cellui qui mieulx lui vient a gré.
Et font ensemble leur demour,
Pareille de cuer et d'amour,
Jusques a la fin de l'annee.
Et quant la saison est finee,
Qu'il veul, il puit son per changier
Et choisir autre sans dangier.
Entre eulx n'en est nulz dangier.
Mais soit faucon ou esprevier,
Sacre, gerfaut ou mylion,
Ou oyselet d'autre fasson,
Certez ceulz font faulceté
Qui premier brisent l'amictié.
Ne le teigne nul a mençonge.
Or vueil retourner a mon songe.
En mon dormant m'estoit advis
Entre lez autres que je vys
Un oyseil assis sur un pin
Qui sembloit faucon pelerin.
D'ellez, de chief et de coursaige,
De piés, de bec et de plumaige,
De long, de gros et de largeur,
De siege, des yeulx, de haulteur
Tresbien le faucon ressembloit,
Hor pres que tiercelet estoit.
Car de ce me prins je bien garde.
Ly oisel faisoit sur sa garde,
En sus des autres tout seulet,
Sans longes et sans chappelet.
Mais il avoit entour ses piés
Bonnes campanez et beaulx giés.
L'aigle, qui bien l'apparcevoit,
Comme celle qui cler y voit,
Le fit devant elle venir
Pour la coustume maintenir.

And from this I had great pleasure,
For it seemed to me, in my heart,
That I understood their speech,
By which I was greatly comforted.
And my comfort was so great
That I forgot about my rings
In order to listen to the birds
And to hear what they were saying.
Thus I learned that they were accustomed
Every year at this celebration
That each of them, one by one,
Should choose as a mate from within its rank
The one who was most pleasing to it.
And together they make their dwelling
Identical in heart and love,
Until the end of the year.
And when the season is ended,
Whoever wishes can change its mate
And choose another without refusal.
Among them there is no reluctance.
But whether falcon or sparrowhawk,
Saker, gerfalcon, or kite,
Or bird of some other sort,
Certainly they commit falsity
Who first breach the bond of friendship.
Let no one consider it a lie.
Now I want to return to my dream.
As I slept, it seemed to me
That among the others, I saw
A bird perched upon a pine
That seemed to be a peregrine.
In wings, in head, and in body,
In feet, in beak, and in plumage,
In length, in weight, and in size,
In its perch, its eyes, its height,
It closely resembled a falcon,
Except that it was a tercel.
For of this I took careful notice.
This bird was keeping watch
All alone above the others,
Without a tether and without a hood,
But it had around its feet
Fine bells and beautiful straps.
The eagle, who was well aware of it,
As she who sees clearly,
Had it come before her
In order to uphold the custom.

Et se lui dist, sans plus targier:
«Pour quoy vien tu si regarder
Nostre fait et nostre conseil,
Ce choisir n'en veulx un pareil,
Ainsy comme ses autres font
Qui si entour assemblé sont?»
«Aigle, fait il, pour Dieu mercy!
Saichés de vray que j'ay chosy
Si bien, si bel et si apoint
Que autre choisir ne vuel je point,
Et se ne puis, pour nul avoir,
Cellui que j'ay choisi avoir.
Ja soit mon affaire petis,
Si sui je dez oiseaulx gentiz,
Et ne sui mie si estrange
Que vouler vueille pour le change.
Le change ne m'est bel ne gens.
Je fus jadis privéz dez gens
Et, se je puis, encor seray.
Doulent sui que je mesarray,
Mais j'avoie de mal envie.
Se sçavoir voulez de ma vie,
Saichez de vray que j'ay esté
Plus d'un yver et d'un esté
En la garde d'un gentilhomme.
Nul besoing est que je le nomme.
Mais il m'a fait et apris,
Et tient mains bons oyseaulx de pris,
Faucons, tiercelés et laniers,
Voulans, reclamez et maniers,
Qui tresbien et haultement voulent,
Quant il fait bon temps et ilz veulent.
Entre tous ses faucons a un,
Et silz n'est mie du commun,
Mais est des autres despareil,
Tout ainsy comme le souleil
Est despareillié de la lune.
Cilz oyseaulz a telle fortune
Qu'il est aimez et chier tenuz
Devant tous autrez plus que nulz.
Tant par est beaul et bien voulant
Que chascun lui est bien vueillant.
Il est en tous ses fais certains
Et a vouler le plus haultains,
Et non obstant sa grant haultour,
Jamais ne feroit un faulx tour.
Tant scet a point de l'elle batre,

And thus she said, without delay,
"Why do you come thus to observe
Our proceedings and our council,
If you do not wish to choose a mate
Just as these others do
Who are assembled all around?"
"Eagle," it said, "For God's mercy,
Know for a truth that I have chosen
So well, so beautifully, and so perfectly
That I do not want to choose another,
And yet I cannot, for anything I own,
Have the one that I have chosen.
Even though my rank is low,
Yet I am one of the noble birds,
And I am not at all so strange
That I want to engage in any ruse.
Change is neither fair nor noble.
I used to be domesticated,
And if I can, I will be again.
I am sorry that I escaped,
But I had a great desire for pain.
If you wish to know about my life,
Know for truth that I have been
For more than a winter and a summer
In the possession of a nobleman.
There is no need for me to name him.
But he brought me up and taught me,
And he owns many good birds of worth,
Falcons male and female,
Flying, called back, and held in hand,
That fly very well and very high
When the weather is good and they so wish.
Among all his falcons there is one,
And it is not at all ordinary
But it is different from the others
Just as much as the sun
Is different from the moon.
This bird has such fortune
That it is loved and held dear
More than any, before all others.
It is so fair and flies so well
That everyone wishes well for it.
It is sure of itself in all it does,
And it is the highest to fly,
And despite its great altitude,
It would never make a false turn.
So well does it know how to beat its wings,

Il seul fait plus que vint et quatre,
Soit pour heron ou pour riviere.
Rien ne part s'il veult qu'il ne fiere,
Sans son corps trop esvertuer.
Mais il n'a cure de tuer,
Ains tient tout en subjection.
Car sa noble condition
Est de vouler tousjours plus hault.
Ja ne sera le jour si chault
Que de l'aler plonger ait cure,
Tant par est de noble nature.
De sa bonté ne fault parler
Pour bien vouler et revoler:
Il n'est oyseil qui mieulx l'endure,
En tant comme le monde dure.
N'il n'est besoing que on le hue,
Car il est tousjours vers la nue.
Et si part malart ou cercelle
Ne oyseil qui par force d'ale
Vueille contre le vent vouler
Pour soy cuidier a eulx sauver,
Cil la le fait tantost remectre,
Puisqu'il s'en vueille entremectre,
Soit de haulteur ou soit de tois.
Et puis si leur est si courtois
Qu'il ne lez fiert ne ne mehaigne.
Ou il ne veult ou il ne daigne,
Mais lez prent on vifz a la main.
Bien voule au tart et mieulx au main.
Bien fait d'esté et mieulx d'iver.
Jamais ne trouve temps diver.
Et si n'aimme change n'esor.
Il n'i a tel mué ne sor.
Cil a tous les autrez passéz.
Point n'est de bien faire lasséz,
Tant est gentil et vertueux,
Le bon, le bel, le gracieux.
Bien pert qu'il est de bon affaire,
Car il n'est nul plus debonnaire,
Plus doulz ne de meilleur coustume.
Et porte la plus belle plume
Que nul oysel puisse porter.
C'est un desduit a deporter
De lui regarder seulement,
Sans avoir plus d'esbatement,
Soit a l'ostel ou soit au champs.
Il n'est nul oysel mieulx sachans

It alone does more than twenty-four,
Whether for heron or water fowl.
Nothing escapes if it wishes to strike,
Without straining its body too greatly.
But it does not care to kill;
Rather it holds all in subjection.
For its noble condition
Is to fly always higher.
Never will the day be so hot
That it desire to dive down from its course,
It is of so noble a nature.
There is no need to speak of its goodness
In flying out or flying back.
There is no bird that does it better
For as long as the world lasts.
And there is no need to urge it on
Because it is always up in the clouds,
And if a mallard or kestrel takes to flight
Or a bird that by force of wing
Wishes to fly against the wind
Thinking to escape from them,
It quickly makes it return to place,
Because it wishes to intervene,
Whether from the height or from the roof.
And yet it is then so courteous to them
That it neither strikes nor injures them.
Either it doesn't want to or doesn't care to,
But they are taken in hand alive.
It flies well late and better early;
It does well in summer and better in winter.
It never finds the weather variable.
And it does not care for ruse or flight.
There is no molted bird or fledgling like it.
It has surpassed all the others.
It is never tired of doing well,
It is so noble and virtuous,
The good, the fair, the gracious one.
It is very clear that it is of high rank,
For there is none more gracious,
More gentle, or of better disposition.
And it wears the most beautiful plumage
That any bird could wear.
It is a delight to enjoy
Just looking at it
Without any other pleasure,
Whether at home or in the field.
There is no bird that is wiser

De bien savoir faire son droit,
Grasieusement et a droit.
N'oncques ne vis si doulz regart
De nul oyseil, se Dieu me gard,
Ne qui tant feust polis et net
En tous lez lieux ou il se met.
Et s'on le veult lorrer ou paistre,
Il scet mieulx sez drois que son maistre.
Le bien de lui et la beaulté
Ne vous auroye pas compté
Entre cy et deux ans entiers,
Mais je vous diray voluntiers
En quel point j'ay mon temps usé.
Si me tiendrez pour excusé
De ce que cy pareil ne quier.
Autre chose ne vous requier.
Saichez de vray que cel oysel
Que lez gens tiennent a si bel
Et a si bon et a si doulx,
C'est cil que j'ay choisi sur tous,
Ja soit ce qu'il ne le scet pas.
Car je feroie grant trespas
Et grant folie et grant oultrage
Vers un oysel de son paraige,
Se pour mon par le demendoie.
Tel ne sui que fere le doye.
Mais pour ce que la norriture
Ne puit apaisier ma nature,
Ne restraindre le grant desir
Que j'ay qu'il me vousist choisir,
Et, d'autre part, j'ay grant paour
Que ce ne fust pour mon peyour
S'il le pouoit appercevoir,
Si que pour faire mon devoir
Et tous sez perilz eschever,
Sur espoir de confort trouver,
Je me suis un poy essouréz,
Et mon cuer lui est demouréz
Qui, nuit et jour, de lui ne part,
Ne choysir ne vueil autre part.
Jamais autre ne choisiray.
Pour lui ma franchise larray
Et tout le desduit du bosquaige.
Si me remectray en servaige,
Soit sur le poing ou soit emmue,
Sans ce que jamais m'en remue.
Il ne m'en chault par quelle voye,

In knowing how to do what it ought,
Graciously and properly.
Never did I see so gentle a look
From any bird, so help me God,
Nor any that was so polite and clean
In every place where it goes.
And if one wants to train or teach it,
It knows what is right better than its master.
Its virtue and its beauty
I couldn't have described to you
If I took two whole years,
But I will tell you willingly
In what way I have spent my time.
Then you will consider me excused
For the fact that I do not seek its equal here.
I don't ask anything else of you.
Know for truth that this bird
That the people consider so beautiful
And so good and so gentle,
Is the one that I have chosen above all,
Although it does not know it.
For I would commit a great offense
And great folly and great presumption
Towards a bird of its descent,
If I asked for it as my mate.
I am not worthy to do so.
But because my upbringing
Cannot subdue my nature
Nor restrain the great desire
That I have for it to choose me,
And, on the other hand, I greatly fear
Lest it turn out worse for me
If it could perceive it,
Thus in order to do what I must
And to avoid all of these perils,
In the hope of finding comfort,
I have taken flight for a while,
And my heart has remained behind,
Which night and day never parts from it,
Nor does it want to be anywhere else.
Never will I choose another.
For it I will give up my freedom
And all the delight of the woods.
And I will return to captivity,
Whether on the fist or in the cage,
Without ever leaving there again.
It doesn't matter to me by what means,

Mais que souvent dez ieulx le voye.
Quar je n'ay plume mehaingnee.
Quant je sui en sa compaignie,
Je suis en parfaicte plaisance
A regarder sa contenance.
Et a veoir ce qu'il scet faire,
Que riens ne me pourroit meffaire.
Tant ayse suy quant ad ce vient
Que de mon mal ne me souvient.
Et se j'eusse cogneu
Le divers temps que j'ay eu
Et celluy que, jour et nuit, ay,
Depuis que de luy m'esloignay,
Saichés bien que par nul party
De luy ne me feusse party.
Mais onques, en tout mon vivant,
Senty n'avoye si avant
Quelle douleur est d'esloignier
Ce qu'on aime de cuer entier.
Or l'ay si avant esprouvé
Que maint mal jour y ay trouvé,
Et bien cognois qu'amour lointainne
Est de doulour rente certainne.
C'est mort de soy enamorer,
Qui vuelt longuement demourer
Sans revenir la ou il ayme.
Souvent convient que las se clame,
S'il n'a cuer d'acier ou de fer,
Car c'est un dez tourmens d'enfer,
Sans reppoux et sans finement.
Je le sçay de droit sentement.
A brief parler et le voir dire,
C'est bien de tous lez maulx le pire.
Et pour ce je retourneray
Le plus briefment que je pourray.
Or vous ay tout compté mon estre,
Si ne vueil plus entre vous estre.»
Lors s'escria a haulte voix:
«A Dieu vous commens; je m'en voys.»
Il print son voul et s'envoula,
Et l'aigle qui premierz parla
Dist, quant elle l'ost escouté,
Que bien avoit son fait compté
Et que loiaulment se pourtoit
L'oysel qui d'eux se departoit.
De celluy fait plus ne parlerent,
Mais tuit a un coup s'envolerent,

As long as I often see it with my eyes.
For I have never hurt a feather.
When I am in its company,
I am in complete pleasure
In looking upon its countenance
And in seeing what it can do,
So that nothing could harm me.
I am so content when I come there
That I do not remember my pain.
And if I had known
The ups and downs that I have had
And that which I have, by night and day,
Since I separated from it,
Know well that on no account
Would I have parted from it.
But never, in all my life,
Had I felt so much before
What a sorrow it is to be apart
From the one that one loves with all one's heart.
Now I have experienced so much since then
That I have had many a painful day,
And I know well that love from afar
Is a sure payment of sorrow.
It is death to be in love
For the one who wishes long to remain
Without returning there where he loves.
Often must he call himself miserable
Unless he has a heart of iron or steel,
For it is one of the torments of hell,
Without respite and without end.
I know it as a true feeling.
To speak briefly and to tell the truth,
It is easily of all pains the worst.
And therefore I will go back
Just as quickly as I can.
Now I have told you all my condition
And I wish no longer to be among you."
Then it cried out in a loud voice,
"I commend you to God; I take my way."
It took to flight and flew away,
And the eagle who spoke first
Said, when she had listened to it,
That it had told its story well
And that it behaved loyally,
The bird that departed from them.
Of this matter they spoke no further,
But all at once they flew away,

Ainsy comme il me sembloit.
Chascun a son per s'asembloit
En voulant parmy le pais,
Et je, qui remains esbais
Et euz du jour dormy partie,
M'esveillay sur leur departie,
Et me retournay sur mon lit,
Gisant a moult peu de delit,
Car lez oyseaulx que je songoie,
Qui d'amour ont douleur et joye,
Me firent, en songent, entendre
Que moult petit font a reprendre
Les gens, se ilz veulent amer.
A tort lez en puit on blasmer,
Mais qu'il droit faire leur vouldroit
Ja nulz ne lez en blasmeroit.
Lez oyseaulx a leur gré choisissent,
Et lez gens pour aimer eslisent
La ou leur plaisance s'acorde.
Dont bien souvent y a discorde,
Car a l'un plaist, a l'autre non.
Chascun quiert ce qui lui est bon.
Maiz quant bon accort y arive,
Il n'est nul qui si aise vive
Comme font cez gens amoureux,
Tant sont lez desduis savoureux.
L'amour des gens fait a parer,
Autre ne cy doit comparer.
Amour est chouse naturelle,
Mais elle ne sera ja telle,
Si loial ne si bien servie,
Ne tant a son droit assouvye,
Qu'entre lez oyseaulx et les bestez
Qui n'ont point de sens en leurz testez,
Et ne doubtent paour ne honte,
Et de dongier ne tiennent compte,
Mais vivent sans entendement.
L'amour dez gens est aultrement.
Gens ont le sens cler et loyal
Pour congnoistre le bien du mal,
Et si scevent, par voye bonne,
Garder le bien quant Dieu leur donne,
Et se le mal leur fault souffrir,
Aussy le sevent ilz couvrir
Et porter en humilité.
Quant gent ont mal, c'est grant pitié.
Tant de biens vueil a cellez gens

So as it seemed to me.
Each one joined with its mate
In flying throughout the country,
And I, who remained troubled
And had slept a part of the day,
Awoke with their departure,
And I turned over in my bed,
Lying with very little joy,
For the birds of which I dreamt,
Who have grief and joy in love,
Made me understand, in dreaming,
That humans do little to reproach
If they wish to love.
Wrongly can one blame them for it,
But whoever would do them justice
Would not blame them for it at all.
The birds choose according to their will,
And people choose to love
There where their pleasure is in accord.
Then very often there is discord,
For it pleases one and not the other.
Everyone seeks what is good for himself.
But when harmony is achieved,
There is no one who lives in such ease
As do these people who are in love,
So delightful are the pleasures.
Love causes people to seek one another.
Nothing else can compare to this.
Love is a natural thing,
But it will never be such,
So loyal nor so well served,
Nor carried out so properly,
As among the birds and the beasts,
Who have no sense in their heads,
And who aren't afraid of fear or shame,
And take no account of disdain,
But live without understanding.
Love among humans is otherwise.
People have sense, clear and loyal,
In order to know good from bad,
And thus they know, by good means,
How to preserve the good that God gives them,
And if they must suffer wrong or pain,
They also know how to hide it
And bear it with humility.
It is a great pity when people have pain.
I wish so much good for these people

Qui en amer usent leur temps,
Que, de leur grief et de leur dueil,
Me vient souvent la larme a l'ueil,
Et si m'antre par my lez vainez
La remenbrance de leurs painez,
Qu'a poy me fait le cuer partir
Dez maulx qu'ilz leur convient souffrir.
En se penser ou lors estoie,
M'estoit advis que je sentoie,
Ainsy que par pitié dou lour,
En partie de la doulour
Et du mal que sez amans ont,
Quant ilz aiment du cur parfont
Et sont loing en estranges terrez,
Pour suir voyaiges ou guerres,
Et ont lez cuers en grant cremour
Pour doubtance de long demour,
Ne pour chose qui leur desplaise.
Le temps retourner ne lez leisse,
Mais leur est Fortune contraire,
Quant ilz ont volunté d'eulx traire
Celle part ou leur cuer lez tire,
Et paour de ce les martire
Qu'ilz ne scevent au revenir
A quoy leur fin pourra venir,
Ne plus que faisoit ly oyseaulx
Qui tant estoit ferme et loiaulx.
Telz gens ont moult poy de confort,
Se Espoir ne lez soustient fort.
Dez oyseaulx ne tiens je plus plait,
Mais du mal des gens me desplet,
Ja soit ce que je ne suy mye
Nesun de ceulx qui ont amie,
Et si ne suy n'aimé n'amis,
Ne oncquez ne m'en entremis,
Ne pas ne me vueil acointier
A moy mesler d'autruy mestier.
Car trop me tenroit on pour nice,
Se je prenoie tel office
Ou je ne sçay chanter ne lire,
Fors ainsy que par ouy dire.
Mais, non obstant ma grant simplece,
Tant est navré qui Amours blesse,
Que j'ay pitié de tous amans,
Soyent englois ou alemens,
De France né ou de Savoye,
Et prie a Dieu qu'il lez avoye

Who spend their time in loving,
That, because of their grief and sorrow,
A tear often comes to my eye,
And then enters into my veins
The remembance of their pains,
Which causes my heart to break a little
Because of the woes that they must suffer.
As I was in this thought,
It seemed to me that I felt,
As if out of pity for them,
A portion of the sorrow
And of the pain that these lovers have,
When they love from deep in their heart
And are far away in foreign lands
To go on trips or undertake wars,
And have their hearts in great dread
For fear of a long stay,
And for anything that might displease them.
Time does not allow them to return,
But Fortune is against them
When they have the wish to go
There where their hearts pull them,
And fear of this makes them suffer,
For they do not know upon returning
What their destiny will be,
Any more than did that bird
Who was so firm and loyal.
Such people have very little comfort
If Hope does not strongly sustain them.
I speak no further of the birds,
But the pain of humans troubles me,
Although I am not at all
One of those who have a lover,
And thus I am neither beloved nor a lover,
Nor did I ever get involved in it,
Nor do I wish to get to know
How to meddle in another's business.
For one would consider me too silly
If I took up such a rite
Where I do not know how to sing or read
Except from what I have heard.
But despite my great simplicity,
So wounded is the one Love hurts
That I have pity on all lovers,
Whether they be English or German,
Born in France or in Savoy,
And I pray to God that he keep them

Et conforte a leurs besoings,
Nommeement ceulx qui sont loings
De la ou leur cuer est assis,
Dont mains sont tristes et pensis.
Et si requier au Dieu d'Amours
Qu'il vueille savoir leurs clamours
Et ouir les pleurs et les plains
Et les regars dont ilz sont plains.
Et face lez cuers souvenens
A cez damez de leurz amans,
Et leur envoie bonnez nouvellez
A ellez d'eux et a eulx d'ellez,
Et les face brief retourner
Et tous leurs fais a bien tourner.
Et quant ilz seront revenus,
Pour si loiaulx soient tenus
Que envieux ne mesdisans
Ne leur puissent estre nuisans,
Mais leur soit mis en habandon
D'amour le gracieux guardon,
Pour avoir parfaitte plaisance
Et chascun jour en acroissance
A honneur et au bien des damez
Et au plaisir de toutes femmes
Qui sont amiez ou amees,
Si que ja n'en soient blasmees.
Et tous ceulx qui amans se clament
Aient joye de ce qu'ilz aiment,
Selon l'estat de leur service,
Gardans lez drois et la franchise
Et tous les poins de loiaulté
Devant promis ou creanté.
Ne ja au Dieu d'Amours ne plaise
Que loial cuer perde sa place
Par nul nouvel entrevenant.
Ce ne seroit pas advenent.
Je ne leur puis de plus aydier
Fors seulement de souhaidier
Aussi comme pour moy feroye,
Se es las d'Amours me feroye
Ou maintez gens ont esté prins,
Qui, en eulz prenant, ont aprins
A sçavoir aimer de cuer fin.
Veés cy de mon songe la fin.

And comfort them according to their need,
Especially those who are far away
From the place where their hearts are set,
For which many are sad and pensive.
And thus I ask the God of Love
To please be aware of their cries
And to hear their weeping and lamenting
And the looks of which they are full.
And that he make the hearts of these women
Mindful of their lovers,
And that he send good news
To each of them about the other,
And that he make them come back quickly
And turn their situation to good.
And when they have returned,
Let them be held so loyal
That the envious and the slanderers
Not be able to do them harm,
But that the gracious rewards of love
Be granted to them in abundance
In order to have perfect pleasure
And every day in greater amount,
To the honor and to the good of the ladies
And to the pleasure of all women
Who are lovers or beloved,
In such a way that they are not blamed.
And may all those who call themselves lovers
Have joy of the ones they love,
According to the degree of their service,
Preserving the rights and the freedom
And every point of loyalty
Formerly promised or affirmed.
And may it never please the God of Love
That a loyal heart lose its place
Because of any new acquaintance.
That would not be right.
I cannot help them any further
Except only to wish
What I would wish for myself
If I placed myself in the bonds of Love
Where many people have been caught,
Who, on being captured, learned
To love with a pure and noble heart.
This is the end of my dream.

78. Le Livre Messire Ode

Je vueil ung livre commencier
Et a ma dame l'envoyer,
Ainsi que je lui ay promis,
Ou seront tous mes faiz escripz.
Non pas tous, maiz une partie
Diray de ma mellencolie.
Amours, par vostre bon vouloir,
Vous a pleu moy faire savoir
Que je choisisse une maistresse.
Choisy l'ay plaine de jeunesse,
De biens, de beaulté acomplie,
De doulceurs et de chiere lie.
Son regard est doulx a merveille.
Sur toutes est la non pareille,
Et pour ce l'ay voulu choisir,
Esperant que deusse advenir
Au haultain bien des amoreux.
Maiz trop me trouve angoisseux
Par hardement de trop parler,
Car dit luy ay tout mon penser,
Cuidant qu'il m'en deust estre mieulx.
Mais Reffuz, le tresenvieulx,
Est contre moy de sa puissance.
Dangier d'autre costé s'avance
Et y est quant g'y doy venir.
Lors ne sçay je que devenir.
Quant a elle cuide parler,
Emprés elle huche Dangier,
Et Reffuz est d'autre cousté.
En ce point suis je gouverné.
Adoncq je n'ose plus mot dire.
Maiz plus me plaist son escondire
Que d'avoir tous les autres biens
Du monde qui point ne sont miens.
Jusqu'a la mort la veuil servir
Et toutes errieres bannir
De moy pour elle seulement.
Sien en vueil estre ligament,
A la servir de cuer et d'ame,
Loyaulment, comme seulle dame
Et maistresse de mon vouloir.
En ce point je veuil remanoir,
Ne jamaiz ne m'en vueil lasser
Pour nul que j'en puisse endurer,
Esperant q'un temps qui vendra

78. The Book of Messire Ode

I wish to begin a book
And to send it to my lady
Just as I promised her,
In which all my works will be inscribed.
Not all but a portion
I will tell of my melancholy.
Love, out of your good will
It pleased you to instruct me
To choose a mistress.
I chose her, full of youth,
Of virtues, of perfect beauty,
Of gentleness and joyful countenance.
Her look is marvelously sweet.
Among all women she is without peer,
And for this reason I wished to choose her,
Hoping that I might arrive
At the supreme reward of lovers.
But I find myself severely distressed
For having dared to say too much,
For I told her all that I was thinking,
Believing that it would be better for me.
But Rejection, the envious one,
Is against me with all its power.
Danger comes forth from the other side,
And it is there when I should be.
Then I don't know what to do.
When I think about speaking to her,
Danger, next to her, cries out,
And Rejection is on the other side.
In this condition am I ruled.
Then I no longer dare to say a word.
But her refusal pleases me more
Than to have all the other goods
In the world that are not mine.
I wish to serve her until death
And banish all other women behind me
In favor of her, exclusively.
I wish to be hers as a liege,
To serve her with heart and soul,
Loyally, as my only lady
And the mistress of my will.
In this state I wish to remain,
Nor do I want ever to tire of it
For anything that I might endure,
Hoping that at some future time

Sa voulenté retournera
Et aura pitié de mes plains
Et de mes maulx dont je me plains.
Maiz l'actente me fait languir
Et trespiteusement fenir
Par Desir, qui m'art et enflamble.
Souvenir avec lui s'assemble.
Penser me font a sa beaulté,
Et par ces deux suis gouverné.
Devant me prennent et derriere.
Perdre me font souvant maniere.
Je pense quant deusse parler.
Je ne puis boire ne menger,
Tant suis de s'amour entrepris.
Amours, pour quoy me suis je prins
A desirer ung si grant bien?
Ma mort vueil et pour mort me tien.
Je ne vaulx nesq'un homme mort,
Car homme qui est sans confort
Ou monde ne peult riens valoir.
Helas! ou est allé Espoir
Qui m'a promis moy conforter?
Il ne me devoit point laissier.
Ainsi le m'avoit il promis.
C'est le meilleur de mes amys.
Je sçay bien, quant il revendra,
Qu'a moy tresfort il tancera
De moy ainsi desesperer,
Maiz je ne sçay quel tour tourner,
Tant me destraint ma maladie.
Je suis en mortel resverie,
Et croy que je feusse ja mort,
Ne feust ung poy de reconfort
Qui par Espoir m'est venu dire
Que j'ay tort de moy desconfire
Ne de mener si dure fin,
Ne d'estre a desespoir enclin.
Et dit, se je puis endurer,
Ma douleur verray retourner
En joye bien prochainement,
Et que des biens treslargement
J'auray d'Amours, quoy que nul die.
Loyaulté me sera amye
Et m'aydera a avenir
Au treshault bien que je desir.
Et ainsi comme je pensoye
Et en espoir me confortoye,

Her will will change
And she will have pity on my plaints
And on the pains of which I complain.
But the wait is making me languish
And come to a very piteous end
Because of Desire, which burns and inflames me.
Memory joins forces with it.
They make me think upon her beauty,
And by these two am I ruled.
They seize me from the front and from behind.
They often make me lose composure.
When I ought to speak, I think.
I can neither eat nor drink,
So much am I overcome by love.
Love, why have I undertaken
To desire so great a good?
I wish my death, and I feel like I'm dead.
I am worth no more than a dead man is,
For a man who is without comfort
In the world cannot be worth anything.
Alas, what has become of Hope
Which promised to comfort me?
It should not have abandoned me.
So had it promised me.
It is the best of my friends.
I know very well that when it returns,
It will blame me very strongly
For despairing in this way,
But I don't know which way to turn,
So much does my malady oppress me.
I am in mortal state of frenzy,
And I believe that I would already be dead
Were it not for a bit of comfort
That came to me from Hope, saying
That I am wrong to become discouraged
And to carry on in so harsh a way
And to be subject to despair.
And it says, if I can endure,
I will see my sorrow turn
Into joy again quite soon,
And that abundantly of the rewards of Love
I will have, whatever anyone says.
Loyalty will be a friend to me
And it will help me to arrive
At the supreme good that I desire.
    And as I was thinking thus
And taking comfort in hope,

Je m'allay sur ung lit gecter
Pour moy ung petit reposer,
Et meiz peine de moy dormir,
Maiz je ne poz, pour Souvenir,
Dormir ne reposer vrayement.
Et lors que je meiz mon pensement
A commancier une ballade,
Et la fiz comme homme malade
Et enregistray en mon livre,
Et, s'il vous plaist, la povez lire.

Balade

Desconforté de joye et de leesse,
Raemply de dueil et de plains doloreux,
Triste, pensif, desgarny de leesse,
Desesperé de tormens amoureux,
Tout esloingné de tous plaisirs joyeulx,
Maintenant, plus que je ne pourroye dire,
De tous tormens suis accueilly du pire.
Actains me truiz de douleur et de rage.
Sans franchise me suis trouvé en servage,
Tant que j'en sens mon cueur ardoir et frire.
De plus en plus ay de maulx l'eritage.
J'ay le rebours de ce que je desire.

Souffreteux suis en ma jeune jeunesse
De ce qu'amant doit estre desireux.
Plus n'en diray, bien sçay ce qui me blesse.
Dolant seroye d'estre si maleureux
Que chascun sceust mon meschief ennuyeux,
Dont j'ay trop plus que ne pourroye escripre. *(see note)*
Ung seul chemin desroye mon couraige,
Me fait languir et passer ce passaige.
Qu'en dictez vous? Me doibt il bien souffire?
Qu'en diray plus? En la fleur de mon eage,
J'ay le rebours de ce que je desire.

Dangier m'assault, Reffuz me nuyt et blece.
Ung jour je suis trop merencolieux
Et l'autre jour Espoir me fait promesse
Que maugré tous, il me fera joyeux.
En ce maintain me fault devenir vieux.
Contre Fortune nul ne puet contredire,
Soit droit, soit tort, soit plaisance ou martire.
Plaisant folye m'a gardé d'estre saige.
Riens ne m'y vault, escu, pavas ne targe.

I threw myself upon a bed
In order to rest myself a bit,
And I tried hard to fall asleep,
But because of Memory,
I could not truly sleep or rest.
And so I set my thought
To beginning a ballade,
And I wrote it like a sick man
And recorded it in my book,
And if you like, you may read it.

Ballade

Forsaken by joy and happiness,
Filled with grief and sorrowful plaints,
Sad, pensive, deprived of happiness,
Driven by love's torments to despair,
Completely removed from all joyous pleasures,
Now, more than I could ever say,
I am assailed by the very worst of torments.
I find myself stricken with grief and rage.
Without liberty, I am found in servitude,
Such that I feel my heart both burn and freeze.
More and more I am the heir of pain.
I have the opposite of what I desire.

In my early youth I am destitute
Of that which a lover ought to desire.
I will say no more; I know well what wounds me.
I would be sorry to be so unfortunate
That everyone knew of my grievous pain,
Of which I have much more than I could write. *(see note)*
A single path leads my heart astray,
Makes me languish and go through this passage.
What do you say? Should I be satisfied?
What more will I say? In the flower of my life,
I have the opposite of what I desire.

Danger attacks me; Rejection hurts and wounds me.
One day I am excessively melancholy
And another day, Hope makes me a promise
That despite all, it will make me joyous.
In this condition I must grow old.
No one can oppose Fortune,
Be it right or wrong, be it pleasure or suffering.
A pleasing folly has kept me from being wise.
No sort of shield does me any good.

Bien suis gardé de chanter ne de rire,
Tant que j'en diz a haulte voix par rage:
«J'ay le rebours de ce que je desire.»

Jeune et gente, ma tresbelle princesse,
De garison ne quier chemin n'adresse
Se non par vous qui estez mon droit mire.
Alegez moy de tous mes maulx du pire.
Et ne souffrez que die plus par rudesse,
«J'ay le rebours de ce que je desire.»

Quant j'euz ma balade achevee
Et en mon livre enregistree,
Je reprins a mener mon dueil,
Disant a Amours: «Dessus le sueil
Je suis de l'Ostel de Tristesse.
Dangier m'assault, Reffuz me blece.
Contre eulx je ne me puis deffendre.
Pieça a eulx m'eust falu rendre
Ne fust Espoir qui me conforte.
De bien servir tousjours m'enhorte,
Mais mon mal si fort me constraint
Et de douleur suis si estraint
Que durer gueres ne pourroye.
Amours, fault il que je soye
Banny du Danjon de Leesse,
Moy qui suis en fleur de jeunesse?
Ayez pitié de ma douleur
Et de ma piteuse clameur.
Ne souffrez que je soye deffait
Quant pour vous ay empris ce fait.
Envoyez Pitié et Humblesse
Hastivement vers ma maistresse
Luy prier qu'a moy secourir
Il luy plaise, par son plaisir,
Car oncques serviteurs, par m'ame,
Ne servy plus loyaulment dame
Que j'ay vouloir de la servir
En tous estaz, et obeir
A tous ses bons commandemens.
C'est mon dieu; a elle m'atens
De moy faire vivre ou mourir
Ou trespiteusement languir,
Lequel que bon lui semblera.
Car mon cueur ne contredira
Riens qui d'elle soit ordonné.
En ce point est ma voulenté.

Well am I kept from singing and from laughing,
So that I say out loud, furiously:
"I have the opposite of what I desire."

Young and gracious one, my beautiful princess,
I do not seek the path or route to healing
Except through you, who are my true physician.
Relieve me of the worst of all my pains.
Allow no more that I say boorishly,
"I have the opposite of what I desire."

When I had finished my ballade
And recorded it in my book,
I began again to bewail my grief,
Saying to Love, "Upon the threshold
I am of the Inn of Sadness.
Danger attacks me, Rejection wounds me.
Against them I cannot defend myself.
I would have had to surrender to them long ago
Were it not for Hope, which comforts me.
It exhorts me still to serve well,
But my pain oppresses me so strongly
And I am so afflicted with sorrow
That I could hardly endure.
Love, must I be banished
From the Tower of Happiness,
I, who am in the flower of youth?
Have pity on my sorrow
And on my piteous cry.
Don't allow me to be undone
When I have undertaken this for you.
Send Pity and Humility
In haste unto my mistress
To beg her that to succor me
It please her, by her pleasure,
For never did a servant, by my soul,
Serve any lady more loyally
Than I wish to serve her
In every circumstance, and to obey
All of her good commands.
She is my god; I count on her
To make me live or die
Or very piteously to languish,
Whichever will seem good to her.
For my heart will not oppose
Anything that is ordained by her.
My will is fixed upon that point.

Et se je meurs en la servant,
De mon ame luy faiz presant.
Je ne luy ay plus que donner.
Dame des dames, seulle sans per,
Vostre serf suis et serf me tien.
Regardez se vous ferez bien
De moy ainsi laisser fenir
Par faulte de moy secourir.»
Ainsi que m'aloye complaignant
Et ma douleur ramantevant
Comme ung homme en resverie,
Enceint de dure maladie,
Someil me prist, si m'endormy.
En mon dormant, ung songe fy,
Et en mon songe me sembloit
Qu'emprés moy ung jardin avoit
Bel et plaisant et gracieux,
Enceint d'arbres, couvert de fleurs.
Es arbres les oyseaulx chantoient,
Et en leur chant se desduisoient.
Le lieu estoit bel a merveilles.
Les chemins estoient de treilles,
Et entre deux, de pavillons.
Et de parquez, carréz et bellons,
Avoit assez, plains de flouretes,
Blanches, yndes et vermeilletes.
De preaux praslez d'erbe vert
Estoit tout le chemin couvert.
La m'allay, ce me fut advis,
Mectre en lieu ou mieulx je choisiz
Qu'on ne me peust aparcevoir
Pour mieulx mon dueil ramantevoir.
Et la recommançay ma plaincte,
Et fez, en façon de complaincte,
Une qu'ay cy mis en escript
Affin que mieulx m'en sovenist.

Complainte

Mon dieu, ma dame, ma maistresse,
A vous me plains de ma tresgrant ardour
Du mal d'amer qui si tresmal me blesse
Et ja tenu m'a long temps en langour.
Et me complain, plain de douleur et plour,
A vous, maistresse, que je clains plus qu'amye
Et clameray tous les jours de ma vie.
Confortez moy que j'aye allegement.

And if I die in serving her,
I make her a present of my soul.
I have nothing more to give her.
Lady of ladies, alone without peer,
I am your serf and a serf I remain.
Consider if you will do well
To let me perish in this way
By failing to come to my aid."
As I thus went on lamenting
And bringing my sorrow back to mind
Like a man in a frenzied state,
Engulfed in great malady,
Sleep took hold of me, and I fell asleep.
In my sleep I had a dream,
And in my dream it seemed to me
That all about me was a garden
Beautiful and pleasant and gracious,
Encircled by trees, covered with flowers.
In the trees the birds were singing,
And in their song they rejoiced.
The place was marvelously beautiful.
The paths were marked by trellises,
And in between, by pavilions.
And of flowerbeds, square and rectangular,
There were quite a few, full of little flowers,
White, violet, and red.
With little meadows of green grass
The entire path was covered.
Then I went, it seemed to me,
To sit in the place where best I found
That no one could perceive me
To better call to mind my grief.
And then I began my lament anew,
And I made, in the manner of a complainte,
One that I have set down here in writing
So that I might better remember it.

Complaint

My god, my lady, my mistress,
To you I complain of my intense burning
From the pain of love which wounds me so grievously
And has already held me long in languor.
And I complain, full of sorrow and tears,
To you, my mistress, whom I call more than friend
And will so call all the days of my life.
Comfort me, so that I might have relief.

Du tout me mect en vostre jugement:
Jugiez de moy comme juge et partie.

Et se me plains et tourmente et crie,
Pardonnez moy, je vous prie humblement,
Car j'ay ung mal qui si tresfort me lie
Qu'avoir leesse ne pourroye nullement
Ne reconfort qui m'aide aucunement
A conforter mon ennuy doloreux.
Que vous diray? Je suis si angoisseux,
Je ne viz mie; je ne foiz que languir.
Si vous supplie, quant me fauldra fenir,
Priez pour moy, s'il vous plaist, amoureux.

Et faictes duel, tous jeunes cuers joyeux,
Que pour amer et servir loyaulment
Fault que deffine en plours et plains piteux,
Et sans avoir secours aucunement
Fors que d'Espoir, qui dit certainement
Qu'i m'aidera a oster le martire
Que mon cuer sent. Maiz il n'est q'un seul mire
Qui mon courroux peust mectre a plaisant vueil.
Pour ce duray, tout en menant mon duel.
Qu'en puis je maiz se je me tiens de rire?

Et se je faiz semblant d'avoir grant ire,
Si poise moy, si m'en peusse tenir.
Maiz ma douleur me va de pire en pire.
Pour ce me fault souspirer et gemir.
En languissant voy qu'il me fault finir,
Et dit mon cueur qu'en langueur finera
Et que du tout leesse laissera.
Maiz ains qu'il meure, diray a ma maistresse:
«Dame sans per, pour vous laisse leesse.
Faictes de moy tout ce qu'il vous plaira.

«Qu'a tousjours maiz mon vouloir si sera
De vous servir, en ce point est mon vueil,
Ne jamaiz jour ne s'en despartira,
En esperant que vostre riant oeil
Et la doulceur de vostre bel acueil
Aient pitié de mon piteux tourment.
Mes griefz douleurs passeray simplement,
Et en chantant ung chant tresdoloreux,
Dy et diray ou que soye, en tous lieux,
Je sui tousjours en vo commandement.»

I place myself entirely in your judgment:
Pass judgment on me as both judge and party.

And if I complain and rage and shout,
Pardon me, I pray you humbly,
For I have a pain that binds me so strongly
That I could have absolutely no joy
Nor comfort that might help me in any way
To relieve my sorrowful affliction.
What will I say to you? I am so distressed,
I do not live at all; all I do is languish.
Thus I beseech you, when it comes for me to die,
Pray for me, please, all you lovers.

And make sorrow, all young joyous hearts,
That for loving and serving loyally
I must end in tears and piteous laments,
And without receiving help in any way
Except from Hope, which says with certainty
That it will help me remove the suffering
That my heart feels. But there is only one physician
That can turn my wrath into a pleasant desire.
Therefore I will endure, while carrying on my grief.
What more can I do if I refrain from laughing?

And if I appear to have great anger,
It troubles me, and yet I could refrain.
But my sorrow is getting worse and worse.
Therefore I must sigh and moan.
I see that I must end in languishing,
And my heart says that in languor it will end
And that it will completely abandon joy.
But before it dies, I will say to my mistress:
"Lady without peer, for you I give up joy.
Do with me anything that you please.

"For thus my wish will be forever more
To serve you, such is my will,
Nor will it ever cease to be so,
Hoping that your laughing eye
And the sweetness of your fair welcome
Might have pity on my piteous suffering.
I will endure my grievous sorrows humbly,
And singing a very sorrowful song,
I say and will say, wherever I might be,
I am always at your command."

Bien estre y doy, sans faire changement,
Du tout en tout, comme a la nom pareille
D'onneur, de bien, de plaisance ensement.
Pourtant souvent en penser me resveille,
Et en pensant souvent je me merveille
De la douleur que me fait endurer,
Veu que pieça luy ay voulu donner
Mon cueur, mon corps, sans faire departie.
A la servir mect tout mon estudie.
C'est mon vouloir, c'est mon loyal penser:

De la servir, honnourer et doubter
A tousjours maiz, tant que j'auray duree.
La clameray, sans nulle autre excepter,
Dame et maistresse et de moy seulle amee.
En ce vouloir feray ma destinee,
En esperant qu'en puisse valoir mieulx.
De plus en plus je vueil estre soingneux
De la servir de toute ma puissance.
En actendant que j'en aye allegrance,
Suis et seray adés plus envieulx

Que puisse faire son vouloir en tous lieux,
Tant que son vueil me vueille retenir
Son serviteur. Lors doubleront mes jeux
Et tornera desplaisance en plaisir.
Ja a grant temps que ne faiz que languir
Et que pieça suis en telle langour
En actendant que, par sa grant doulceur,
Elle me vueille aucun confort donner.
Sans despartir, tousjours la vueil clamer
Mon tresdoulx cueur et ma loyalle amour.

Soiez piteuse et plaine de doulceur,
Dame sans per, de tous biens acomplie.
Aiez pitié de la tresgrant ardour
Du mal d'amours qui ainsi fort me lie.
Venez vers moy dire: «Je te deslie.»
Autre que vous ne me peult conforter.
De moy povez a vo gré ordonner.
Ja a grant temps que je suis en servage
Tant que j'en pers force, couleur, et langage.
En soupirant me souhaide en la mer!

Dictes s'ay tort de moy desconforter
Et en plourant, de maudire ma vie.
Car oncq amant ne souffrist tel amer

So should I be, without changing,
Completely, to the one who is without equal
In honor, in goodness, in charm as well.
Often, however, I lie awake in thought,
And in thinking, I often marvel
At the sorrow that she makes me endure,
Given that long ago I wished to give to her
My heart, my body, fully and exclusively.
I put all my effort into serving her.
That is my wish; that is my loyal intention:

To serve her, honor her, and fear her
Forever more, as long as I last.
I will call her, without any exception,
Lady, mistress, and my only beloved.
In this wish I will make my destiny,
Hoping that I might deserve better.
I wish to be more and more attentive
In serving her with all of my power.
Awaiting that I might have some joy,
I am and will be even more desirous

To carry out her wish in every place,
So that her will might wish to retain me
As her servant. Then my stakes will double
And my displeasure will turn into pleasure.
For a long time now, all I do is languish
And I have long been in such a state of languor
While awaiting that, out of her great gentleness,
She might wish to give me some comfort.
Without reserve, I wish always to call her
My most gentle heart and my loyal love.

Have pity and be full of gentleness,
Lady without peer, complete in every virtue.
Have pity on the great burning
Of the pain of love that binds me so strongly.
Come to me, saying: "I release you."
No one else but you can comfort me.
You can rule me according to your will.
For a long time now I have been in servitude
So greatly that I lose strength, color, and speech.
Sighing, I wish that I were far at sea!

Say if I am wrong to be discouraged
And while weeping, to curse my life.
For no lover ever suffered such bitterness

Comme je faiz. Je ne sçay que je die!
A vous me rens; ne me desertés mie!
Mon cueur, mon corps, du tout je vous presente,
Piteusement, loing de joyeuse sente.
Treshumblement je vous viens requerir
Que me vueillez vo servant retenir,
Tresbelle, bonne, jeune, joyeuse, gente.

Ma complaincte ne puis plus soustenir,
A dire vray, que la mort si me chasse
Tresardanment, maiz je me vueil tenir
Garny d'Espoir, lui priant qu'il pourchasse
Envers ma dame mon bien, et qu'il deschasse
Du tout en tout de moy la desplaisance.
Ravy je suis sans avoir soustenance.
Je ne sçay plus que puisse devenir.
Tout gemissant et plain d'ardant desir,
En souppirant, j'ay delaissié plaisance.

Ainsi que ma plainte escripsoie
Et en mon livre la mectoye,
Je viz venir tres liement
Ung qui chantoit joyeusement.
De sa chanson les diz estoient:

Chançon

Je me doy bien tenir en joye,
Quant je voy chascun souffreteux
Et des bien d'Amours douloreux,
Moy qui ay ce que desiroie.

Souhaidier mieulx je ne pourroye.
Je passe les autres eureux.
Je me doy bien tenir en joye,
Quant je voy chascun souffreteux.

Je souhaide que je vouldroie
A trestous loyaulx amoreux
Dames pour les faire joyeulx.
Tant qu'est a moy, ou que je soye,

Je me doy bien tenir en joye,
Quant je voy chascun souffreteux
Et des bien d'Amours douloreux,
Moy qui ay ce que desiroie.

As I do. I don't know what I am saying!
I surrender to you; do not desert me!
My heart, my body, I present entirely to you,
Piteously, far from the path of joy.
Most humbly do I come to beseech you
That you please retain me as your servant.
My beautiful, good, young, joyous, gracious lady.

I can sustain my complaint no longer,
To tell the truth, for death pursues me
Most ardently, but I want to consider myself
Furnished with Hope, praying it that it obtain
From my lady my reward, and that it expel
Unhappiness from me entirely.
I am carried off without anything to sustain me.
I know no longer what I might become.
Moaning and full of burning desire,
Sighing, I have abandoned pleasure.

As I was writing down my plaint
And placing it in my book,
I saw come very happily
One who sang joyously.
The words of his song were:

Song

Well should I consider myself in joy,
When I see everyone who is destitute
And who grieves for the rewards of love,
I who have what I desired.

I could not wish for better.
I surpass the others who are lucky.
Well should I consider myself in joy,
When I see everyone who is destitute.

I wish that I could grant
To all faithful lovers
Ladies to make them joyous.
As for me, wherever I am,

Well should I consider myself in joy,
When I see everyone who is destitute
And who grieves for the rewards of love,
I who have what I desired.

Aprés qu'il eust dit sa chançon,
Il escouta ly osillon
Qui chantoient tresdoulcement.
C'estoit ung grant esbatement.
Et se print a faire ung chappel
Qui fut, ce me semble, tresbel,
Car assez eut de quoy le faire.
De fleurs y avoit mainte paire.
Sur sa teste tantost le mist
Et puis sur l'erbe s'assist
Et commença une balade.
Faicte n'estoit d'omme malade.
La balade ycy trouverez.
S'il vous plaist, lire la pourrez.

Balade

Je mercy Amours et ma dame
Qui me tiennent en tel leesse,
Car ung seul desplaisir, par m'ame,
N'ay en moy de nulle tristesse.
Je ne sens douleur ne detresse.
Des amans suis le plus eureux.
Qu'est ce que d'estre douloreux?
Quant a moy, je ne le sçay mie,
Mais d'esbatre suis tressoingneux.
Je n'ay nulle autre maladie.

Pour ce escript sera sur ma lame
Quant Mort sera de moy maistresse
Que loyaulment, sans nul diffame,
Ay servy tousjours ma princesse
Trestous les temps de ma jeunesse,
Sans estre de mal angoysseux
Et de nulle riens envieux.
Jugiez: n'ay je pas bonne vie
D'estre tousjours ainsi joyeulx?
Je n'ay nulle autre maladie.

Se plaigne qui veult et se clame
De Dangier, Reffuz et Destresse.
Je ne les loe ne les blasme,
Car point ilz ne me font de presse.
Bel Acueil conduit ma deesse,
Doulx Regard gouverne ses yeulx,
Et mes amys y sont tous deux.
La loyaulté n'est point faillie.

After he had sung his song,
He listened to the birds
Who sang very sweetly.
It was a great pleasure.
And he set about making a floral chaplet
Which was very beautiful, it seems to me,
For he had enough with which to make it.
Of flowers there were many a pair.
Upon his head he quickly placed it
And then sat down on the grass
And he began a ballade.
It wasn't made by a sickly man.
You will find the ballade here.
You will be able to read it, if you like.

Ballade

I give thanks to Love and to my lady
Who keep me in such happiness,
For not a single displeasure, by my soul,
Do I have, from any sadness.
I feel neither sorrow nor distress.
I am the luckiest of lovers.
What is it to be sorrowful?
As for me, I don't know at all,
But I am occupied with pleasure.
I have no other malady.

Thus it will be written on my tomb
When Death becomes my mistress
That loyally, with no dishonor,
I always served my princess
The entire time of my youth,
Without being distressed by pain
And desirous of nothing.
You judge: don't I have a good life
Always to be in such great joy?
I have no other malady.

Let him who wishes complain and protest
About Danger, Rejection, and Distress.
I neither praise nor blame them,
For they do not oppress me at all.
Fair Welcome guides my goddess,
Sweet Regard governs her eyes,
And both of these are friends to me.
Loyalty has not been lacking.

Doy je pas bien dire en tous lieux:
Je n'ay nulle autre maladie?

Prince amoureux, Dieu gard mon ame
Et mon corps des faulx envieux,
Et doint a tous vrays amoureux
De plaisance la seigneurie,
Car, quant a moy, se m'aist Dieux,
Je n'ay nulle autre maladie.

A son semblant, il n'estoit mie
Assailly de mellencolie
Ainsi que suis pour le present.
Car s'il y vint joyeusement,
Il s'en va plus joyeulx assez.
De mener joye n'est lassez.
Il ne craint maladie ne mort.
En s'en allant s'efforçoit fort
De chanter, maiz tost fust en bois,
Entendre ne pouoie sa voix.
Lors reprains ma douleur a plaindre
Piteusement et sans me faindre
De crier a Amours mercy
Et a ma belle dame aussi.
Maiz je ne sçay qu'ilz en feront,
Ne se de moy mercy aront.
Ilz me peuent de tous poins deffaire
Ou en pou d'eure me reffaire,
Lequel que bon leur semblera,
Car mon vouloir ne changera
Pour mal que je puisse endurer.
Et, pour mieulx semblant demonstrer
Que trop m'est dure ma penance,
Vestu de noir, par desplaisance,
Me suis, sans prendre autre couleur,
Jusques a tant que ma douleur
Cessera et viengne en leesse
Pour le vouloir de ma maistresse.
Et tant suis de mon deuil content
Et me plaist tant en me blessant,
Quant je pençay que c'est pour celle
Qui sur toutes est depareille.
«Adoncq, dy je a par moy, amis,
N'es-tu content de t'estre mis
A celle ou tous biens habonde,
Fleur de beaulté de tout le monde?
Par bien servir tu advendras

Should I not say in every place:
I have no other malady?

Prince of Love, may God protect my soul
And body from false envious ones,
And may he grant to all true lovers
The seigniory of pleasure,
For as for me, so help me God,
I have no other malady.

From his appearance, he wasn't at all
Afflicted with melancholy
As I am at present.
For if he came joyously,
He goes away more joyous still.
He is not weary of carrying on his joy.
He does not fear sickness or death.
As he left, he sang loud and vigorously,
But soon he was in the woods,
And I could not hear his voice.
Then I resumed complaining of my sorrow
Piteously, and without hesitating
To call upon Love for mercy
And upon my beautiful lady too.
　But I do not know what they will do,
Nor if they will have mercy on me.
They can in every way destroy me
Or in little time restore me,
Whichever seems good to them,
For my desire will not change
For any pain that I might endure.
And in order better to show
That my suffering is too harsh for me,
Out of distress I have dressed in black,
Without wearing any other color,
Until such time that my sorrow ceases
And I arrive at happiness
By the desire of my mistress.
And I am so content with my grief
And so much does it please while wounding me,
When I considered that it is for her
Who above all women is without peer.
"Thus," I say to myself, "My friend,
Aren't you content to have placed yourself
With her in whom all virtues abound,
The flower of beauty of the entire world?
By serving well you will arrive

Aux biens que tu demanderas.»
Ainsi me sert une heure Espoir.
L'autre me quert sus Desespoir.
Desir m'assault et me fait guerre.
Souvenir souvant me fait braire
Et dire: «Helas! quant reverray je
Ma dame, ne quant parleray je
A sa plaisant belle beaulté?
Mes yeulx seront en obscurté
Et piteusement languiray
Jusques ad ce que la verray.
Quant y seray, ce sçay je bien,
Son vouloir ne sera le mien.
Ainsi ne sçay je lequel faire
D'y aler ou de moy retraire.»
    Lors pensay que je escriproye
Et que mes lectres lui envoyroie.

Lectres

Mon dieu, ma dame, ma maistresse,
A vostre tresplaisant jeunesse
Me recommande autant de foiz
Que l'on pourroit mectre de poix
L'ung sur l'autre jusques aux cieulx,
Tresdesirant de bien en mieulx
Oyr de voz doulces nouvelles,
Priant Dieu qu'elles soient telles
Que vous soyez tousjours en joye,
Car ainsi le desireroye.
Et s'il vous plaist de vostre humblesse,
Oyr ma piteuse destresse,
Vueillez sçavoir, ma redoubtee
Et ma dame tresbien amee,
Que mon cueur ne fait que languir,
Plaindre, plourer, souvant gemir,
Tant ay mis mon vueil fermement
A vous servir tresloyaulment
De cueur, de corps et de pensee.
Si vous supply, ma seule amee,
Que soit vostre doulx plaisir
De moy faire ung pou rejoir.
Si chanteray treslieement.
Je vueil chanter joyeusement *(see note)*
Et monstrer par joyeulx semblant
Que j'ay espoir d'avoir leesse
Et que, du gré de ma maistresse,

At the rewards that you will seek."
Thus at times does Hope serve me.
At other times Despair overcomes me.
Desire attacks and makes war upon me.
Memory often makes me cry out
And say, "Alas! When will I see again
My lady, and when will I speak
To her charming, fair beauty?
My eyes will be in darkness
And piteously will I languish
Until the time that I see her again.
When I am there, this know I well,
Her wish will not be mine.
Thus I don't know what to do,
To go there or to draw further away."
Then I thought that I would write
And that I would send my letter to her.

Letter

My god, my lady, my mistress,
To your very charming youth
I commend myself as many times
As one could place peas
One upon another up to the sky,
Desiring ever more and more
To hear sweet news of you,
Praying God that it be such
That you are still in joy,
For thus would I desire it.
And if you like, out of your humbleness,
To hear of my piteous distress,
Please know, my dreaded one
And my well beloved lady,
That my heart does nothing but languish,
Complain, weep, and often moan,
So firmly have I set my will
On serving you very loyally
In heart, in body, and in thought.
Thus I beseech you, my only beloved,
That it might be your sweet pleasure
To cause me to rejoice a bit.
Then will I sing very happily.
I wish to sing joyously *(see note)*
And to show by my joyous expression
That I have hope of gaining happiness
And that, by my mistress's will,

J'auray des biens treslargement.
Faictes moy de mercy present,
Belle et douce bien acomplie.
Faictes moy faire chiere lie.
Nulle que vous n'en a pouoir.
Faictes moy devestir le noir
Et me revestés de leesse.
Ne me souffrez plus en tristesse.
Remectez en joye mes plains.
A vous seule servant me clains,
Vous suppliant treshumblement
Que me tenez vostre servant.
Lors auray de richesse assez,
Car jamaiz ne seray lasséz
De vous cherir, servir et craindre.
Jamaiz nul jour ne me vueil faindre
D'acomplir vostre bon vouloir,
Vous faisant, ma dame, savoir
Qu'il me semble qu'auriés tort
De souffrir que j'eusse la mort,
Vous qui me povez secourir.
Or en faictes vostre plaisir,
Car se je muir, je dy, par m'ame,
Car c'est pour la plus belle dame
Qui marchast oncques dessus terre.
Pour Dieu, ne vous vueille desplaire,
Mon dieu, ma dame, mon seul mire,
Se m'enhardiz de vous escripre.
Je ne sçay si m'en avendra
Pis ou mieulx, lequel ce sera.
Et pour ce plus pour le present
Ne vous escripz de mon torment,
Maiz je prie Dieu de tresbon cueur
Que joye, santé et honneur
Vous doint et des biens a largesse,
Et voulenté que vostre humblesse
Si ait pitié de ma clamour,
Affin que cesse ma doulour.
Escript au lieu que vous dira
Cellui qui les vous portera.

Quant j'euz toute ma lectre dicte,
Close, seellee et escripte,
Je pensay que je l'envoyroye
Tout au plus tost que je pourroye
Vers ma dame hastivement.
Lors appellay tout maintenant

I will have an abundance of rewards.
Make me a gift of your mercy,
Oh lady, fair and gentle in every way.
Make me put on a happy countenance.
None but you has the power to do so.
Make me remove my black attire
And dress me in happiness instead.
Don't allow me to remain in sadness.
Turn my plaints into joy.
I call myself your servant alone,
Beseeching you very humbly
That you consider me your servant.
Then I will have wealth enough,
For never will I grow tired
Of cherishing, serving, and fearing you.
Not a single day do I wish to fail
To carry out your good wish,
Letting you know, my lady,
That it seems to me that you would do wrong
To allow me to suffer death,
You who can rescue me.
Now do what you please about it,
For if I die, upon my soul, I say
That it is for the most beautiful lady
Who ever walked upon this earth.
For God's sake, may it not displease you,
My god, my lady, my only physician,
If I embolden myself to write to you.
I don't know if it will turn out
Worse or better for me, which it will be.
And therefore no more for the present
Do I write to you about my torment,
But I pray earnestly to God
That he give you joy, health, and honor
And rewards in great abundance,
And a willingness that your humbleness
Thus have pity on my cries,
So that my sorrow might cease.
Written in the place that
He who carries this letter will tell you.

When I had composed my entire letter,
Closed it, sealed, and copied it,
I thought that I would send it
Just as soon as I could
Unto my lady in all haste.
Then I called at once

Ung mien tresloyal serviteur
Que j'aymoie de tout mon cueur,
Qui autrefoiz avoit esté
Vers celle ou est ma voulenté,
Et lui diz que tantost alast
Vers ma dame, et se hastast
Bien a haste de retourner,
Et s'a elle pouoit parler,
Qu'il luy requist treshumblement
Qu'amaindrir voulsist mon tourment
Et abaisier mes piteux plains
Et la douleur ou je remains.
Mon serviteur de moy partist
Et lui diz qu'il luy souvenist
De ce que dit je luy avoie.
Adonc print a aller sa voye
La ou il s'en devoit aler.
Seul demouray en mon vergier
Et a par moy diz: «Beaulx doulx dieux,
Seray je courroucé ou joyeulx?
Auray je joye ou desplaisir?
Hé, Dieu, quant pourra il venir?
J'ay espoir qu'il m'apportera
Nouvelle qui bien me plaira.
Seroit bien ma dame piteuse
De ma douleur tresangoisseuse?
Hé! plust a Dieu qu'il feist ainsi!
Amours, ayez de moy mercy!
Secourez moy a ceste foiz!»
Lors entrouuay auprés d'ung bois
Une voix, si me fut advis,
Qui me dist: «Beau, doulx amys,
Chante et mect peine de guerir,
Car je te dy, et sans mentir,
Que de ta dame auras grant bien
Et te retendra pour le sien.»
Plus n'en dist; ne sçay ou alla.
Maiz je sçay bien que de cela
Je me tins ung pou resjouy.
Maiz tantost qu'il se fut party,
Desespoir revint par derriere
Pour moy faire changer maniere.
Et lors ne sceuz je plus que dire.
Trop fut doloreux mon martire.

Ha, dame, fault il que je soye
Bouté hors de l'Ostel de Joye,
Par bien servir, par fort amer

A very loyal servant of mine
Whom I loved with all my heart,
Who formerly had been
To her who is the object of my wish,
And I told him to go at once
To my lady, and to hasten
As quickly as possible to return,
And if he was able to speak to her,
That he request her most humbly
That she wish to reduce my torment
And to ease my piteous laments
And the sorrow in which I remain.
My servant took his leave from me
And I told him to remember
What I had said to him.
Then he set out upon his way
There where he was supposed to go.
Alone I remained in my garden,
And I said to myself, "Fair sweet gods,
Will I be distressed or joyous?
Will I have joy or unhappiness?
Oh, God, when will he return?
I hope that he will bring to me
Tidings that will please me well.
Would my lady really have pity
Upon my very painful grief?
Oh, would to God that He bring it about!
Love, have mercy upon me!
Come to my aid at this time!"
Then I heard near a wood
A voice, so as it seemed to me,
That said to me, "Fair sweet friend,
Sing and make an effort to recover,
For I say to you, and without lying,
That from your lady you will have great good
And she will take you for her own."
It said no more; I don't know where it went.
But I know well that because of this
I felt myself a little gladdened.
But just as soon as it was gone,
Despair returned from behind
In order to make me change my mood.
And then I no longer knew what to say.
Too painful was my suffering.
    Oh lady, must I be expelled
From the Inn of Joy,
For serving well, for loving strongly

Vostre belle beaulté sans per?
Me lairez vous par desespoir
Si longuement vestu de noir
User tous les temps de ma vie?
Ha, Mort, fay de moy departie.
Ma douleur m'est trop ennuyeuse
Et trop durement angoisseuse.
Moy plaignant, feiz une chanson
Dont j'ay escript cy la fachon,
Maiz point ne l'ay voulu chanter.

Chanson

Je ne sçay plus que demander
Quant riens ne me voulez donner.
Ma demande ne vauldroit riens.
Deserté je suis de tous biens
Aujourd'uy plus que devant yer.

Mon dueil se prent a efforcer
Et ma joye a racourcer.
Pitié ne veult estre des miens.
Je ne sçay plus que demander
Quant riens ne me voulez donner.
Ma demande ne vauldroit riens.

Ne me laissez desesperer,
Maiz me vueillez reconforter.
A vous seulle servant me tiens,
Et humblement requerir viens
Mort ou mercy, pour m'abregier.

Je ne sçay plus que demander
Quant riens ne me voulez donner.
Ma demande ne vauldroit riens.
Deserté je suis de tous biens,
Aujourd'uy plus que devant yer.

Mieulx vault taire que folie dire.
Je me sçay bien tenir de rire
De ce que j'ay dit mon vouloir
A celle qui a le pouoir
De remectre mon cueur en joye.
Maiz je suis plus que ne souloie,
Pensifz et mellencolieux
Depuis que lui diz mes douleurs.
Maiz je cuidoie le mieulx faire.

Your fair beauty without peer?
Will you let me spend my whole life
So long a time dressed in black
Because of despair?
Oh Death, bring about my end.
My sorrow is too painful
And causes me too great an anguish.
    Complaining thus, I made a song
Of which I have written here the words,
But I did not wish at all to sing it.

Song

I know no longer what to ask
When nothing do you wish to grant.
My asking would amount to nought.
Deprived I am of every good
Today more than ever before.

My grief begins to grow stronger
And my joy to decrease.
Pity does not want to take my side.
I know no longer what to ask
When nothing do you wish to grant.
My asking would amount to nought.

Do not allow me to despair,
But instead, please comfort me.
I hold myself your servant alone
And humbly do I come to ask,
In short, for death or mercy.

I know no longer what to ask
When nothing do you wish to grant.
My asking would amount to nought.
Deprived I am of every good,
Today more than ever before.

Better to be silent than speak folly.
I can easily refrain from laughing
About the fact that I told my wish
To her who has the power
To return my heart to joy.
But more than I was accustomed,
I am pensive and melancholy
Since I told her of my sorrows.
But I believed to be doing the best.

Or ne m'en puis je retraire.
Ainsi que menoye tel fin,
Plain de lermes, le chief enclin,
Vy entrer dedans le vergier
Ung jeune joliz escuier
Qui durement se complaignoit
Et bien douloreux ressembloit.
Et disoit en façon de plainte:
«Amours, je seuffre douleur mainte.
Jadiz soloye chanter et rire,
Et Douleur me veult desconfire
A tort et sans nulle achoison.
Ceuffreres vous tel desraison,
Moy qui vous serfz si loyaulment?
Vostre hostel vauldroit piz vrayement
Se j'avoye descort a Leesse.
Amours, remectez a l'adresse
Ma dame de moy secourir.
Lors me verrez bien resjouir
Et faire corner menestrelz.
Amours, je vous supply, souffrez
Que de vous aye allegement.»
Ainsi qu'il s'alloit complaignant
Vint a luy une damoiselle,
Jeune, gente, jolie et belle,
Et luy dist: «Ma dame m'envoye
Vous dire que soyez en joye.
Or sus, avecques moy venez
Et plus ne vous desconfortez.»
Moult doulcement la mercya
Et avecques elle s'en ala.
Et moy, que demouré tout seul,
Recommençay mon piteux duel,
Disant, «Amours, vous despartés
Des biens largement et assez
A tout le monde fors qu'a moy.
Helas! si ne sçay je pourquoy.
Je ne cuide avoir forfait,
Envers vous riens ne meffait
Dont je deusse avoir tel peine
Qu'il n'est heure en la sepmaine
Que mon mal ne voise en croissant.
Mes jours finent en languissant.
Ha! Mort, venez! A vous me rens!»
Lors ou vergier entra dedans
Mon serviteur, secretement,
Et me salua humblement.

Now I cannot take it back.
While I carried on in this way,
Full of tears, my head inclined,
I saw enter into the garden
A handsome young squire
Who was complaining bitterly
And seemed to be very sorrowful.
And he said, in the manner of a lament:
"Love, I suffer many a sorrow.
Formerly I would sing and laugh,
And Sorrow wishes to destroy me
Wrongly and without any cause.
Will you allow something so unjust,
For me, who serve you so loyally?
Being in your service would be worth very little
If Happiness and I were not in accord.
Love, set my lady back
On the path of helping me.
Then you will see me greatly rejoice
And make the minstrels blow their horns.
Love, I beseech you, allow me
To have some relief from you."
While he went, lamenting thus,
A young woman came up to him,
Young, gracious, pretty, and fair,
And said to him, "My lady sends me
To tell you to be in joy.
Now get up, come with me
And don't be distressed any longer."
He thanked her very gently
And he went away with her.
And I, who remained alone,
Recommenced my piteous grief,
Saying, "Love, you distribute your goods
Abundantly and sufficiently
To everyone except to me.
Alas! I don't know why it's so.
I don't think that I have committed a fault
Or done anything wrong to you
For which I ought to have such punishment
That there is not an hour in the week
That my pain does not keep growing.
My days end in languishing.
Oh Death, come! I surrender to you!"
Then entered within the garden
My servant, secretly,
And humbly he greeted me.

Si luy demanday, «Quelz nouvelles?»
Il me dist que bonnes et belles:
Que ma dame me saluoit
Et que mes lectres prins avoit
Et fait lui avoit bonne chiere.
Mais Dangier si estoit derriere
Qu'a elle parler ne pouvoit
Ne luy dire ce qu'il vouloit,
Fors seulement au despartir,
Luy dist que se vouloie venir
En ung lieu ou empris avoye,
Que d'elle bonne chiere aroye.
Plus a elle il ne parla.
Congié print et s'en retourna.
Quant il ot dit tout son rapport,
Adonc le conjuray tresfort
Qu'il me dist qui lui en sembloit
Et se bien ou mal me vouloit.
Lors me jura par son serement
Qu'il luy est adviz que vrayement
Que j'aroye une foiz sa grace.
    Dieu vueille que ainsi se face
Que sa grace puisse acquerir.
C'est tout le bien que je desir.
Et se une foiz la puis avoir,
Je feray mon loyal devoir
De la servir si loyaulment
De cueur, de corps, de pensement,
Qu'oncques dame ne fut cherie,
Craincte, doubtee ne servie
Ainsi que je la serviray,
Car tout son vueil acompliray
A mon pouoir, de bien en mieulx,
Tant que son cueur sera joyeulx
D'avoir le mien pour le servir.
Ha! Amours, laissez moy venir
Aux biens de vostre seigneurie.
Ostez moy de mellencolie
Et mectez mon cueur hors d'ennoy.
    Lors commençay a faire ung lay
Et l'ay nommé cy en escript
«Lay de plour,» actendant respit.

Lay

Amours, Amours, jadiz souloie
Chanter, dancer et mener joye,

Then I asked, "What news?"
He told me that it was good and fair:
That my lady greeted me
And that she had taken my letter
And had made him good cheer.
But Danger was so close behind
That he could not speak to her
Nor tell her what he wished,
Except only as he left,
She told him if I wished to come
To a place that I had chosen,
That I would have good cheer from her.
No more did he speak to her.
He took his leave and returned.
When he had given his whole report,
Then I begged him very strongly
To tell me how she seemed
And if she wished me good or ill.
Then he swore to me with an oath
That truly it appeared to him
That one day I would have her grace.
    God wish that it be so
That I might obtain her grace.
It's the only reward that I desire.
And if one day I can have it,
I will do my loyal duty
To serve her so loyally
In heart, in body, in thought,
That never was any lady cherished,
Feared, dreaded, or served
As I will serve her,
For I will carry out her every wish
Within my power, better and better,
So that her heart will be joyous
To have my heart to serve it.
Oh, Love! Let me come
To the rewards of your domain.
Take away my melancholy
And put my heart beyond reach of pain.
    Then I began to write a lay
And I named it here in writing
"The Lai of Tears," awaiting relief.

Lai

Love, Love, formerly I used to
Sing, dance, and carry on joy,

Et maintenant
Douleur m'assault et me guerroye.
De Desespoir suis a la voye.
Par hardement
De trop parler, suis maintenant
Assailly doloreusement
De Desconfort,
Qui me maine si durement
Que mort seray prochainement
Par son effort.

Se je muir, n'aurés vous pas tort
De souffrir que j'endure mort
Pour bien servir?
Je diray que Loyaulté dort
Quant ne me donne reconfort
Pour resjouir
Mon cueur, qui ne fait que languir
Par le pourchas d'Ardant Desir.
Et nuit et jour
Ne fait que plourer et gemir,
Ne nul bien ne peult recueillir
Fors que douleur.

Ayez pitié de ma clamour,
Ma maistresse et ma seule amour.
Soyez piteuse
De me veoir en telle langour
Et d'oyr mon trespiteux plour.
Gente, joyeuse,
Soiez de moy guerir soingneuse.
Belle, plaisant et gracieuse,
Vous ferés bien:
Mectez ma vie tenebreuse
En parfaicte vie joyeuse.
Vostre me tieng.

Mon cueur est vostre, non pas mien,
Car vostre gracieux maintien
Le m'a osté
Et l'a prins et vueil qu'i soit sien.
Donnez luy ou leesse ou rien.
Ma voulenté
Est d'endurer la cruaulté
D'Amours, pensant que Loyaulté
Me secourra;
Et me donrra joyeuseté,

And now
Sorrow assails and makes war upon me.
I am on the path of Despair.
Because of my boldness
In saying too much, I am now
Assailed sorrowfully
By Distress,
Which treats me so harshly
That soon will I be dead
By its efforts.

If I die, will you not be wrong
To allow me to suffer death
For serving well?
I will say that Loyalty is asleep
When it does not give me comfort
To gladden
My heart, which does nothing but languish
At the instigation of Burning Desire.
Both night and day,
It does nothing but cry and moan,
Nor can it collect any reward
Other than sorrow.

Have pity on my cry,
My mistress and my only love.
Take pity
To see me in such languishing
And to hear my piteous weeping.
Gracious, joyful lady,
Be attentive to healing me.
Fair, charming, and gracious one,
You will do well:
Turn my darkened life
Into a perfect life of joy.
Take me as your own.

My heart is yours, not my own,
For your gracious conduct
Took it from me
And seized it and wants it as its own.
Give it either happiness or nothing.
My wish
Is to endure the cruelty
Of Love, thinking that Loyalty
Will aid me;
And that she will give me joy,

Celle ou remaint toute beaulté,
Quant lui plaira.

Ma douleur se retournera
En leesse, et revendra
Mon dueil en joye.
Espoir me dist qu'ainsi sera.
Bel Accueil dist qu'il luy dira
Qu'amé je soye.
Helas! s'estre amé je pouoye,
Plus rien je ne demanderoye.
J'aroye assés.
Mais Reffuz tresfort me guerroye,
Que je ne sçay que dire doye,
Tant suis mactéz.

Ne doy je mie estre lasséz
D'avoir tant de maulx enduréz
Et tant de paine?
Dieu amoureux, reconfortez
Mon cueur qui est desconfortéz,
Car Mort le maine
Et veult mener a son demaine.
A! Pitié! Dame souveraine!
Faictes mon dueil
Cesser une foiz la sepmaine.
Mectez moy hors de ceste paine
Que je recueil

Ou je suis mort dessus le sueil
Par Desir, dont suis en l'escueil.
Et je ne puys,
Se n'est par vostre tresdoulx vueil,
Garyr. Je suis, plus que ne sueil,
Prouchain de l'uis
De Desespoir. Assailly suis
De Desconfort. Et je ne truis
Qui me sequeure,
Combien que a la mort je suis.
Si fauldra il que soye conduiz
A son demeure.

Ne doye je mauldire l'eure
Par qui gemis souvant et pleure,
Et le regard
Qui tant pleu m'a a desmesure?
Par luy ay eu cest encloeure.

The one in whom resides all beauty,
When it pleases her.

My sorrow will then be turned
Into happiness, and my grief
Will turn into joy.
Hope tells me that it will be so.
Fair Welcome says that it will instruct her
That I be loved.
Alas! if only I could be loved,
I would ask for nothing more.
I would have enough.
But Rejection wars against me strongly,
So that I don't know what I should say,
So completely am I beaten.

Should I not be worn out
From having endured so many pains
And so much suffering?
God of Love, comfort
My heart which is distressed,
For Death rules it
And wishes to lead it into his domain.
Oh, pity! my sovereign lady,
Make my grief
Cease just once a week.
Release me from this suffering
That I receive

There where I am dead upon the threshold
Because of Desire, in whose grip I am.
And I cannot,
Unless it is by your sweet will,
Recover. I am, more than I am accustomed,
Near to the door
Of Despair. I am assailed
By Discouragement. And I don't find
Anyone to help me,
However close I am to death.
Thus I will have to be led off
To its abode.

Should I not curse the fate
By which I often moan and cry,
And the look
Which pleased me so excessively?
From it I received this wound.

Ce fut le dart
Qui m'a navré et main et tart.
Par luy mon cueur tressault et art.
Dieu amoureux,
Seray je de joye bastart?
Haroy je bien gecté hazart
D'estre joyeulx?

N'ay je esté mellencolieux,
Jeune, gente, belle aux beaulx yeulx,
Longue saison?
Ne me souffrez plus envieux.
Par Dieu, belle, vous ferés mieulx,
Car sans raison
Je suis long temps sans garison
Et ay des maulx a grant foison,
Dont je souppire
De ce que je pers ma saison.
En douleur suis en garnison.
Doy je bien rire?

Dictes, me doit il bien souffire?
Je sens de tous les maulz le pire.
Ne fust Espoir,
Mort fusse, sans plus contredire.
Mais il dit qu'i me doibt souffire
De remanoir
Son serviteur, vestu de noir,
Actendant de Mercy avoir
Quant lui plaira.
Et que ce soit son bon vouloir;
Ma leesse, a dire voir,
Retournera.

Faire en peult ce qu'elle vouldra.
Ma voulenté ne changera
Que pelerin
Je ne soye le temps qui vendra.
J'ay espoir que mieulx m'en sera
En la parfin.
Si prie de cueur saint Valentin
Qu'a moy secourir soit enclin
Contre douleur
Qui me tient et seoir et matin.
Et pour ce cy vueil faire fin
Du Lay de Plour.

It was the dart
Which wounded me both early and late.
Because of it, my heart trembles and burns.
God of Love,
Will I be Joy's bastard child?
Will I have rolled an unlucky number
In the game of joy?

Haven't I been melancholy,
Oh young, gracious beauty with fair eyes,
For a long time?
Leave me no longer in a state of desire.
By God, fair one, you will do better,
For without reason
I am long without healing
And I have an abundance of pain,
For which I sigh
For the fact that I lose my well-being.
I am locked up in sorrow.
Should I then laugh?

Tell me, should I be satisfied?
I feel the worst of all pains.
Were it not for Hope,
I would be dead, without further denial.
But it tells me that it should suffice
For me
To remain its servant, dressed in black,
Waiting to have Mercy
When it pleases her.
And may this be her wish;
My happiness, to tell the truth,
Will return.

She can do whatever she likes.
My wish will not change
To be a pilgrim
During the time to come.
I hope that it will be better for me
In the end.
Thus I pray from my heart to Saint Valentine
That he be disposed to succor me
Against the sorrow
Which possesses me both evening and morning.
And thus do I wish to bring to an end
The Lai of Tears.

Alors que j'euz mon lay finé
Et en mon livre enregistré,
En mon dormant m'estoit advis
Qu'aprochoie prés du pays
Ou demouroit ma seule joye,
Celle qui tant veoir desiroye.
Lors pensay que je l'yroye voir
Pour ma douleur ramantevoir,
Savoir s'il m'en seroit de mieulx.
    Maiz je la treuve, se m'aist Dieux,
Si environnee de Reffuz
Que je en suis du tout esperduz.
Maiz ses reffuz sont si plaisans
Et ses dangiers si advenans
Que plus me plaist son escondire
Que tous les biens qu'on pourroit dire
Avoir, s'il ne me venoit d'elle.
Or est empiré ma querrelle,
Car jadiz vivoye en espoir.
Maintenant suis en desespoir.
Car l'autre yer, quant je me party,
Sans congié d'elle desparty,
Cuidant mussier ma maladie.
Maiz je congneuz tost ma folie
Et sçay qu'elle en eust desplaisir.
Lors luy envoyay requerir
Qu'il luy pleust le me pardonner
Et ma douleur reconforter.
J'euz le pardon sans reconfort,
Et sceuz qu'elle n'estoit d'accord
De me vouloir sien retenir.
Pour ce piteusement languir
Me fault sans avoir garison
Des griefz maulx dont j'en ay foison.
Pour ce j'ay fait une balade.
Languissant, durement malade,
L'ay escript et mis en mon livre.
Si vous plaist, vous la povez lire.

Balade

Mort et non mort, languissant en tristesse,
Et esloingné de tous biens amoureux,
Vestu de noir et tout nu de leesse,
Environné de Reffuz envieux,
Plain de penser tresmellencolieux
Suy pour ma dame qui ne me veult amer.

Then when I had finished my lai
And recorded it in my book,
As I was sleeping, it seemed to me
That I drew near to the country
Where resided my only joy,
She whom I so much desired to see.
Then I thought that I would go see her
In order to remind her of my sorrow
And to see if I would fare any better.
But I find her, so help me God,
So well surrounded by Rejection
That I am completely discomfited.
But her rebuffs are so pleasing
And her disdain is so appealing
That her refusal pleases me more
Than all the goods that one could think
Of having, if they came not from her.
Thus has my case grown worse,
For formerly I lived in hope.
Now I am in despair.
For the other day, when I departed,
I left without taking leave of her,
Thinking to hide my malady.
But I quickly recognized my folly
And I know that she was displeased.
Then I sent to her to ask
That it please her to pardon me
And to relieve my sorrow.
I had the pardon without the relief,
And I learned that she was not disposed
To wish to keep me as her own.
Therefore piteously must I languish
Without having any cure
For the grievous pains of which I have so many.
Therefore I have composed a ballade.
Languishing, extremely ill,
I wrote it and put it in my book.
If you like, you may read it.

Ballade

Dead and not dead, languishing in sadness,
And far removed from all rewards of love,
Dressed in black and naked of happiness,
Surrounded by envious Rejection,
Full of most melancholy thought
Am I for my lady, who does not wish to love me.

Helas! Amours, vueillez luy conseiller
Que son vouloir soit et sa doulce grace
De moy guerir et mon mal conforter,
Car ma douleur de tout mon cueur efface.

Laz! fauldra il que fine ma jeunesse
En plours, en plains, en soupirs doloreux?
Aray je ja de reconfort l'adresse?
Sera tousjours mon cueur si angoisseux,
Jeune, gente, doulce, belle, aux beaulx yeulx?
Sans espoir, suis prés de desesperer.
Vous plaist il bien me laisser definer?
Vostre vouloir est il que je trespasse?
Confortez moy, qu'i m'en est bien mestier,
Car ma douleur du tout mon cuer efface.

J'envoye vers vous requerir, vostre humblesse,
Pardon de ce que suis malgracieulx.
Car mon grief mal me destraint et me blesse
Si durement que ne sçay, se m'aist Dieux,
Que faire doye, tant suis fort desireux
De acquerir ce que ne puis trouver:
C'est vostre amour, belle dame sans per,
Maiz prés de moy ne voulez estre en place,
Dont je sens bien qu'il me fault enrager,
Car ma douleur du tout mon cuer efface.

Mon dieu, ma dame, ma tresdoulce maistresse,
Guerir ne puis de ma dure destresse
Se n'est par vous. Mandez moy que je face.
Confortez moy, s'il vous plaist, ma deesse,
Car ma douleur du tout mon cueur efface.

Ainsi que finoie ma balade,
De douleur durement malade,
Souspiroie moult tendrement,
En regrectant piteusement
Les douleurs que reçoy pour elle,
En disant a par moy, «C'est celle
Qui de biens toutes autres passe.
C'est le rubiz qui tous efface!»
Ainsi qu'estoie en ce penser,
Vy entrer dedans le vergier
Ung messagier qui vint vers moy,
Disant, «Douleur m'envoye a toy
Et te mande qu'il vient logier
Dedans ton cueur sans atargier,

Alas! Love, please counsel her
That her will and her sweet grace might be
To cure me and relieve my pain,
For my sorrow totally blots out my heart.

Alas! Am I to end my youth
In tears, in plaints, in mournful sighs?
Will I never find the way to relief?
Will my heart remain forever in such anguish,
Oh young, gracious, gentle beauty with fair eyes?
Lacking hope, I am near to despairing.
Does it please you well to let me meet my end?
Is it your will that I should perish?
Comfort me, for I need it badly,
For my sorrow totally blots out my heart.

I send to you to ask, your humbleness,
For pardon that I have been ungracious.
For my grievous pain constrains and wounds me
So greatly that, so help me God,
I know not what to do, so greatly do I desire
To obtain that which I cannot find:
It is your love, fair lady without peer,
But you do not wish to be anywhere near to me,
For which I feel that I surely must go mad,
For my sorrow totally blots out my heart.

My God, my lady, my most gentle mistress,
I cannot recover from my harsh distress
If not through you. Tell me what to do.
Comfort me, please, my goddess,
For my sorrow totally blots out my heart.

When thus I finished my ballade,
Extremely ill with sorrow,
I sighed very tenderly,
Lamenting piteously
The sorrows that I receive for her,
Saying to myself, "She is the one
Who surpasses all other women in goodness.
She is the ruby who eclipses all."
While I was in this thought,
I saw enter into the garden
A messenger who came to me,
Saying, "Sorrow sends me to you
And declares to you that it comes to lodge
Within your heart without delay,

Et avec luy Reffuz sera,
Ne Dangier pas ne lessera.
Avec foison de soudoiers,
Et tantost les apparceverez.
Et si m'a ditque Souvenir,
Acompaigné d'Ardant Desir,
De vostre cueur ne bougeroit
Et compaignie lui tiendroit.»
Plus n'en dist; de moy se partist,
Ne ne sceuz tantost qu'il devint.
Lors commançay crier, «Helas!
Amours, suis je dedans voz las
Envelopé si durement
Que mon cueur ne sent que torment?
De jour en jour ma douleur croist,
N'un seul plaisir il ne reçoit.
Quant de ma dame suis prochains,
De s'amour me trouve loingtains,
Et quant loing suis, Ardant Desir
De la veoir me fait souvenir.»
Et pour ce, durement malade,
Ay cy escript une balade.

Balade

Doleur me mande qu'il retient sa forteresse
Dedans mon cueur, pour estre en garnison,
Et qu'avec luy, il retiendra Tristesse.
Ces deux auront soudoiers a foison.
Car avec eulx, pour fournir la maison,
Sera Desir, pour faire l'assaillie,
Et Souvenir, le vaillant champion.
Ces deux desja ont leur place choisie.

Ilz ont baillé la grosse tour maitresse
A Desconfort et le maistre donjon,
Et ont mandé Desespoir qu'il s'appresse
Et qu'il se haste, car il en est saison.
Dangier sera logié, car c'est raison,
Et avec luy Reffuz, n'en doubtés mie.
Chacun aura en sa main ung baston,
Ces deux desja ont leur place choisie.

Tous ceulx la ont juré que se Leesse
Aprouche prés, ilz l'auront en prison.
Maiz j'ay grant paour que gueres ne s'apresse
Se par Pitié je ne truis garison.

And with it will be Rejection,
Nor will it leave Danger behind.
Together with a multitude of soldiers,
You will soon perceive them.
And it also told me that Memory,
Accompanied by Burning Desire,
Would not budge from your heart
And would keep it company."
He said no more; he departed from me,
Nor did I know what happened to him.
Then I began to cry, "Alas!
Love, am I within your bonds
So strongly wrapped
That my heart feels only torment?
From day to day my sorrow grows,
And it receives not a single pleasure.
When I am close to my lady,
I find myself distant from her love,
And when I am far, Burning Desire
Makes me remember seeing her."
And thus, grievously ill,
I have written here a ballade.

Ballade

Sorrow declares to me that it keeps its fortress
Within my heart, and will be garrisoned there,
And that with it, it will retain Sadness.
These two will have soldiers aplenty.
For with them, in order to strengthen the house,
Will be Desire, to carry out the assault,
And Memory, the valiant champion.
These two have already chosen their position.

They have handed over the large main tower
And the main donjon to Discouragement,
And they have ordered Despair to draw near
And to hasten, for now is its time.
Danger will be given lodging, for it is proper,
And with it Rejection, have no doubt.
Each will bear a club in its hand.
These two have already chosen their position.

All of these have sworn that if Happiness
Comes near, they'll throw it into prison.
But I greatly fear that it will hardly approach
Unless from Pity I find some relief.

Helas! Amours, vous faictes desraison
De me tenir en si piteuse vie,
En plours, en plains; c'est ma destruction.
Ces deux desja ont leur place choisie.

Balade

De plus en plus j'apparçoy ma doulour
Renouveller et accroistre mes plains.
Je sens mon cuer dedans le Lac de Plour,
Et de plourer mes yeulx en sont destains.
Mon cueur est ja de tous poins si estains,
Je suis muet quant je deusse parler,
Vueiller me faut lors que deusse dormer,
Et tout ce fait celle qui est sans per,
Qui en ce point me veult faire languir.

Desir me tient en ses laz nuyt et jour,
Et Souvenir me prent entre ses mains.
Bel Acueil vient m'acueillir en sa tour,
En me disant, «Tu voiz que ne me fains
De toy amer. Pour bien amé te clains.
Maiz plus avant ne te vueil accorder,
Ne nul autre ne vueil mien retenir.»
Tout ce me dist celle qui est sans per,
Qui en ce point me veult faire languir.

Comment pourray je delaisser ma clamour
Ne les pensers dont suis si fort actains?
Comment auray je puissance ne vigour
De soustenir les maulx dont suis estrains
Ne la tristesse dont suis tout en tout tains
Quant ma princesse si ne me veult donner
Le don d'«amy», ne pour sien retenir?
Par elle fault mon cueur desesperer
Qui en ce point me veult faire languir.

Balade

Puisqu'a la belle plaist moy faire finir,
J'en suis content, ainsi m'aist vrayement Dieux,
Et ayme mieulx pour elle recueillir
Autant de maulx que fist onc amoureux
Que par nul autre redevenir joyeux.
Or en face tout a son bon vouloir,
Car en ce point mon cueur vueil remanoir.
Mes yeulx le veullent et mon penser aussi.

Alas! Love, you do great wrong
To keep me in so piteous a state,
In tears, in plaints; it is my destruction.
These two have already chosen their position.

Ballade

More and more I see my sorrow
Renew and my laments increase.
I feel my heart within the Lake of Tears,
And my eyes are all washed out from weeping.
My heart is already in every way so lifeless,
I am completely mute when I should speak,
I must stay awake when I am supposed to sleep,
And all this does she who is without peer,
Who in this state wishes to make me languish.

Desire holds me in its bonds by night and day,
And Memory seizes me between its hands.
Fair Welcome comes to welcome me into its tower,
Saying to me, "You see that I am not slow
To love you. I declare you to be well loved.
But more than that I do not wish to grant,
Nor do I wish to keep any other as my own."
All this says to me she who is without peer,
Who in this state wishes to make me languish.

How will I be able to leave off my cries
And the thoughts by which I am so strongly afflicted?
How will I have the power and strength
To bear the pains by which I am oppressed
And the sadness with which I am totally stricken
When my princess does not wish to grant
The gift of "lover," nor keep me as her own?
My heart is doomed to despair because of her
Who in this state wishes to make me languish.

Ballade

Since it pleases the fair one to have me die,
I am content, so truly help me God,
And I would rather receive because of her
As many pains as a lover ever did
Than from another woman to have joy.
So let her do anything she pleases,
For in this state my heart wishes to stay.
My eyes desire it and my thought as well.

Et dient eulx deux, «On ne pourroit veoir
Plus belle dame, de tous biens sans nul sy.»

Sa grant beaulté me mect le souvenir
Dedans mon cueur qui me tient en tous lieux,
Et d'autre part, me suyt Ardant Desir,
Qui me contraint d'estre fort desireux
A revoyer son gent corps gracieux.
Et son reffuz me mect en desespoir
Quant ne luy plaist pour sien moy recevoir
Ne de mon mal avoir nulle mercy.
Non obstant, on ne pourroit veoir
Plus belle dame, de tous biens sans nul sy.

Que vous diray? Je ne foiz que gemir
Et souspirer, comme tresdoloureux.
J'ay tous les maulx que on pourroit sentir.
Je suis pensifz et mellencolieux.
De la servir je suis tresenvieux,
Et si crains fort prés d'elle remanoir,
Car j'ay doubte qu'on puisse aparcevoir
La voulenté qu'ay eue jusqu'a cy
D'elle amer, car on ne peult veoir
Plus belle dame, de tous biens sans nul sy.

Ainsi comme je baladoye
En songant, et me complaignoye,
Advis m'estoit qu'estoie vers celle
Qui est du monde la plus belle,
Et que mercy lui requeroye,
Qu'il luy pleust moy remectre en joye,
En luy disant, comme tout sien:
«Mon cueur est vostre; il n'est pas mien.
Je vous prie, vueillez le garder.»
Lors me faisoit ung doulx dangier
Et ung si gracieux reffuz
Que j'estoye du tout esperduz,
En me disant, «Je ne vueil mie
Garder tout, maiz une partie
De vostre cueur bien garderay,
Et l'autre si vous renderay.»
Mais recevoir ne le vouloie,
Ne dire rien ne luy savoie.
Maiz plus avant elle disoit
Que nul sien elle ne retendroit,
Ne ne seroit plus point qu'a moy.
Adonc me taisoie tout coy

And they both say, "One could never see
A fairer lady, faultless in every way."

Her great beauty places the memory
Within my heart which binds me everywhere,
And furthermore, Burning Desire pursues me,
Which compels me strongly to desire
To see her noble gracious self again.
And her rejection puts me in despair
When she does not wish to take me as her own
Nor to have any mercy on my pain.
Nevertheless, one could not see
A fairer lady, faultless in every way.

What will I tell you? All I do is moan
And sigh, as one who is very sorrowful.
I have all the pains that one could ever feel.
I am pensive and melancholy.
I have a great desire to serve her,
And yet I greatly fear remaining near her,
For I am afraid that someone could perceive
The wish that I have had until now
To love her, for one can not see
A fairer lady, faultless in every way.

While I was composing my ballades
In my dream, and while lamenting,
It seemed to me that I drew near to her
Who is the fairest lady in the world,
And that I asked her for her mercy,
That it please her to restore me to joy,
Saying to her, as one entirely hers:
"My heart is yours; it is not my own.
I beg you, please keep it and protect it."
Then she responded with a sweet disdain
And with so gracious a rebuff
That I was entirely confounded,
Saying to me, "I do not want
To keep it all, but one portion
Of your heart I will surely keep,
And the other I will return to you."
But I did not wish to accept it,
Nor could I say anything to her.
But she then went on to say
That she would have no one as her own,
Nor would she ever be only mine.
Then I fell completely silent

Ne plus ne luy savoie que dire.
Maiz, affin qu'on ne veist mon ire,
Adieu humblement luy disoie,
Et, en luy disant, je veoye
Qu'elle pensoit tresdurement.
    Helas! quel est son pensement?
Est il piteux de mon martire?
Je ne sçay que penser ne dire.
Je vueil en la servant finer.
Je n'oseroye retourner
Vers elle en jour de ma vie,
Qu'on ne congneust ma maladie.
Loing d'elle ne pourroye vivre.
Ainsi me vois je desconfire
Et mectre a mort a mes deux mains.
A! Amours, a bon droit me plains,
De vous, se me laisez mourir
Si piteusement et fenir
Que mon ame en soit dampnee
Et ma vie deshonnoree
De moy mectre mesmes a mort.
Il vault mieulx que, par desconfort,
Je laisse de tous poins le monde
Et que moy mesmes me confonde.
Or seray je deshonnoré,
En disant que, par lascheté,
Seray esloingné de la guerre.
Las! je ne sçay garison querre.
Je n'ay vouloir a riens penser
Fors seulement a abreger
Ma vie pour haster ma mort.
    Ainsi qu'estoye en tel descort,
Je pensay que je requerroye
Ung de combatre, et escriproye
Devers luy tout ysnellement
Pour faire mon definement,
A mon pouoir, plus honnorable
Et a mon cueur plus agreable
De definer en ce party
Que nul des deux autres party.
Lors feiz unes lectres pour armes,
Seellees du seel de mes armes,
Lesquelles sont cy en escript
Affin que mieulx m'en souvenist.

And I didn't know what more to say to her.
But so that no one perceive my anger,
I humbly said goodbye to her,
And while speaking to her, I saw
That she was very deep in thought.
Alas! What is her thought?
Is it piteous of my suffering?
I don't know what to think or say.
I want to die in serving her.
I would not dare return to her
Any day of my life,
Lest someone perceive my malady.
Far from her I could not live.
Thus I am going to destroy myself
And put myself to death with my own two hands.
Oh, Love! I rightly complain about you,
If you allow me to die
And end so piteously
That my soul will be damned
And my life dishonored
For having put myself to death.
It is better that, out of discouragement,
I leave the world entirely
And that I destroy myself.
Then I will be dishonored,
When they say that out of cowardice
I will have fled from the battle.
Alas! I don't know how to seek a cure.
I have no wish to think of anything
Except only how to shorten my life
In order to hasten my death.
While I was in such a turmoil,
I thought that I would challenge
Someone to combat, and that I'd write
To him very quickly
In order to make my death
More honorable, to the extent I could,
And more agreeable to my heart
To end in this way
Than either of the two other options.
Then I composed a summons to arms,
Sealed with the seal of my arms,
Which is here in writing
So that I might better remember it.

Lectres Closes

Ou nom de Dieu, de Nostre Dame et de ma dame saincte Katherine, pour l'amour de ma mortel folie, a vous sire de Cornoaille, envoye mes lectres faisans savoir, comme a ung des plus vaillans chevaliers et des plus renomméz du party du roy d'Angleterre, que je, pour l'achoison de mon cuer que j'ay perdu nouvellement, ay empris de vous requerir par ces presentes de combatre. Et ne le tenez pour orgueil, que affin que saichez pourquoy j'ay entrepris ceste querelle, vueillez savoir que j'ay amé et ameray toute ma vie la non pareille dame du monde. Or est ainsi qu'il ne luy plaist mon cueur tenir pour serviteur, et a ce puis apparcevoir qu'elle veult abreger ma mort. Et puisqu'il est ainsi que celle qui de tous biens les autres passe desire mon definement, vous envoye requerir de mon tresdoloreux oultrage. Car je sçay bien que les biens sont en vous si grans que, quant au fait des armes de vous, ne vendroy je a au dessus, se ce n'estoit que ma seulle maistresse ne fust piteuse de mon deffinement. Se n'est par elle, je ne puis riens valoir. En elle maint ma vertu et ma force. Demouré suis sans cueur, sans honneur, sans pouoir. Or povez veoir que n'aurez guere affaire a moy confire. Maiz nostre jeu sera ainsi party. Quant vous m'aurez oultré et desconfit, vous ne prendrez fors que la vie de moy. Car en ce point vueil ma vie finer. Et s'il estoit ainsi que celle qui a le pouoir de moy remectre mon cueur en joye par son bien me donnoit vertu de vous mectre a desconfiture, je ne vouldroie de vous tant seulement avoir, sans plus, que ung dyament pour envoyer a celle qui desconfit vous auroit. Et affin que je maintiengne ces lectres vrayes, les ay seellees du propre seel de mes armes.

Quant j'euz toutes mes lectres dictes *(see note)*
Et dedans mon livre escriptes,
Mon cueur si se print a songier,
En maudissant tresfort Dangier,
Qui me mect a destruction.
Lors me vint en advision
Qu'Espoir si me juroit moult fort
Que de ma dame auroye confort
Et seroye pour amy claméz
Et de s'amour reconfortéz,
Et que tresfort luy desplaisoit
Du mal que mon cueur recevoit.
Ainsi me tient Espoir en vie.
Autrement ne vesquisse mye.
Et ainsi qu'en ce point estoie
Et en Espoir me confortoye,
Je regarday tout bellement
Ung qui estoit secrettement
Dedans le vergier embuschié
Et durement estoit courroucie.
Quant il vist qu'aparceu l'avoie,
Il dist, «Amis, Dieu vous doint joye!
Qu'avez de vous desconforter

Letter

In the name of God, of our Lady, and of my lady St. Katherine, out of love of my mortal folly, to you, Lord of Cornwall, I send my letter, informing you, as one of the most worthy and most renowned knights of the party of the king of England, that, on account of my heart which I have newly lost, I have undertaken to challenge you to combat by this letter. And do not take it as an act of pride, for, in order that you might know why I have undertaken this challenge, please know that I have loved and will love all my life the most peerless lady in the world. But such it is that she does not wish to take my heart as a servant, and from this I can see that she wishes to hasten my death. And since it is so, that she who surpasses all others in virtue desires my end, I write to challenge you out of my most sorrowful presumption. For I know well that your virtues are so great that, as for your feats of arms, I will never prevail, if it were not that my only mistress took pity on my end. If it is not through her, I can be worth nothing. In her resides my strength and my force. I am left without heart, without honor, without power. Thus you can see that you will have hardly any trouble in overcoming me. But our match will be carried out in this way. When you have surpassed and overcome me, you will not take anything but my life. For in this way I wish to end my life. And if it were such that she who has the power to return my heart to joy by her virtue gave me the strength to put you to defeat, I would not wish to have from you, without anything else, but a diamond to send to her who will have overcome you. And so that I might keep this letter unaltered, I have sealed it with the true seal of my arms.

When I had composed my entire letter *(see note)*
And written it within my book,
My heart then began to dream,
Cursing Danger very strongly,
Which leads me to destruction.
Then it came to me in a vision
That Hope then swore to me very strongly
That I would have comfort from my lady
And that I would be claimed as friend
And comforted with her love,
And that she was greatly displeased
With the pain that my heart received.
Thus does Hope keep me alive.
Otherwise I might not live at all.
And while I was in this state
And comforted myself with Hope,
I looked very amicably
At one who was secretly
Hidden within the garden
And who was greatly troubled.
When he saw that I had noticed him,
He said, "Friend, God give you joy!
What reason do you have to be distressed

Si durement et regrecter
Les maulx qui vous viennent d'Amours?
Quelx besoingnes sont ce qu'amours?
Jamaiz je n'en oy parler.
Ce sont choses pour enrager.
Je le voy a vostre maniere,
Qui faictes si piteuse chiere.
Je cuidoye que nul n'eust tristesse,
Douleur, desplaisir ne destresse
Fors moy tout seul, tant seulement,
Qui en reçoy si largement
Que je m'en tiens trop bien de rire.
Maiz s'il vous plaisoit a moy dire
L'achoison de vostre douleur,
Se faire vous pouoie doulceur,
De tresbon cueur je le feroye.»
Lors doulcement les mercyoye,
Luy disant que nul reconfort
Je ne demande que la mort,
Car le mire qui garir peult
Le mal dont mon cueur si se deult
Veult qu'en douleur languisse ainsi.
«Maiz dictes moy vostre party
Et l'achoison de vostre plainte.
Car advis m'est que seuffrez mainte
Dure destresse en vostre cueur.
Car se je pouoye par honneur
Vous conforter, je le feroye,
Et a mon pouoir, vous donroye
Conseil de vostre garison.
Or me dictes vostre raison,
S'il vous plaist, et je vous en prie.»
Lors me disoit par mocquerie,
«Helas! comment m'ahideriés vous?
Vous avez tant a faire a vous
Que ne savez quel tour torner.
Comment me pourroit conseiller
Ung qui aydier ne se sauroit,
Combien que faire le vouldroit?»
«Doulx frere, adonc je luy disoie,
Peult estre que mieulx vous saroye
Conseiller que je ne foiz moy.
Dictes moy, s'il vous plaist, pourquoy
Ainsi vous vous desconfortez.
Et aprés, se sçavoir voulez
De mon mal tout la verité,
Je le vous diray en briefté.»

So greatly and to protest
The pains that come to you from Love?
What are these cares that are called love?
I never heard speak of them.
These are things to make one mad.
I can see it in your manner,
You who have so piteous an expression.
I thought that no one had sadness,
Sorrow, displeasure, or distress
Except myself, exclusively,
Who partake of these so abundantly
That I am kept too well from laughing.
But if it pleased you to tell me
The reason for your sorrow,
If I could offer any relief,
I would do so with good heart."
Then I gently thanked him,
Telling him that I ask for no comfort
Other than my death,
For the physician who can heal
The pain from which my heart so suffers
Wants me to languish thus in sorrow.
"But tell me about your case," I said,
"And the reason for your complaint.
For it seems to me that you suffer many
A harsh distress within your heart.
For if I could out of respect
Comfort you, I would do so,
And within my power, I'd give you
Advice with regard to your cure.
So tell me your story,
Please, I beg you."
Then he said to me in mockery,
"Alas! How would you help me?
You have so much to do yourself
That you don't know which way to turn.
How could anyone counsel me
Who doesn't know how to help himself,
However much he wanted to?"
"Sweet brother," then I said to him,
"Perhaps I could counsel you
Better than I do myself.
Tell me, please, why
You are so distressed.
And after, if you wish to know
The whole truth about my pain,
I will tell you briefly."

Lors disoit, «Puisque le voulez,
Dire le vous vueil. Escoutés!

Balade

«A l'entree de ma jeunesse,
A mon premier commancement,
J'estoie destraint de leesse
Et de trouver esbatement.
J'avoye hostel bel et plaisant
Prés de bois et plains de jardins
Ou je m'aloie deduisant.
De mon deduit tresmal m'est pris!

«Ung jour que j'estoie sans presse
En ung jardin, tout privement,
Je regarday a la tournesse
Et vy voler si gentement
Ung esprevier, en menassant
Trestous les oyseaulx du pourpris,
Car j'ay prins grant soulassement.
De mon deduit tresmal m'est prins!

«Au plus tost me mis en l'adresse
De regarder voye comment
Prendre le pourroye, maiz tristesse
M'en est venue nouvellement
Que je l'ay prins, maiz malement
Le garday, comme m'est advis.
Dont je pleuray et diz souvant,
«De mon deduit tresmal m'est prins!»

«Avant que je le peusse prendre,
Ne qu'a moy il se voulsist rendre,
Maintes foiz en euz assez peine.
Il n'estoit heure en la sepmaine
Que ne feusse, seoir et matin,
Enfermé dedans le jardin,
Et ne faisoie qu'estudier
Comment peusse cest esprevier
Acoincter ne actraire a moy.
Trop bien vennoit au prés de moy,
Maiz prendre je ne le pouoie,
Ne laisser je ne le vouloie,
Tant avoie parfait desir
De le vouloir mien acquerir.
Tant me plaisoit parfaictement

Then he said, "Since you wish it,
I wish to tell you. Listen!

Ballade

"At the beginning of my youth,
When I was first starting out,
I was captivated by happiness
And by the pursuit of pleasure.
I had a fair and pleasant lodging
Near to a wood and replete with gardens
Where I went to amuse myself.
My joy turned out very badly for me!

"One day, when I, carefree,
Was in a garden, all by myself,
I looked up towards a little tower
And saw fly by very nobly
A sparrowhawk, which threatened
All the birds in the enclosure,
From which I took great solace.
My joy turned out very badly for me!

"Immediately I set about
To see if I could find a way
To capture it, but sadness
Came upon me quickly,
For I captured it, but badly
Did I keep it, it seems to me.
For which I wept and often said,
'My joy turned out very badly for me!'

"Before I was able to capture it,
And before it would surrender to me,
Many times I had a great deal of pain.
There was not an hour in the week
That I wasn't, in evening and morning,
Closed up inside the garden,
And all I did was to study
How I could get to know the sparrowhawk
And attract it to me.
It would indeed come up close to me,
But I wasn't able to capture it,
Nor did I wish to let it go,
So much did I have a complete desire
To wish to obtain it for my own.
So completely did it please me

Que je miz tout mon pensement,
A lui, sans penser autre rien,
Pour l'amour de son beau maintien.
Je mectoie paine de lui plaire
Et me gardoie de lui desplaire.
Je fuz long temps en ce party,
Qu'onques ung jour ne me party
D'emprés de ce que tant amoye,
Pour ce que prendre ne le pouvoye.
En ce faisant euz assez paine.
Or m'avint en une sepmaine,
Par ung lundy assez matin,
L'endemain de saint Valentin
Que tous oyseaulx veullent chanter,
Ainsi qu'estoie alé jouer
Ou jardin comme es autres foiz,
Je viz cest esprevier courtois
Qui vint vouler dessus ma main.
Maiz pour maleureux je me claim
Que autrement ne l'ay gardé.
Je suis de malvaise heure né
D'avoir ung si grant bien conquis,
Pour le perdre comme chetis,
Car jamaiz nul ne vit oysel
Si gent, si plaisant, ne si bel,
Ne de si trescourtois affere.
Ses faiz devoient a chascun plaire.
Long temps de luy j'euz grant leesse
En luy faisant toute humblesse
Et doulceur que faire pouoie.
Durement de mon cueur l'amoye
Et luy moy, ce m'estoit advis.
Ainsi estoit le jeu partiz
Tresloyaulment d'entre nous deux.
A lui plaisoient tous mes jeux.
D'autre accointier ne se vouloit.
Ne nul autre ne le portoit
Fors moy tout seul tant seulement.
Je le garday treslonguement.
Ou qu'i vollast, si estoit il
Si franc, si noble et si gentil
Que tousjours a moy revenoit,
Et point changer ne me vouloit.
En ce point passay mon enfance.
Or m'avint ung jour par mescheance
Qu'estoie dedans le jardin
Si viz ung faulcon pelerin

That I gave it all my thought,
Without thinking of anything else,
Out of love of its beautiful demeanor.
I took great pains to please it
And kept myself from displeasing it.
I was in this state for a long time,
For never a day did I depart
From near that which I loved so much,
Because I could not capture it.
In so doing I had considerable pain.
Then it happened to me one week,
On a Monday, early in the morning,
The day after Saint Valentine's Day,
When all the birds want to sing,
Just as I had gone to play
In the garden as at other times,
I saw this courteous sparrowhawk
Come alight upon my hand.
But I call myself unlucky
That otherwise I didn't keep it.
I was born in an unlucky hour
To have won so great a reward,
Only to lose it like a wretch.
For never did anyone see a bird
So noble, so pleasing, nor so fair,
Nor of so courteous a bearing.
Its nature would please everyone.
For a long time I had great joy from it
In showing it all the humbleness
And gentleness that I could.
I loved it greatly from my heart
And it loved me, it seemed to me.
Thus was the game begun
Most loyally between us two.
It was pleased with all my games.
It cared not to know anyone else.
Nor did anyone else carry it
Except for myself alone.
I kept it for a very long time.
Wherever it flew, it was
So well-bred, so noble, and so gracious
That it always came back to me,
And did not wish to change me for another.
In this state did I spend my youth.
Then it happened one day by mischance
That I was inside the garden
And I saw a peregrine falcon

Qui de voller faisoit merveilles.
Je me boutay dessoubz les treilles
Pour regarder sa contenance,
Et prins en luy tant de plaisance
Que je pensay que se pouoie
L'avoir, que plus riche seroie
Que d'avoir tout l'argent du monde.
Convoitise, que Dieu confonde,
Me fist a lui si fort penser
Que j'obliay mon esprevier.
Quant a mon esprevier venoye,
Trop bien de luy apparcevoye
Qu'il m'avoit ung pou estrangié,
Maiz j'estoie si tresenraigié
De vouloir prendre ce faulcon
Que j'en seiché comme ung baston.
Maiz ainsi que j'estoie ung seoir
Ou jardin pour mieulx le veoir,
Je viz ung tiercellet venir,
Qui bien sembloit, a son venir,
Oysel de noble et hault affaire.
Quant fut venu, c'estoit la paire.
Ilz se prindrent a festoier
Et leurs becz ensemble touchier.
De leurs elles s'entracolloient.
Ces deux oyseaulx se festoioyent
Si bien que c'estoit grant merveilles.
Et puis se mirent sur leurs elles
Et ensemble leur chemin tindrent,
Ne sceu quel part ne qu'ilz devindrent.
Mais quant je viz que perdu avoye
Le faulcon, se Dieu me doint joye,
Je fuz couroucié si fermement
Que je plouray moult tendrement.
Maiz mon dueil ne me mist guere a croistre
Quant je peuz clerement congnoistre
Qu'avoie perdu double perte,
Et s'estoit a bonne desserte.
Quant je vins ou laissié avoie
Mon esprevier, et le cuidoie
Trouver ainsi comme autresfoiz,
Je regarday et puis congnoiz
Que de la perche estoit party,
Qui me fust trespiteux party.
Adonc congneuz ma guignardie
Et ma mortelle couardie,
Que j'avoye, pour vouloir changier,

That performed wonders in flying.
I placed myself beneath the arbor
In order to watch its behavior,
And I took such pleasure in it
That I thought that if I could have it,
That I would be richer than if I had
All the money in the world.
Covetousness, which may God confound,
Made me think about it so much
That I forgot my sparrowhawk.
When I came back to my sparrowhawk,
I perceived all too well
That it had grown a bit cool to me,
But I was so foolishly mad
With wanting to capture the falcon
That I became as dry as a stick.
But one evening, while I was in the garden
In order to see the falcon better,
I saw a male peregrine come,
Which clearly seemed, when it arrived,
A bird of high and noble rank.
When it had come, they made a pair.
They began to celebrate
And to touch their beaks together.
They embraced each other with their wings.
These two birds celebrated
So much that it was a great wonder.
And then they took to their wings
And together they took their way,
I knew not where nor what became of them.
But when I saw that I had lost
The falcon, may God give me joy,
I was so terribly upset
That I cried very tenderly.
But hardly had my grief begun to grow
When I could clearly recognize
That I had suffered a double loss,
And it was my just deserts.
When I came back to where I had left
My sparrowhawk, and thought
To find it there just as before,
I looked about and realized
That it had left its perch,
Which was to me a piteous case.
Thus I recognized my coquetry
And my mortal stupidity,
And that I had, for wanting to change,

Perdu du tout mon esprevier,
Ne le faulcon pour pris n'avoye.
Et pour ce rien je ne vouldroie
Fors que la mort; tant seullement.
Je vueil finer piteusement,
En serchant se j'ourray nouvelles
Qui de ma perte me soient belles.
Car se recouvrer le pouoye,
Plus sagement le garderoye,
Sans enfraindre ma loyaulté.
Mal fut tournee faulseté,
Qui en ce point me fait languir.
Je suis par faulceté martir.
Ha! mauldicte soit guinardie!
Nul ne peut maintenir sa vie
Qui ne s'en repent au derrain.
De leesse suis mort de fain
Et ja tant en estoie raemply.
Ha! Loyaulté, je te supply,
Ne me mectz pour ce fait a mort,
Combien que j'aye si grant tort
Envers toy et si fort meffait
Qu'amander ne pourroye le fait,
Ce se n'estoit, par vostre humblesse
Qu'eussiés pitié de ma tristesse.
Et loyaulment vous jureroye
Que jamaiz ne me mefferoye
Envers vous en jour de ma vie.
Pour ce je diz ma maladie
Et mon mal. Ne sçay si vous plaist
Ou se mon parler vous desplaist.
Pour ce fineray ma raison.
Ouy vous avez l'achoison
Et la raison de ma complainte
Que je faiz sans pensee fainte.
Or m'en dictes la vostre aussi.
Si sera nostre jeu party.»

Balade

Lors luy disoie, «Beaulx amys,
J'ay bien ouy vostre clamour,
Et suis de vous fort esbahiz
Dont vous prenez telle doulour.
Il me semble que c'est foulleur
Pour ung oysel mener tel fin,

Completely lost my sparrowhawk,
And I hadn't caught the falcon at all.
And therefore I wanted nothing else
Except to die; that is all.
I wish to end pitifully,
While seeking if I might hear
Good news about what I have lost.
For if I could get it back,
I would take care of it more wisely,
Without breaching my loyalty.
My falsehood turned out very badly,
Which makes me languish in this state.
I am forced to suffer because of falsehood.
Oh, cursed be flirtation!
No one can lead such a life
Who doesn't regret it in the end.
I am dead of hunger for joy
And formerly I was so well filled.
Oh, Loyalty, I beseech you,
Do not put me to death for this,
However much I was in the wrong
Towards you, and so badly erred
That I could never make up for it,
If it were not that, out of your humbleness,
You had pity on my sadness.
And I would swear to you loyally
That never would I do wrong
To you any day of my life.
Thus I tell of my malady
And of my pain. I don't know if you're pleased
Or if my speech displeases you.
With this I will finish my story.
You have heard the cause
And the reason for my complaint
Which I make without any feigning.
Now tell me yours as well.
And then our exchange will be complete."

Ballade

Then I said to him, "Fair friend,
Well have I heard your cry,
And I am very greatly dismayed
That you experience such sorrow.
It seems to me to be a folly
To carry on so for a bird,

Que d'en perdre force et vigour
En souspirant seoir et matin.

«Nous savons bien que pour deduis
On ne peut avoir point d'onneur.
Qui vous a en ce point conduiz,
De prendre en oyseaulx tel amour
Ne d'estre d'eulx en tel ardour
Qu'a eulx soiez de tout enclin,
Tant qu'en perdez force et vigour
En souspirant seoir et matin?

«Ce penser ou vous estes mis
Trop a fait en vous long sejour,
Ainsi comme il m'est advis.
Je diroye que c'est le meilleur
Que vous preissiés ung autre tour.
C'est mon conseil, beaulx doulx cousin,
Puisqu'en perdez force et vigour
En souspirant seoir et matin.»

«Et s'il vous plaist savoir mes plains
Ne les maulx dont je me complains,
Sachiés que c'est pour une dame
Qui est de beaulté, par mon ame,
Seulle sans per, la non pareille.
C'est bien l'estoille despareille
Qui de clarté les autres passe.
C'est celle qui toutes efface
De tous biens que Dieu ne Nature
Pourroit mectre en creature.
C'est celle qui a tous doit plaire.
Se Dieu l'avoit encores affaire,
Il n'en sauroit faire une telle.
Elle est gente, joyeuse et belle.
Tant est plaisant son regarder
Et advenant son doulx parler
Qu'a chascun plaist sa contenance.
C'est la deesse de plaisance,
C'est le tresor de courtoisie,
C'est le dieu de joyeuse vie,
C'est d'onneur la droicte princesse,
C'est Alixandre de largesse.
C'est tous les biens qu'on pourroit dire.
Je n'en saroye tant escripre
Qu'en elle n'en ait assés plus.
Maiz tant y a que son reffuz

To the point of losing strength and vigor,
Sighing in both evening and morning.

"We know well that in amusement
One cannot win any honor.
Who has led you to this state,
To have for birds so great a love
And to be for them in such a fever
That you be completely subject to them,
So much that you lose both strength and vigor,
Sighing in both evening and morning?

"This state of mind in which you are placed
Has lingered with you much too long,
So does it seem to me.
I would say that it's for the best
That you take a different turn.
That's my advice, my fair sweet cousin,
Since you lose both strength and vigor,
Sighing in both evening and morning.

"And if you'd like to know my plaints
And the pains of which I complain,
Know that it is for a lady
Who, by my soul, in beauty is
Alone without equal, the peerless one.
She is the star distinct and different
That surpasses all others in brightness.
She is the one who outshines them all
In all the goods that God and Nature
Could place in any creature.
She is the one with whom all must be pleased.
If God still had it to do,
He could never make another such.
She is gracious, joyful, and fair.
So charming is her look
And so appealing her sweet speech
That her demeanor pleases all.
She is the goddess of pleasantness,
She is the treasure of courtesy,
She is the god of joyous life,
She is the very princess of honor,
She's an Alexander of generosity.
She is all the virtues that one could name.
I wouldn't know how to describe so many
That she not have a great deal more.
But there are so many that her rebuff

Me fait piteusement languir,
Quant ne lui plaist moy sien tenir,
Son humble et loyal serviteur.
C'est l'achoison de ma douleur.
C'est ce pourquoy j'ay tel destresse,
Combien qu'Espoir me fait promesse
Que d'elle je seray amé
Et de mon mal reconforté.
Et me promect Espoir pour vray
Que bien tost je m'apparcevray
Du bon vouloir qu'elle a a moy.
Et si m'a juré par sa foy
Que nagueres qu'elle disoit
Que mieulx amer ne me sauroit,
Et qu'il n'est en ce monde femme
Qui peust plus amer, par son ame,
Homme du monde qu'elle fait moy.
Et si dist, je ne sçay pourquoy,
Que dire ne me vouldroit mie
L'amour dont elle est assaillie.
En ce point veult Espoir que soye,
Més Desir, qui mon cueur mestroie,
Me fait s'amours tant desirer
Que souvent m'en fault souspirer
Et dire «helas!» et main et seoir.

Chançon

«En languissant, j'actens vostre vouloir
Dedans ces bois assez secretement,
Ne n'ay a qui prendre esbatement.
Seul suis de gens, acompaigné d'Espoir,

«Qui a mon cueur fait souvent assavoir
Qu'il est aymé. Nonobstant vrayement,
En languissant, j'actens vostre vouloir
Dedans ces bois assez secretement.

«S'il estoit vray que peusse parcevoir
Que m'amyssiés plus que nul seulement,
J'aroye Leesse bien a commandement
Et chanteroie, en chassant Desespoir,

«En languissant, j'actens vostre vouloir
Dedans ces bois assez secretement,
Ne n'ay a qui prendre esbatement.
Seul suis de gens, acompaigné d'Espoir.

Makes me languish piteously,
When she doesn't wish to consider me her own,
Her humble and loyal servant.
That is the reason for my grief.
That is why I have such distress,
However much Hope promises me
That I will be loved by her
And comforted for my pain.
And Hope does promise me in truth
That very soon I will perceive
The good will that she has for me.
And it has sworn to me by its faith
That not long ago she said
That she could not love me better,
And that there is no woman in the world
Who can love an earthly man more,
By her soul, than she loves me.
And it also says, I don't know why,
That she wouldn't like at all to tell me
Of the love by which she is assailed.
Hope wants me to be in that condition,
But Desire, which rules my heart,
Makes me desire her love so much
That often I am forced to sigh
And say 'alas' both morning and night.

Song

"Languishing, I await your will
Within these woods, quite secretly.
No one is here to provide me pleasure.
I am all alone except for Hope,

"Which often lets my heart know
That it is loved. Truly nonetheless,
Languishing, I await your will
Within these woods, quite secretly.

"If it were true that I could see
That you loved me more than anyone else,
I would have Joy at my command
And I would sing, driving out Despair,

"Languishing, I await your will
Within these woods, quite secretly.
No one is here to provide me pleasure.
I am all alone except for Hope.

«Que voulés vous que je vous die?
Frere, toute ma maladie
Me vient par elle seulement.
De moy peult faire jugement:
Elle est juge et si est partie.
Qu'en dictes vous? Ne doy je mie
Me plaindre et estre doloreux?
Se j'estoie si maleureux
Que de moy Espoir se partist,
Mourir vouldroie sans respit.
Espoir si me fait soustenir.
Autrement me faulcist fenir.
Et se Dieu veult qu'avoir je puisse
S'amour, je ne seray si nice
Que feustes de vostre esprevier,
Qui le laissates pour changier.
Jamais changer ne la vouldroye.
A mon pouoir la serviroye
De tout mon cueur si loyaulment
Sans avoir ung seul pensement
A nulle autre fors que a celle.
Vous avez ouy ma querelle.
N'ay je mieulx cause de me plaindre
Et de bien amer, sans me faindre,
Que vous n'avez, qui amez tant
Ung oysel qui s'en va vollant?
Vueillez m'en dire vostre advis,
Beau frere et beaulx doulx amis.»
«Frere, plus ne me puis defffendre.
De ma querelle me fault rendre.
J'ay debatu par poetrie
Et ainsi que par rimerie
La douleur que mon cueur sentoit,
Feignant que par deduit s'estoit.
Mon cueur est a destruction.
Maiz dire vous vueil l'achoison
Dont m'est venu ce desconfort
Pour quoy je me souhaide mort.
L'esprevier que je vous ay dit,
Ou prenoie tout mon deduit,
Si estoit une demoiselle,
Gente de corps, durement belle,
Qu'aymee avoie en ma jeunesse.
Si en souffry mainte destresse
Avant que d'elle fusse amé
Ne de mon mal reconforté.
Toutesvoyes m'en prist il si bien

"What do you want me to say to you?
Brother, all my malady
Comes from her alone.
She can pass judgment on me:
She is both judge and one of the parties.
What do you say? Should I not
Complain and be sorrowful?
If I were so unlucky
That Hope departed from me,
I would want to die without delay.
Thus does Hope sustain me.
Otherwise I would have to meet my end.
And if God wants me to have
Her love, I will never be as foolish
As you were with your sparrowhawk,
Who left it in order to choose another.
Never would I want to change.
I would serve her as best I could
With all my heart so loyally
Without ever having a single thought
For anyone else except for her.
You have heard my case.
Don't I have better cause to complain
And to love well, without relenting,
Than you do, who love so greatly
A bird that flies away?
Please tell me what you think about this,
Fair brother and fair sweet friend."
"Brother, I can defend myself no more.
I have to give up in my dispute.
I have laid out in poetry
And likewise in rhyme
The sorrow that my heart was feeling,
Pretending that it was for fun.
My heart is at the point of destruction.
But I want to tell you the cause
For which this distress has come upon me
For which I wish myself dead.
The sparrowhawk of which I spoke,
In which I took all my pleasure,
Was in fact a young woman,
Gracious of body, extremely fair,
That I had loved in my youth,
And I suffered much distress
Before I was loved by her
And relieved of my pain.
Nonetheless, it turned out so well for me

Q'une foiz me retint pour sien.
Et perdue l'ay par guinardie,
Dont je mauldiz souvent ma vie.
Maiz pour finer nostre debat,
Je me tien pour eschec et mat,
Et dy qu'il n'est ou monde dame,
Damoiselle, ne autre femme,
Qui en riens n'en sceust comparer
A celle que vous oy louer.
Toutes lui deussent faire hommage
Et se tenir en son servage.
Et pour ce me dirés, beau frere,
La douleur qui vous est amere.
Sans vous bouger de loyaulté,
Pensez que serés conforté,
Car il a en vous assez bien
Pour avoir compaignie du sien.»
Plus n'en disoit, ce m'est advis,
Et me laissoit tout esbahiz,
Ainsi seulet que par devant,
Et se partoit, ne scez commant.
Si n'euz gueres esté tout seul
Qu'avis me fut que trop grant dueil
Faisoit mon Corps et se plaignoit
De mon Cueur, qui lassié l'avoit.
Mon Cueur disoit qu'il avoit tort
De prendre si grant desconfort,
Et faisoit, en façon de plaincte,
L'ung de l'autre une complaincte.
Et s'ennuyer ne vous vouloit,
Voir la pourrés ycy endroit.

Complainte

N'a pas long temps, qu'en maniere de plainte,
Mon Corps parloit a mon Cueur fierement,
En lui disant, «Je seuffre douleur mainte.
Je voiz, je viens, je n'ay reposement.
Tu as empris ung si hault pensement
Et commencié une si haulte emprise
Qu'il m'en fauldra finer piteusement.
Mal fut pour moy en toy tel pensee mise.

«Je vy ung temps que souloie estre fort
Et maintenant ne me puis soustenir.
J'use mes jours en douleurs sans deport,
Et tout par toy, qui t'es voulu partir

That finally she took me as her own.
And I lost her because of flirtation,
For which I often curse my life.
But to bring our debate to an end,
I consider myself checkmated,
And I say that there's no lady in the world,
No maiden, or any other woman,
That one could compare in any way
To her whom I heard you praise.
All women ought to pay her homage
And put themselves in her service.
And thus you will tell me, fair brother,
Of the sorrow that is bitter for you.
Without varying in loyalty,
Think that you will be relieved,
For there is enough good in you
To keep company with hers."
He said no more, it seems to me,
And he left me completely dismayed,
Just as lonely as before,
And he went away, I don't know how.
Hardly had I been left alone
When it seemed to me that my Body felt
A very great grief, and that it complained
About my Heart, which had abandoned it.
My Heart said that the Body was wrong
To feel such great distress,
And each, in the form of a lament,
Made a complaint about the other,
And if it wouldn't bore you,
You will be able to see it here.

Complaint

Not long ago, in the style of a lament,
My Body spoke sharply to my Heart,
Saying, "I suffer many a grief.
I go, I come, I have no rest.
You have conceived so high an idea
And undertaken so high a task
That I will be forced to end piteously.
It was bad luck for me you got such an idea.

"I knew a time when I used to be strong
And now I cannot hold myself up.
I spend my days in sorrow without relief,
And it is all due to you, who wanted to depart

De dedens moy et par mes yeulx saillir.
Ce me sera une dure saillie.
Mort en seray; lors te fauldra querir
Ung autre corps se tu veulz avoir vie.

«Je sçay trop bien qu'il n'est en ma puissance
De longuement tel douleur endurer.
J'ay bien cent yeulx enclos dedens ma pense,
Qui jour et nuit ne font que regarder,
Ne ne me laissent tant soit pou reposer.
Tousjours en a troys ou quatre vueillans
Pour regarder la grant beaulté sans per
De ma dame et ses faiz advenans.»

Lors respondoit mon Cueur: «Je me merveille
Que tu ne prens a ta paine plaisir,
Quant tu scez bien que c'est la non pareille
D'onneur, de biens que on pourroit choisir.
Se par tes yeulx me suis voulu partir,
En esperant de acquerir sa grace
Par fort amer, par loyaulment server
Sa grant beaulté qui toutes autres passe,

«Ne doiz tu bien endurer ta destresse
Pour les grans biens qui venir t'en pourront?
Se tu saurez congnoistre la leesse
Qui par tes yeulx une foiz te vendront
Et le plaisir qu'avoir ilz te feront,
En leurs regard tu devroyes prendre joye.
Car, quant a eulx, point ne se lasseront
De regarder de tous biens la monjoye.

«Tu vas disant que tu as dedens toy
Plus de cent yeulx. Je les y feiz venir
Prendre logis au premier jour de may.
Scés tu pourquoy? Affin que retenir
T'en voulsisses et tousjours souvenir
Des treshaulx biens qu'oye veu le matin.
Ce sont ceulx la que je vueil acquerir,
Pour quy j'en prins a estre pellerin.»

«Ha, beau doulx Cueur, vueillez moy conforter.
Je ne puis plus en moy prendre confort.
Venez vous en dedens moy bouter.
Laissiés ce fait dont sommes en discort.
Par Dieu, je pense que vous avez grant tort
Car il me semble qu'elle ne puet amer,

From inside of me and leap out through my eyes.
This will be a hard escape for me.
I will be dead; then you will have to seek
Another body if you want to stay alive.

"I know too well it's not within my power
To endure such sorrow for a long time.
I have easily a hundred eyes within my mind
That day and night do nothing but look,
And do not let me rest, however little.
There are always three or four that stay awake
To look at the great beauty without peer
Of my lady, and at her pleasing features."

Then my Heart replied, "I am surprised
That you do not take pleasure from your pain,
When you know well that she is without equal
In honor, in any virtue that one could choose.
If through your eyes I wished to take my leave,
In hoping to obtain her grace
By loving strongly, by serving loyally
Her great beauty, which surpasses every other,

"Shouldn't you put up with your distress
For the great rewards that can come to you?
If you will be able to know the happiness
That by your eyes will come to you one day
And the pleasure that they will make you have,
You ought to take great joy in their looking.
For, as for them, they will never tire
Of looking at the summit of all good.

"You go about saying that you have within you
More than a hundred eyes. I made them come there
To take up lodging on the first of May.
Do you know why? So that you might wish
To hold onto and always keep in mind
The great good that I had seen that morning.
That is the good that I want to obtain,
For which I have undertaken to be a pilgrim."

"Oh fair sweet Heart, please comfort me.
I can no longer find comfort on my own.
Come put yourself back inside of me.
Abandon this act on which we're in discord.
By God, I think that you are very wrong
For it seems to me that she cannot love,

Et ne lui chault se vous recevez mort.
Elle est contente de vous faire enragier.

«Par plusieurs foiz vous luy avez requis
Que il luy pleust vous donner allegrance.
Maiz j'apperçoy que tousjours me va pis.
De plus en plus va croistre ma meschance.
De tant qu'elle est non pareille de France,
Deust elle estre de mes maulx plus piteuse,
Moy, qui la sers de toute ma puissance,
Comme ma dame et princesse amoureuse.

«Je sçay trop bien se vous creez Espoir,
A l'endemain, il vous decevra
Et vous fera maintenir et vouloir.
Maiz j'ay grant doubte que riens ne vous tendra.
C'est son affaire, je le sçay despieça.
Maintes gens sont trompés par tel maniere.
Or en faictes tout ce qu'il vous plaira,
De reffuser ou faire ma priere.»

«N'en parler plus, Corps; c'est ma voulenté
De la servir en gardant loyaulté.
Ne dedans vous plus ne retournray
Jusques a tant qu'avec moy amenray
Le noble cueur de ma belle princesse.
En cest espoir, obliés la destresse
Que vous avez, que s'acquerir pouoye
Le don d' «amy», plus riche vous feroye
Que vous ne feustes en jour de vostre vie.
Vous n'eustes oncques tant de mellencolie,
D'ennuy, de dueil, ne de douloreux plains,
Que recevrez de joie entre les mains
Se ma maistresse me vouloit bien amer.
Vous n'avez corps ou vous peussiés logier
La grant leesse que de moy vous vendroit
Se son servant retenir me vouloit.
Se Dieu vouloit que tant luy peusse plaire
Que ses deux yeulx me voulsissent actraire
Dedans son cueur, lors vers vous revenroye,
Et puis après, savez que je feroye?
Nous deux ensemble luy jurerions homage,
De nous tenir tousjours en son servage.
Et se la foy de nous receue avoit
Et par son gré peurmettre nous vouloit
De nous tenir pour siens toute no vie,
Jamaiz n'aurions peine ne maladie.

And she doesn't care if you receive your death.
She is content to make you go mad.

"Many a time have you entreated her
That it please her to give you happiness.
But I perceive that it just gets worse for me.
My hardship just increases more and more.
Inasmuch as she is without peer in France.
She ought to be more pitiful of my pains,
I, who serve her with all my power
As my lady and as my princess of love.

"I know too well that if you believe Hope,
The next day it will deceive you
And it will make you linger in desire.
But I fear greatly it will give you nothing.
That's its business; I have known it long.
Many people are fooled by its manner.
Now do anything you please about it,
To refuse or carry out my prayer."

"Body, say no more; it is my wish
To serve her while maintaining loyalty.
Nor will I ever come back within you
Until the time that I bring with me
The noble heart of my beautiful princess.
In this hope, forget the distress
That you are having, for if I could obtain
The gift of 'lover,' I would make you richer
Than you have been at any time in your life.
You have never had as much melancholy,
Affliction, grief, or sorrowful laments,
As you will receive of joy between your hands
If my mistress wished to love me well.
You have no body in which you could lodge
The great happiness that would come to you from me
If she wished to retain me as her servant.
If God wished that it might please her such
That her two eyes wanted to draw me
Within her heart, then I'd come back to you,
And afterwards, do you know what I would do?
We two together would swear homage to her,
To always hold ourselves in her service.
And if she accepted our pledge of faith
And by her will wanted to permit us
To consider ourselves as hers for all our life,
Never would we have pain or malady.

Et jour et nuit serions raempliz de joye.
Quoy qu'avenir a vous n'a moy en doye.
En ce vouloir feray ma destinee,
Ne ja changer ne verray ma pensee.
Endurés, Corps, je vous prie, le grant bien
Qui m'en vendra, s'il vous plaist: que soie sien.»
Lors respondit le Corps, «Beaulx doulz amys,
Tant a de biens ou vous estes assis
Que retirer jamaiz ne vous vouldroye.
Maiz, en espoir que je doye avoir joye,
Je vueil chanter tresmellencolieux.

Chançon

«Mon Cueur est sailly par mes yeulx,
Car mon Corps n'a point de souloie,
Ne retraire ne le vouldroie.
Logier ne le saroye mieulx.

«Il est logié, ainsi m'aist Dieux,
En droit tresor de toute joye.
Mon Cueur est sailly par mes yeulx,
Car mon Corps n'a point de souloie.

«Combien que soye douloreux,
Si ay je espoir qu'avenir doye,
De plus en plus que ne souloie,
Au haultain bien des amoureux.

«Mon Cueur est sailly par mes yeulx,
Car mon Corps n'a point de souloie,
Ne retraire ne le vouldroie.
Logier ne le saroye mieulx.

«Cueur, faictes vostre voulenté.
Maintenés vous en loyaulté.
Traveillez moy tant que vouldrés.
Foible suy et fort empiréz,
Mais nonobstant j'endureray
Trestout au mieulx que je pourray
La chose qu'avez entreprise.
Vostre pensée est bien mise.
Tenez vous y, c'est mon conseil,
Puisque c'est le dieu despareil
De toutes les dames qui sont,
Qui furent ne jamaiz seront
En tous lieux que dire on pourroit,

And day and night we would be filled with joy.
Whatever might happen to you or me.
In this wish I will make my destiny,
And I will never see my thought change.
Endure, Body, I beg you, please, the great reward
That will come to me: that I be hers."
Then the Body answered, "Fair sweet friend,
There is so much good where you are placed
That I would never wish to draw you back.
But in the hope that I might have joy,
Very melancholy, I wish to sing.

Song

"My heart has leapt out through my eyes,
For which my body has no consolation.
Nor do I wish to draw it back.
I don't know where to lodge it better.

"It is lodged, so help me God,
In the true treasury of all joy.
My heart has leapt out through me eyes,
For which my body has no consolation.

"However sorrowful I am,
Yet I have hope that I might come,
More and more than I was accustomed,
To the supreme reward of lovers.

"My heart has leapt out through my eyes,
For which my body has no consolation.
Nor do I wish to draw it back.
I don't know where to lodge it better.

"Heart, do what you will.
Maintain yourself in loyalty.
Torment me as much as you want.
I am weak and badly injured,
But nonetheless I will endure
The very best that I am able
The thing that you have undertaken.
Your intention is well placed.
Hold to it is my advice,
For she's the god without peer
Of all the ladies who are now,
Who were, or who will ever be
In all the places that one could name,

Ne nul tant dire ne sauroit
Que en a, sur Dieu et sur mon ame.
C'est la plus non pareille dame
Qui soit et qui jamaiz sera.
Et pour ce, vive qui pourra,
Je suis prest de tout endurer
Et par souffrir me conforter
Comme faisoit Palamidés.

Chançon

«J'ay fait mon tresor de souhaiz
Et si me suis garny d'Espoir
Pour resister contre Douloir
Et encontre ses rudes faiz.

«Desconfort ne me laisse en paix,
Maiz guerre je luy vueil mouvoir.
J'ay fait mon tresor de souhaiz
Et si me suis garny d'Espoir.

«Et pour ce me vueil desormais
Vestir de blanc en lieu de noir,
Pour l'esperance qu'ay d'avoir
Allegement de mes regrés.

«J'ay fait mon tresor de souhaiz
Et si me suis garny d'Espoir
Pour resister contre Douloir
Et encontre ses rudes faiz.»

Le Cueur le Corps remercioit
De ce que son plaisir estoit
D'estre vray martir par amours.
Nonobstant les ardant tours
Qu'amours lui faisoit endurer,
Si ne se vouloit il bouger.
«Ainsi sommes d'accort nous deux
D'estre tousjours si desireux
De la cherir, servir et craindre.
Nul de nous deux ne se veult faindre
D'acomplir son plaisant vouloir,
Luy suppliant que recevoir
Luy plaise en gré noz piteux faiz
Et amendrir noz griefz regrectz,
Et en chantant luy requerir:

And none could ever name as many
As there are, upon God and my soul.
She is the most peerless lady
Who is and who will ever be.
And therefore, let him live who can,
I am ready to endure all
And by suffering to console myself
As did Palamedes.

Song

"I have made my treasury of wishes,
And I have equipped myself with Hope
In order to resist against Sorrow
And against its harsh attacks.

"Distress does not leave me in peace,
But I wish to wage war upon it.
I have made my treasury of wishes,
And I have equipped myself with Hope.

"And therefore from now on I want
To dress in white instead of black,
For the hope I have of obtaining
Some relief from my complaints.

"I have made my treasury of wishes,
And I have equipped myself with Hope
In order to resist against Sorrow
And against its harsh attacks."

The Heart thanked the Body
That it was its pleasure
To be a true martyr for love.
Despite the harsh turns
That love made it suffer,
Yet it didn't wish to budge.
"Thus are we both in accord
Always to be just as desirous
Of cherishing, serving, and fearing her.
Neither of us wants to be slow
To carry out her charming wish,
Beseeching her that it please her
Willingly to accept our piteous deeds
And to reduce our grievous sorrows,
And in singing, to ask of her:

Chançon

«Mectez nous en droit souvenir
Du parfont de vostre pensee.
Nostre princesse desiree,
Faictes nous devers vous venir.

«Car nous ne faisons que languir,
Jour et nuyt, seoir et mastinee,
Mectez nous en droit souvenir
Du parfont de vostre pensee.

«Acompaignéz d'Ardant Desir,
Endurons nostre destinee.
En presentant, tresbien amee,
Cette chanson pour requerir:

«Mectez nous en droit souvenir
Du parfont de vostre pensee.
Nostre princesse desiree,
Faictes nous devers vous venir.»

Quant nostre debat fut finé
Et en ce livre enregistré,
Il avint que je m'esveillay,
Et lors en tour moy regarday
Et viz que j'estoie tout seul,
Si pensay que faire mon dueil
Je feroye secrectement,
Si diz «helas!» piteusement,
«Amours, Amours, tant travaillier
M'avez fait qu'a ce resveiller
Me fault faire de vous complaincte.
Mon dormir n'est que une estraincte.
Quant on cuide que je repose
Pour ce qu'on voit ma veue close,
Lors est ce que croist mon travail,
Qu'oncques maiz ne viz le pareil.
L'ueil de mon corps n'a nul repos,
Car il est en Desir encloz,
Qui tousjours fait veoir sa mort,
Et si est de l'avoir d'accord.
Et pour ce nul ne m'en doit plaindre,
Car Raison veult mon mal estraindre,
Maiz souffrir ne le voulez mye,
Tant me plaist ma plaisant folie.
Je l'appelle folie plaisant

Song

"Place us in the true memory
Of the depth of your thought.
Oh princess that we desire,
Make us come before you.

"For all we do is languish,
Day and night, eve and morn.
Place us in the true memory
Of the depth of your thought.

"Accompanied by Burning Desire
We endure our destiny.
Offering, oh dearly beloved,
This song, in order to ask:

"Place us in the true memory
Of the depth of your thought.
Oh princess that we desire,
Make us come before you."

When our debate was ended
And recorded in this book,
It happened that I awoke,
And then I looked around me
And I saw that I was all alone,
And I thought that I would conduct
My grief in private,
So I said piteously, "Alas,
Love, Love, you have made me suffer
So much that upon awakening,
I must make a complaint about you.
My sleep is nothing but a torment.
When one thinks that I am resting
Because one sees my eyes are closed,
That is when my suffering increases
Such that I never saw the like.
The eye of my body has no rest
For it is enclosed in Desire,
Which constantly makes it see its death,
And yet it agrees to have it.
And therefore no one should reproach me,
For Reason wishes to end my pain,
But you, Love, don't want to allow it,
So much does my pleasing folly please me.
I call it a pleasing folly

Combien qu'elle soit desplaisant.
En m'actrayant me desconfit
Et du tout son reffuz m'occist.
Amours, mal fut vostre maniere
De faire tel dame murtriere,
Et si ne peut de mon mal maiz.
Je ressemble Palamidés,
Qui vouloit, sanz avoir partie,
Amer tous les temps de sa vie.
Ma voulenté est d'ainsi faire.
Jamaiz jour ne m'en vueil retraire.
(Si dit on bien quelque hutin
Piteusement a la parfin.)
Pour tel fait fut mis a mort,
Et fut de ce faire d'accord.
Helas! et tant ma mort vouldroie.
Autre rien ne souheteroie
Se non tant seulement mourir.
Ha! Mort, que ne faiz tu fenir
Ma vie, qu'est trop ennuyeuse
Et trop durement doloreuse?
Tout m'ennuye, quant que je voy.
En lieu de plaisir j'ay ennoy.
Ha! Amours, et vous, ma maistresse,
Ay je desservy tel destresse
Pour bien vous loyaulment servir?
J'ay tousjours voulu acomplir
Trestous voz bons commandemens.
Ha, Amours, il n'a pas long temps
Que j'euz le plus grant desplaisir
Gueres qu'il me pourroit venir,
Car en dormant, me fut advis
Que le cueur, que devant je diz
A ma maistresse entierement,
Estoit perdu, ne sçay comment.
Et me sembloit que le veoie
Martirer, et lors requeroye
A ceulx qui luy faisoient la paine
Que, pour la Vierge souverayne,
Leur pleust me faire tel doulceur
De me rendre ce doulant cueur,
Et qu'assez avoit eu martire.
Baillié me fut sans escondire.
Quant je l'euz, comme tresdollant
D'une piece en feiz present
A ma dame, seulle amee,
Et croy qu'elle s'en soit coursee.

However unpleasant it may be.
In drawing me in, it throws me down
And it slays me with its full rebuff.
Love, evil was your manner
To make such a lady a murderess,
And yet she can do nothing for my pain.
I resemble Palamedes,
Who wished, without anything in return,
To love for all his life.
My will is to do the same.
Not a single day do I wish to withdraw.
(Thus one says some sort of noise
Piteously in the end.)
For such a deed he was put to death,
And he was in agreement with it.
Alas! And so much would I like my death,
I would not wish for anything else
Except only to die.
Oh Death, why do you not end
My life, which is too distressful
And too greatly sorrowful?
Everything bothers me, whatever I see.
Instead of pleasure I have aggravation.
Oh Love, and you, my mistress,
Have I deserved such distress
For having served you loyally?
I have always wanted to carry out
All of your good commands.
Oh Love, it was not long ago
I had the greatest unhappiness
That ever could befall me,
For while sleeping, it seemed to me
That my heart, which formerly I said
Belonged to my mistress totally,
Was lost, I don't know how.
And it seemed to me that I saw it
Suffering, and then I asked
Of those who inflicted this pain
That, for the Sovereign Virgin,
They might please be so kind
As to return to me this grieving heart,
And that it had had suffering enough.
It was given to me without refusal.
When I got it, I very sorrowfully
Made a present of a piece of it
To my lady, my only beloved,
And I think that it made her angry.

De son courroux me desplaisoit,
Ma douleur trop empiroit
Se j'avoye fait, pensé ne dicte
Chose dont elle fust despite.
Soit droit soit tort, je lui vueil plaire
Et me garder de luy desplaire.
Et aussi scez je de verité
Que en luy a tant loyaulté
Qu'en mal dire on ne pourroit
Se mentir d'elle on ne vouloit.
Et de tant que j'ay en pensee
De quoy elle s'estoit yree,
Humblement l'en crie mercy.
Et prie Amours que, pour cecy,
Ne me mecte hors de la grace
De celle de tous qui bien passe
Les dames qui furent ne sont
Ne qui jamaiz aprés seront,
Nonobstant que sa bien vueillance
Je n'euz oncques ne n'ay esperance,
Au semblant que je truiz en elle,
Que jamaiz ne puis ma querelle
Mectre a fin, comme je desire.
Maiz il me doit sans plus souffire,
De garder que ne luy desplaise,
Et se pour luy seuffre mesaise,
Nonpourtant je ne lairray mie
De la servir toute ma vie.
Amours, j'ay bien la congnoissance
Que ne vaulx d'avoir esperance
D'estre d'elle amy clamé.
Pou de chose est de ma bonté
Au regard de sa grant valeur,
De sa beaulté, de sa doulceur.
Et pour ce, Amours, je vous supplie
Seullement que, pour courtoisie,
Me gardez de sa desplaisance
S'avoir ne puis sa bien vueillance,
Et me donnez pouoir de faire
Tousjours chose qui lui peust plaire.
Amours, je suis tresvolentiers
L'ung de voz pouvres souldoiers,
Que n'ay ne gaige ne parement,
Et me souffist tant seulement
Que vous congnoissiés mon service,
Moy, qui vous serf sans nul office.
Servy vous ay sans ordonnance,

I was displeased by her anger,
And my sorrow grew much worse
If I had done, thought, or said
Anything for which she was annoyed.
Be it right or wrong, I wish to please her
And keep myself from displeasing her.
And I also know in truth
That there is so much loyalty in her
That one could never speak ill of it
If one didn't want to lie about her.
And for anything that I have in mind
For which she had become angry,
Humbly I beg mercy for it.
And I pray to Love that, for this,
It not put me beyond the grace
Of the one among all who surpasses
The ladies who were and are
And who will ever be afterwards,
Notwithstanding that her good will
I never had, nor do I have hope,
From what I can see in her,
That I can ever bring to an end
My suit in the way that I desire.
But it should satisfy me, without more,
To keep from displeasing her,
And if for her I suffer discomfort,
Nonetheless I will not leave off
From serving her for my whole life.
Love, I understand well
That I am not worthy to have hope
That she declare me her lover.
My virtues are insignificant
Compared to her great worth,
To her beauty, and to her gentleness.
And therefore, Love, I beg you
Only that out of courtesy
You preserve me from her displeasure
If I cannot have her good will,
And give me the power to perform
Each day something that can please her.
Love, I am very willingly
One of your poor foot-soldiers,
Who have neither salary nor equipment,
And I am satisfied
Only that you recognize my service,
I, who serve you without office.
I have served you without orders,

Sans avoir confort qu'esperance.
Encores n'ay je retenue.
Je ne sçay si j'aroye perdue
Ma peine pour vous bien servir.
Point ne le dy pour repentir,
Ne jamaiz ne le m'ourrez dire.
Nonobstant mon piteux martire,
Je suis de ma paine content.
Je suis tout en commandement
De celle qui me fait avoir
Le mal dont je me doy douloir.
Je vueil tout ce qu'elle vouldra
Et faire quanque luy plaira,
Ou vivre en dueil ou en leesse.
Seulle la vueil tenir maistresse.
Je suis son serf sans afranchir,
Ne ne vueil nulle autre choisir.
Elle est ma tresdoulce ennemye,
Et de mon cueur mortel amye.
Elle m'a tout. Je n'ay rien mien.
Et si ne me veult tenir sien.
Mais sien seray, vueil ou non vueille,
Ne lairray pour rien qui me vueille.
C'est une amour sans despartie
Qui durera toute ma vie.
Et pour s'amour, comment qu'il est,
Je vueil faire cy ung souhaist:
Plust a Dieu que, par vision,
Peusse savoir s'oppinion.
Je doubte qu'elle me het
Pour ce qu'envers luy ay meffait.»
Et tant pour le traveil qu'avoye
Que pour le desir, que vouloie
En mon dormant ung songe faire,
Je m'endormy, et n'y mis guere,
Et en mon dormant, je veoye, *(see note)*
Chevauchant par une saulsoye,
Dangier. Si me prins a gemir
Et penser au mal que j'avoye
Et la douleur qui me faisoit sentir
Tant pour amer et loyaulment servir
La non pareille qui soit dessoubz les cieulx
D'onneur, de bien, de regart gracieux.
La pareille ne pourroit on trouver.
Si dist mon cueur, qui la veult honnorer,
Servir, doubter, plus qu'autre, se m'aist Dieux.

Without having comfort or hope.
Still do I have no reward.
I do not know if I would have wasted
My pain for serving you well.
I say it not at all with regret,
Nor ever will you hear me say it.
Despite my piteous suffering,
I am content with my pain.
I am totally at the command
Of her who causes me to have
The pain of which I must lament.
I want everything that she would like
And to do whatever will please her.
Whether to live in grief or in happiness.
Her alone do I wish to consider my mistress.
I am her serf without liberty,
Nor do I want to choose another.
She is my most sweet enemy,
And of my heart the cruel friend.
She has me totally. I have nothing that is mine.
And yet she does not wish to consider me her own.
But I will be hers, whether she wish it or not,
Nor will I cease for anything that she wishes of me.
It is a indivisible love
Which will last for all my life.
And for her love, however it is,
I want here to make one wish:
May it please God that in a vision
I might know how she feels.
I fear that she hates me
Because I have offended her."
And as much for the torment that I had
As for the desire, that I wished
In sleeping to have a dream,
I fell asleep, and with no effort,
And while I was sleeping, I saw, *(see note)*
Galloping through a willow grove,
Danger. Then I began to sigh
And to think about the pain I felt
And the sorrow that it made me feel
So greatly for loving and serving loyally
The most peerless one beneath the heavens
In honor, in virtue, in gracious look.
One would not be able to find her equal.
So says my heart, which wants to honor her,
Serve her, fear her, more than any other, so help me God.

Pour ce en espoir me vueil tenir joyeulx,
En actendant d'avoir allegement
De ma maistresse aux tresbeaulx rians yeulx,
Car sa doulceur ne veult mon finement.
Confort me dit et me va conseillant
Que je la serve mon vivant sans faulser.
Je l'en croyray; point ne m'en vueil lasser
De la servir, tant que je auray duree,
De cueur, de corps, de vouloir, de pensee,
Pour quelque mal que j'en puisse endurer,

En attendant que, par son doulx parler,
Mes griefz douleurs se tournent a leesse,
Et que mon cueur y puisse demourer
Et estre hors de paine et de tristesse.
Car j'ay esté si longtemps en destresse
Qu'ay obliay joye et esbatement.
Dancer, chanter, je souloie en mon temps,
Et maintenant me fault courroux mener.
Maiz j'ay espouoir de ce temps recouvrer,
Maulgré jaloux et les faulx medisans,

Qui m'ont esté a leur pouoir nuysans.
Maiz, maulgré eulx, je serviray la belle
Que j'ay aymé et honnoré longtemps.
Et nullement ne puis bonne nouvelle
Ouir n'avoir, s'elle ne me vient d'elle.
En elle maint ou ma mort ou ma vie.
Riche d'onneur, de loyaulté garnie,
Aiez pitié de mes dures doulours
Et du torment avec plains et plours
Que j'ay pour vous. Et si ne m'en plains mye,

Car je sçay bien qu'en une heure et demye
Povez mon mal retourner en doulceur.
Ma princesse. Doncq ne vueillez mie
Que tout mon temps soit en telle langueur,
Maiz m'alegiez et ostez la douleur
Qu'au cueur je sens, que plus n'en puis sans mort.
Belle et doulce ou gist tout mon confort,
Reconfortez ce pouvre souffreteux
Qui est tousjours a son pouoir soingneux
De vous servir, soit a droit, soit a tort.

Ma seulle dame ou gist tout mon confort,
Par vostre gré escoutez la complaincte
De moy, qui n'ay aucun deport,

Therefore in hope I want to remain joyous,
While awaiting that I have relief
From my mistress with the beautiful laughing eyes,
For her sweetness does not wish my death.
Comfort tells me and comes to advise me
That I serve her all my life without betrayal.
I will believe it; I don't want at all to be neglectful
In serving her, as long as I shall endure,
In heart, in body, in will, in thought,
For whatever pain that I might endure,

While awaiting that, by means of her sweet speech,
My grievous sorrows turn to happiness,
And that my heart might there remain
And be free from pain and from sadness.
For I have been so long in distress
That I have forgotten joy and amusement.
I used to dance and sing in my time,
And now I must go about in anger.
But I have hope of bringing back that time,
Despite the jealous and the lying slanderers

Who have been harming me as best they can.
But despite them, I will serve the fair one
Whom I have loved and honored for a long time.
And in no way can I ever hear or have
Good tidings if they do not come from her.
In her resides my death or my life.
Lady rich in honor, adorned with loyalty,
Have pity on my harsh sorrows
And on the torment with laments and tears
That I have for you. And yet I do not complain,

For I know well that in an hour and a half,
You can turn my pain into sweetness,
My princess. Therefore please don't wish
That all my time be spent in such languor,
But relieve me and remove the sorrow
That I feel in my heart, for I can bear no more without dying.
Fair gentle one, in whom lies all my comfort,
Console this poor destitute one
Who is always within his power attentive
To serve you, whether for right or wrong.

My only lady in whom lies all my comfort,
If you please, listen to the plaint
Of myself, who has no amusement,

Et desconfort a ma doulceur destaincte.
Tous autres maulx ont si ma teste actainte,
Plus ne puis vivre, se je n'ay allegence.
Mon bien joyeulx et ma seulle plaisance,
Faictes de moy tout a vostre talent,
Car, se je meur, je peuz dire vrayement
Que seuffre mort pour la meilleur de France.

Ma seulle amour, ou je mis ma fiancé, *(see note)*
Faictes de moy tout a vostre plaisance.
Pour vous amer, je languis, en verité.
Et languiray tant que seray renté
De vostre amour et que me donnez grace
D'oster de moy, comme infortuné,
Paine et soucy, et que je les deschace,
Et desplaisir qui longtemps si me chasse
Et m'a chassié a oster de baudour,
Et ja de fait m'a mis en tel ardour
Que je n'ay plus bon jour ne bonne nuit.
Dangier m'aprouche, et Dangier si me nuit
Que loisir n'ay de compter ma clamour.

Il fault que fine, je ne puis trouver tour.
Je dy adieu a bonne compaignie
Et a vous, dame, des bonnes la meilleur.
Je prens congié de vostre chiere lie.
Orrant, plourant, menant piteuse vie,
Fault que departe de grans biens amoureux.
Si vous supply, compaignons gracieux,
Prigent, Regnault et Jamect ensement,
Voz maistresses servez soingneusement.
Quoy qu'on en die, vous n'en vauldrez que mieulx.

Et tout ainsi que je me complaignoye,
J'ouy passer dessus moy une voix
Qui me disoit: «Amys, ne te desvoye!
Le Dieu d'Amours si t'en sera courtois,
Et m'envoie cy pour t'oster le doulx poiz
Qu'as dessus toy et la mellencolie.
Lieuve tost sus et mene bonne vie!
Confortez toy, mectz peine de guerir!
Tu te doiz bien plus qu'oncques maiz esjouir
Car tu auras d'onneur la seigneurie.»

Quant je l'oy, j'estoye en pasmerie.
Si prins adonc a ma teste lever
Veoir se verroye la voix qu'avoye ouye,

And distress has extinguished my sweetness.
All other pains have so afflicted my head,
I can live no longer if I don't have relief.
My joyous good and my only pleasure,
Do with me anything you wish,
For if I die, I can say truly
That I suffer death for the best woman in France.

1947 My only love, to whom I am committed, *(see note)*
1949 Do with me according to your pleasure.
1956 In order to love you, I languish, in truth,
And I will languish, until I am granted
Your love and until you give me the grace
Of removing from me, as an ill-fated one,
Pain and care, and until I expel them
Along with the unhappiness that long pursues me
And has sought to remove me from all joy;
And indeed it has so enflamed me
That I no longer have a good day or good night.
Danger draws near me, and Danger so injures me
That I don't have time to tell of my complaint.

I must come to an end. I can find no release.
I say farewell to the good company
And to you, my lady, the best of the good.
I take my leave of your happy face.
Praying, weeping, leading a piteous life,
I must depart from the great rewards of love.
Thus I beseech you, gracious companions,
Prigent, Regnault, and Jamect together,
Serve your mistresses attentively.
Whatever anyone says, you will only be better for it.

And just as I was lamenting in this way,
I heard a voice coming from above me
That said to me, "Friend, don't be discouraged.
The God of Love will be courteous to you,
And he sends me here to remove the sweet burden
That you have upon you, and the melancholy.
Get up at once and lead a happy life!
Take comfort, and take pains to recover!
You ought more than ever to rejoice,
For you will have the seignory of honor."

When I heard it, I swooned,
Yet then I began to raise up my head
To see if I could see the voice I'd heard,

Car voulentiers eusse voulu parler
Plus longuement et la araisonner
Pour demander quelle seroit ma fin.
Point ne la viz, maiz quant vint le matin,
De mes maulx fu allegré grandement.
J'en mercyay Amours piteusement.
Cela m'avint le jour saint Valentin.

Balade

Jeune, gente, belle, doulce maniere,
Riant regart, bel acueil, doulx parler,
Je viens vers vous, faisant piteuse chiere,
Prendre congié et moy recommander
A vo doulceur qui me peult conforter.
Faictes de moy tout ce qu'il vous plaira,
Que jamaiz jour mon vueil ne changera.
Car a ce faire mon vueil est tout fermé,
De vous servir tousjours en loyaulté.
Ou que je voise, mon cueur vous demourra.

Helas! pourquoy estes vers moy si fiere
Qu'i ne vous plaist mon parler escouter?
Ne pourquoy m'est vostre humblesse si chiere
Qu'i me convient durement achapter
Ung doulx semblant, quant le puis recouvrer?
Et si ne sçay quant vostre vueil sera
De m'octroyer ce qu'ay requis pieça
Pour faiz ou mal que j'ay ja enduré.
Car, par ma foy, mon bien et ma chierté,
Ou que je voise, mon cueur vous demourra.

Mes plains, mes plours sont bien boutés arriere.
Trop pou vous chault de me voir tormenter,
Ne de conforter ma piteuse priere
Et la douleur qu'i me fait endurer,
Belle et doulce, pour vous vouloir amer.
Je sçay trop bien que briefment me fauldra
Finer d'ennuy. Oncques nul n'endura
Si grant peine, pour en dire verité,
Maiz tout en voit a vostre voulenté.
Ou que je voise, mon cueur vous demourra.

Ma princesse, ma voulenté entiere
Est et sera vous craindre et redoubter.
Et se je n'ose a vous souvant parler,
Ce poise moy, maiz, quant il vous plaira,

For willingly would I have wished to speak
At greater length and converse with it
In order to ask what would be my end.
I didn't see it, but when the morning came,
I was greatly relieved of my pain.
Piteously I gave thanks to Love.
This happened to me on Saint Valentine's Day.

Ballade

Young, noble, beautiful, a sweet manner,
A laughing look, fair welcome, sweet speech,
I come to you, making piteous cheer,
To take my leave and to recommend myself
To your gentleness, which can comfort me.
Do with me anything you please,
For never will my wish ever change.
For my will is completely determined to do this:
To serve you always in loyalty.
Wherever I go, my heart will stay with you.

Alas, why are you so haughty towards me
That it doesn't please you to listen to me speak?
And why is your humbleness so dear
That I am forced to buy so painfully
A gentle look, when I can even obtain it?
And I do not know when it will be your will
To grant me that which I have long requested
For the pains or hurt that I have already endured.
For by my faith, my good and my treasure,
Wherever I go, my heart will stay with you.

My plaints, my tears, are completely brushed aside.
Very little does it matter to you to see me tormented
Or to comfort my piteous prayer
And the sorrow that I am made to endure,
Fair gentle one, for wanting to love you.
I know very well that soon I will be forced
To die of sorrow. Never did anyone endure
So great a pain, to tell the truth,
But may it all go according to your will.
Wherever I go, my heart will stay with you.

My princess, my entire will
Is and will be to fear you and dread you,
And if I do not dare to speak to you often,
This troubles me, but when it pleases you,

Mon dueil ferez en reconfort tourner.
Si vous povez de moy tout asseurer,
Ou que je voise, mon cueur vous demourra.

Chançon

Adieu, gent corps, jeune, joyeulx,
Adieu, doulx regart gracieulx,
Adieu, ma tresbelle maistresse.
Je prens congié par grant destresse
Et m'en voiz mellencolieux.

Je delaisse tous biens eureux,
Et si me pars tous souffreteux,
Pensant au grief mal qui me blesse.
Adieu, gent corps, jeune, joyeulx,
Adieu, doulx regart gracieulx,
Adieu, ma tresbelle maistresse.

S'Umble Vouloir ne m'est piteux
D'alegier mon mal angoisseux,
Je suis forbanny de leesse,
Sans jamaiz retrouver l'adresse
De revenir n'en riz, n'en jeux.

Adieu, gent corps, jeune, joyeulx,
Adieu, doulx regart gracieulx,
Adieu, ma tresbelle maistresse.
Je prens congié par grant destresse
Et m'en voiz mellencolieux.

Complaincte

Plus ne pourroit avoir mon cueur destresse, *(see note)*
Ne desplaisir, ne torment envieulx.
Quoy que j'ay bien desja la congnoissance
Que sans pitié est le dieu que je croy.
Maiz j'ay espoir de faire le pourquoy
Mon entrecrist sera vers moy piteux.
A tout le moins ne tendra point a moy
Se je ne suis sans raison maleureux.

Plus ne me puis tenir que je ne die
Que mon dieu est des autres dieux deesse,
Faicte des fees et venu de faairie,
Plaine de biens, d'onneur et de largesse.
Celle doit bien estre a tous maistresse.

You will make my sorrow turn into comfort.
Thus you can be fully certain of me:
Wherever I go, my heart will stay with you.

Song

Farewell, noble one, young and joyous,
Farewell, sweet gracious look,
Farewell, my very beautiful mistress.
I take my leave in great distress
And melancholy, I depart.

I leave behind all happiness,
And thus I go completely destitute,
Thinking of the grievous pain that afflicts me.
Farewell, noble one, young and joyous,
Farewell, sweet gracious look,
Farewell, my very beautiful mistress.

If Humble Will does not have pity on me
In order to relieve my sorrowful pain,
I am banished from happiness
Without ever finding the way or means
To return either to laughter or to play.

Farewell, noble one, young and joyous,
Farewell, sweet gracious look,
Farewell, my very beautiful mistress.
I take my leave in great distress
And melancholy, I depart.

Complaint

My heart can no longer bear distress *(see note)*
Or unhappiness, or the torment of desire.
Although I already recognize well
That the god in whom I believe is without pity.
But I hope to provide a reason why
My intercessor will have pity on me.
At the very least he will not blame me
If I am not unhappy for no reason.

No longer can I refrain from saying
That my god is the goddess of the other gods,
Made by fairies and come from an enchanted land,
Full of virtues, of honor and of largesse.
She ought well be the mistress of all.

Son vueil sans plus peut chascun enrichir.
Il peut sans plus souffir de la servir
Pour les grans biens, beaultés qui sont en elle.
On la doit bien nommer, et sans mentir,
Dame des dames, des bonnes la plus belle.

Ainsi m'aist Dieux, que je croy fermement,
Se Dieu avoit perdue Nostre Dame,
Qu'i s'en vendroit embas, ne sçay comment,
Ne ne prendroit ja pour luy autre femme
Que ma maistresse, qui m'est et dieu et dame.
Maiz cuidés vous que je luy laisse aller,
Se par force le pouoye destourner?
Et d'autre part a tant de serviteurs
Que ung seul dieu ne l'en pourroit mener,
S'avec luy n'avoit des enchanteurs.

Maintes gens sont devenuz par clergie
Hors de leur sens et perdu tout leur savoir,
Maiz j'ay empris une trop grant folie
D'amer celle qui d'amer n'a vouloir.
Je pers le sens, la force et le pouoir.
Mal eust sur moy Amours tant de puissance
De m'asservir a la non per de France.
Serf demourray, sans jamaiz afranchir.
Quoy que ce soit a mon cueur grant vaillance,
Si m'en fault il mainte douleur souffrir.

Encores ce de quoy plus me merveil,
C'est qu'Amours n'a nul pouoir sur elle.
Seulle veult estre sans choisir nul pareil.
Nul oncques maiz n'y ot parler de telle.
Qui me pourra aider a ma querelle?
Qui me pourra faire abaisser mon dueil?
Qui lui pourra dire ce que je vueil?
Car d'escouter est si tresdangereuse.
Quant luy vueil dire le mal que je recueil,
Craincte me dist que n'est de riens piteuse.

Taire me fault de luy dire mes plains,
Que je ne puis du dire trouver place.
Et, d'autre part, si durement la crains,
Car se j'avoie temps, loisir et espace,
Si n'oseroye. Or regardés que face.
Suy je en bon point? Jugiez, se vous aist Dieux.
Sont bien vengéz de moy les envieulx?
Il m'est advis qu'il leur doit bien souffire.

Her wish alone can enrich everyone.
By itself, it can be enough to serve her
For the great virtues and beauties that reside in her.
One ought well to call her, and without lying,
Lady of ladies, the most beautiful of the good.

So help me God, I firmly believe,
If God had lost Our Lady,
That if he would then come down, I know not how,
He would not choose for himself any other woman
But my mistress, who is to me both god and lady.
But do you think that I would let her go
If I by force were able to prevent it?
And furthermore, she has so many attendants
That one god alone couldn't lead her off
Unless he had with him some magicians.

Many people have gone out of their minds
From study and have lost all that they knew.
But I have undertaken too great a folly
In loving her who has no wish to love.
I lose my wits, my strength, and my power.
Wickedly did Love have such power over me
As to subject me to the one without peer in France.
I will remain her subject, without ever gaining freedom.
Although to my heart this is something of great worth,
Yet I am forced to suffer many a sorrow.

There is still this of which I marvel more:
It is that Love has no power over her.
She wishes to remain alone without choosing an equal.
Never did anyone hear of such a woman.
Who will be able to aid me in my cause?
Who will be able to reduce my grief?
Who will be able to tell her what I want?
For she is very disdainful of listening.
When I want to tell of the pain that I receive,
Fear tells me that she has no pity at all.

I must desist from telling her my complaints,
For I cannot find an opportunity for speaking.
And furthermore, so greatly do I fear her,
For if I had the time, leisure, and space,
I would not dare. Now watch what I do.
Am I in a good state? Judge, so help you God.
Do the envious have their vengeance upon me?
It seems to me that it ought to suffice them.

J'ayme ma mort. Demanderoient ilz mieulx?
Et si ne scet quel douleur j'ay mon mire.

Plus ne me vueil de ma douleur complaindre.
Endurer vueil, soit a droit ou a tort,
Et bien amer tousjours maiz, sans me faindre,
Celle qui est consentant de ma mort.
Mon cueur le veult et j'en suis bien d'accord.
Si prie a Dieu qu'i me garde de faire
Ne dire chose qui lui puisse desplaire.
Et s'ainsi est que je ne puisse avoir
Sa bienvueillance, de quoy ne me puis taire,
Dieu me gart d'estre en son maulvaiz vouloir.

Balade

Doulce durté, ma tresmortel amye,
Mon bien, mon mal, ma maistresse, ma joye,
Mon tout, ma tresdoulce ennemye,
Ma balade humblement vous envoye
Vous supplier qu'il vous plaise que soye
De ma douleur par vous reconforté.
Qu'ainsi m'aist Dieux, mon bien et ma cherté,
Nulle que vous n'a sur moy le pouoir
De moy guerir, car je suis ahurté.
Et pour cela me tiens vestu de noir.

Plus pense aux biens de vostre seigneurie,
A la beaulté dont vous estes montjoye,
Aux plaisans jeux dont vous estes garnie,
Mon mal me plaist, ne guerir ne vouldroye
Se n'est par vous, quoy qu'avenir m'en doye.
Jamaiz changer ne vueil ma voulenté.
Mon cueur le veult et je l'ay accordé,
Quoy que m'ayez de tout banny d'espoir
Par ung reffuz assez prés du fossé.
Et pour cela me tiens vestu de noir.

Helas! ma dame, ay je mort desservie
Pour vous amer tant que plus ne pourroye?
Vostre pitié me sera elle faillie?
Ay je riens fait que faire je ne doye?
Mort ou mercy, plus ne souhaderoye.
A vous me rens, recevez moy en gré.
Faictes moy riche dont j'ay grant pouvreté.
C'est la leesse que par vous puis avoir.

I love my death. Would they ask for more?
And my doctor does not know what pain I bear.

I wish no longer to complain of my sorrow.
I want to endure, whether for right or wrong,
And to love well forever more, without slacking,
The one who is consenting to my death.
My heart wishes it, and I fully agree.
Thus I pray to God that he keep me from doing
Or saying anything that might displease her.
And if it is such that I cannot have
Her good will, about which I cannot be silent,
May God keep me from being in her ill will.

Ballade

Sweet harshness, my very deadly friend,
My good, my ill, my mistress, my joy,
My all, my very sweet enemy,
My ballad humbly I send to you
To pray you that it please you that I be
Consoled of my sorrow by you.
For so help me God, my good and my treasure,
No woman but you has the power over me
To heal me, for I am stricken.
And for that reason I remain dressed in black.

The more I think about the benefits of your lordship,
About the beauty of which you are the peak,
About the charming play with which you are adorned,
My pain pleases me, nor would I wish to recover
If not through you, whatever should happen to me.
I never wish to change my desire.
My heart wishes it and I have agreed,
Although you have completely banished me from hope
By a rejection near enough to the ditch or moat.
And for that reason I remain dressed in black.

Alas, my lady, have I deserved death
For loving you until I could no more?
Will your pity be denied to me?
Have I done anything I shouldn't do?
Death or mercy, I would not wish for more.
I surrender to you; accept me willingly.
Make me rich in that of which I am poor:
It is the happiness that I can have through you.

Je suis en dueil, presque desesperé.
Et pour cela me tiens vestu de noir.

Autre Balade

Las! je suis en dueil vestu de noir.
Vostre doulceur me peult bien revestir
A leesse et chasser desespoir
Hors de mon cueur pour me faire esjouir.
Vous me povez de plaisance bannir
Ou conforter mon doloreux torment.
Vostre serf suis, maiz c'est si loyaulment
Qu'a nulle rien ne puis prendre plaisir
Qu'a vous amer, ma dame, seulement.

Il a longtemps que j'ay mis mon vouloir
A vous amer et loyaulment servir.
Guion pieça le vous feist assavoir,
Maiz se j'avoye puissance ne loisir
Ne hardement de mon fait regehir,
Plus vous vouldroie dire mon pensement
Qu'autre le deist. Maiz pensez seurement
Que jamaiz jour n'auray autre desir
Qu'a vous amer, ma dame, seulement.

Las! ma maistresse, se je avoye le pouoir
Que ciel et terre je peusse despartir,
S'il vous plaisoit tout en gré recevoir,
Tout seroit vostre, sans riens ailleurs partir.
Aiez pitié de moy qui suis martir,
Ma seule amour, mon dieu, mon sauvement.
Ne me laissez finer piteusement.
Car espoir ay de nul bien desservir
Qu'a vous amer, ma dame, seulement.

Autre Balade

Helas! ma dame, pour qui me fault gemir
Par maintes foiz et souvent souspirer,
Aiez pitié de vostre vray martir,
Qui humblement veulz son temps definer
En vous servant, sans jamaiz autre amer,
Quoy que diez qu'avenir ne me pourroit
Vostre doulx cuer, pour ce doy bien porter:
«En cest hostel, pitié goute n'y voit.»

I am in grief, almost in despair,
And for that reason I remain dressed in black.

Another Ballade

Alas, in grief I am dressed in black.
Your gentleness can very well dress me instead
In happiness and can chase despair
Out of my heart in order to make me joyful.
You can banish me from pleasure
Or comfort my sorrowful torment.
I am your subject, but it is so loyally
That I cannot take pleasure in anything
Except to love you, my lady, exclusively.

It has been a long time since I set my mind
On loving you and serving you loyally.
Guion let you know this long ago,
But if I had the power or the leisure
Or the courage to describe my state,
I would wish to tell you more of my thought
Than another said. But think assuredly
That never will I have any other desire
Except to love you, my lady, exclusively.

Alas, my mistress, if I had the power
That I could parcel out the heaven and earth,
If it pleased you to accept all willingly,
All would be yours undividedly.
Have pity on me, who is a sufferer,
My only love, my god, my salvation.
Do not let me end piteously.
For I have hope of winning no other reward
Except to love you, my lady, exclusively.

Another Ballade

Alas, my lady, for whom I am forced to moan
On many occasions and often to sigh,
Have pity on your true sufferer,
Who humbly wishes to end his days
In serving you, without ever loving another,
Although you say that your gentle heart
Could never belong to me; therefore I must bear:
"In this house he finds not a drop of pity."

Tout mon regard et tout mon souvenir
Si est en vous, ma deesse sans per.
Tout mon confort me peult de vous venir,
N'autre que vous ne me peult conforter.
Ma garison se peult en vous trouver.
Maiz dit m'avez, quoy que n'ayez pas droit,
Que je puis bien en devise porter:
«En cest hostel, pitié goute n'y voit.»

Pouoir avez de moy faire fenir
Piteusement et mes jours abregier,
Et, d'autre part, par vous puis recueillir
La garison que je doy desirer.
Vous me povez bannir ou rappeller.
Humble vers vous seray commant qu'il soit,
Nonobstant ce qu'il me fault porter:
«En cest hostel, pitié goute n'y veoit.»

Balade

N'a pas longtemps que mon cueur vous faisoit
Une requeste assez piteusement,
Car en humblesse bien fort vous supplioit
Que souffrissiés au moins tant seulement
Qu'il vous servist jusques au deffinement.
Maiz vostre gré n'a voulu consentir
Que j'eusse espoir d'avoir allegement,
Et en ce point m'a faillu despartir.

Et par Dieu, belle, se vostre vueil estoit
D'estre piteuse de mon tresdoulx torment,
A ceste foiz ma douleur cesseroit.
Lors me tendroie trop plus joyeusement
Que je ne faiz, car tout mon penseement
Seroit de vous en leesse servir.
Maiz de vous n'ay nul reconfortement,
Et en ce point m'a faillu despartir.

Maiz nonobstant, soit a tort, soit a droit,
Demourer vueil en vostre jugement.
Mon cuer est vostre et sera ou qu'il soit,
Quoy qu'en ayez fait le despartement.
Par Dieu, ma dame, je ne vueil nullement
Autre que vous pour maistresse tenir.
Si m'avez dit que je foiz follement,
Et en ce point m'a faillu despartir.

All my thoughts and all my memory
Are thus on you, my goddess without equal.
All my comfort can come to me from you.
No one else but you can console me.
My healing can be found in you.
But you have told me, although you are not right,
That I can well bear as a motto:
"In this house he finds not a drop of pity."

You have the power to make me end
Piteously and to shorten my days,
And on the other hand, from you I can receive
The healing that I ought to desire.
You can banish me or call me back.
I will be humble to you however it is,
Despite what I am forced to bear:
"In this house he finds not a drop of pity."

Ballade

Not long ago, my heart made to you
A request, rather piteously,
For humbly it beseeched you very strongly
That you allow at least only
That it might serve you until the end.
But your will did not wish to consent
That I have hope of having any relief,
And in that state, I was forced to leave.

And by God, fair one, if your will were
To have pity on my very sweet torment,
At that time my sorrow would come to an end.
Then I would act much more joyously
Than I do now, for all of my thought
Would be in happiness to serve you.
But from you I have no consolation,
And in that state, I was forced to leave.

But nonetheless, whether wrong or right,
I wish to remain under your judgment.
My heart is yours and will be, wherever it is,
Although you have brought about our separation.
By God, my lady, in no way do I wish
To have as mistress anyone but you.
Yet you have told me that I act foolishly,
And in that state, I was forced to leave.

Complaincte

A vous, belle, tresdoulce dame,
A qui j'ay donné corps et ame,
Cueur et tout ce que je puis avoir,
Faiz oroison et vous reclame
Comme celle par qui j'enflame
Du desir d'amoureux vouloir.
Plaise vous mon fait pourveoir,
Car de tous biens suis despourveu,
Ne n'ay d'avoir nul bien espoir.
Confort ne me veult recevoir.
Je suis de tristesse vestu.

Helas! je mis mon pensement
A vous amer tresloyaulment,
Ne je n'ay nulle autre pensee.
Je parle aux gens le plus souvent
Et si ne sçay quoy ne comment,
Fors que trestout a la volee.
M'amour est en vous arrestee.
Je vous voy tousjours, ce me semble.
Laz! vendra jamais la journee,
Ma princesse tresdesiree,
Que je nous puisse veoir ensemble?

Il m'est advis, ainsi m'aist Dieux,
Que j'ay tousjours devant les yeulx
Vostre non pareille beaulté,
De qui chascun est amoureux,
Les jeunes, aussi sont les vieulx.
Quant ainsi y suis ahurté,
Ne n'a d'autre amer voulenté,
Le cueur qui le me peust souffrir,
Tant m'a conquis vostre bonté,
Que du tout m'y suis ahurté,
Sans jamaiz jour en despartir.

On me peult crier en l'oreille,
Maiz nulle rien ne me resveille
Que vostre bonne renommee.
En veillant ou quant je someille,
Si ay je tousjours la merveille
Des biens dont vous estes louee,
Ma maistresse tresredoubtee,
Tant est vostre corps et esperit.
Ne seuffrez que ma destinee

Complaint

To you, beautiful, very gentle lady,
To whom I have given body and soul,
Heart and all that I can possess,
I make my prayer, and I call upon you
As she by whom I am inflamed
With the desire of a loving will.
May it please you to consider my state,
For I am deprived of all good,
Nor do I have hope of any benefit.
Comfort does not wish to receive me.
I am dressed in sadness.

Alas! I set my thought
On loving you very loyally,
And I have no other thought.
Most often I speak to people
And yet do not know what or how,
Except that I do so distractedly.
My love is fixed upon you.
I see you always, it seems to me.
Alas! Will the day ever come,
My greatly desired princess,
That I might be able to see us together?

It seems to me, so help me God,
That I have always before my eyes
Your beauty without equal,
With which everyone is in love,
The young and the old as well.
When I am stricken thus
And the heart which allows me to suffer it
Has no wish to love any other,
So much has your goodness conquered me
That I am fully overcome by it,
Without ever forsaking it a single day.

One can cry aloud into my ear,
But nothing can awaken me
Except your great renown.
In waking or when I am asleep,
I am in constant wonderment
Of the virtues for which you are praised,
My very formidable mistress,
Such is your body and your mind.
Do not allow that my destiny

Soit par vous en douleur finee.
D'autre ne puis avoir respit.

Las! comment peussiés vous savoir
La douleur et le desespouoir
En quoy je suis pour vous amer?
Je n'ay du dire le pouoir
Et congnoiz que n'avez vouloir
De moy ouyr ne escoucter.
Dont vous peut venir tel amer?
Comment le peult Amours souffrir?
Mieulx me vaulsist estre en la mer
Et du tout le monde laissier,
Quant g'y seuffre tel desplaisir.

Mais dont me vient la maladie?
Puisqu'il convient que je le die,
C'est pour celle que je choisy,
De tous biens la mieulx acomplie
Qui soit ne fut jamaiz en vie,
Ainsi m'aist Dieux qu'il est ainsi.
Et puisqu'Amours m'a asservy
A celle querre pour le mieulx,
Si seray du tout sans nul sy,
Actendant sa doulce mercy
Dont maintes gens sont convoiteux.

Las! me vendroit il bien meschance
De choisir la non per de France,
Et de qui on dit plus de bien?
Mon mal me deust estre plaisance,
Et me deust estre souffisance
D'estre tant seulement tout sien.
Car d'elle mieulx vault ung seul rien
Que d'autre ce qu'on pourroit dire.
Et pour ce la mort point ne craing,
Maiz je luy rens ce qui fut mien,
Puisque trouver je ne puis mire.

Las! maintes gens sont par oultrage
Pieça mors, dont c'est dommaige,
Ou par l'oultrage de la mort.
Et moy qui n'ay nul aventage
De bien, mais languis en servage,
Ne puis mourir n'a droit n'a tort.
Je vif en dueil sans reconfort,
Je suis pres de desesperé,

Be ended in sadness because of you.
From another I cannot have relief.

Alas! How could you know
The sorrow and the despair
In which I am for loving you?
I do not have the power to say,
And I realize that you don't have the wish
To hear me or to listen to me.
From where can such harshness come to you?
How can Love allow it?
It would be better for me to be at sea
And to leave behind the entire world
When I suffer such unhappiness.

But whence does this malady come to me?
For it is necessary that I say it:
It is for her whom I chose,
The most perfected in all virtues
Who is and ever was in life,
So help me God that it is so.
And since Love has commanded me
To seek her for my own good,
So will I be unconditionally,
Awaiting her sweet mercy
Of which many are covetous.

Alas! Would it really be misfortune
For me to choose the one without peer in France
And of whom one says more of good?
My pain should be to me a pleasure,
And it ought to be enough for me
To be so exclusively completely hers.
For just a single thing from her is worth more
Than whatever one could name from another.
And therefore I don't fear death at all,
But I surrender to it that which was mine,
Because I can not find a physician.

Alas! Many people have been killed
By violence, which is a pity,
Or by the ravages of death.
And I, who have no excess of well-being
But who languish in servitude,
Cannot die for right or wrong.
I live in grief without consolation.
I am near to despair

Se Pitié n'est vers moy d'accord.
Maiz je pense que Pitié dort,
Dont je suis tout desconforté.

Balade

Ma princesse, tant que je reverray
Voz beaulx yeulx doulx, vostre doulce maniere,
Piteusement en douleur languiray,
Ne plus n'auray une liesse entiere.
Mes yeulx seront de tous poins sans lumiere.
Vostre esloingner me fait mortel traveil,
Ne je n'ay plus confort que regarder
De nuit la lune et de jour le souleil.

Et se m'aist Dieux que je vous serviray,
S'il le convient, sans nulle pensee fiere,
Que vostre vueil du tout accompliray.
Soiez de moy ou piteuse ou murtriere.
Ma voulenté est en vous toute entiere,
Ne ja n'auray de dormir tel sommeil
Que je ne vueille une foiz regarder
De nuit la lune et de jour le souleil.

Savez pourquoy je les regarderay,
M'amour qui estes de mon pouvre cueur biere?
Car advis m'est que mieulx vous verray.
Veoir le povez, pour ce vous foiz priere
Que mon regard tire par une archiere
En vostre cueur, qui n'a point de pareil.
Lors saurez vous pourquoy vueil regarder
De nuit la lune et de jour le souleil.

Complainte

N'a pas longtemps que je cuidoye
Estre hors du dangier d'Amours,
Et des amoureux me mocquoye
Quant leur veoie faire leurs tours.
Maiz or suis je tout a rebours,
Car j'ay entreprins la folie
De ceste meschant aymerie,
Dont il me fault, a dire veoir,
Souvent parler en resverie.
C'est maulvaiz mal que de renchoir.

If Pity isn't favorable to me.
But I think that Pity is asleep,
For which I am completely discouraged.

Ballade

My princess, until I see again
Your beautiful sweet eyes, your gentle manner,
Piteously in sorrow will I languish,
Nor will I have complete happiness ever again.
My eyes will be completely without light.
Your departure causes me a mortal torment,
Nor do I have any comfort except to look
By night at the moon and by day at the sun.

And so help me God, I will serve you,
If necessary, with no proud thought,
And carry out your will in every way.
Be to me either piteous or a murderer.
My will is entirely with you,
And I will not have in sleeping such a rest
That I do not wish sometime to look
By night at the moon and by day at the sun.

Do you know why I will look at them,
My love, you who are the tomb of my poor heart?
Because it seems to me that I will see you better.
You can see it; therefore I pray to you
That my look shoot by means of an archer
Into your heart, which has absolutely no equal.
Then will you know why I wish to look
By night at the moon and by day at the sun.

Complaint

It wasn't long ago that I thought
To be beyond the power of Love,
And I used to make fun of lovers
When I saw them playing their games.
But now I am all upside down,
For I have undertaken the folly
Of this nasty love business,
For which I am forced, to tell the truth,
Often to speak as if in a daze.
It is a terrible pain to succumb again.

Je suis trop pis que ne souloie.
J'ay de mes souhaiz le rebours.
J'ay pis que dire ne pourroye,
Torment, desplaisir et doulours,
Sans esperance de secours
Trouver vers ma mortel amye,
Car de mercy est desgarnie.
Maiz sa doulceur me donne espoir
De guerir de ma maladie.
C'est maulvaiz mal que de renchoir.

La beaulté et ma seulle joye
Me fera definer mes jours.
Quant elle vient, ou que je soye,
Estre prés pour oyr mes plours,
En luy ne treuve nul secours
Pour m'oster de forcenerie.
Ouir ne veult rien que je die.
Las! comment pourra elle savoir
Mon penser et ma muserie?
C'est maulvais mal que de renchoir.

Maiz plus me plaist, par mon serement,
En avoir douloreux tourment
Et en souffrir mainte destresse
Pour l'aymer fort et loyaulment
Et la veir tant seulement,
Mon dieu et ma seulle princesse,
Que d'autre toute la leesse
Avoir que souhaidier pourroye.
Mon cueur du tout lui fait promesse
Qu'autre ne prandra a maistresse,
Pour nul mal qu'endurer en doye.

Car j'ay trop bien la congnoissance
Qu'il n'a point de pareille en France
De tout bien que dire on pourroit.
Sa beaulté et sa contenance
Me font avoir mal en plaisance.
Se chascun bien la congnoissoit,
Tout le monde estre vouldroit
A elle, ainsi m'aist Dieux.
Ja loyaulté ne l'en tendroit,
Ne par faulx tenuz n'en seroit,
Car c'est le dieu des autres dieux.

I am much worse off than I used to be.
I have the opposite of what I wish for.
I have worse than I could say,
Torture, unhappiness, and sorrows,
Without hope of finding help
From my deadly friend,
For she is bereft of mercy.
But her sweetness gives me hope
Of healing from my malady.
It is a terrible pain to succumb again.

The beauty and my only joy
Will make me end my days.
When she happens, wherever I am,
To be ready to hear my tears,
In her I don't find any help
To free me of my madness.
She doesn't want to hear anything I say.
Alas, how will she know
My thought and my imaginings?
It is a terrible pain to succumb again.

But more does it please me, by my oath,
To have a sorrowful torment
And to suffer many a distress
For loving her strongly and loyally
And only just to see her,
My god and my only princess,
Than to have from another
All the happiness that I could wish.
My heart fully makes her a promise
That it will not take another as a mistress
For any pain that I must endure.

For I recognize very well
That there is absolutely no equal in France
In any virtue that one could name.
Her beauty and her manner
Make me experience pain in pleasure.
If everybody knew her well,
Everyone would want to belong
To her, so help me God.
Loyalty to her would never be lacking,
Nor would she ever be had by the false,
For she is the god of other gods.

Et puisqu'elle a tant de beaulté,
D'onneur, de gracieuseté,
Que de biens c'est la non pareille,
Ne doy je estre reconforté
Se je seuffre mal et durté
Et se j'ay la puce en l'oreille?
Se pour s'amour je me resveille
Alors que je deusse dormir,
Il ne m'en chault, car c'est pour celle
Qui est du monde la plus belle,
Et pour ce m'en doy resjouir.

Par Dieu, Amours, je ne vouldroie,
Ne pour rien ne me tendroye,
Que d'elle ne fusse amoureux
Pour chose qu'avenir m'en doye.
Ne cesseray, ou que je soye,
De la servir de bien en mieulx.
Et s'il plairoit a ses beaulx yeulx
Monstrer que de moy fust contente,
J'en seroye plus desireux
D'acomplir son vueil en tous lieux,
Et y mectroye toute m'entente.

Et plust a Dieu qu'elle sceust bien
Comme mon cueur est du tout sien,
Maugré les jaloux plains d'envie.
Sur toutes a elle me tien.
Je ne pense a nulle rien
Qu'a sa treshaulte seigneurie
Et aux biens dont elle est garnie,
Esperant que ung temps vendra,
Ne laisseray pour jalousie,
Qu'elle me soit dame et amye.
Maiz je ne sçay quant ce sera.

Seroit bien Amours si contraire
Vers moy et de si rude affaire
De m'avoir pourchassié ma mort?
Amours m'a fait, pour lui complaire,
De toutes autres me retraire
Pour la servir jusqu'a la mort,
Et ad ce faire suis d'accord.
Or m'en doint Dieux telle nouvelle
Que j'en puisse prendre confort,
Car sien seray, soit droit ou tort,
Quant c'est des bonnes la plus belle.

And since she has so much beauty,
Honor, and graciousness
That in virtues she is without peer,
Should I not be comforted
If I suffer pain and harshness
And if I have a flea in my ear?
If for love I lie awake
When I am supposed to be sleeping,
I do not care, for it is for her
Who is the most beautiful in the world,
And for that reason I ought to rejoice.

By God, Love, I would not wish,
Nor for anything would I restrain myself,
That I was not in love with her
For anything that might happen to me.
I will not cease, wherever I am,
To serve her better and better.
And if it would be pleasing to her sweet eyes
To show that she was happy with me,
I would be more desirous
To carry out her will in every place
And there I would set all my effort.

And may it please God that she know well
How my heart is entirely hers
Despite the jealous who are full of envy.
I belong to her above all women.
I do not think about anything
Except about her great lordship
And about the virtues with which she is adorned,
Hoping that a time will come –
And I will not quit out of jealousy –
That she is my lady and my friend.
But I do not know when this will be.

Would Love indeed be so opposed
To me and of so cruel a nature
As to have pursued my death?
Love caused me, to please himself,
From all other women to withdraw
In order to serve her until death,
And I am in agreement to do so.
Now may God bring to me such tidings
That I can take some comfort,
For I will be hers, whether right or wrong,
When she is the most beautiful of good women.

Amours, se peusse tant veiller
Qu'en veillant peusse espier
Une estoille qui voulsist cheoir,
Tost me verriés agenoillier
Et envers les dieux supplier
Qu'ilz me voulsissent pourveoir.
Car ma dame m'a dit, pour voir,
Que ce que on requiert adoncques,
Le requerant le doit avoir.
Et j'en vueil la verité savoir,
Pour ce que je ne le sceuz oncques.

Chançon

Belle, des bonnes non pareille,
Pourquoy m'entra tant en l'oreille
Le bien de vostre renommee?
Las! que n'estoit ma veue troublee
Quant je viz de vous la merveille!

Car en veillant mon cueur sommeille,
Et en dormant il me resveille,
Pensant a ma folle pensee.
Belle, des bonnes non pareille,
Pourquoy m'entra tant en l'oreille
Le bien de vostre renommee?

Pieça sçavez que m'appareille,
Seulle des autres despareille,
A vous servir, toute louee.
Mort ou mercy me soit donnee.
Ne souffrez plus que me traveille.

Belle, des bonnes non pareille.
Pourquoy m'entra tant en l'oreille
Le bien de vostre renommee?
Las! que n'estoit ma veue troublee
Quant je viz de vous la merveille!

Chançon

Si fort m'ont pleu les tresors des hauls biens
Qui sont en vous, ainsi vrayement m'aist Dieux,
Que, sans cesser, j'ay esté envieux
D'estre tout vostre, et pour vostre me tiens.

Love, if I could stay awake
Until waking I could catch sight
Of a star that was about to fall,
At once you would see me kneel down
And pray to the gods
That they please watch over me.
For my lady told me, in truth,
That what one asks for then,
The petitioner ought to have it.
And I hope to learn the truth of this,
Because I never did find out.

Song

Fair one, without peer among good women,
Why entered so strongly into my ear
The goodness of your reputation?
Alas, how my sight was disturbed
When I saw the wondrousness of you!

For in waking my heart is asleep,
And while sleeping it awakens me,
Thinking on my foolish thought.
Fair one, without peer among good women,
Why entered so strongly into my ear
The goodness of your reputation?

You who are alone without equal among other women
Have long known that I am ready
To serve you, fully praised lady.
May death or mercy be given to me.
Don't allow me to be tortured any further.

Fair one, without peer among good women,
Why entered so strongly into my ear
The goodness of your reputation?
Alas, how my sight was disturbed
When I saw the wondrousness of you!

Song

So greatly pleased me the treasure of great virtues
That you possess, so truly help me God,
That without cease, I have desired
To be fully yours, and yours I hold myself to be.

Le cueur, le corps qui jadis furent miens
Veullent tous deux que vous soiez mon mieulx,
Si fort m'ont pleu les tresors des hauls biens
Qui sont en vous, ainsi vrayement m'aist Dieux.

Las! je suis riens et ne me donnez riens
Qui conforter puist mon mal envieux.
Et si soutien mon mal tresangoisseux
Bien doulcement, car par vous le soustiens.

Si fort m'ont pleu les tresors des hauls biens
Qui sont en vous, ainsi vrayement m'aist Dieux,
Que, sans cesser, j'ay esté envieux
D'estre tout vostre, et pour vostre me tiens.

Chançon

Celle qui est belle, doulce et plaisant,
Toute bonne, des autres non pareille,
Vostre renom m'a tout emply l'oreille,
Mes yeulx ne voient que vous que j'ayme tant.

Desir me va nuyt et jour atisant
Et me dit: «Ayme, car je le te conseille,
Celle qui est belle, doulce et plaisant,
Toute bonne, des autres non pareille.

Puisqu'Amours, a qui suis obeissant,
Veult que du tout a amer m'appareille,
J'aymeray tant que ce sera merveille,
Et serviray, son honneur acroissant,

Celle qui est belle, doulce et plaisant,
Toute bonne, des autres non pareille.
Vostre renom m'a tout emply l'oreille.
Mes yeulx ne voient que vous que j'ayme tant.

The heart, the body that formerly were mine
Both wish that you be my greater good,
So greatly pleased me the treasure of great virtues
That you possess, so truly help me God.

Alas, I am nothing and you give me nothing
That might console the pain of my desire.
And yet I bear my very sorrowful pain
Very sweetly, for through you I endure it.

So greatly pleased me the treasure of great virtues
That you possess, so truly help me God,
That without cease, I have desired
To be fully yours, and yours I hold myself to be.

Song

She who is beautiful, sweet, and charming,
Fully good, without equal among others,
Your renown has fully filled my ear.
My eyes see only you, whom I love so.

Desire comes to afflict me night and day
And says to me, "Love, for so I advise you,
Her who is beautiful, sweet, and charming,
Fully good, without equal among others."

Since Love, to whom I am obedient,
Wishes me to be fully ready to love,
I will love so much that it will be a wonder,
And I will serve, to the increase of her honor,

Her who is beautiful, sweet, and charming,
Fully good, without equal among others.
Your renown has fully filled my ear.
My eyes see only you, whom I love so.

Explanatory Notes

Abbreviations: **A**: Lausanne, Bibliothèque Cantonale et Universitaire, MS 350, second quarter 15th century; **B**: Paris, Bibliothèque nationale, f. fr. 1727, mid 15th century; **C**: Paris, Bibliothèque nationale, f. fr. 1131, mid 15th century; **D**: Paris, Bibliothèque nationale, f. fr. 24440, 15th century; **E**: Barcelona, Biblioteca de Catalunya, MS 8, Catalan, 1420–30; **F**: Paris, Bibliothèque Nationale, f. fr. 2201, early 15th century; **K**: Lausanne, Bibliothèque Cantonale et Universitaire, IS 4254, 15th century; **N**: Brussels, Bibliothèque royale Albert 1er, MS 10961–10970, c. 1465; **P**: Philadelphia, University of Pennsylvania, Van Pelt Library, MS Codex 902 (formerly Fr. MS 15), 1395–1400; ***100B***: *Les Cent Ballades*; **Basso**: "L'envol et l'ancrage"; ***BD***: Chaucer, *The Book of the Duchess*; **Berguerand**: Berguerand, *Duel*; **Boulton**: *Song*; **Braddy**: Braddy, *Chaucer and Graunson*; **Carden**: "Le *Livre Messire Ode* d'Oton de Grandson; ***CA***: Gower, *Confessio Amantis*; ***DL***: Guillaume de Machaut, *Dit dou lyon*; ***DLA***: Guillaume de Machaut, *Dit de l'alerion*; ***FA***: *La fonteinne amoureuse*; ***FC***: Wimsatt, *French Contemporaries*; **GW:** Granson, *Poésies*, ed. Grenier-Winther; ***LGW***: Chaucer, *The Legend of Good Women*; ***PA***: Froissart, *Paradis d'Amour*; ***PF***: Chaucer, *The Parliament of Fowls*; **Piaget**: Grandson, *Vie et poésies*, ed. Piaget; ***PL***: Guillume de Machaut, *Poésies Lyriques*; **Poirion**: Poirion, *Poète et prince*; ***TC***: Chaucer, *Troilus and Criseyde*; ***RR***: Guillaume de Lorris and Jean de Meun, *Le Roman de la rose*; ***VD***: Guillaume de Machaut, *Le livre dou voir dit.*

1–9 Rondels

On the form of the *rondeau*, see the Introduction, p. 16. The manuscripts differ greatly in their presentation of the refrain. In manuscript *A*, it must be assumed: the ten unique lines of the poem are presented in a single block, in almost all cases with a paragraph mark (¶) to indicate the beginning of each stanza (as in the ballades in this manuscript) but with no signal that the opening lines are to be repeated. In the two rondeaux that appear in manuscript *F* (*4* and *9*), the repetition of the entire first stanza at the end of the poem is indicated by the first word or words plus "&c," while in the interior of the poem, the same abbreviation occurs for each repeated line, including each line of the 4-line refrain in *9*.13–16. In manuscript *D*, which we have used as our base for *Le Livre Messire Ode*, the first words of the refrain appear as an abbreviation for the rest, in one case only within the second stanza (at *78*.2042), in three cases only for the final stanza (at *78*.599, 1452, and 1723), and in the other six instances in both positions. Manuscript *N*, a partial copy of *Le Livre Messire Ode*, contains three rondeaux. In none of the three does it indicate the repetition in the second stanza. In one instance (at line 344), a single line stands for the repeated final stanza; in the other two, the repeated final stanza is written out in full (at 599–603 and 1452–55). We have taken the broadest view, adopting all of the scribes' indications of repetition in every case: thus in each of the rondeaux here and in *Le Livre Messire Ode*, we have silently inserted or expanded the refrain in both positions, repeating the opening lines of the initial stanza at the end of the second stanza and the entire initial stanza at the end. On the rondeaux containing 5-line stanzas, see the note to ***78***.591–93. On the variations in scribal presentation of the refrains, see Poirion, pp. 336–39.

2. Rondel: «Avril, qui vest de verdure»

9 *Figure*. *Figure* did not take on its modern meaning of "face" until the sixteenth century (Rey, *Dictionnaire Historique*). For "face," Granson uses *vis*, *visage*, *face*, or *viaire* instead. *Figure* still had the more general meaning of "form" (in addition to specific contextual senses), but like *corps* (see Greimas, *Moyen*), when referring to the human form, it could be used simply to mean "person" or "individual," without necessarily the implications of physicality of modern English "figure" or "body" (Godefroy, *Dictionnaire*). So have we taken it, here and in ***30***.8; see also ***61***.14.

3. Rondel: «Je ne voy riens qui me doie suffire»

9–10 *Riens qui soit bel a mon cuer ne puit luire / Tout ce qui puit gecter mon cuer d'esmay*. The sense is clear here, though the grammar is a bit obscure. The missing negative (or "I lack") in line 10 is somehow to be inferred from line 9.

4. Rondel: «S'il ne vous plaist que j'aye mieulx»

9 *Belle, tournez vers moy voz yeux*. Compare the identical line in ***75***.1 and ***75***.216. Jung ("Répertoire," p. 95) notes that ***4*** immediately follows ***75*** in manuscript A, the only one of four copies of ***75*** that contains line 216, and he suggests that this rondeau is actually the conclusion of the lai that precedes it.

12 *Et puis faitez de moy voz jeux*. We have translated this line literally in recognition that it might possibly be ambiguous. *Jeu* more commonly has a positive sense in Granson, suggesting innocent amusement, as in ***78***.1268, 2049, and 2137, and the "jeu sans vilennie [game without wickedness]" of ***61***.5; but the game played by Love in ***50***.24 suggests something more like the cat and mouse image invoked by our translation.

6. Rondel: «Comment seroit que je fusse joieulx?»

12–13 *Avec Danger qui tant est envieux, / Comment seroit que je fusse joieulx*. On the continuation of the sentence from one stanza to the next, see the note to ***46***.10–11 below.

8. Rondel: «Ce premier jour que l'an se renouvelle»

This is one of four poems by Granson with a New Year's setting; see also ***13***, ***69***, and ***70***. For other examples in which a poet offers a New Year's gift, see Poirion, pp. 117–18.

11 *Regart . . . Bel Parler*. These two personifications of the lady's actions towards the lover are typical of figures used commonly by fourteenth-century lyricists, building upon the allegorical narrative of the lover's approach to the lady in the *RR*. See the note to ***21***, below.

9. Rondel: «Adieu, Jeunesse, m'amie»

For a very different take on the effects of aging see ***15*** and ***25***. This poem extends the normal form of the rondeau by taking the second appearance of the complete refrain as the first in a new sequence of four stanzas, as is common in the virelais. The extra length allows a greater complexity of feeling than is typical of the rondeau, especially in the sixth stanza.

21 *druerie*. Neither *druerie* (which we have translated as "gallantry") nor its root *dru(e)*, from an Old Provençal word for "lover," occurs anywhere else in Granson's poetry. *Druerie* is more common in the romances, and like the rest of this poem, it evokes a setting of flirtation and of amorous relations very different from that of the suffering unrequited lover of the majority of Granson's poems.

10. Vyrelay: «Je vous aime, je vous desir»

On the form of the virelai, see the Introduction, pp. 16–17. Of the three copies of this virelai that survive, only that in manuscript *F* contains any indication that the refrain is to be repeated at the end, in the form "Je vous &c," the same way that the scribe of this manuscript indicates the repetition of the initial stanza in the rondeaux. See the note to ***1–9*** above.

12. Balade: «J'ay tout perdu; le festu est rompu»

1 *d'amor*. Both Piaget and GW preserve the manuscript reading *de mort* [of death] instead of the emendation adopted here, *d'amor* [of love].

4 *amis*. *Amis* can be used in Middle French to mean simply "friend," as at 23.1, ***39***.12, 46.8, or ***70***.45, but in contexts involving the lover's relation with his lady, it generally means one who has been accepted as a lover, as opposed to *amant*, one whose love may be but is not necessarily returned. As such, it also occurs in the feminine form *amie* (e.g., in ***23***.13, ***48***.27, and ***77***.391–93). If they did not sound too juvenile, we might have used "boyfriend" and

"girlfriend" in the translation. Since the only other choice in English appears to be "lover," the distinction from *amant* and the implication of reciprocity are lost. Exactly what is implied by the *don d'ami* (literally, the "gift of or from [a] friend"), here and in ***78***.991 and 1613, is somewhat more elusive. The closest to this expression that we are aware of in Machaut occurs in a ballade in which he refers to the "don d'amie," in the feminine, where the sense is evidently "the gift of (having a) (girl)friend" (*PL* 1:101, number XVCI; *Louange des Dames*, p. 87, number 146; line 6). In Granson's use, the *don d'ami* appears instead to be the lady's acceptance of the lover as her "boyfriend" as in ***46***.27–28; hence our punctuation and our translation, "the gift of 'lover.'"

7 *le festu est rompu*. *La paille est rompue*, the modern equivalent of this expression, is still recognized by older speakers of French as meaning "our friendship is at an end." Godefroy (*Dictionnaire*, s.v. *festu*) also provides "l'engagement est annulé" (roughly, "the deal is off").

10 *corps*. On *corps* [person], see the note to ***2***.9.

12–13 *En maudiray Desir qui m'a surpris, / Quant Doulx Espoir m'a son arc destendu*. The relation between Hope and Desire is one of the recurring themes in Machaut's *dits amoureux*. For Machaut, however, Hope typically constitutes the antidote to Desire rather than its cause, as in these lines. See Kelly, *Imagination*, pp. 130–50.

15–16 *Tristam . . . Yseult*. Tristam (or Tristan) and Iseult are the hero and heroine of one of the best-known French romances, the earliest surviving versions of which, by Béroul and Thomas of Britain, date from the mid twelfth century. Granson makes two direct references to them, here and in ***18***.17–18. In *Le Livre Messire Ode*, he makes two further references to Palamedes, Tristam's rival for Iseult's love; see the note to lines ***78***.1758–66 below. As in the case of the other figures that he names, it is not necessary to suppose that Granson was directly familiar with any of these earlier texts: the stories themselves were already well known and the names frequently cited. Machaut, for instance, cites Tristam and Lancelot together as examples of true lovers in *DL*, line 1321; *Le Jugement du Roi de Navarre*, lines 2841 and 2957; and *Le Confort d'Ami*, line 2803.

13. BALADE: «A CE PLAISANT PREMIER JOUR DE L'ANNEE»

On the New Year's setting see the note to ***8***, above.

1 *que j'aim plus qu'autre ne que moy*. Compare Machaut, *Balade notée* XLV, line 7, "Que j'aim cent fois plus qu'autre ne que moy" (*PL*, 2:564).

10 *noir*. Even if *noir* [black] is meant in a literal rather than metaphorical sense, it may not necessarily have to be taken as an indication of mourning rather than of sadness more generally. In *Le Livre Messire Ode* (***78***.421, 485–86 et al.), the narrator chooses to dress in black as a token of his sorrow at being

rejected by his lady. Compare also Christine de Pisan's Balade LXXXVIII, "Qu'en puis je mais, se je porte le noir" (*Œuvres poétiques*, 1:88).

14. BALADE: «EN GRANT DESDUIT ET EN DOULCE PLAISANCE»

Though addressed to his lady in the final stanza, this poem more closely resembles the praises of loyalty and the celebrations of the rewards of love that are more common in the "wisdom" poems such as ***23***.

15. BALADE: «CAR J'AY PERDU MA JEUNESSE, MA JOYE»

Granson constructs a topographical allegory of the speaker's sadness and distress that provides a counter-image to the literary gardens of the type that appears in *RR*. Compare the God of Love's tower in ***56***.11–18. For a different response to the effects of aging compare ***9***.

7 *Jeunesse*. *Jeunesse* here may be either the speaker's youth (that is, he has grown old) or merely his youthfulness, as in ***74***.129, a sense that is perhaps more consistent with "my joy."

16. BALADE: «OR VUEILLE DIEUX QUE BREFMENT LE REVOYE»

This is one of five of Granson's ballades spoken by a woman, as indicated by the masculine forms that she uses to refer to her lover (in lines 1, 15, 19 and the refrain) and the feminine forms that she uses for herself (in lines 4, 5, and 20). (*Luy* in lines 8 and 12 is not unambiguously masculine in Granson's French, though it certainly is here; compare ***20***.6, ***74***.127 et al.) Compare ***20***, ***32***, ***34***, and ***50***. Machaut has nearly three dozen poems spoken by a woman, not counting those attributed to Toute Belle that occur only in *VD*. The pains of separation are a recurring theme in Granson's work, as in Machaut's; compare ***24***, ***28***, and ***57***. Each case, however, presumes a different narrative setting. Here an evidently happy relationship is disturbed by the male partner's leaving.

17. BALADE: «QUE NULLE AUTRE JAMAIS NE CHOISIRAY»

For a similar (if not as extensive) use of anaphora compare ***28*** and ***46***. Citing this poem, Poirion (p. 465) lists Granson with other poets who "ont fait un usage immodéré de la répétition [made immoderate use of repetition]."

In manuscript *F*, this poem is entitled "Balade de Saint Valentin," and Saint Valentine replaces the God of Love as the speaker's witness in line 23. Overlooking the latter, Wimsatt (*FC*, p. 236) observes that "a strong indirect association" with the Saint Valentine feast is provided by the repeated "Je vous choisy." On Saint Valentine, see the Introduction, pp. 32–34.

18. Balade: «A Dalida, Jhezabel, et Thays»

This is one of two of Granson's ballades employing a *vers coupé* (a shorter line, of only seven syllables instead of ten) in the fifth line of each stanza. Compare ***32***.

1–3 *Lucresce . . . Hecuba . . . Hilie*. Lucrece (or Lucretia) is the virtuous wife who committed suicide after being raped by the son of the king of Rome, as recounted by Livy (*The History of Rome*, Book I, chapters 57–60). Hecuba is the wife of King Priam of Troy in all versions of the story of the Trojan War. "Hilie" may be Helie or Helia, one of the "Heliades," daughters of Helios and sisters to Phaeton, who on mourning their brother's death are turned into poplar trees, weeping tears of amber (see Hyginus, *Fabulae* 154), though we do not know of any source for the celebration of her chastity. Both Chaucer (*LGW* F 1680–1885) and Gower (*CA* 7.4754–5130, and 8.2632–39) tell the story of Lucresce and speak of Hecuba variously, but neither mentions Helia.

8 *Dalida, Jhezabel, et Thays*. Delilah is the temptress who betrays Samson to the Philistines in Judges XVI. Jezebel is the wife of Ahab, king of Israel (1 Kings XVI–2 Kings IX); she is a worshipper of Baal and a sorceress. Thaïs is a celebrated courtesan and companion of Alexander the Great.

17–19 On Tristan and Iseult see the note to ***12***.15–16, above. The reference to the fountain is an allusion to one of the best-known (and in the Middle Ages, most frequently illustrated) episodes in the story, when King Mark, Iseult's husband, spies on the two lovers during their rendezvous at a fountain or spring. Detecting his presence, they conduct a conversation that is calculated to persuade him of Iseult's fidelity. The story of Jason and Medea is told by many classical authors, among them Ovid (in both the *Metamorphoses* and the *Heroides*), Hesiod, and Hyginus, and among other medieval authors, by Benoît de Sainte-Maure (*Roman de Troie*, lines 715–2044), Guido delle Colonne (*Historia Destructionis Troiae*, 2.169–393), Chaucer (*LGW* F 1580–1678), and Gower (*CA* 3.3247–4373). See also ***20***.1–2. Paris's kidnapping of Helen is the immediate cause of the Trojan War, and was also well known from both classical and medieval sources.

20. Balade: «Ainsi le fait cuer plain de fausseté»

This ballade is spoken by a woman, as indicated not only by the comparison to Medea in line 1 but also by the feminine grammatical forms in lines 12 and 15 and the masculine forms to refer to her lover in 10, 17, and 22. Compare ***16***, ***32***, ***34***, and ***50***.

1–2 *A Medee me puis bien comparer, / Qui a grant tort fu de Jason traie*. For Jason and Medea, see the note to ***18***.17–19, above. Here the reference is to the unhappy ending of their story rather than to its happier beginning.

21. BALADE: «POUR MIEX GARDER DE MA DAME LE FORT»

Dangier, in line 7, is the personification of the woman's reluctance, standoffishness, or resistance to the lover's entreaties. Along with *Malebouche* (Evil Tongue), *Honte* (Shame), and *Peor* (Fear), it guards the rosebud and thus serves to frustrate the lover's intentions in *RR*, while *Bel Acueil* (Fair Welcome), *Franchise* (Generosity), and *Pitié* (Pity) encourage him or come to his aid. These figures all stand for attributes of the woman herself as the lover experiences her. Later narrative *dits* enlarge the allegorical tableau to include figures such as *Durté* (Harshness), *Courtoisie* (Courtesy), *Merci* (Mercy) and *Grace* on the lady's side, and *Désir*, *Esperance* or *Espoir* (Hope), *Dous Penser* (Sweet Thought) and *Dous Regard* (Sweet Sight) as representations of the emotional experience of the lover. These all became staples of the fourteenth-century lyric. Along with *Danger*, Granson here deploys *Pitié*, *Franchise*, *Désir* and *Doulx Expoir* in an allegory of a siege of the lady's "fortress."

7–8 *Contre Dangier, qui a toute heure veille, / Pour miex garder de ma dame le fort.* This is one of three examples of a two-line refrain. The others are at ***27***.7–8 and ***43***.8–9.

22. BALADE: «S'A MA CAUSE PERDOIT SA BONNE FAME»

Male Bouche (Evil Tongue) is one of the guardians of the rosebud in *RR* (see the note to ***21*** above), but in later poetry it takes on a life of its own as the personification of gossip or slander. This is the figure's only appearance in Granson. On the fear of or the effects of slander in the form of the *mesdisans* (also a common theme in Machaut), compare ***32***.4–6, ***35***.13, ***49***.14, and ***57***.28. See also ***73***.138 and ***77***.423–24.

23. BALADE: «VOUS N'EN POVEZ TOUSDIZ QUE MIEX VALOIR»

This is one of five ballades (along with ***33***, ***44***, ***56***, and ***58***; one could also add ***18*** and parts of others) in which the poet offers his advice on the nature or conduct of love, as opposed to dwelling on his own (normally troubled) experience. Their lessons vary: here, as in ***44***, he extols virtuous conduct as a prerequisite for rewards in love.

24. BALADE: «CAR JE LANGUIS EN TROP DURE TRISTOUR»

The pains of separation are a recurring theme in Granson; compare ***16***, ***28***, and ***57***. Here the lover is forced to separate from a woman who does not even know of his love for her.

1–8 The anacoluthon in this stanza — the fact that the first two lines do not seem to be part of the same grammatical structure as the clause that follows — could be resolved by emending *ou maint* in line 2 to *remaint*, a verb that

Granson uses elsewhere (in ***35***.19, ***77***.316, ***78***.537, and 748), and thus by deleting "where" from the translation.

25. Balade: «Car de presant, je veul tout le contraire»

See ***9*** for a somewhat different take on aging. It is easy to suppose that Granson might have been thinking about his own experience in this poem, for it could hardly have been written by a poet who was young, but the juxtaposition with ***9*** suggests that we shouldn't take either completely literally. It is more interesting to ponder the poet's use of a lyric form for what is in effect a renunciation of his earlier poetry.

3 *Et me tenoie liéz, jolis et gais*. This is not, of course, the impression created by the vast majority of the poems to which he refers, another reminder not to take either this poem or those as a precise biographical record.

9–16 Berguerand (p. 137) (like Piaget, p. 142) sees in this stanza an allusion to the troubles of Granson's final years, when he was forced to defend himself against a charge of complicity in the death of Count Amadeus VII, and more specifically a possible admission that he had blindly allowed himself to fall into the trap of a judicial duel laid by his adversaries. The third stanza of this ballade, however, is much less suggestive either of the circumstances or of the options that Granson faced as the duel approached. Compare ***47***.

17–19 For readers of the English poet John Gower, these lines will recall the conclusion of the *CA*, in which the narrator, forced into confrontation with his old age, is urged by Venus to make a "beau retret" (8.2416) and to "preie hierafter for the pes" (8.2913). However striking the verbal similarity, the two passages in Gower are five hundred lines apart, the sentiments are otherwise very different, and it is difficult to establish any direct connection between Granson and Gower, even in Gower's lyric sequence, the *Cinkante Balades*. If there were a borrowing, it would be difficult to tell in which direction it went, since the *CA* may have been complete as early as 1390.

27. Balade amoreuse: «Car vrayement ce martelé me tue»

This ballade contains one of Granson's more extravagant images, of an anvil in his heart, being pounded by the hammers of his desire. (For another, see ***59***.11–12.) While the refrain is memorable, it is not clear that the poet has been able to sustain the metaphor, particularly in lines 9–10.

7–8 *Languir me fault ou a la mort aler, / Car vrayement ce martelé me tue*. One of three examples of a 2-line refrain. See ***21***.7–8 and ***43***.8–9.

9–10 *Celle enclume qu'en mon cuer est entee, / C'est le cler vis de ma dame honnorer. Honnoree* [honored], rhyming with the preceding and following lines, would be easier to deal with: "It is the bright face of my honored lady." The infinitive *honnorer*, however, is required by the *abab* rhyme scheme. Without *pour*, it expresses only the action in French and not the purpose, and the phrase might better be translated as "the honoring of the bright face of my lady." It is difficult, however, to associate that action with the concrete image of the anvil.

28. BALADE: «CAR LOIN DE VOUS VIVRE JE NE POURROYE»

For the use of anaphora compare ***17*** and ***46***. If we are correct in taking *pansés* in line 7 as an imperative, this is the only of Granson's poems about separation in which it is apparently the lady who must depart. Compare ***16***, ***24***, and ***57***.

7 *Pansés*. *Pansés* might be a plural noun meaning "thoughts," but the *–és* spelling also occurs on second-person formal verbs in the same manuscript in ***32***.23, ***34***.21, ***50***.11, and ***64***.31. The imperative, "think about returning," certainly makes more sense with the line that follows than the speaker's farewell to his own "thoughts of returning."

30. BALADE: «QUANT JE PENSE A VO DOULCE FIGURE»

8 *figure*. On *figure*, see the note to ***2***.9.

32. BALADE: «FOY, LOIAULTÉ, SANS FAULCER, VOUS TENDRAY»

This is one of five of Granson's ballades spoken by a woman, as signaled by the masculine forms of the address to *Tresdoulz amis*; compare the opening of ***34*** and ***50***; see also ***16*** and ***20***. The only other indication of gender in this case is the masculine form *certain* in line 23. This is the only of Granson's poems in which the woman must defend her reputation against slanderers. This is also one of only two of Granson's ballades employing a *vers coupé* (a shorter line, of only seven syllables instead of ten) in the fifth line of each stanza. Compare ***18***.

33. BALADE: «DON DE MERCY AINÇOIS QUE ON LE DEPRIE»

This is one of five ballades (along with ***23***, ***44***, ***56***, and ***58***) in which the poet offers his advice on the nature or conduct of love. Each adopts a somewhat different tone. Here the poet's advice is more practical than in the others, urging a reluctant lover not to hesitate to make his desire known.

34. Balade: «Se je m'en plains, ce ne fait a blasmer»

This is one of five ballades by Granson that are spoken by a woman, as signaled by the opening address to *doulz amis*; compare the opening of ***32*** and ***50***; see also ***16*** and ***20***. She also uses feminine grammatical forms to refer to herself and to her rival in lines 5, 6, and 10. Here, as in ***20***, she blames her lover for his disloyalty and falsehood.

35. Balade: «Prouchaine mort en lieu de garison»

This is the first of the six ballades that are presented under the single title "Les six balades ensuivans [The sequence of six ballades]" in manuscript *F*. The others are ***52***, ***63***, ***62***, ***51***, and ***66***. As noted in the Introduction (pp. 19–20), this group constitutes a unity neither thematically nor formally, consisting as it does of three different stanza forms of different lengths (but compare Carden, "Oton de Grandson," p. 143, for whom the six ballades "develop an extended complaint"). Two of these poems (***35*** and ***63***) appear only in manuscript *F*. The other four appear in manuscript *A*, but not grouped together and in a different order; one of these (***66***) contains a third stanza that is lacking in *F*. None of the six appears in manuscript *P*, and only ***52*** appears in any other copy. Since this sequence has a far more dubious status than the "Cinq balades ensuivans" (see the note to ***37–41***, below), we have not preserved it here, and we have adhered to our decision to present the individual poems in order of length and for the text, to privilege *A* over *F*.

11–14 *Se non par mort . . . par traison*. The fear of slander is a recurring theme in Granson; see the note to ***22***, above. This is his strongest statement of its impact upon the lover. There is no reference to the slanderers, however, in any of the other five poems that make up the "Six balades ensuivans."

36. Balade: «Par vo douceur, tresbelle et bonne nee»

23 *Et qu'il vous pleust mon fait recommender*. There is a missing negative in this line unless the *se . . . ne* [if . . . not] of line 22 is understood to be a single conjunction, "unless," that governs both clauses.

37–41. Cinq balades ensuivans

The title, "Cinq balades ensuivans [Sequence of Five Ballades]," appears only in manuscript *F*, but as noted in the Introduction (p. 20), there is good evidence that the five were planned as a group, especially in the fact that all use a stanza form that Granson employs nowhere else. This group also has better manuscript authority than the "Six balades ensuivans" (see the note to ***35***, above). The same five poems appear together in the same order (though without a title) in manuscript *P*, which we have used as our base. (We thus preserve the titles as they appear in *P*.) In manuscript *A*, the poems also appear in the same order, and the first three are grouped together. In GW's edition, which preserves the order in *A*, the five are GW21, GW22, GW23, GW27, and GW31. There is also another copy of ***41***, the last poem in the group, earlier in *A*, GW2. In manuscript *E*, the first four of these poems appear together and in order; the fifth appears separate from and before the rest, putting them in the same order as in *A* if one uses the first of the two copies of ***41*** in *A* rather than the second.

This group of poems has been studied most closely by those examining its relation to Chaucer's "Complaint of Venus." See Braddy, pp. 61–64; Piaget, pp. 171–74; Wimsatt, *FC*, pp. 213–19; Phillips, "Complaint of Venus," and Scattergood, "Chaucer's Complaint of Venus." Wimsatt, *Poems of "Ch,"* pp. 59–65, offers a text and a modern English translation based, like ours, on manuscript *P*. For his argument that *P* contains the text that is closest to Chaucer's, see the Introduction, note 92.

38. *BALADE*: «CAR TROP PAR EST SON CUER PLAIN DE REFFUS»

21–24 The same motif occurs in ***65***.25–28. It takes a more extravagant form in ***78***.2075–84.

39. *BALADE*: «PRIEZ POUR MOY, TOUS LES LOYAULX AMANS»

For the allegorical struggle between *Danger* and his allies on the one hand and *Pitié* and *Mercy* on the other see the note to ***21*** above.

5 *Et si vous dy qu'il a passé sept ans*. There are four such references to the length of the speaker's relationship with his lady in Granson's ballades: ***53***.7 (one year in MS *P*, "about six years" in MS *A*), ***54***.14 (three years), here (seven years), and ***60***.1 (seven and a half years). One could use these references to construct a chronology only by making two equally dubious assumptions: (1) that Granson was referring to his own actual experience so openly, and (2) that in all four poems the same lady was involved.

41. *BALADE*: «DE LI SERVIR NE SERAY JAMAIS LAS»

Wimsatt (*FC*, pp. 215–17) reprints this ballade along with the corresponding stanzas from Chaucer's "Complaint of Venus," and he notes that in choice of rhymes, in the phonetic subtlety of the refrain, and in the graceful conclusion, Granson "appears to advantage in this pair."

13–24 *Or ayme, Cuer . . . jamais las*. Compare the personification of the heart in ***53*** and ***64*** and the debate between Heart and Body in ***78***.1534–1726.

42. Balade: «Desloiaulté en l'amoureuse vie»

This poem, together with ***68*** "Le Dit de Loiauté," may well be Granson's response to the invitation in the one-hundredth of the *Cent ballades* to offer advice on whether or not to adhere to *Loyauté* that is posed by the contrasting views of the old knight and the young lady in the bulk of the ninety-nine ballades that precede. Here Granson seems to address directly those among the thirteen respondents whose poems are included at the end of the *Cent ballades* who side with the lady, who argues not so much for disloyalty *per se* as for protecting oneself from the pains of unreciprocated love by playing the field. Without citing either the knight or any of the other respondents directly, Granson holds to the view, also expressed elsewhere in his ballades, that loyalty constitutes the only proper service to love.

25–28 *Princesse d'Amours . . . l'amoureuse vie*. Four of the last five responses in *Le livre des cent ballades* also end with an envoy (the only ballades in the collection to do so), one of them (the twelfth) also addressed to "Princesse."

43. Balade: «Fors que d'amours et de ma belle dame»

8–9 *Que de riens plus ne me souvient, par m'ame, / Fors que d'amours et de ma belle dame*. One of three examples of a two-line refrain. See ***21***.7–8 and ***27***.7–8.

44. Balade: «Ainsi puet il don d'amours desservir»

This is one of five ballades (along with ***23***, ***33***, ***56***, and ***58***) in which the poet offers his advice on the nature or conduct of love. Their lessons vary: here, as in ***23***, he extols virtuous conduct as the surest way to rewards in love.

45. Balade: «Que mon cuer voit tousdiz, ou que je soye»

Poirion (p. 468) cites this poem in his discussion of what he regards as the overuse of personification in the fourteenth-century lyric.

1–4 *J'ay en mon cuer un oeil . . . voit tout cler*. The image of the eyes of his heart recurs in ***52***.7; compare also ***67***.8–9.

46. Balade: «Ma belle dame et ma loyal amie»

1–5 *Je vous mercy . . . grant doulçour*. For the use of anaphora compare ***17*** and ***28***.

4 *flour*. One expects "flower" in the translation, certainly the more common meaning at the time, but "flour" is also attested from at least the twelfth

century (see Rey, *Dictionnaire historique*) and appears to be more suited to the context here.

10–11 *Ma belle dame et ma loyal amie, / Se plus souvent n'oyez de moy nouvelle*. This is one of the very few clear examples in Granson's shorter poems in which the sentence continues from one stanza to the next, something that is normally prevented in the ballades by the closure that is created by the refrain. The lack of semantic weight in the refrain to this poem opens the way to the exception. For an example in a rondeau, see ***6***.12–13. Such enjambment is also rare in Granson's longer stanza forms: for the few examples, see ***75***.32–33, ***76***.96–97 and 144–45. It is more common in the lyrics included in *Le Livre Messire Ode*: see ***78***.276–77 and 286–87 (two successive stanzas); 773–74; 1565–66; and 1906–7, 1916–17, and 1926–27 (three stanzas in a row); and in rondeaux, ***78***.343–44, 1443–44, 1451–52, and 2497–98 (the very last lyric in the poem).

21–26 For the personifications see the note to ***21*** above.

47. BALADE: «CAR JE LANGUIS PAR DEFFAULT DE RAISON»

This is the one ballade that contains what appear to be specific references to events in Granson's own life (see Piaget, pp. 142–43), particularly in lines 11–18, which describe the circumstances that he faced after he was accused of complicity in the death of Count Amadeus VII in 1391. Forced into exile that year, he was disinherited of his property in 1393, and then, after the judgment against him was reversed by Charles VI in 1395, he was forced to defend himself anew when he was challenged to a judicial duel by one of his longtime enemies. It is not impossible that the poem was written while he was still in exile, but if, as appears, lines 14–16 refer specifically to the challenge to a duel, then the poem must date from the period after his return to Savoy in late 1395 or early 1396, and thus not long before his death in August of 1397. The most complete source for the details of the final years of Granson's life is Berguerand, upon whom we have relied heavily in the notes that follow. See also Piaget, pp. 20–67, and Chaubet, "Duel."

11 *Jeune seigneur*. Amadeus VIII, the son of the deceased count, was only eight years old when his father died and Granson went into exile, and only fourteen at the time of the duel in which Granson was killed. Until Amadeus VII's death, Granson served as a member of the count's Council (Berguerand, p. 113). After his exile, the exact role of the Council in the outcome of the affair is not documented, but two of its members, Raoul de Gruyère and Jean de la Baume, had unsuccessfully brought challenge in 1390 to Granson's right to property he inherited through his wife, and they profited from his exile to acquire that which they had failed to obtain earlier. They thus stood to lose if his property were restored upon his return (Berguerand, pp. 20, 106–8, 113).

Conceil de volunté. Perhaps "willful council." Compare Machaut, *Balade notée* XVIII, lines 15–16, "Mais seulement de volenté / Ma dame m'a congié donné," where *de volenté* seems to imply "without good reason" (*PL*, 2:549).

12 *Gens ennuyeux et commun trop puissant.* In addition to Raoul de Gruyère and Jean de la Baume, Granson's enemies would of course have included Gérard d'Estavayer, who made the formal challenge to a duel and who also had taken possession of one of Granson's properties upon his exile (Berguerand, p. 20). The communes exercised their influence and authority through the *États de Vaud*, a representative assembly in existence since at least 1361 (Holenstein, "Assemblée"). They sided against Granson from the very beginning, ordering the confiscation of his property in 1393 and later helping to finance d'Estavayer in his pursuit of his claim by judicial duel (Berguerand, pp. 117–27).

14–18 *Et vont . . . grant dilacion.* The challenge to Granson's honor might refer to any time when he thought that he was falsely accused, but the vow to defend it, the reference to *l'espreuve certainne*, and the appeal to God in the final stanza point to the period after his return from exile and more specifically to the events that preceded the duel in which he was killed. In his formal response to the challenge to a duel, Granson used some of the same language that he employs here in his statement of his willingness to defend himself:

> Je suis en la misericorde de celluy qui est plus plains de mercy que je ne puis estre pecheable, et *je me fie en luy* de cestuy fait, car *il m'en sera vray juge*. . . . Et il n'est pas en la puissance de celluy qui m'a appelé, s'il ne vous plaist, qu'il puisse avoir plus de *dilacion*. Et je qui suis deffendant n'en requiert point, et Dieu le scet, non pas par orgueil, ne par envye que j'aye de tollir la vie de nul Crestien, fors que ainsy que je suis contrains de *deffendre ma vie et mon honneur* et l'estat en quoy Dieu m'a convoqué
>
> [And I place myself at the mercy of Him who is more full of mercy than I can be guilty of sin, and *I trust in Him* in this affair, for *He will be a true judge* of it for me. . . And it is not in the power of him who has summoned me, if it doesn't please you, to have any more *delay*. And I who am the defendant do not seek any, and God knows, not because of pride or because of any desire that I might have to take the life of a Christian, but only because I am required to *defend my life and my honor* and the state in which God has placed me]
>
> (Berguerand, pp. 156–57).

The same passage can be found in Piaget, p. 60, and Chaubet, "Duel," pp. 33–34.

17 *Le juge fault que ne lez y amainne.* For the construction compare ***67***.27. Is Granson making an appeal to anyone in particular in this line? During the minority of Amadeus VIII, final authority over the county rested with Philippe le Hardi, the Duke of Burgundy (Berguerand, pp. 24, 130), who was among those who had already found Granson innocent of the charges against him, and to whom Granson makes an indirect appeal in his formal response to d'Estavayer's challenge (Berguerand, p. 153). Granson might reasonably have hoped, therefore, for the Duke's intervention against those whom he names in lines 11–12. Berguerand speculates that by this time, Philippe may have lost interest in the case or may even have seen an advantage in Granson's loss (Berguerand, p. 130).

49. Balade: «Je n'ay riens fait qu'Amours ne m'ait fait faire»

This poem forms a pair with ***50***, each employing the same refrain (nearly; see note to ***49***.30), and the second containing the woman's response to the lover's complaint in the first. The two appear in sequence in three of the four copies in which they occur (on manuscript *F*, see the note to ***50*** below), but not in manuscript *A*, which we use as our base. As model for this exchange, one might cite the ballade double in Machaut's *Louange des dames (PL*, 1:41–42, number XXVI; *Louange des dames*, p. 105, number 214) or the sequence of three ballades with the same refrain among his *ballades notées* (*PL*, 2:543–45, numbers IX–XI), in both of which, however, the lover and his lady offer mutual affirmations of affection.

1–2 *Ay my! quel mal, quel ennuy, quel doleur, / Quel grant meschief, quel soussy ne quel pene*. Poirion (p. 249) cites these lines for their similarity to Froissart's *Espinette amoureuse*, line 3828, and Christine de Pisan's Balade V, lines 1–2 (*Œuvres poétiques*, 1:5).

30 *Je n'ay riens fait qu'Amours ne me fait faire*. The change of tense in the third occurrence of the refrain is without precedent, but it is confirmed in all four manuscript copies of the poem, and it is the form that is taken up by the lady in her response in ***50***.

50. Balade: «Je n'ay riens fait qu'Amours ne me fait faire»

This is one of five ballades by Granson that are spoken by a woman, as signaled by the opening address to *doulz amis*. Compare the opening of ***32*** and ***34***; see also ***16*** and ***20***. She also uses a feminine grammatical form to refer to herself in line 29 and masculine forms to refer to her new lover in lines 13 and 15. This is certainly one of the most remarkable of Granson's poems, as the lady makes a spirited and unapologetic response to the lover's reproach of her inconstancy in ***49***, reusing the same refrain and turning it against him. For possible models for the exchange, see the note to ***49*** above. The two poems appear together in three of the four manuscripts in which they occur (see the note to ***49***), and in each, ***50*** is labeled *Response*. Manuscript *F*, however, contains only the initial stanza. The lady's briefer reply in this copy is in its own way even more effective since it is all the more dismissive of her lover's complaint.

19 *Je respondray que droit a droit revient*. The same expression occurs in the refrain to *Cent ballades* XLI, where the context is the rightful punishment suffered by one who is disloyal in love. "What goes around, comes around" might be a suitable equivalent.

51. Balade: «Dame, de moy plus que nulle autre amee»

This is the fifth of the six poems grouped together in manuscript *F* under the title "Les six balades ensuivans." See the note to ***35***, above.

52. Balade: «Il m'est advis que vostre beauté voye»

This is the second of the six poems grouped together in manuscript *F* under the title "Les six balades ensuivans." See the note to ***35***, above.

7 *Dez yeux du cuer*. For the image of the eyes of his heart, compare ***45***.1–4 and ***67***.8–9.

12 *doulour*. The emendation of *doulour* [sorrow] to *douçour* or *doulçour* [sweetness] is very tempting, but *doulour* is confirmed by all three manuscripts.

53. Balade: «Puis qu'il lui plaist, il me soufist»

This is one of two of Granson's independent ballades in octosyllables; the other is ***65***. Granson also uses octosyllables in the ballades in ***78*** *Le Livre Messire Ode* that begin at lines 362, 1195, 1365 and (if it is to be considered a ballade) 2342 (see note to ***78***.2342–2448 below). The tug-of-war between the speaker and his heart anticipates the debate between the Body and the Heart in *Le Livre Messire Ode*, ***78***.1534–1726. A different personification of the speaker's heart is found in ***64***. See also ***41***.13–24.

Consistent with the editorial policy of this edition, we present this ballade as it appears in MS *P*. Those who studied this manuscript previously — Piaget, for his edition (Grandson, *Vie et poésies*), Mudge, "Pennsylvania," and Wimsatt, *Poem's of "Ch"* — all failed to notice that this was another version of a poem that also appears in *A*. Piaget doesn't include it in his list of the works of Granson contained in the manuscript (pp. 115–16), and Mudge and Wimsatt, in their catalogs of the contents of *P*, do not attribute it to Granson. In addition to some small textual differences, the copy in *P* also contains an envoy that does not appear in *A*:

> Princesse, on me veult marier,
> Mais savez vous qu'il en sera?
> Mon corps sans cuer espousera,
> Car long temps a qu'il vous promist
> Qu'a tous jours mais vostre sera.
> Puis qu'il lui plaist, il me souffist.
>
> [Princess, they want me to marry,
> But do you know how it will be?
> My body will marry without the heart,
> For long ago it promised you
> That it would be yours forever.
> Since it pleases my heart, that's enough for me.]

We place it here in the notes because the ascription to Granson is somewhat more doubtful. The circumstances it describes cannot literally be true: Granson married only once, in 1365, when we assume he was quite young (and before it was customary for a ballade to have an envoy), and his wife survived him. The specificity of the pose would be very unusual, however, if it did not refer to a real event. The sudden change in tone and the seeming inconsistency between the *long temps* [a long time] of the third to last line and the *un an* [one year] of line 7 of the ballade, while certainly not unique, suggest that the envoy may have been added later and by another hand. If it is original, then we might have to presume that the envoy was deliberately omitted in *A* (though the time reference in *A* poses less of a problem; see the note to line seven below). *A* also omits the envoy to ***56*** which is included in all four of the other copies of that poem, including *P*.

1 *Pourquoy virent onques mes yeulx*. The opening line is nearly identical to that of one of Machaut's ballades, "Helas! pour quoy virent onques mi oueil" (Machaut, *Poesies lyriques*, 1.69, number LIII; *Louange des dames*, p. 73, number 92). There is no similarity in what follows.

7 *Car onques puis d'un an an sa*. MS *A* reads instead *environ six an en ça* [about six years ago]. See the note to ***39***.5, above.

54. BALADE: «UN SEUL CONFORT DE MA TRESBELLE DAME»

14 *Car il y a trois ans entierement*. See the note to ***39***.5 above.

56. BALADE: «CAR LE COUROUX N'Y VAULT PAS UNE MAILLE»

This is one of five ballades (along with ***23***, ***33***, ***44***, and ***58***) in which the poet offers his advice on the nature or conduct of love. Of the five, it takes the most realistic, or perhaps we should say resigned, view of the fortunes of love. It is the only of the five to appear in manuscript *F*, where it stands first, and both Piaget ("Oton de Granson," p. 408) and Kosta-Théfaine ("Du chant d'amour," pp. 301–02) suggest that it constitutes a kind of prologue to that collection.

10 *Car le couroux n'y vault pas une maille*. The expression is proverbial. Compare *Cent ballades* XXXIII, line 12: "Mais on n'en dourroit une maille [But no one would give a stitch]."

11–18 *Le Dieu d'Amours . . . la ne s'en saille*. Compare the allegorical tower and garden in ***15*** and the inn and tower in ***78***.148–60. Attwood ("Dialectique," p. 90) notes that the God of Love's house recalls Fortune's house in Alain de Lille's *Anticlaudianus*, Book VIII; in *RR*, lines 6049–88, and in Christine de Pisan's *Mutacion de Fortune*.

31–35 *Gens et gentes . . . une maille*. Though not as precise, the speaker's claim here comes close to the narrator's admission in ***77***.391–407 that he himself has no experience in love but that he seeks comfort for those who are lovers. This is a note that occurs nowhere else in Granson's shorter poems.

57. Le Desert («Fors que la mort prouchainement»)

This is the only of Granson's ballades to bear an actual title. A *desert* might be a desert or wasteland (as in ***15***.2); as an adjective, however, applied to humans, it can also mean "the one who has lost everything." The latter appears to be the primary sense in this case, though the former might also be present, as the speaker's place of exile, by implication. The need for the lover to depart from a lady from whom he has received much joy in love because of fear of slander (see the note to ***22*** above) distinguishes this poem from others in which Granson writes of the pains of separation; compare ***16***, ***24***, and ***28***.

58. Balade: «D'un tel amer que faire tous honnis»

This is one of five ballades (along with ***23***, ***33***, ***44***, and ***56***) in which the poet offers his advice on the nature or conduct of love. Here he offers a defense both of a young woman's right to fall in love and of the virtuous nature of *bonne amour* (line 13).

59. Balade: «Qui fondre peust et lui renouveller»

11–12 *Il me fauldroit avoir un corps de cire / Qui fondre peust et lui renouveller*. This poem contains another of Granson's more extravagant images, that of a body of wax that can be melted and reformed. Compare ***27***. The image of melting wax (but not of being reshaped) can also be found in one of the poems ascribed to "Ch" in manuscript P (see Wimsatt, *Poems of "Ch,"* p. 10); and in Christine de Pisan's Balade XXV (*Oeuvres poétiques*, 1:26).

21 *Si fais assez ne pie peuent souffire*. See the Textual Notes for the readings in the three different manuscripts. None offers an acceptable meaning.

60. Balade amoreuse: «Pardonnés moy, besoing le me fait faire» (1)

This is the first of two poems (with ***61***) that appear consecutively and with the same title, "Balade de Saint Valentin Double," in manuscripts *F* and *K*. In manuscript *E* the two appear in sequence as a single poem, entitled simply "Granson." Both poems appear in manuscript *A*, which we have used as our base, but separated by thirteen folios and five other poems and with the titles that we have printed here. The two poems have the same stanza form, the same rhyme scheme, and the same refrain, and while one is addressed to the lady and the other to Love, they complement one another. The significance of the specific day in ***60***.3 is explained by the reference to Saint Valentine and his feast in ***61***.1–2, and the statement about having chosen his lady "long ago" in ***61***.13–14 is consistent with the more specific reference to the seven and a half years that have passed in ***60***.1–2. For a very different pair of ballades see ***49–50***. For precedents for the *balade double* see the Introduction, p. 19. On Saint Valentine, see the Introduction, pp. 32–34. Wimsatt (*FC*, pp. 234–35) suggests that this may be the earliest of the surviving Saint Valentine poems on the basis of its appearance in manuscript *E*, but see the Introduction, note 40. He also observes that it contains "the most extensive reference . . . to the saint and his feast."

1 *Il a passé des ans sept et demy*. See the note to ***39***.5 above.

61. Balade Granson: «Pardonnez moy, besoing le me fait faire» (2)

This is the second part of what is entitled in manuscripts *F* and *K* a "Balade Double." See the note to ***60***.

1 *Saint Valentin*. On St. Valentine, see the Introduction, pp. 32–34. The only other reference to the saint in Granson's rondeaux or ballades occurs in ***17***, and only in manuscript *F*. See the note to ***17*** above.

62. Balade: «Trop plus de biens que penser ne sauroye»

This is the fourth of the six poems grouped together in manuscript *F* under the title "Les six balades ensuivans." See the note to ***35***, above.

3–4 *M'amour, m'espoir, mon plaisir, ma pensee, / Mon cur, ma joye, tout mon esbatement*. For the enumeration in these lines, Poirion (*Poète et prince*, p. 463) cites Machaut's refrain, "Mon cuer, m'amour, ma joie et mon espoir" (*PL*, 1:93, number LXXXVI; *Louange des dames*, p. 82, number 128) and other poems by Machaut, Froissart, Christine de Pisan, Chartier, and Charles d'Orléans.

63. Balade: «Ma seule dame, plus que nulle autre amee»

This is the third of the six poems grouped together in manuscript *F* under the title "Les six balades ensuivans." See the note to ***35***, above.

1–6 To make sense of this sentence, the temporal reference in line 6 must go with the verb in line 2.

64. Balade: «Faitez de moy tout ce qu'il vous plaira»

On the relation between the eyes and the heart compare ***70***.32–48.

2 *Mon cuer le veult et vers moy le pourchace*. For the personification of the heart, compare ***41***.13–24, ***53***, and the debate between Heart and Body in ***78***.1534–1726.

65. Balade: «Je n'en congnoiz nulle si belle»

This is one of only two of Granson's independent ballades in octosyllables; see the note to ***53***.

7 *Pymalion*. Pygmalion is the sculptor whose statue of a beautiful young woman is brought to life by Venus in response to his prayers. See Ovid, *Metamorphoses*, 10.243–92 and *RR*, lines 20787–21153.

25–28 *Et se le Dieu d'Amours . . . preste d'escondire*. Compare ***38***.21–24.

66. Balade: «Car quanque voy ne me fait que desplaire»

This is the last of the six poems grouped together in manuscript *F* under the title "Les six balades ensuivans." See the note to ***35***, above.

67. Balade: «Ma seule amour, en quelque lieu que je soye»

This is the only of Granson's ballades to use a 14-line stanza. The rhyme scheme, *ababbccddeefef*, derives from the shorter ballade forms and owes nothing at all to the sonnet. In the only manuscript in which this poem appears (*F*), it consists of only two stanzas plus the envoy.

8 *des yeux de ma pensee*. Compare "the eyes of my heart," ***45***.1–4.

27 *Car mon mal fault qui ne croit tant ne quant*. For the construction, compare ***47***.17.

68. Le Dit de Loiauté

This is the shortest of Granson's poems in couplets; it is the only one that uses only two rhymes throughout. Though it makes no direct allusion to any of the poems in *100B* and though not itself in ballade form, this poem may constitute another contribution to the debate between *Loiauté* and its opposite initiated by the authors of that collection; see the note to ***42*** above.

9 *Fors ung tout seul d'autre nature*. One might expect *fors a ung tout seul* [except to one alone], completing the thought from the preceding line. As it is, it is not clear what *ung*, as another object of the verb *a* [has] in line 3, refers to, nor why it might be something in which *Loiauté* takes comfort and pleasure (lines 10–12). To make that change while preserving the meter, however, would also require altering *d'autre nature* to remove one syllable.

69. L'ESTRAINE DU JOUR DE L'AN

This is one of four poems by Granson with a New Year's setting; see also ***8***, ***13***, and ***70***. An *estraine*, as Granson uses it in the title, is a New Year's gift. He uses the related verb, "to give a New Year's gift," in lines 22 and 41, and also in ***70***.14. *Estraine* can also mean "luck, fortune," in either good contexts (this poem, line 3) or bad (***49***.15). Both senses appear to be present in ***70***.17. For other examples in which a poet offers a New Year's gift, see Poirion, pp. 117–18.

1–7 *Joye, santé . . . ma doulce dame*. These lines closely recall the conventional opening formulas of the New Year's poems of Christine de Pisan ("Bon jour, bon an, bon mois, bonne novelle"; *Œuvres poétiques*, 2:229) and Jean de Garencières ("Honneur, sancté, parfaicte joye"; *Poésies complètes*, p. 54), both cited by Poirion, p. 117.

37–38 *Vous le sarez, se je puis vivre, / Mieulx par mes fais que par mon livre*. Piaget (p. 144) takes these lines as an allusion to Granson's own *Livre Messire Ode* (***78***). See the Introduction, p. 13.

70. LA COMPLAINTE DE L'AN NOUVEL

On the New Year's setting see the note to ***69***. The *complainte* of the title does not imply a fixed metrical form; here, as in ***72*** and ***76***, Granson uses the same 8-line stanza (rhyming *ababbcbc*) that he used in more than a third of his ballades, though without maintaining the same rhymes in each stanza. The narrative frame in which the knight's complaint is set, however slight, opens the way to comparison with other contemporary *dits amoureux* and with their counterparts in English, and this poem has received greatest attention from those studying its relation to Chaucer's *BD*. See in particular Braddy (*Chaucer*, pp. 57–61), who assumes Granson's priority, and Wimsatt *(French Love Poets*, pp. 143–46, and *FC*, p. 220), who argues for Chaucer's. As noted in the Introduction (pp. 30–31), there is no good external evidence of chronology to help decide the case. Most of the details that the two poems share, moreover, might plausibly be derived separately from Machaut's *FA*, which certainly preceded both. In all three poems, the poet overhears a knight bewailing his misfortune and introduces himself to comfort him.

1–5 *Jadis m'avint . . . l'an doit commencier*. Braddy (*Chaucer*, pp. 58–59) notes that both Granson's and Chaucer's poems are set in a wood (*BD*, line 444), and that "the poet, in both accounts, is described as moody and longing for diversion" ("merancolie," line 1; "melancolye," *BD*, line 23). Machaut's poet also suffers from *merencolie* (*FA*, line 67), but he overhears the knight's complaint through a window from an adjacent room. Braddy also claims that in both Granson's and Chaucer's poems the time is "towards morning." While true of Chaucer's (line 292) and Machaut's (line 1041), Granson's seems to be set in the evening.

9 *Le chevalier disoit en sa complainte*. In Machaut's and Chaucer's poems, as in Granson's, the knight's lament is labeled a *complainte* (*FA*, lines 214, 231, 1047; *BD*, line 487). He speaks it aloud without realizing that he is overheard until the poet steps forth to greet him.

10–56 The *complaintes* in Machaut's, Granson's, and Chaucer's poems differ greatly — Machaut's recounting the anxiety surrounding an upcoming separation, Granson's the pangs of unrequited love, and Chaucer's the grief at a lady's death — and have no apparent relation to one another.

17 *la bonne estraine*. While "good fortune" appears to be the primary sense here, one cannot use *estraine* in this context without also invoking the notion of the New Year's gift as in line 14. See the note to ***69*** above.

32–48 For the personification of the heart and the eyes in these lines, compare ***64***.

61–64 *Et quant son plaint recommencier . . . sa complainte cesser*. The consolation offered in Granson's poem is perfunctory, to say the least, compared to both Machaut's and Chaucer's, in each of which the conversation between poet and knight constitutes the longest part of the poem.

71. Le Souhait de Saint Valentin

The initials of the first six lines of this poem spell out ISABEL; compare ***74*** and ***77***, and see the Introduction, pp. 34–36. On the Valentine's Day setting (line 64, but which is mentioned in the title only in manuscript *F*), see the Introduction, pp. 32–34.

63–64 *Mais que ce fust ce samedi matin, / Pour ce qu'il est le jour saint Valentin*. Piaget dismisses the value of the indication of the day of the week on which Saint Valentine's day fell, here and in ***78***.1245–46, for determining the date of composition of these poems (p. 163n2), countering his own earlier suggestion ("Oton de Granson," p. 410n). (Compare Galway, "Isabel of France," p. 276.) His skepticism is all the more justified in view of the lack of certainty that the saint's feast was observed on February 14; see the Introduction, pp. 32–34.

72. Complainte de Saint Valentin

On the Valentine's Day setting (which is invoked only in the title to this poem and in only two of the three manuscripts in which it appears), see the Introduction, pp. 32–34. The *complainte* was not a fixed genre metrically. This poem on the lover's separation from his lady contains fifteen 8-line stanzas rhyming *ababbcbc* (as in ***70*** and ***76***), the form that Granson used for more than a third of his ballades. They occur in five groups of three stanzas, each group using identical rhymes, and thus the poem might be seen as a sequence of five ballades without refrains.

25 *Hors du pais me fault aler*. Braddy takes this line as a reference to Granson's forced exile in 1391 (Braddy, p. 73). Cartier agrees, but notes that if that is so, then Granson's lady must be a *Savoyarde*, not the Spanish princess who Braddy identifies as Granson's "Isabel" ("Messire," p. 14). Even if there is an autobiographical reference here, there were many instances in the life of the poet when he might have had to leave a lady friend behind.

48 *paradis des amoureux*. Piaget ("Oton de Grandson," p. 422) suggests a possible allusion to Froissart's *PA*.

73. LA PASTOURELLE GRANSON

On the lack of formal models for this poem, see the Introduction, pp. 26–27. Except for the brief narrative setting in the opening, the entire poem consists of the dialogue between the shepherd and shepherdess in alternating stanzas. Granson uses a 10-line stanza with the same rhyme scheme as in all but one of his 10-line ballades, but without refrain. Though Granson's most popular work (judging from the number of surviving copies) and one of his most original, the poem has attracted little critical comment, even among those who have studied the fourteenth century *pastourelle*, perhaps because it fits so poorly among the more conventional *pastourelles* of Granson's time. The shepherdess in particular is worthy of attention, both for the right she claims to govern her own behavior and for the cleverness of her replies.

79 *On doit d'onneur suyr la feste*. For the variants, see the Textual Notes. The reading in manuscript *P*, which we have used as our base, "En doit don fuir la feste," is defective both metrically and grammatically. The alternative reading in manuscripts *A* and *F*, "On doit honneur fuir la feste," is better metrically, but it gives two subjects for *doit*, and whichever one chooses, the statement does not appear consistent with the point that the shepherdess is making. There is no satisfactory solution. For all but the subject (for which *on* is more consistent with the *ses* in the following line), we adopt the reading of the later manuscript *C* (which offers "Je doybz donneur suyr la feste") because it suits the sense, though it may well represent a scribe's attempt to resolve the difficulty.

91–100 *Si Bel Acuel . . . veir et parler*. Piaget ("Oton de Granson," p. 405n1) cites Christine de Pisan's Balade XXVI (*Œuvres poétiques*, 1:27) as an analogue to this stanza, though there the lady makes a much stronger commitment to the lover that she addresses. Another analogue can be found in Machaut's *Remède de Fortune*, lines 4197–4218, though there too the lady is much more reassuring than in this case.

141–50 *Je maintien d'Amours . . . porroit aidier*. In this remarkable stanza, the shepherd proceeds dizzyingly from the school-masters who denounce braggarts of the shepherdess's last speech to (1) the facts of their situation, which are his masters and teach a different lesson, to (2) the school of Loyalty, where the lessons are guided by self-interest (justifying his distrust), to (3) the school in which he wishes to study the "Book of Joy," to (4) a reaffirmation of his wish to find joy only with his shepherdess.

151–60 *Nul ne puet . . . appercevoir*. The shepherdess is a bit elusive in her reply, but she seems to be saying that the shepherd would be happier if he didn't look so closely into her behavior, or at least learned to look the other way. That certainly seems to be how he understands her in his reply in the next stanza.

171–90 *Et puis que . . . trouveroit*. The last two stanzas are not only inconclusive; they also seem to be disconnected from the stanzas that precede. One is tempted to speculate either that something has been lost or that the poet didn't finish everything that he planned. Piaget compares the sentiment expressed here to the opening lines of ***56*** ("Oton de Granson," p. 408).

74. COMPLAINTE DE GRANSSON

The initial letters of the twelve stanzas of this poem spell out ISABEL EN TOVT [Isabel entirely, or Isabel in every way]. (No distinction is made between consonant *v* and vowel *u* at this time.) Compare ***71*** and ***77***; on the possible designee, see the Introduction, pp. 34–36. This is Granson's only use of the stanza form found in this poem: four quatrains with a *vers coupé*, with only two rhymes, in symmetrical arrangement (*aaab aaab bbba bbba*). Machaut used this form in poems inserted in both *FA* (235–1034, 2207–2526) and *VD* (4042–89, 5885–6076) and elsewhere; examples also occur in Froissart, Pisan, and Chartier. See Piaget, "Oton de Granson," pp. 433–34n; Earp, *Guillaume de Machaut*, pp. 206–07; and Poirion, pp. 407–08.

29 *Je pris congie de ce tresdoulz enfant*. Galway ("Isabel of France," p. 274) cites this line with others in her argument that the "Isabel" of the anagram was the daughter of Charles VI, who was born in 1389 and who was married to Richard II of England when she was not yet seven.

75. LE LAY DE DESIR EN COMPLAINTE

On the form of the *lai* see the Introduction, pp. 25–26. In the number of stanzas (12), the variety of stanza forms, the symmetry of each, and the repetition of the form of the first stanza in the last, models can be found in Machaut, Deschamps, and Froissart (see Poirion, p. 190). In content, a close model for the implied narrative situation can be found in the *lai* that provides the spring to the plot in Machaut's *Remède de Fortune*, in which the narrator, also afflicted by *désir* (lines 515, 519, 639), is torn between his fear of the lady's refusal if he should make his love known (lines 545–58) and his wish to reveal it to her (lines 530–36). (Here Wimsatt and Kibler offer a misleading translation; because of the subjunctive in line 535, it ought to be "[That is] all I want, except that in some manner, my dear lady . . . know that she is my first love and my last.") In Machaut's *dit*, the *lai* itself serves as the means by which the lady learns of the narrator's love. In Granson's *lai*, the speaker makes his silent plea that his lady do the same.

1 *Belle, tournez vers moy vos yeulx*. Compare ***4***.9 and the note to ***75***.200–16 below.

62 *lais*. *Lais* could be "lais," the type of poem, as in line 59 (Modern French *lai*); "lay," that is, "secular" (also *lai* in Modern French); or as we have translated it, "rough" (Modern French *laid*). Similarly in line 63, *homs lais* could be either "layman" or "an ugly man." No doubt all of these are meant to be suggested.

153 GW suggests that there is a line missing here in all four copies that contain this passage, providing the fifth rhyme in *–ent*. With line 155 we resume the numbering as in her edition.

161–64 *Maistre Guillaume de Machaut . . . de rigour*. Piaget (p. 166) suggests that Granson may be alluding here to Machaut's *Dit dou vergier*, in which one does indeed find a description of the effects of Desire (lines 549–70), but in view of his casual use of citations (see the next two notes), it's possible that the reference is less precise. Desire is one of the recurring motifs of Machaut's *dits*; see the note to ***12***.12–13 above.

165–71 *Et Guillaume de Saint Amour . . . nul sejour*. Guillaume de Saint-Amour was a thirteenth-century scholastic whose only known work, in Latin, is a polemic against the mendicant orders. Only his picturesque name (from the town in which he was born) explains why he might be cited as an expert on desire or why, before Granson's time, he replaces Guillaume de Lorris in the passage naming the author in some manuscripts of *RR*. See Langlois (*Manuscrits*, pp. 11, 25, and 83).

183 *li bons maistres*. The "good master" would be Jean de Meun, who wrote the long continuation to *RR* during the last third of the thirteenth century. Nowhere in his more than seventeen thousand lines, however, does he make any comment on the burning of desire. Compare Piaget, pp. 165–66.

200–16 *Ne doy je bien estre joyeux . . . vos yeulx*. The final stanza repeats both the form and the rhymes of the first sixteen lines of the poem. Line 216, moreover, is identical to line 1, bringing the poem to a close where it began. This line is the seventeenth in what should be a 16-line stanza, and it appears only in manuscript *A*, one of the four manuscripts that contain this poem, but it is required to complete the clause that seems to begin in line 214. In the same manuscript, this poem is immediately followed by ***4***, a rondeau in which the same line occurs at the beginning of the third stanza (see ***4***.9). Jung ("Répertoire," p. 95) suggests that the rondeau is actually the conclusion to this *lai*.

76. COMPLAINTE DE SAINT VALLENTIN GARENSON

The *complainte* of the title occupies only the first eleven stanzas. With the twelfth, the poem switches to narrative as Saint Valentine and the God of Love appear in order to comfort the speaker. On Saint Valentine, see the Introduction, pp. 32–34. This is the only of Granson's poems in which the saint actually appears; it is also set on the day of his feast (line 272). Like

70, this poem has been examined most closely by those studying the sources for Chaucer's *BD*, though the similarity involves little more than the mourning of a lady's death. Braddy, pp. 59–60, argues for Granson's priority and Wimsatt (*French Love Poets*, pp. 144–46) argues for Chaucer's. Wimsatt also suggests Granson's use of the anonymous *Le Songe vert* and possibly Machaut's *Jugement du roi de Behaingne*. See the Introduction, p. 31. As in ***70*** and ***72***, Granson uses the 8-line stanza that he also used in more than a third of his ballades.

1–8 *Je voy que chascun amoureux . . . maistresse*. Kelly (*Saint Valentine*, pp. 67–68) cites this passage in his argument that the feast of Saint Valentine was not yet linked to February 14.

125–26 *A la non pareille beaulté / Qu'on peut en ce monde choisir*. Our translation skips over an awkwardness in the French, in which, because of the clause that follows, *non pareille* [peerless] seems to be treated as a superlative (i.e., "the most peerless beauty that one can find in France").

163–66 *Viens vers celle . . . renommee*. See the Textual Notes for variants. We have reconstructed this passage primarily on the basis of manuscript *B*, but with two important emendations even of that copy. The variation among the surviving copies must derive from a confusion in the underlying prototype, and the reading that we offer may well owe as much to the scribes as to the author.

77. LE SONGE SAINT VALENTIN

The title refers to the fact that the dream that the narrator relates takes place on the feast of Saint Valentine (line 22); by implication, though Granson never states so directly, this is also the day on which the birds meet to choose their mates (see lines 86–90). The assembly of the birds draws this poem very close to the final episode of Chaucer's *PF*, and Granson's poem has received greatest attention from those exploring its relation to Chaucer's. As with regard to ***76***, Braddy, pp. 64–66, assumes Granson's priority, while Wimsatt (*FC*, pp. 220–27) argues for Chaucer's, in part because of the debt he perceives to other works by Chaucer of even later date, including *BD*, *TC*, and "probably" *The House of Fame*. Wimsatt also notes (pp. 236–37) that this is the only of Granson's Valentine poems that refers to the mating of the birds (but see the note to ***78***.1247 below). He dates both this poem and ***78*** *Le Livre Messire Ode*, in which he also finds evidence of dependence on Chaucer's *TC*, to the period 1386–92. He also notes a general similarity to Machaut's *DLA* (pp. 227, 334n25). On Chaucer and Granson see also the Introduction, p. 29–34. Windeatt (*Chaucer's Dream Poetry*, pp. 120–32) offers a prose translation of Granson's poem, which simply skips, however, the more puzzling passages.

1–6 The initial letters of these lines spell out ISABEL. Compare ***71*** and ***74***, and on the designee, see the Introduction, pp. 34–36.

1–28 Wimsatt (*FC*, pp. 224–25) compares this passage to the opening of both Chaucer's *BD* and Froissart's *PA*.

23–26 *Celle nuit . . . toutez passees*. Braddy, p. 65, notes the similarity to Chaucer's *PF*, lines 85–89. Wimsatt (*FC*, pp. 225–26) sees an inconsistency between these lines and the opening passage on the comforts of reflection, and also, if they imply the pains of an unrequited love, with the narrator's denial of any knowledge of love in lines 390–406.

29–33 *Et me . . . aler cherchier*. Wimsatt (*FC*, p. 334n25) draws attention to the parallel between line 29 and *RR*, line 26; and between lines 30–33 and the Middle English *Pearl*, lines 9–10.

73 *L'aigle tenoit son per prez d'elle*. The gender of the birds poses certain challenges for the translator. *Aigle* (eagle) is grammatically feminine in Middle French (like Latin *aquila*), and the feminine pronouns in lines 73, 122–23, and 307 do not necessarily therefore indicate the eagle's sex. *Per*, the word used to refer to the eagle's mate in line 73, though grammatically masculine, also does not necessarily resolve the issue, but we have chosen to follow the grammar and to regard the eagle as a "she." On the tercel and the falcon, see the note to **77**.107–14 below.

99 *Sacre*. A saker is a type of falcon; all of the species mentioned here are birds of prey.

107–14 *Un oyseil assis . . . tiercelet estoit*. The tercel (Granson's *tiercelet*, line 114) is by definition a male. The falcon (*faucon*) that it loves, however, though it must be female, is grammatically masculine and is referred to with masculine pronouns and adjective forms throughout. Similarly, in the bird episode in *Le Livre Messire Ode*, the man's second love is a *faucon* (lines 1280, 1295; grammatically masculine), but he loses it to a *tiercellet* (grammatically masculine and another male, line 1299). In the translation, we have chosen to preserve the birdness of both tercel and falcon by designating them both as "it," perhaps inconsistently with the choice we made regarding the eagle; see the note to **77**.73 above. See also the note to **77**.113–14 below.

113–14 *Tresbien le faucon ressembloit, / Hor pres que tiercelet estoit*. Among peregrines, the female is considerably larger and stronger than the male; compare the tercel's praise of the falcon's strength and hunting ability in lines 165–201. This sexual dimorphism helps explain this passage and justifies our translation "except that it was a tercel," that is, "except that it was male" (not "but it was almost a tercel").

126–30 *Pour quoy vien . . . entour assemblé sont?*. For Braddy, p. 66, the refusal of the eagle in Chaucer's *PF* to choose a mate is proof of Chaucer's dependence upon Granson, in which the tercel makes a similar refusal, since this is the feature than most distinguishes these two poems from other accounts of assemblies of birds.

140–41 *change*. *Change* is being used in two senses here, and we may have them reversed: the term is used in hunting (as still in modern French) to refer to an animal's attempt to deflect its pursuer onto another prey, and more generally, it may be used for any type of change, for instance in the object of one's affection.

157 *Entre tous ses faucons a un*. On the gender of the falcon see the note to **77**.107–14.

165–201 On the female falcon's skill at hunting see the note to **77**.113–14 above. Wimsatt (*FC*, p. 227) notes Granson's emphasis on the avian attributes of his birds, as in Machaut's *DLA*, in contrast to Chaucer's anthropomorphic description of the birds' love relationships.

302–03 *Sine vueil plus entre vous estre / Lors s'escria a haulte voix*. Wimsatt (*FC*, p. 334n25) notes the parallel to Machaut's *DL*, lines 312–13.

390–406 Wimsatt (*FC*, pp. 221–23, 334n28) labels the narrator's stance here, joining his own incapacity for love (which has no contemporary French precedent) with his concern for other lovers, a "patently Chaucerian feature," and he links it particularly to *TC*, 1.15–18, though he judges it less necessary and "poorly timed" in Granson's case. If Granson did have *TC* in mind here, that would settle the question of the priority of this poem and *PF*, which was written earlier. Gilbert, however, observes a close verbal resemblance to *PF*, lines 512–18, and he assumes Chaucer to be the borrower ("'Turtil Trewe,'" p. 165).

404–05 *Soyent englois ou alemens, / De France né ou de Savoye*. As Piaget notes (p. 141), this is the only reference in Granson's poetry to his native Savoy. Carden ("Oton de Grandson," p. 145) finds a "subtle hint of the poet's love relationship" with Isabel of Bavaria, Queen of France, in these two lines, *englois* and *Savoye* referring to the poet himself, and *alemens* and *France* referring to Isabel (though that is not where she was born). Compare the note to **77**.1–6 above.

410–25 *Dont mains sont tristes . . . en habandon*. Wimsatt (*FC*, pp. 223–24) notes the "emotive" value of the narrator's final prayer, which also confirms the essentially lyric nature of the *dits amoureux*.

78. Le Livre Messire Ode

As noted in the Introduction (p. 29), the closest model for this poem is Machaut's *VD*, but with substantial differences. Basso (pp. 157–59) points out that even in following Machaut, Granson sometimes reverses the image that he borrows from his source. The imitation of the formal model of *VD* is also rather loose. As Wimsatt observes, Granson is rather less careful than Machaut about distinguishing the embedded lyrics from the narrative (in couplets) about their composition: there are instances (e.g. lines 1195–1218) where a lyric simply continues the narrative, while elsewhere, couplets are used "where we might expect a stanzaic piece" (e.g. lines 452–519). Such a blending, together with "the fragmentation of the *Livre* into numerous set pieces, . . . actually represents a logical development of the long love poem in the Middle French mode. The essential nature of the works is lyric" (*FC*, p. 231). The lyric basis of the *Livre* is also the burden of much of the small body of commentary on the poem, which has focused in different ways on its lack of narrative development and its lack of closure. Boulton, for instance, notes that the poem from the very beginning presents a record of the narrator's "current distress, rather than the history of the love affair," and thus is destined to end without resolution (p. 224). Granson "seems to have renounced the progression of the *complainte-comfort* structure [more typical of the *dits amoureux*] in favor of the stasis inherent in the lyric *complainte*" (p. 228). For Arden ("Love's Martyrs"), the poem reconfigures the experience described by its predecessors into a type of game, "a perpetual pattern of suffering and submission played out in the mind of the lover" in which the lady, only a "mute idol," "must keep the game going by a delicate balance between cruelty and kindness, so that the lover may continue to proclaim his pain forever" (p. 107). "Anything that ends the game is to be avoided" (p. 115), and for this reason Granson left his poem unfinished (p. 118). Basso also finds that the work "presents itself as unfinished" (p. 149), and she describes its lack of development in contrast to Machaut's *DLA*, in which the four birds represent the growth in the narrator's understanding both of love and of himself. Carden, however, who examines the manifestations of the first-person in the poem in relation to earlier poetry, finds a coherent pattern in the progress from the dream-vision in which the poet-narrator is distinguished from the lover that he observes, in the manner of a typical *dit*, to the final group of lyrics, in which the voices of poet and lover are again united as in the poem's opening.

Among other possible sources, Wimsatt (*FC*, pp. 227–34) lists Machaut's *Remede de Fortune*, *FA*, and *DLA*, Froissart's *PA*, and Chaucer's *TC* and *BD*. Specific passages are cited below.

For the line numbering in this edition and in GW's, whose numbering we have retained, compared to Piaget's, see the Concordance on p. 393 below.

Title The poem contains no title and no indication of authorship in any of the manuscripts in which it appears. The title by which it is now known, *Le Livre Messire Ode*, is entirely Piaget's invention, based on a line in Martin Le Franc's *Le Champion des Dames* which may or may not refer to this poem, even if it is by Granson. For the problems of attribution, see the Introduction, pp. 14–15.

1–188 Boulton notes that Granson "begins his *Livre* in the present, and gives only enough history to account for his melancholy state" (p. 224). For Arden, this opening section introduces the motifs — particularly the interplay of suffering and hope and the paradox of the lover's willing submission to his lady's will — that are developed during the remainder of the poem ("Love's Martyrs," pp. 108–12). Specific details of the introduction are recalled in the first dream, which appears to recapitulate in greater detail the narrator's revelation of his love to his lady. See the note to lines 189–1726 below.

1–4 Basso (p. 159n2) notes the similarity of these lines to Machaut's *VD*, lines 11–12, though in this case, the narrator evidently intends to make a written request for love where the spoken word has failed (p. 150). Boulton observes that "although he intends to send [his book] to her, we never actually learn its fate" (p. 224). The promise that he refers to here is also not recorded, and in his later comments on the composition of the poem, he doesn't refer again to the purpose of presenting it to her. Compare, for example, lines 215–16, 1088–89. For Carden (pp. 80–81), the opening lines establish the narrator both as poet and as lover, roles that are conventionally distinguished in the *dit* and that are separated in the dream that follows.

4 *faiz*. *Faiz* most often means simply "acts" or "deeds" (e.g. at ***69***.38), but in specific contexts it can also signify "nature" or "features" (***37***.5, ***72***.59, ***78***.1260) or "attacks" (***59***.15, ***78***.1683). In contexts related to writing, as here and in ***75***.58, it refers primarily to a poet's compositions, his or her "works."

5–6 *Non pas tous, maiz une partie / Diray de ma mellencolie*. Basso (p. 159) cites these lines for contrast to *VD* 513–15, in which Machaut promises to include everything he has done or said.

7–9 *Amours . . . une maistresse*. Piaget (p. 145) takes these lines as a reference to ***76*** (see particularly lines 105–06); see the Introduction, p. 14.

120 Though there is no break in the sense, a line rhyming in *–ire* lacks in both manuscripts that contain this passage. With 122, we resume the line numbering as in GW.

189–1726 The largest part of the poem is made up of the first dream. As Wimsatt notes (*FC*, p. 231), each of the separate encounters in the dream refers in some way to the narrator's love for his lady, though as Basso suggests (p. 154), the narrator doesn't seem to realize it. Boulton points out that unlike the dream visions of Granson's predecessors, this one offers no relief to the narrator but only serves to "remind him of his sorrow" (p. 224). Attwood ("Dialectique amoureuse," pp. 96–100) describes the dialogue structure of most of the dream, referring also to the *mise en abîme* of the narrator's experience in his encounter with the young squire in lines 614–43. For Carden (p. 81), the dream episode is a fictive space that "allows the poet to explore his lyric subjectivity, heightening the distance between his historical identity and the one that he constructs in the text" (all subsequent translations are by the editors).

The narrative portion of the dream up to line 850 appears to recapitulate in greater detail the narrator's revelation of his love to his lady, the event that has caused him such distress as the poem begins. Some of the verbal correspondences are quite precise: compare lines 19 and 707–8 (and also 507); 21 and 612; and 32–34 and 848–50. The same gallery of personifications also appears (though each also occurs later in the poem): compare lines 22–23 *et al.* (*Reffuz*) and 759, 844, and 875; 24 (*Dangier*) and 665; 51–52 (*Desir* and *Souvenir*) and 438–39, 721, 775; 66 (*Espoir*) and 436–37, 555–68, 706, 753, 812; 88 (*Loyauté*) and 745.

213 *Et la recommançay ma plaincte*. Carden (p. 82) notes that from the very beginning of the dream, the distinction between the waking narrator and the character of whom he dreams is effaced.

217–326 Like all but one of Granson's poems that are labeled *complaintes* (the exception is ***74***), this one uses a stanza form that Granson also employs in his ballades, here an 11-line stanza rhyming *ababbccddc* (compare ***58***). With the *complainte* (not in fact so labeled) in 1887–1996 below, it is one of only two that use concatenation of the rhyme, as the *c*-rhyme in each stanza becomes the *a*-rhyme of the next. An exception occurs in the second to last stanza (lines 307–16), where it is the *d*-rhyme that becomes both the *a*-rhyme and the *d*-rhyme of the final stanza (lines 317–26).

226 *partie*. That is, in the judicial metaphor employed here, one of the parties to the dispute as well as the judge. Compare 1460.

236 *Priez pour moy, s'il vous plaist, amoureux*. Compare ***39***.8.

267–96 These three stanzas are linked by the continuation of the sentence from one stanza to the next. See 1907–36 below and the note to ***46***.10–11.

327–28 *Ainsi que ma plainte escripsoie / Et en mon livre la mectoye*. As Boulton notes, with reference to lines 834–35 and 1123–24 (pp. 225–26), Granson here blurs the distinction between waking and sleeping, as he records the poem in his book while in his dream. Compare the lines that precede the *complainte* (215–16), where the transcription is set outside the dream; and also the note to 213 above.

332 *Je me doy bien tenir en joye*. Though the rhyme is imperfect, this appears to be the first instance in the poem in which the opening line of an inserted lyric also supplies the second line of a couplet. See the note to line 583 below.

421–22 *Vestu de noir, par desplaisance, / Me suis, sans prendre autre couleur*. Wimsatt (*FC*, p. 227) traces the motif of dressing in black to Chaucer's *BD*, though in Granson's poem it "symbolizes unhappiness rather than bereavement." Compare lines 485–86.

452–519 Wimsatt (*FC*, p. 230) notes the use of couplets "where we might expect a stanzaic piece."

475 Though there is no break in the sense, a line rhyming in *–ant* lacks in both manuscripts that contain this passage, unless Granson, either accidentally or intentionally, wrote three lines in succession with the same rhyme (474–77). With 477, we resume the line numbering as in GW.

571 *l'Ostel de Joye*. Compare the "Inn of Sadness," line 149 and the "Tower of Happiness," line 159.

583 *Je ne sçay plus que demander*. The opening line not only provides the *a*-rhyme for this rondeau; it also supplies the second line of the couplet that begins with line 582, thus anchoring the inserted lyric to this point in the text. There are four other similar examples in the *Livre Messire Ode*, at lines 1440, 1643, 1680, and 1711, and another at line 332, though there the rhyme is imperfect. In all but one of these, both lines of the couplet (and thus the rest of the lyric) are in octosyllables, but in 1439–40, the first line is octosyllabic while the second (and the rest of the *chanson*) are in decasyllables. See also the note to lines 1881–91, where Granson may or may not use a similar device to attach a lyric to the narrative.

591–93 In the three rondeaux that contain 5-line stanzas (here and at 2034–54 and 2449–69 below), there is no indication in the manuscripts whether the partial repetition of the refrain in the second stanza should consist of the first two lines or the first three. (On the scribal presentation of the refrains, see the note to ***1–9***, above.) Only in the third example is the third line required for the sense. The resulting 6-line stanza could not have been sung to the same melody as the other stanzas, but the rhyme scheme *aabaab* is more satisfying than the 5-line *aabaa* that would result if only the first two lines were used. In expanding the scribes' abbreviations, we have chosen the 3-line alternative for all three of these poems here.

612 *Maiz je cuidoie le mieulx faire*. Compare line 21. See the note to lines 189–1726 above.

702–833 The "Lay de Plour" shares its title with two poems by Machaut (numbers XIX and XXII in *PL*, 2:434–42 and 459–66) and another by Deschamps (*Œuvres Complètes*, 2:306). See Poirion, pp. 419–20, who also sees the influence of Machaut's complainte "Amours, tu m'as tant esté dure" *(PL*, 1:241–49); and Betemps, "Les lais de plour," who also sees "echoes" of other of Machaut's works, including his ballades and *Le Jugement dou Roy de Behaingne*. As noted in the Introduction (pp. 25–26), the stanza form that Granson employs here is a shorter version of the *lai* stanza, with twelve lines instead of sixteen — *aab aab bbc bbc* — and with concatenation, as the *c*-rhyme of each stanza is carried over to become the *a*-rhyme of the next.

707–08 *Par hardement / De trop parler, suis maintenant*. Compare line 19. See the note to lines 189–1726 above.

738 *Mon cueur est vostre, non pas mien*. Piaget notes the similarity to *RR*, line 1983: "Li cuers est vostres, non pas miens" (p. 165).

759 *Mais Reffuz tresfort me guerroye*. Compare lines 22–23. See the note to lines 189–1726 above.

828–31 *saint Valentin*. This is the first of three references to Saint Valentine in this poem. See also lines 1246–47 and 1996, and the Introduction, pp. 32–34.

848–50 Compare lines 32–34. See the note to lines 189–1726 above.

991 *don d'amy*. See the note to ***12***.4 above.

1024–50 Boulton (p. 224) notes that this is the only time in the poem that the narrator addresses his lady directly. Basso (pp. 151–52) sees in the lady's return of the narrator's heart her desire that he be more himself if he wishes her to love him, a lesson that he does not understand.

1089 ff. Machaut's *VD*, which is the closest model for the quasi-autobiographical narrative in this poem, contains 46 inserted letters in prose.

sire de Cornoaille. Wimsatt (*FC*, p. 232) identifies the "Lord of Cornwall" as John of Cornwall, "a well-known military figure in the service of Edward III" (actually Edward's younger brother), who died, however, in 1337. After John's death, the title of Duke of Cornwall was held by Edward the Black Prince, and on his death in 1376, it passed to Edward's son Richard, who became king a year later on the death of Edward III. If there is a "Lord of Cornwall" during the time when we must suppose this poem to have been written, it is Richard

II of England. If the reference is not deliberately fictitious, perhaps Granson was more familiar with British geography than he was with the peerage.

1123 At the conclusion of the prose passage, we resume the line numbering following GW.

1125–34 Is this a dream within a dream? The boundaries between sleeping and waking again become blurred, as they do in the immediately preceding lines, in which the writing of the book evidently occurs within the dream. See the note to lines 327–28, above.

1139–1523 The man's account of his courting of the sparrowhawk and the falcon recalls the four episodes in which the narrator pursues different birds in Machaut's *DLA*. Compare also the different use of avian imagery in ***77*** *Le Songe Saint Valentin*. Wimsatt sees in the dialogue frame of this episode a "clear evocation" of the situation in Chaucer's *BD* (*FC*, pp. 227–28). Boulton labels the entire episode "a *dit*, though it is not separated from the rest of the text" (p. 224). Carden describes the whole passage as a *jeu parti*, the judge of which must be the absent lady of line 1452, and like the dialogue between Heart and Body that follows, it marks a transition from a narrative mode to the lyric mode in which the poem ends (pp. 85–86).

1178–92 According to Wimsatt, the model for this passage is found in Chaucer's *TC*, 1.622–69 (*FC*, pp. 228–29).

1195–1218 There is some uncertainty about the *c*-rhyme in this ballade. In the first stanza, manuscript *B* (which we use as our base) has *jardins/pris*, but in the second and third stanzas *pourpris/prins* and *advis/prins*. As GW notes in her edition, there exists a form *jardil* which (though not otherwise attested in Granson) could give *jardis* in the plural, fixing the first rhyme. The second and third stanzas could be corrected by changing *prins* to the more common form *pris*. Manuscript *N*, which contains the only other copy of this poem, does not help in resolving the issue because it gives *jardins/prins* in the first stanza, *pourpris/prist* in the second, and *advis/prins* (as in *B*) in the third.

Wimsatt notes the highly unusual use of a lyric piece as part of narrative, here and in lines 1365–88 below (*FC*, pp. 230–31). For Carden, this ballade "inaugurates the collapse of the formal and generic system that has defined the text to this point," as the poet moves from the model of the *dit* to one more like the *100B* (p. 84).

1244–51 Kelly cites this passage in his argument that the feast of Saint Valentine was not yet linked to February 14 when Chaucer and Granson wrote (*Saint Valentine*, pp. 68–69). See also the note to ***71***.63–64.

1247 *Que tous oyseaulx veullent chanter*. Manuscript *N* (the only other copy to contain this passage) reads "prennent leur per [choose their mates]." This is the only place outside of ***77*** "Le Songe Saint Valentin" in which Granson makes any association between Saint Valentine and the birds.

1296 *Que j'en seiché comme ung baston*. For the expression, see Froissart, *Œuvres*, 9:280 (on the effects of poisoning on the young Charles V) and Chaucer's

Knight's Tale, I(A)1362 (on Arcite's love-sickness). Machaut too uses the verb *sechier* "to become dry" to describe the effects of desire (*PL,* Balade XXII, line 3, [1:37] and Balade LXXXVII, line 10 [1:94]; *Louange des dames,* number 125, line 3 [p. 82] and number 134, line 10 [p. 84]).

1325 *ma guignarde*. *La Guignarde* [The Coquette] is the name given to the woman who argues against the strict need for loyalty in *100B*. Carden sees a broader allusion to that work in the contrast between the bird-lover's disloyalty and the absolute fidelity of the narrator (p. 85).

1365–88 For Wimsatt, the comic obtuseness of the narrator here evokes Chaucer's *BD,* lines 740–41 (*FC,* p. 229). For Basso, the narrator's superficial understanding reflects his rejection of what he might have learned both about the power of language and about the reasons for the ineffectiveness of his own quest from Machaut's *DLA* (pp. 155–57). See also the note to lines 1195–1218 above.

1440 *En languissant, j'actens vostre vouloir*. This is one of several instances in the poem in which the opening line of an inserted lyric also supplies the second line of a couplet, but it is the only one in which the two lines of the couplet are of different length. See the note to 583 above.

1460 *partie*. See the note to 226 above.

1481 From this point on, manuscript *B* is the only witness. The generally poor quality of this copy tempts one to emend the text in more than the most obvious ways. We note some of the possibilities below.

1534–1726 The dialogue of the Heart and the Body constitutes virtually another separate *dit* within the *Livre Messire Ode*, though it is not marked off from the rest of the text. It begins with a nine-stanza *complainte*, and it incorporates three rondeaux (marked, like the others in the *Livre*, as *chançons* [songs]), the first of which, though attributed to the Body, is about the body and the heart, and the second of which cannot be ascribed to either. As analogues to this episode, Attwood ("Dialectique," p. 100) cites examples by Charles d'Orléans, René d'Anjou, and François Villon, all of which are later than Granson's. In this episode, according to Boulton, Granson "attempts to resolve his ambivalent feelings about love, to reconcile the ideal with the actual misery he experiences." The apparent resolution in favor of love at the end "is illusory, for the poet resumes his reproaches to love immediately upon awakening" (p. 226). For Basso, the splitting of the narrator into two represents the fact that he can only exist outside himself, in the identity that he obtains from another, in contrast to the self-knowledge gained by the narrator of Machaut's *DLA* (pp. 152–53).

1613 *d' «amy»*. See the note to ***12***.4, above.

1637–38 Manuscript *B*, the only copy to contain this passage, inserts a speaker marker (*Le Corps* ["The Body"]) between lines 1637 and 1638. It is unnecessary since the speaker is identified in the text, and we have omitted it rather than supplying the five other speaker markers that would be necessary for consistency.

1654 *Au haultain bien des amoureux*. Compare line 17.

1679 *Comme faisoit Palamidés*. See note to lines 1758–66 below.

1680 *J'ay fait mon tresor de souhaiz*. The manuscript reads "Jay fait mon souhait," a line that is defective metrically, being three syllables short. In the two places where the scribe indicates the repetition of the refrain, however, he has written "Jay fait mon tresor &c." Piaget (p. 447) suggests the combined reading "J'ay fait mon tresor de souhaiz" which we adopt here.

1758–66 *Palamidés*. Palamades, here and in line 1679, is Tristam's rival for Iseult's love; see the note to ***12***.15–16. He first appears in the *Prose Tristan* in the early thirteenth-century. He is cited elsewhere as an example of devoted suffering, e.g., in *100B*, p. 204, but in no known version of the story does he die because of his love, much less by his own consent.

1763–64 *Si dit on bien quelque hutin / Piteusement a la parfin*. It is tempting to take this couplet as an insertion by a bored or exasperated scribe, for whatever it means, it interrupts the comparison between the speaker and Palamedes. (Hence our parentheses.) Dismissing it, however, does not resolve all of the issues that it poses. *Hutin* ordinarily means "noise" or "quarrel" (as in *100B*, LXIII, line 4), and it sits uncomfortably with the verb *dire*, "to say," suggesting that even if it is an insertion, there has been some kind of disruption in the text. *Hutin* is also the name that is given to the old knight who defends *loiauté* in *100B* in three of the responses appended at the end (pp. 201, 224, 227). Could the original of this line have been another allusion to that earlier work? (Compare the note to line 1325 above.)

1846 *qu'esperance*. After *sans*, one would expect to find *n'esperance*. We retain the manuscript reading, but our translation reflects our understanding of the sense.

1881–91 In manuscript *B* (the only copy to contain this portion of the poem), these lines appear without any indication of a gap, and so we present them here, though we retain the line numbering from GW. They can be read straight through with no break in the sense, though strictly speaking, one would expect to find the preposition *a* repeated before *la douleur* in 1890 if it were part of the sentence that begins in 1883. 1883 and 1885 both lack their rhymes, however, and 1890 suddenly switches from octosyllables to decasyllables. Lines 1890–96, though beginning with three couplets, match the rhyme scheme of the last seven lines of a 10-line stanza like the nine stanzas that immediately follow, *(aba)bbccddc*. Those stanzas appear to make up a typical *complainte*, though it is not given a title. Both Piaget and GW assume that at least five lines have been lost here, the rhyming octosyllabic lines for 1883 and 1885 and the three decasyllabic lines at the beginning of the first stanza of the complaint, along with the title with which such lyrics normally begin in the *Livre Messire Ode*. They thus insert the title, "Complainte," and they insert lines of dots to replace what they suppose to be missing lines. In their support, one could point not only to the missing preposition but also to the complete abandonment of the image of Danger on his horse in lines 1881–83, to the unusual switch from the past tense to the present that occurs between lines 1883 and 1896, and to the fact that the complaint, with its allusion to "lying slanderers" (line 1916) and to the narrator's imminent departure (lines 1968–72, a theme that is also picked up in the two lyrics that follow), seems to be part of a different narrative from the one that immediately precedes. One could also cite the evident incompleteness or damage in another stanza of the complaint and in another of the poems that follow; see the notes to lines 1947–66 and 2055–64 below. The apparent gap suggests both that the narrative that begins in lines 1877–81 remains unfinished and that in an early copy, the group of poems that begins with this complaint might have lain apart before becoming attached to this text. And if that is the case, it is impossible to tell how many additional complete stanzas or even complete poems might also have been lost.

Line 1883 does rhyme, however, with 1890 (as here numbered), and the missing rhyme for 1885 could actually be supplied by 1882. In other words, strictly in terms of rhyme, lines 1882–85 could supply the missing three lines (the initial *aba*) for the 10-line stanza 1882–96 (though again they don't have the required number of syllables). If that were so, then 1882 would function both as the second line of a couplet (1881–82) and as the opening line (providing the *a*-rhyme) of the 10-line stanza 1882–96. There are five and perhaps six examples earlier in the poem in which the opening line of a lyric also provides the second line for a couplet; see the note to line 583 above. In one of these, at line 1440, the second line of the couplet (the opening line of the lyric) is longer than the preceding line with which it is paired (it is decasyllabic rather than octosyllabic). In none of these, however, does the sentence continue directly from the narrative into the lyric as it does here, and not even in 1440 is the metrical form of the lyric disrupted for even a single line, much less for three. Nonetheless, Granson, who has already shown a willingness to blend narrative into lyric (see the note to lines 1195–1218 above), may here take that blending one step further as he merges his couplets into a typical stanza form.

If that seems less likely an explanation, then the continuity of both sense and rhyme in lines 1881–85 is due either to extraordinary good luck or to an active scribal effort to paper over the incomplete passage at some point in the history of the text. What one decides can affect, or be determined by, how one reads the last two stanzas of the complaint, which pose another set of issues of their own. See the note to lines 1977–96 below.

1907–36 These four stanzas are linked by the continuation of the sentence from one stanza to the next. See 267–96 above and the note to ***46***.10–11.

1921 *n'avoir*. After *ouir* [hear], one would expect *ne voir* [or see], but we retain the reading of the manuscript.

1939 Though there is no evident gap in the sense, this line is two syllables short, suggesting a loss. Both Piaget and GW insert *joieulx* before *deport*.

1947–66 Piaget treats this passage as a single 13-line stanza in the midst of the 10-line stanzas that make up the rest of this complaint. The rhyme scheme, *aabbcbccddeed*, is not one that Granson (or any other poet that we know) used elsewhere. GW (whose line numbering we retain) presents the last ten lines of this passage as a regular 10-line stanza rhyming (like those that precede and follow) *ababbccddc*, and she treats the first three lines as the remnants of a defective stanza, lacking a line between 1947 and the line that follows, and lacking six lines before the third surviving line, which, judging from the concatenation of the rhyme and the repetition of the verb in the very next line, appears to be the last line of the stanza. If there is a gap, it is impossible to determine whether lines have been lost or the poet simply never finished writing them.

1974 *Regnault*. Piaget (p. 153) suggests that "Regnault" may refer to Regnaut de Trie, who provided the first of the responses to the *100B*, defending the position of La Guignarde (pp. 201–02). Otherwise, if these names refer to specific real individuals, they are now unknown.

1977–96 Line 1977 introduces 20 lines of past tense narrative in the same stanza form as the narrator's complaint that precedes. There are other examples of the insertion of lyric within narrative in the *Livre Messire Ode* (see the note to lines 1195–1218 above), and there are similar switches from present tense to past throughout the *Livre*, as, for instance, at line 91 and, even more like the present passage, at line 189. But for the switch to narrative within a stanzaic lyric the best precedent is provided by ***76*** "Complainte de Saint Vallentin Garenson," in which the transition is marked by a shorter but otherwise identical line, "Ainsi que je me complaingnoie" (89). The final line of the second stanza (1996), with its reference to Saint Valentine's Day, resembles the final line of that poem and also that of ***69*** and ***71***, which similarly set the scene on a particular day; and with the coming of morning and the relief of the narrator's pain in the lines that precede, it appears to mark a conclusion. But to what? To this particular lyric within the *Livre*? To the *Livre* as a whole? Or to what may originally have been a separate poem (more like ***76***) that happens to have been inserted here? Directly related is the question of whether the coming of morning in line 1988 is meant to mark the end of the dream that begins in line 1881. So is it understood by both Carden (p. 87) and Basso (pp. 148–49), who see the remaining thirteen lyrics as occurring within a final period of wakefulness. Boulton, on the other hand, evidently sees the second dream as incorporating all of the following lyrics, noting, however, that line 1996 "seems to conclude the narrative part of the *dit*" (pp. 226–27).

1978–86 The voice that the narrator hears here resembles that of lines 555–61, and in both cases we are probably to associate it with *Espoir* [Hope]; compare lines 78–90.

1996–2501 The thirteen lyrics that conclude the *Livre* in manuscript *B* (the only copy that proceeds this far) are not linked by any narrative. Some repeated imagery suggests that they were indeed meant to be part of the same work. Both sections refer to the lady as "princesse" (e.g., lines 139, 375, 990 *et al.*, and in the additional lyrics, lines 1929, 2027, 2250, 2318, 2377); and the references to her as "la meilleur de France [the best woman in France]" (line 1946) and "la non per de France [the one without peer in France]" (lines 2091, 2297) who has "point de pareille en France [no equal in France]" (line 2384) echo line 1594, where she is "non pareille de France [without peer in France]." (In his other poems, Granson addresses his "princesse" only in the envoys to ***42***, ***57***, ***64***, and ***66***, and nowhere else does he place the lady in France.) The exact relationship between these poems and the preceding narrative is nonetheless difficult to define. The first two refer to the narrator's imminent departure (lines 2000, 2034–38), a theme that occurs only in the immediately preceding complaint and nowhere else in the *Livre* (see the note to lines 1881–91 above); while two of the ballades that follow contain references to the narrator dressing in black (lines 2134, 2155; compare 421 *et al.*), which suggest that they might have been meant to be included in an earlier part of the poem since the debate between the Heart and the Body leads to a resolve to resume dressing in white at line 1689. Other possible recollections of the earlier narrative are far from precise; see the notes to lines 2166 and 2207–13 below. In other respects, this last group of poems differs very little from what precedes. For Boulton, "the lover's situation remains essentially unchanged, and the lyrics reflect his lack of progress" (p. 228), and for Basso too, "the quest for love thus appears to be a failure" (p. 149). For Carden, who sees the entire group as constituting a final waking scene, following the end of the second dream (see the note to lines 1977–96 above), these final lyrics provide a fit conclusion as they recall and comment upon the preceding elements of the *Livre* in the authoritative voice of the poet with which the work begins (pp. 87–88).

2042–44 See the note to lines 591–93.

2055–64 If lines 2055–56 belong to the same stanza as the lines that follow, at least two lines lack following line 2056, though there is no indication of a gap in the manuscript. But if they do, then according to the rhyme scheme of the rest of this complaint (*ababbccdcd*), 2056 should rhyme with line 2059 (as we continue to follow the line numbering in GW), and it does not. One could emend 2056 in order to fix the rhyme, but the stanza would still be two lines short (which GW marks with two lines of dots). It is possible that portions of two separate stanzas (or more) have been lost at this point, unless the poet simply left this portion of the poem unfinished.

2075–84 It is not unusual for Granson to refer to the lady as either a god or a goddess (as in, for instance, lines 2066, 2178, 2191, 2377, and 2393), and twice before he imagines her being courted by the God of Love (***38***.21–24, ***65***.25–28). But nowhere else does he suggest that she might make an appropriate mistress for God, much less that He might be prevented from having her.

2108 *Car se j'avoie temps, loisir et espace*. After *si* [so] in 2107, one expects *que* [that] rather than *car* [for], but we retain the reading of the manuscript.

2134 *Et pour cela me tiens vestu de noir*. The narrator's claim to remain dressed in black, here and in line 2155, contradicts his resolution to set aside his black clothes for white in 1688–89, suggesting that this and other of these final lyrics might originally have been intended for inclusion earlier in the poem.

2143 *Par ung reffuz assez prés du fossé*. We offer a literal translation, not at all sure of exactly what is meant. *Fosse* (rather than *fossé*, which is required by the rhyme) might mean "a grave" (see Godefroy, *Dictionnaire*, vol. 9 [Supplement]), preparing line 2145, but the construction is still puzzling.

2155 *Las! je suis en dueil vestu de noir*. See the note to line 2134.

2166 *Guion pieça le vous feist assavoir*. This line might possibly refer to the episode described in lines 520–32, though the messenger (the narrator's servant) is not there named.

2206–13 This stanza recalls both the episode in lines 1024–50 and the debate between Heart and Body in lines 1534–1726, but it does not correspond in detail to either.

2323 *Vostre esloingner me fait mortel traveil*. We retain the reading of the manuscript here, though we know of no other use of *eloingner* as a noun, and there is no other reference in the poem to the woman departing. *Vous eloingner* [departing from you] is just as good metrically and would better suit the context.

2326 *Et se m'aist Dieux que je vous serviray*. For the construction (*se m'aist Dieux* followed by *que*), compare lines 2075, 2290.

2336 *mieulx*. Our emendation here (*mieulx* for *mienne*) is greater than what we have normally allowed ourselves, but it appears to be compelled by both grammar and sense. *Mienne*, the feminine form of the possessive pronoun "mine," is grammatically redundant since the object of the first person verb *verray* is already provided by *vous*. Its referent is also unclear: the only nearby feminine noun is *Amour*, which is being used as a vocative, however, to refer to the lady herself, not to the narrator's emotional state. *Mieux* ("better") poses no such problems, and it completes the thought, though it may not remove all of the challenges in this stanza. The referent of *le* ("it") in the next line is still somewhat obscure, and the clause that follows presents a rather unusual image.

2342–2448 This passage is headed (in the one manuscript that contains it) "Complainte." It begins, however, with three 10-line stanzas rhyming *ababbccdcd* and ending in the same line, thus matching the form of a ballade with its refrain. The remaining seven stanzas contain eleven lines, rhyming *aabaabbcbbc* (a stanza form that Granson uses elsewhere only in the complaint in lines 2230–2317). There is, however, no break in the sense between stanzas three and four. GW divides the passage into two poems, inserting the title "Ballade" before line 2342 and "Complainte" before line 2372. We present it here as it appears in the manuscript.

2399 *Et se j'ay la puce en l'oreille?*. This proverbial expression can evidently mean both "to be afflicted with desire" (Rey, *Dictionnaire historique*), as suggested by the preceding lines, and "to lie awake" (Greimas, *Moyen*), as suggested by the lines that follow.

2457–59 See the note to lines 591–93.

2486 *Celle*. French *celle* can function either as subject or as object; in English, we are unable to maintain the consistency of the refrain as we must choose between *she* and *her*. The difference in the function of the pronoun between lines 2486 and 2498 also requires a change in the punctuation of the refrain in both languages.

Textual Notes

Abbreviations: A: Lausanne, Bibliothèque Cantonale et Universitaire, MS 350; **B**: Paris, Bibliothèque nationale, fr. 1727; **C**: Paris, Bibliothèque nationale, fr. 1131; **D**: Paris, Bibliothèque nationale, fr. 24440; **E**: Barcelona, Biblioteca de Catalunya, MS 8, Catalan, 1420–30; **F**: Paris, Bibliothèque Nationale, fr. 2201; **G**: London, Westminster Abbey Library, MS 21; **H**: Paris, Bibliothèque nationale, fr. 833, c. 1500; **J**: Paris, Bibliothèque nationale, fr. 1952, 16th century; **K**: Lausanne, Bibliothèque Cantonale et Universitaire, IS 4254; **L**: Paris, Bibliothèque nationale, Rothschild MS I.I.9; **M**: Carpentras, Bibliothèque Inguimbertine, MS fr. 390; **N**: Brussels, Bibliothèque royale Albert 1er, MS 10961–10970, c. 1465; **O**: Karlsruhe, Badische Landesbibliothek, MS 410, c. 1430; **P**: Philadelphia, University of Pennsylvania, Van Pelt Library, MS Codex 902 (formerly Fr. MS 15), 1395–1400; **Q**: Berne, Burgerbibliothek da la Bourgeoisie, MS 473, 1400–40; **R**: Turin, Archivio di Stato, MS J. b. IX. 10; **S**: Paris, Bibliothèque nationale, fr. 24404 (16th century addition); **T**: Besançon, Bibliothèque Municipale, MS 556, 1826; **V**: Carpentras, Bibliothèque Inguimbertine, MS 411; **W**: Brussels, Bibliothèque royale Albert 1er, MS IV 541, 1564–81; **Y**: Turin, Biblioteca Nazionale e Universitaria, MS L.II.12.

For each poem, we provide the following:
Other editions: The location of the poem in the editions of Grenier-Winther (GW) and Piaget.
Base MS: The manuscript from which our text is taken, using the sigla listed on this page.
Other copies: The other manuscripts in which the poem appears, with the line numbers for excerpts.
Selected variants: Most of the notes record the editors' emendations. A small number (for instance, regarding the titles) record alternative readings when we did not emend the base text. We do not, however, provide a complete list of variants, for which one may consult Grenier-Winther's edition. Each note consists of a line number, a lemma (the reading from our text), the manuscript source for the reading that we have chosen, selected readings from other manuscripts; and the reading from the base manuscript when it was rejected. If no manuscript source is listed following the lemma, the adopted reading is the editors' conjecture.
Other comments on the text, as required.

1. Rondeau: «Se Dieu eust oblié 'non'»

GW16, Piaget p. 304.
Base MS A. No other copies.

2. *Rondel*: «Avril, qui vest de verdure»

GW18, Piaget p. 306.
Base MS A. No other copies.

3. *Rondel*: «Je ne voy riens qui me doie suffire»

GW19, Piaget p. 307.
Base MS A. No other copies.

6 *com*. A: lacks.
9, 10 *cuer*. Instead of writing out the word, the scribe has drawn a small heart.

4. *Rondel*: «S'il ne vous plaist que j'aye mieulx»

GW40, Piaget p. 241.
Base MS A. Other copies: F.

3, 15 *Mais*. So F; A: lacks.
10 *quele*. So F; *quel* A.

5. *Rondel*: «Bien appert, Belle, a vo bonté»

GW54, Piaget p. 346.
Base MS A. Other copies: T.

6. *Rondel*: «Comment seroit que je fusse joieulx?»

GW56, Piaget p. 349.
Base MS A. No other copies.

7. *Rondel*: «Belle, pour hair faulceté»

GW58, Piaget p. 349.
Base MS A. No other copies.

1 *pour*. A: lacks.

8. Rondel: «Ce premier jour que l'an se renouvelle»

GW61, Piaget p. 350.
Base MS A. No other copies.

5 *seule celle*. A: *seule et celle*.

9. Rondel: «Adieu, Jeunesse, m'amie»

GW88, Piaget p. 267.
Base MS F. No other copies.

10. Vyrelay: «Je vous aime, je vous desir»

GW46, Piaget p. 304.
Base MS A. Other copies: F, T.

17–21 *Je vous aime . . . et mourir*. So F. A, T: lacks.

11. Balade: «Se je m'en dueil, nul ne m'en doit blasmer»

GW66, Piaget p. 359.
Base MS P. Other copies: A.

12. Balade: «J'ay tout perdu; le festu est rompu»

GW13, Piaget p. 300.
Base MS A. No other copies.

1 *d'amor*. A: *de mort*.

13. Balade: «A ce plaisant premier jour de l'annee»

GW52, Piaget p. 344.
Base MS A. No other copies.

7 *l'annee*. A: *lanne*.
15 *playt*. A: *play*.

14. Balade: «En grant desduit et en doulce plaisance»

GW53, Piaget p. 345.
Base MS A. Other copies: T.

6	*Puet*. A, T: *Pour*.
17	*desordoner*. A, T: *desordene*.

15. Balade: «Car j'ay perdu ma jeunesse, ma joye»

GW55, Piaget p. 347.
Base MS A. No other copies.

16. Balade: «Or vueille Dieux que brefment le revoye»

GW72, Piaget p. 370.
Base MS A. No other copies.

1	*ami*. A: *amis*.
21	*le*. A: *la*.

17. Balade: «Que nulle autre jamais ne choisiray»

GW26, Piaget p. 226.
Base MS P. Other copies: A, F, R.

Title	*Balade*. So P. A: *Balade amoureuse*. F: *Balade de Saint Valentin*.
23	*Le Dieu d'Amours*. So P, A. F, R: *Saint Valentin*.

18. Balade: «A Dalida, Jhezabel, et Thays»

GW77, Piaget p. 379.
Base MS P. Other copies: A, R.

19. Balade: «Plus m'escondit, plus la vueil tenir chiere»

GW69, Piaget p. 364.
Base MS P. Other copies: A, R.

12	*deust*. So A. P: *deux*.
15	*n'estuet*. So A. P: *n'estoit*.
21	*pis aler*. So A. P: *parler*.

20. *BALADE*: «AINSI LE FAIT CUER PLAIN DE FAUSSETÉ»

GW74, Piaget p. 373.
Base MS P. Other copies: A.

21. *BALADE*: «POUR MIEX GARDER DE MA DAME LE FORT»

GW63, Piaget p. 353.
Base MS P. Other copies: A.

17 *sy*. So A. P: *car*.

22. *BALADE*: «S'A MA CAUSE PERDOIT SA BONNE FAME»

GW64, Piaget p. 355.
Base MS P. Other copies: A.

11 *Que*. So A. P: *Quune*.

23. *BALADE*: «VOUS N'EN POVEZ TOUSDIZ QUE MIEX VALOIR»

GW17, Piaget p. 305.
Base MS P. Other copies: A.

24. *BALADE*: «CAR JE LANGUIS EN TROP DURE TRISTOUR»

GW3, Piaget p. 284.
Base MS A. No other copies.

25. *BALADE*: «CAR DE PRESANT, JE VEUL TOUT LE CONTRAIRE»

GW10, Piaget p. 304.
Base MS A. No other copies.

2 *amours*. A: *amour*.
7 *tourné*. A: *tourner*.
18 *recours*. A: *recorps*.

26. Balade: «Mais vous m'avez tousjours respondu 'non'»

GW15, Piaget p. 303.
Base MS A. No other copies.

17 *plus belle*. A: *trop plus belle*.

27. Balade amoreuse: «Car vrayement ce martelé me tue»

GW28, Piaget p. 325.
Base MS A. No other copies.

4 *mail*. A: *mal*.

28. Balade: «Car loin de vous vivre je ne pourroye»

GW32, Piaget p. 327.
Base MS A. No other copies.

19 *vueil*. A: *veult*.

29. Balade: «En languissant defineront my jour»

GW62, Piaget p. 351.
Base MS A. No other copies.

30. Balade: «Quant je pense a vo doulce figure»

GW65, Piaget p. 357.
Base MS A. No other copies.

9 *mets*. A: *met*.

31. Balade: «Vous vueil servir tresamoureusement»

GW67, Piaget p. 360.
Base MS A. No other copies.

32. BALADE: «FOY, LOIAULTÉ, SANS FAULCER, VOUS TENDRAY»

GW71, Piaget p. 368.
Base MS A. No other copies.

33. BALADE: «DON DE MERCY AINÇOIS QUE ON LE DEPRIE»

GW73, Piaget p. 371.
Base MS A. No other copies.

22 *ce qui*. A: *ce*.

34. BALADE: «SE JE M'EN PLAINS, CE NE FAIT A BLASMER»

GW76, Piaget p. 377.
Base MS A. No other copies.

1 *vous*. A: lacks.
4 *je*. A: *et*.
16 *m'en*. A: *me*.

35. BALADE: «PROUCHAINE MORT EN LIEU DE GARISON»

GW80, Piaget p. 214.
Base MS F. No other copies.

Title *Balade*. F: *Les six balades ensuivans*.

36. BALADE: «PAR VO DOUCEUR, TRESBELLE ET BONNE NEE»

GW83, Piaget p. 242.
Base MS F. No other copies.

37–41. CINQ BALADES ENSUIVANS

Heading *Cinq balades ensuivans*. So F. A, E, P: lacks.

37. Balade: «Car chascun a joye de li loer»

GW21, Piaget p. 209.
Base MS P. Other copies: A, E, F.

Title *Balade*. So P. A: *Balade amoureuse*.

38. Balade: «Car trop par est son cuer plain de reffus»

GW22, Piaget p. 210.
Base MS P. Other copies: A, E, F.

Title *Balade*. So P. A: *Balade amoureuse*.

39. Balade: «Priez pour moy, tous les loyaulx amans»

GW23, Piaget p. 211.
Base MS P. Other copies: A, E, F.

Title *Balade*. So P. A: *Balade amoureuse*.

40. Balade: «Tout a rebours de ce qu'on vuelt trouver»

GW27, Piaget p. 211.
Base MS P. Other copies: A, E, F.

41. Balade: «De li servir ne seray jamais las»

GW2, 31, Piaget p. 212.
Base MS P. Other copies: A (twice, A1 and A2), E, F.

Title *Balade*. So A1, P. A2: *Balade amoureuse Granson*.
3 *j'ay*. So A1, A2, E, F. P: *a*.

42. Balade: «Desloiaulté en l'amoureuse vie»

GW68, Piaget p. 362.
Base MS P. Other copies: A.

4 *soubz*. So A. P: *sur*.
25–28 *Princesse d'Amours . . . l'amoureuse vie*. So A. P: lacks.

43. BALADE: «FORS QUE D'AMOURS ET DE MA BELLE DAME»

GW45, Piaget p. 338.
Base MS P. Other copies: A.

44. BALADE: «AINSI PUET IL DON D'AMOURS DESSERVIR»

GW75, Piaget p. 375.
Base MS P. Other copies: A.

45. BALADE: «QUE MON CUER VOIT TOUSDIZ, OU QUE JE SOYE»

GW42, Piaget p. 334.
Base MS P. Other copies: A.

24 *Qu'en*. So A. P: *Que*.

46. BALADE: «MA BELLE DAME ET MA LOYAL AMIE»

GW14, Piaget p. 301.
Base MS P. Other copies: A.

47. BALADE: «CAR JE LANGUIS PAR DEFFAULT DE RAISON»

GW4, Piaget p. 286.
Base MS A. No other copies.

48. BALADE: «C'EST MON TALANT, BELLE DAME SANS PER»

GW33, Piaget p. 328.
Base MS A. No other copies.

3 *choisyr*. A: *choisy*.
28 *serez*. A: *sarez*.

49. BALADE: «JE N'AY RIENS FAIT QU'AMOURS NE M'AIT FAIT FAIRE»

GW41, Piaget p. 237.
Base MS A. Other copies: F, L, Q.

Title *Balade*. So F, L. Q: *Aultre Balade*. A: lacks.

50. BALADE: «JE N'AY RIENS FAIT QU'AMOURS NE ME FAIT FAIRE»

GW41 (from Q), GW49 (from A), Piaget pp. 238, 342.
Base MS A. Other copies: F (lines 1–10), L, Q.

Title	*Balade*. So A. F: *Response*. L: *Ballade et Response*. Q: *Response de la dame*.
11	*ou temps dont vo parlés*. So Q. A: *ung temps de vous parler*.
17	*face et*. So Q. A: *faciez*.

51. BALADE: «DAME, DE MOY PLUS QUE NULLE AUTRE AMEE»

GW57, Piaget p. 218.
Base MS A. Other copies: F.

Title	*Balade*. So A. F: lacks.
15	*puist*. So F. P: *puisse*.

52. BALADE: «IL M'EST ADVIS QUE VOSTRE BEAUTÉ VOYE»

GW60, Piaget p. 215.
Base MS A. Other copies: F, R.

Title	*Balade*. So A, R. F: lacks.
5	*penser*. So F. R: *panser*. A: *pensee*.
26	*peust*. So F. R: *en peust*. A: *on peust*.

53. BALADE: «PUIS QU'IL LUI PLAIST, IL ME SOUFFIST»

GW89, Piaget p. 277.
Base MS P. Other copies: A.

10	*souffist*. So A. P: *souffit*.
22	*vueilliez*. So A. P: *vueille*.

54. BALADE: «UN SEUL CONFORT DE MA TRESBELLE DAME»

GW78, Piaget p. 205.
Base MS F. Other copies: E.

Title	*Balade*. E: *Autre*. F: lacks.

55. BALADE: «DE MIEULX EN MIEULX SERVIRAY MA MAISTRESSE»

GW79, Piaget p. 207.
Base MS F. Other copies: G.

Title	*Balade*. F, G: lacks.
1	*Amours Amours*. So G. F: *Amours*.

56. BALADE: «CAR LE COUROUX N'Y VAULT PAS UNE MAILLE»

GW43, Piaget p. 197.
Base MS P. Other copies: A, E, F, L.

8	*qui*. So E F. A, P: *quil*.
18	*s'en*. So A. P: *sans*.
	saille. So A, F. P: *saillie*.

57. LE DESERT («FORS QUE LA MORT PROUCHAINEMENT»)

GW85, Piaget p. 248.
Base MS F. No other copies.

9	*pour*. F: *pas*.
25	*vous*. F: *me*.

58. BALADE: «D'UN TEL AMER QUE FAIRE TOUS HONNIS»

GW70, Piaget p. 366.
Base MS A. Other copies: R.

8	*estre*. So R. A: *est*.
27	*D'amourettes et la doulce savour*. So R. A: lacks.

59. BALADE: «QUI FONDRE PEUST ET LUI RENOUVELLER»

GW47, Piaget p. 340.
Base MS P. Other copies: A, E.

21	*Si fais assez ne pie peuent souffire*. So P. A: *Sy fais assaus ne me doivent suffire*. E: *Ses fais asses ne me point soffire*.

60. Balade amoreuse: «Pardonnés moy, besoing le me fait faire» (1)

GW24, Piaget p. 256.
Base MS A. Other copies: E, F, G, K, V.

Title — *Balade amoreuse*. So A (which also contains 61, but not immediately afterwards). F, K: *Balade de saint valentin double* (where it is followed by 61, bearing the same title). E: *Granson* (where it is immediately followed by 61 without a separate title). G: *Balade* (which does not contain 61).
16 — *l'avoient*. So E, F, G, K, V. A: *l'avoie*.

61. Balade Granson: «Pardonnez moy, besoing le me fait faire» (2)

GW30, Piaget p. 257.
Base MS A. Other copies: E, F, K.

Title — *Balade granson*. So A. F, K: *Balade de saint valentin double* (See note on the title to 60).
7 — *aourer*. So F, K. A: *ouvrer*.

62. Balade: «Trop plus de biens que penser ne sauroye»

GW59, Piaget p. 217.
Base MS A. Other copies: F.

Title — *Balade*. So A. F: lacks.
2 — *soient*. So F. A: *soye*.
9 — *de plaisir*. So F. A: *desplaisir*.
10 — *d'une*. So F. A: *dun*.
24 — *sauroye*. F: *saroye*. A: *pourroye*.

63. Balade: «Ma seule dame, plus que nulle autre amee»

GW81, Piaget p. 216.
Base MS F. No other copies.

Title — *Balade*. F: lacks.
15 — *fois*. F: lacks.

64. Balade: «Faitez de moy tout ce qu'il vous plaira»

GW48, Piaget p. 246.
Base MS A. Other copies: F.

65. BALADE: «JE N'EN CONGNOIZ NULLE SI BELLE»

GW84, Piaget p. 244.
Base MS F. No other copies.

66. BALADE: «CAR QUANQUE VOY NE ME FAIT QUE DESPLAIRE»

GW50, Piaget p. 219.
Base MS A. Other copies: F (1–24 and 36–43 only).

Title	*Balade*. So A. F: lacks.
10	*Ont*. So F. A: *On*.
43	*quanque*. A: *quaque*.

67. BALADE: «MA SEULE AMOUR, EN QUELQUE LIEU QUE JE SOYE»

GW82, Piaget p. 239.
Base MS F. No other copies.

7	*qu'a*. F: *que*.

68. LE DIT DE LOIAUTÉ

GW44, Piaget p. 336.
Base MS A. No other copies.

25	*aigait*. A: *aigard*.
26–27	*Ne nul engin . . . nuysance*. The order of these lines is reversed in A, disturbing the rhyme scheme.
28	*percevance*. A: *perceverance*.
32	*est*. A: *et*.

69. L'ESTRAINE DU JOUR DE L'AN

GW38, Piaget p. 254.
Base MS P. Other copies: A, F, K.

Title	*L'Estraine du jour de l'an*. So P, F. A: *L'Estrainne de gransson*. K: *L'Estrainne du jour de l'an granson*.
30	*qui*. So A, F, K. P: *quil*.

70. La Complainte de l'an nouvel

GW51, Piaget p. 199.
Base MS P. Other copies: A, E (lines 1–44 only, each stanza followed by another attributed to "Lesparra"), F, K, W.

Title *La complainte de l'an nouvel*. So A, E, P. F: *La complainte de lan nouvel que gransson fost pour un chevalier quil escoutait complaindre*. K: *Cy commence la complainte de lan nouvel que granson fist pour un chevalier quil lescoutoit se plaindre pres dun bouquet*.

71. Le Souhait de Saint Valentin

GW29, Piaget p. 202.
Base MS P. Other copies A, F.

Title *Le Souhait de Saint Valentin*. So F. A: *Souhait*. P: *Le Souhait en complainte*.
28 *que le*. So A, F. P: *quelle*.
32 *comme a elle le*. So A. F: *comme elle le*. P: *comme a le*.
45 *d'omme si fins*. So A, F. P: *du me si fins*.

72. Complainte de Saint Valentin

GW20, Piaget p. 221.
Base MS A. Other copies: F, K.

Title *Complainte de Saint Valentin*. So F. K: *Cy apres s'ensuit la complainte Saint Vallentin*. A: lacks.
16 *En*. So F, K. A: *Et*.
32 *Vostre*. So F, K. A: *Vrostre*.
65 *amez*. So F, K. A: *avez*.
70 *monstrez*. So F, K. A: *monstrer*.

73. La Pastourelle Granson

GW34, Piaget p. 269.
Base MS: P. Other copies: A, C, D, E (lacks lines 51–100), F, H, K, M.

Title *La pastourelle granson*. So A, C (in a later hand), D, F, M, K. H: *La pastourelle de granson*. P: *Complainte de pastour et de pastourelle amoureuse*.
5 *ouy*. So A, D, E, F, H, K, M. P: *ainsi*.
6 *Au*. So A, C, D, E, F, H, K, M. P: *Du*.
after 10 *La Bergiere*. Speaker markers: D (in margin), E H. A, C, K, P: lack.
18 *En*. So C, D, E, F, H, K, M. P: *Et*.

33	*contenance*. So A, C, D, E, F, H, K, M. P: *ordenance*.
70	*souvant*. So A, F, K. C, D, H: *tousjours*. M: *tousdis*. P: lacks.
79	*On*. So A, D, F, H, K, M. C: *Je*. P: *En*.
	d'onneur. So C. D, H: *a honneur*. A, F, K, M: *honneur*. P: *don*.
	suyr. So C. D, H, K: *faire*. A, F, M, P: *fuir*.
80	*Et*. So C, D, H, M. A, F, K, P: *Ne*.
84	*l'esay*. So A, C, D, F, H, K, M. P: *le say*.
104	*Nulz*. So A, C, D, E, F, H, K. P: *Ceulz*.
105	*recevoir*. So A, C, D, E, F, H, K, M. P: *decevoir*.
128	*qui*. So A, C, D, E, F, H, K, M. P: *quil*.
153	*fait*. So A, C, E, F, H, K, M. P: *font*.
159	*qui*. So A, C, E, F, H, K, M. P: *quil*.
172	*veulent*. So A, C, E, F, H, K, M. P: *voulant*.

74. COMPLAINTE DE GRANSSON

GW1, Piaget p. 259.
Base MS P. Other copies: A, E, F, K.

Title	*Complainte de gransson*. So F, K. A: *Lay en complainte*. E: *Congie que prist Micer Otto de Granson de sa dame*. P: *Complainte*.
25	*de moy mon cuer plourant*. So A. P: *de mon cuer tout plourant*.
65	*vit*. So A F K. P: *vif*.
110	*corps*. So A, E. P, F, K: *cuer*.
	cuer. So A, E. P, F, K: *corps*.
155	*et*. So A, E, F, K. P: *a*.
184	*Loing*. So F, K. P: *Long*.

75. LE LAY DE DESIR EN COMPLAINTE

GW39, Piaget p. 229.
Base MS P. Other copies: A, F, K, R (lines 95–125), S (lines 1–131).

6	*qui*. So C, F, K, S. A, P: *quil*.
107	*aterminer*. So A, F, K, R. P, S: *aterminer et finer*.
129–32	*Dont je seray . . . faite*. So A. P: lacks.
173	*trovez . . . en*. So A. F, K, P: *tournez . . . a*.
186	*texte*. So A, F, K. P: *teuxte*.
210	*me*. So A. P, F, K: *tel*.
213	*defrire*. So F, K. P: *deffraire*.
216	*Belle, tournez vers moy vos yeulx*. So A. P F K: lacks.

76. COMPLAINTE DE SAINT VALLENTIN GARENSON

GW90, Piaget p. 183.
Base MS D. Other copies: B, G (lines 1–128), H.

Title	*Complainte de Saint Vallentin Garenson*. So D. H: *La complainte de saint Valentin gransson compilee par M. alain ch*. B: *Autre complainte de nouvelle acointance*. G: lacks.
3	*chascun*. So B, G. D: *le temps*.
6	*me*. So G, H. D: *moy*. B: *my*.
83	*doulceur*. So B, H. D, G: *douleur*.
104	*conseil*. So B. D, G, H: *confort*.
151	*n'eschive*. D: *mescheve*. H: *meschive*.
153	*Car*. So B, H. D: *Par*.
163	*Viens*. So B. D, H: lacks.
	la merveille. So B. D, H: *la grant merveille*.
164	*Volle tousjours et volera*. So B. D, H: *De tout bien par tout volera*.
165	*En*. B, D, H: *Et*.
166	*Ou on*. D: *On en*. B: *Lon on*. H: *Et on*.
196	*s'entente*. So B. D: *m'entente*.
211	*si joyeuse*. So B, H. D: *sioieuse*.
268	*consentir*. D: *consenter*.

77. LE SONGE SAINT VALENTIN

GW25, Piaget p. 309.
Base MS A. Other copies: F (lines 402–50).

4	*en grant sejour*. A: *grant sejour*.
22	*la Saint Valentin*. A: *Saint Valentin*.
39	*riviers*. A: *rivieres*.
140	*vouler*. A: *voule*.
168	*vouler*. A: *voules*.
189	*si*. A: *sil*.
345	*Qu'entre*. A: *Entre*.
347	*doubtent*. A: *doubte*.
372	*aiment*. A: *aime*.
407	*conforte*. A, F: *conforter*.
417	*envoie*. A, F: *envoit*.

78. LE LIVRE MESSIRE ODE

GW91, Piaget p. 383.
Base MS: B. Other MSS: G (lines 702–833), J (lines 1–326, 872–966, 994–1089), N (lines 1–1480), O (lines 1–32, 617–57, 762–815, 917–54, 1066–1114).

Title *Le Livre Messire Ode*. Supplied by Piaget. No manuscript authority.
45 *q'un*. So N. B: *qum*.
63 *nesq'un*. So N. B: *nesqum*.
117–58 *Plus n'en diray . . . je soye*. So N. B: lacks (42 lines, the equivalent of one average manuscript page).
122 *desroye*. N: *desroyr*. J: *desiouyz*.
159 B resumes.
172 *obeir*. So J, N. B: *obeiz*.
179 *Riens qui*. So J, N. B: *Bien que*.
187 *laisser*. J: *laiser*. N: *laissier*. B: *laissez*.
192 *Enceint*. So N. J: *ensaint*. B: *Au saint*.
198 *Enceint d'arbres*. So N. J: *ensains darbres*. B: *enceinr dabres*.
200 *desduisoient*. So J, N. B: *desduiroient*.
206 *Blanches*. So J, N. B: *Blandes*.
216 *Affin que mieulx m'en sovenist*. So J, N. B: lacks.
217 *Complainte*. So J. B, N: lacks.
222 *clains*. So N. J: *clame*. B: *clamy*.
225 *me*. So J, N. B: lacks.
239 *plours et*. So J, N. B: *plus en*.
245 *duray*. B, J, N: *diray*.
249 *douleur me*. So J, N. B: *doulce*.
261 *doulceur*. So J, N. B: *douleur*.
265 *Dy et diray ou que soye, en tous lieux*. So J, N. B: lacks.
270 *Pourtant souvent en penser me resveille*. So J, N. B: *Pour pensay maintesfoiz m'a resveillay*.
277 *De la servir, honnourer et doubter*. So J. N: *De la cherir, obeir, crainte, et doubter*. B: *De la cherir, prandre, craindre, obeir, doubter*.
303 *ordonner*. So J, N. B: *ordonnez*.
309 *souffrist*. So J. B: *souffrir*.
329 *tres liement*. So N. B: *treslierment*.
332 *Chançon*. J: *Ballade*. B, N: lacks.
349 *osillon*. So N. B: *orillon*.
361 *S'il vous plaist, lire la pourrez*. So N. B: lacks.
394 *Et doint a tous vrays amoureux*. So N. B: lacks.
395 *la*. So N. B: *de*.
509 *Pis*. So N. B: *Puis*.
517 *Affin que cesse ma doulour*. So N. B: lacks.
556 *voix*. So N. B: *foiz*.
574 *Me*. So N. B: *Ne*.
589 *racourcer*. So N. B: *recommancier*.
613 *ne m'en*. So N. B: *n'en*.
628 *descort*. So N, O. B: *desconfort*.
632 *corner*. So N, O. B: *cornes*.
655 *finent*. So N, O. B: *furent*.
718 *donne*. So G, N. B: *donnay*.
726 *Ayez pitié de ma clamour*. So N. B, G: lacks.
744 *Est*. So G, N. B: *Et*.

763 *endurez*. So N, O. B: *endurer*.
767 *le*. So G, N, O. B: *la*.
778 *Garyr*. B, G, N, O: *Gary*.
795 *Seray*. So G, N, O. B: *Seroye*.
798 *N'ay*. So G, N, O. B: *Ne*.
811–14 *Je sens . . . doibt souffire*. So N (very similar in G and O). B: lacks.
835 *enregistré*. So N. B: *enregistray*.
840–41 *Lors pensay . . . ramantevoir*. So N. B: *Pour ma douleur ramantevoir / Me sembla que la veyre ne oir*.
842 *s'il*. So N. B: *il*.
878 *conseiller*. So J, N. B: *conseillez*.
888 *laisser*. So N. B: *laissez*.
917 *vint*. So J, N, O. B: *vient*.
949 *Et Souvenir, le vaillant champion*. So J, N, O. B: *Et avec lui Reffus, son compagnon*.
960 *Aprouche*. So J, N. B: *Apresse*.
l'auront. So N. B: *auront*.
981 *accorder*. So N. B: *agorder*.
1006 *suyt*. So J, N. B: *fait*.
1009 *me*. So J, N. B: *ne*.
1019 *fort*. So J, N. B: *fors*.
1037 *Garder*. So J, N. B: *Gardez*.
1058 *ne pourroye*. So J, N. B: *ne me pourroye*.
1070 *deshonnoré*. So J, N, O. B: *deshonnoray*.
1083–84 *Et a mon cueur . . . ce party*. These two lines are reversed in B, spoiling both rhymes.
prose *sire de Cornoaille*. So N, O. B: lacks.
prose *de mon cuer*. So N, O. B: lacks.
prose *celle qui*. So N, O. B: lacks.
prose *les*. So N. B: *vous*.
1145 *desconforter*. So N. B: *reconfortez*.
1162 *mercyoye*. So N. B: *mercyroye*.
1190 *se sçavoir*. So N. B: *ce savez*.
1224 *Enfermé dedans le jardin*. So N. B: lacks.
1233 *me plaisoit*. So N. B: *le plairoit*.
1247 *veullent chanter*. So B. N: *prennent leur per*.
1256 *chetis*. So N. B: *conquis*.
1278 *m'avint*. So N. B: *n'avint*.
1299 *Je viz ung tiercellet venir*. So N. B: lacks.
1306 *festoioyent*. So N. B: *festoient*.
1325 *guignardie*. So N. B: *grinardie*.
1350 *pourroye*. So N. B: *pouvoie*.
1373 *Nous*. So N. B: *Ne*.
1384 *diroye*. So N. B: *disoie*.
1396 *celle*. So N. B: *celles*.
1420 *qu'Espoir*. So N. B: lacks.
1423 *Espoir*. So N. B: *espouoir*.

1443, 1455	*gens*. So N. B: *sens*.
1513	*se*. B: *ceulx*.
1521	*tout*. B: *tous*.
1535	*Corps*. B: *Cueur*.
	Cueur. B: *Corps*.
1541	*pensee*. B: *penser*.
1546	*De*. B: lacks.
1567	*qui*. B: *quen*.
1575	*y*. B: *luy*.
1578	*et tousjours*. B: *et tousjours et toujours*.
1587	*puet*. B: *point*.
1591	*luy pleust vous*. B: *vous pleust luy*.
1608	*retournray*. B: *retourray*.
1617	*recevrez*. B: *recevray*.
1620	*vous*. B: *me*.
1625	*savez*. B: *savoir*.
1638	B: *Le Corps* (speaker marker, omitted here).
1645	*Ne*. B: *Ne le*.
1680	*J'ay fait mon tresor de souhaiz*. B: *Jai fait mon souhait*.
1686, 1692	*J'ay fait mon tresor de souhaiz*. B: *Jay fait mon tresor &c*.
1707	*Luy*. B: *Leur*.
1720	*Endurons*. B: *En duron*.
1721	*En presentant*. B: *Presentement*.
1728	*enregistré*. B: *enregistray*.
1735	*travaillier*. B: *travailliez*.
1749	*souffrir*. B: *souffrez*.
1771	*qu'est*. B: *est*.
1781	*desplaisir*. B: *plaisir*.
1799	*desplaisoit*. B: *desplairoit*.
1807	*Qu'en*. B: *Que on*.
1821	*a fin*. B: *affin*.
1823	*desplaise*. B: *desplaire*.
1838	*peust*. B: *pleust*.
1859	*vivre*. B: *livre*.
1862	*nulle autre*. B: *autre nulle*.
1867	*non*. B: *nom*.
1978	*passer*. B: *passez*.
1988	*lever*. B: *la lever*.
2019	*de comforter*. B: *descomforter*.
2031	*ferez*. B: *fera*.
	reconfort. B: lacks.
2065	*Plus*. B: *puis*.
2083	*ne l'en*. B: *le ne len*.
2114	*scet*. B: *scay*.
2153	*desesperé*. B: *desesperee*.
2170	*Qu'autre*. B: *quentre*.
2172	*amer*. B: *amez*.

2173 *avoye.* B: *savoye.*
2198 *Pouoir.* B: *pouez.*
2221 *Et.* B: lacks.
2228 *m'avez.* B: *ma vous.*
2237 *despourveu.* B: *despourveue.*
2253 *tousjours devant.* B: *devant tousjours.*
2258 *n'a.* B: *nay.*
2266 *veillant.* B: *vueillant.*
2305 *qui.* B: *quil.*
2311 *lauguis.* B: *languir.*
2336 *mieulx.* B: *mienne.*
2341 *souleil.* B: *sommeil.*
2344 *me.* B: *ne.*
2361 *mal que.* B: *mal de que.*
2363 *definer.* B: *desiner.*
2387 *Me font.* B: *ne fait.*
2409 *Ne.* B: *Je.*
2416 *plust.* B: *plus.*
2419 *elle.* B: *elles.*
2425 *me.* B: *ne me.*
2428 *si.* B: *sa.*
2438 *peusse.* B: *pense.*
2456 *folle.* B: *folie.*
2461 *Seulle.* B: *semble.*
2469 *Chançon.* B: lacks.
2486 *Chançon.* B: lacks.

CONCORDANCE TO GRENIER-WINTHER'S EDITION

The location of each poem included in the present edition in both Piaget's and Grenier-Winther's editions is recorded in the Textual Notes. The following table lists the poems in the order of their appearance in Grenier-Winther's, with either a reference to the numbering in this edition or a brief explanation for the omission.

Grenier-Winther	*This Edition*
1	74
2	41
3	24
4	47
5	Machaut[1]
6	Machaut
7	Machaut
8	Machaut
9	Machaut
10	25
11	Machaut
12	Machaut
13	12
14	46
15	26
16	1
17	23
18	2
19	3
20	72
21	37
22	38
23	39
24	60
25	77
26	17
27	40
28	27

[1] See the Introduction, p. 7 and n34.

Grenier-Winther	*This Edition*
29	71
30	61
31	41
32	28
33	48
34	73
35	Machaut
36	Machaut
37	Machaut
38	69
39	75
40	4
41	49
42	45
43	56
44	68
45	43
46	10
47	59
48	64
49	50
50	66
51	70
52	13
53	14
54	5
55	15
56	6
57	51
58	7
59	62
60	52
61	8
62	29
63	21
64	22
65	30
66	11
67	31
68	42
69	19
70	58
71	32
72	16
73	33
74	20

Grenier-Winther	*This Edition*
75	44
76	34
77	18
78	54
79	55
80	35
81	63
82	67
83	36
84	65
85	57
86	Deschamps (?)[2]
87	Deschamps
88	9
89	53
90	76
91	78
92	MS B; not attributed to Granson
93	MS B; not attributed to Granson
94	MS E; headed "Glen Balada"; not otherwise attributed to Granson[3]
95	MS E; not attributed to Granson
96	MS E; not attributed to Granson
97	MS E; not attributed to Granson
98	MS E; not attributed to Granson
99	MS E; elsewhere attributed to Garencières; MS E; the *tençon* with "Lesparra."
100	Only the six stanzas drawn from ***70*** attibutable to Granson
101	MS C; only lines 1-21 (from ***75)*** likely to be Granson's[4]
102	MSS C, D, H; not attributed to Granson
103	MSS C, D; not attributed to Granson

[2] See the Introduction, p. 5 and n29.

[3] On the poems in MS E, see the Introduction, pp. 8–9.

[4] See the Introduction, p. 11.

Le Livre Messire Ode: Concordance to Piaget's Edition

The line numbering in Piaget's edition of *Le Livre Messire Ode*, which is the version that is cited in the existing commentary, differs from that in Grenier-Winther's edition, which we have adopted here, for four reasons. (1) Grenier-Winther includes in her numbering more of the lines that one infers from the rhymes are missing than Piaget does. (2) Grenier-Winther provides the full last stanza of the rondeaux (as we do as well), where Piaget gives only the initial line. (3) The prose passage that follows line 1089 (1080 in Piaget) takes up four more lines in Piaget's edition than it does in Grenier-Winther's and fewer lines in our edition because of our larger pages. (4) Piaget makes two errors in his numbering, dropping a line between his 1665 and 1670 and another between his 1695 and 1700. To locate here a passage cited from Piaget's edition, it is thus necessary to add to his line numbers, as follows:

Piaget's numbering	*Grenier-Winther's numbering*	*difference*
1–120	1–120	none
121–343	122–344	+1
344–471	348–475	+4
472–594	477–599	+5
595–1080	604–1089	+9
1118–1447	1123–1452	+5
1448–1647	1456–1655	+8
1648–1668	1659–1679	+11
1670–1682	1680–1692	+10
1683–1698	1696–1711	+13
1700–1711	1712–1723	+12
1712–1932	1727–1947	+15
1933	1949	+16
1934–2028	1956–2050	+22
2029–2439	2055–2465	+26
2440–2452	2470–2482	+30
2453–2465	2486–2498	+33
not included	2499–2501	

Index of First Lines

French

ENGLISH

Index of Titles

French

ENGLISH

BIBLIOGRAPHY

Alain de Lille. *Anticlaudianus*. Trans. James J. Sheridan. Toronto: Pontifical Institute of Medieval Studies, 1973.

Arden, Heather. "Othon de Grandson and Christine de Pizan: Love's Martyrs." In Kosta–Théfaine, *Othon de Grandson*. Pp. 103–21.

Attwood, Catherine. "La dialectique amoureuse chez Othon de Grandson." In Kosta–Théfaine, *Othon de Grandson*. Pp. 85–101.

Bartolini, Lionel. "Neuchâtel, Isabelle de." In *Dictionnaire historique de la Suisse*. Ed. Marco Jorio and Christian Sonderegger. <http://www.hls-dhs-dss.ch/textes/f/F44489.php>. 4 July 2013.

Basso, Hélène. "L'envol et l'ancrage : Le quête amoureuse comme épreuve de soi dans *Le dit de l'alérion* de Guillaume de Machaut et *Le livre Messire Ode* d'Othon de Grandson." In Kosta–Théfaine, *Othon de Grandson*. Pp. 137–63.

Bennett, J. A. W. Review of *Chaucer and the French Poet Graunson*, by Haldeen Braddy. *Medium Ævum* 18 (1949), 35–37.

Benoît de Sainte-Maure. *Le Roman de Troie*. Ed. Léopold Constans. 6 vols. Société des Anciens Textes Français. Paris: Firmin–Didot, 1904–12. Reprint, New York: Johnson, 1968.

Berguerand, Claude. *Le duel d'Othon de Grandson (1397): Mort d'un chevalier–poète vaudois à la fin du Moyen Age*. Lausanne: Université de Lausanne, 2008.

Betemps, Isabelle. "Les lais de plour: Guillaume de Machaut et Oton de Grandson." In *Guillaume de Machaut: 1300–2000*. Ed. Jacqueline Cerquiglini–Toulet and Nigel Wilkins. Paris: Presses de l'Université de Paris–Sorbonne, 2002. Pp. 95–106.

Boulton, Maureen. *The Song in the Story: Lyric Insertions in French Narrative Fiction, 1200–1400*. Philadelphia, PA: University of Pennsylvania Press, 1993.

Braddy, Haldeen. "Messire Oton de Graunson, Chaucer's Savoyard Friend." *Studies in Philology* 35 (1938), 515–31.

———. *Chaucer and the French Poet Graunson*. Baton Rouge, LA: Louisiana State University Press, 1947.

Butterfield, Ardis. *The Familiar Enemy: Chaucer, Language, and Nation in the Hundred Years War*. Oxford: Oxford University Press, 2009.

Carden, Sally Tartline. "Le *Livre Messire Ode* d'Oton de Grandson: Un interrogatoire poétique." *Moyen Français* 35–36 (1996), 79–89.

———. "Oton de Grandson." In *Literature of the French and Occitan Middle Ages: Eleventh to Fifteenth Centuries*. Ed. Deborah Sinnreich–Levi and Ian S. Laurie. Vol. 208 of *The Dictionary of Literary Biography*. Detroit, MI: Gale, 1999. Pp. 141–148.

Cartier, Normand R. "Oton de Grandson et sa princesse." *Romania* 85 (1964), 1–16.

Les cent ballades: Poème du XIVe siècle par Jean le Seneschal. Ed. Gaston Raynaud. Société des Anciens Textes Français. Paris: Firmin Didot, 1905. Reprint, New York: Johnson, 1968.

Cerquiglini, Jacqueline. "Le rondeau." In *La littérature française aux XIVe et XVe siècles*, Ed. Daniel Poirion. Vol. 1, *Partie historique*. Grundriss der Romanischen Literaturen des Mittelalters 8. Heidelberg: Winter, 1988. Pp. 45–58.

Chartier, Alain. *Poetical Works*. Ed. J. C. Laidlaw. Cambridge: Cambridge University Press, 1974.

Chaubet, Daniel. "Le duel Othon de Grandson — Gérard d'Estavayer du 7 août 1397: une conséquence des événements qui agitèrent la Savoie dans les dernières années du XIVe siècle." In Kosta–Théfaine, *Othon de Grandson*. Pp. 11–42.

Chaucer, Geoffrey. *The Parlement of Foulys*. Ed. D. S. Brewer. London: Nelson, 1960.

———. *The Riverside Chaucer*. Ed. Larry D. Benson. Third ed. Boston: Houghton Mifflin, 1987.

Christine de Pisan. *Le Livre de la mutacion de Fortune*. Ed. Suzanne Solente. 4 vols. Société des Anciens Textes Français. Paris: Firmin–Didot, 1959–66.

———. *Œuvres poétiques*. Ed. Maurice Roy. 3 vols. Société des Anciens Textes Français. Paris: Firmin Didot, 1886–96. Reprint, New York: Johnson, 1965.

Clanvowe, Sir John. *The Works of Sir John Clanvowe*. Ed. V. J. Scattergood. Cambridge: Brewer, 1975.

Pearl. Ed. E. V. Gordon. Oxford: Clarendon Press, 1953.

Courvoisier, Jean. *Panorama de l'histoire Neuchâteloise*. Neuchâtel: Baconnière, 1972.

Crow, Martin M., and Clair C. Olson. *Chaucer Life Records*. London: Oxford University Press, 1966.

Deschamps, Eustache. *Œuvres complètes*. Ed. Auguste-Henry-Édouard Queux de Saint-Hilaire and Gaston Raynaud. 11 vols. Société des Anciens Textes Français. Paris: Firmin Didot, 1878–1903. Reprint, New York: Johnson, 1966.

Earp, Lawrence. "Lyrics for Reading and Lyrics for Singing in Late Medieval France: The Development of the Dance Lyric from Adam de la Halle to Guillaume de Machaut." In *The Union of Words and Music in Medieval Poetry*. Ed. Rebecca A. Baltzer, Thomas Cable, and James I. Wimsatt. Austin, TX: University of Texas Press, 1991. Pp. 101–31.

———. *Guillaume de Machaut: A Guide to Research*. New York: Garland, 1995.

Froissart, Jean. *Œuvres*. Ed. Kervyn de Lettenhove. 28 vols. Brussels: Devaux, 1867–77.

———. *L'Espinette amoureuse*. Ed. Anthime Fourrier. Paris: Klincksieck, 1962.

Galway, Margaret. "Chaucer, Graunson, and Isabel of France." *Review of English Studies* 24 (1948), 273–80.

Garencières, Jean de. *Le chevalier poète Jehan de Garencières (1372–1415): sa vie et ses poésies complètes*. Ed. Young Abernathy Neal. Paris: Nizet, 1953.

Gilbert, A.J. "Chaucer, Grandson and the 'Turtil Trewe'." *Notes and Queries* 19 (1972), 165.

Godefroy, Frédéric. *Dictionnaire de l'ancienne langue française et de tous ses dialectes du IXe au XVe siècles*. 10 vols. Paris: Vieweg and Paris: Bouillon, 1881–1902.

Gower, John. *The Complete Works of John Gower*. Ed. G. C. Macaulay. 4 vols. Oxford: Clarendon Press, 1899–1902.

———. *Confessio Amantis*. Ed. Russell A. Peck, with Latin translations by Andrew Galloway. 3 vols. Kalamazoo, MI: Medieval Institute Publications, 2000–06.

———. *The French Balades*. Ed. and trans. R. F. Yeager. Kalamazoo, MI: Medieval Institute Publications, 2011.

Grandson, Oton de. *Oton de Grandson: sa vie et ses poésies*. Ed. Arthur Piaget. Lausanne: Payot, 1941.

———. "A Critical Edition of the Poetry of Oton de Grandson, MS. *L*." Ed. Caroline A. Cunningham. Ph.D. Dissertation: University of North Carolina at Chapel Hill, 1987. *DAI* 48.9A (1988), p. 2332A.

Granson, Oton de. *Poésies*. Ed. Joan Grenier–Winther. Classiques français du moyen âge 162. Paris: Champion, 2010.

Greimas, Algirdas Julien. *Dictionnaire de l'ancien français*. Third ed. Paris: Larousse, 2004.

Greimas, Algirdas Julien and Teresa Mary Keane. *Grand dictionnaire moyen français*. Second ed. Paris: Larousse, 2007.

Grenier–Winther, Joan. "On the Authorship of *La Belle dame qui eut mercy*." In Kosta–Théfaine, *Othon de Grandson*. Pp. 43–74.

Guido delle Colonne. *Historia Destructionis Troiae*. Trans. Mary Elizabeth Meek. Bloomington, IN: Indiana University Press, 1974.

Guillaume de Lorris and Jean de Meun. *Le Roman de la rose*. Ed. Félix Lecoy. 3 vols. Classiques français du moyen âge 92, 95, 98. Paris: Champion, 1965–70.

Guillaume de Machaut. *Œuvres*. Ed. Ernest Hoepffner. 3 vols. Société des Anciens Textes Français. Paris; Firmin Didot, 1908–21. Reprint, New York: Johnson, 1965.

———. *La louange des dames*. Ed. Nigel Wilkins. New York: Barnes & Noble, 1973.

———. *Le jugement du roy de Behaigne and Remede de Fortune*. Ed. and trans. James I. Wimsatt and William W. Kibler. The Chaucer Library. Athens: University of Georgia Press, 1988.

———. *The Judgment of the King of Navarre (Le Jugement du Roi de Navarre)*. Ed. and trans. R. Barton Palmer. New York: Garland, 1988.

———. *The Fountain of Love (La fonteinne amoureuse) and Two Other Love Vision Poems* [*Prologue* and *Dit dou vergier*]. Ed. and trans. R. Barton Palmer. New York: Garland, 1993.

———. *Le livre dou voir dit (The Book of the True Poem)*. Ed. Daniel Leech-Wilkinson. Trans. R. Barton Palmer. New York: Garland, 1998.

———. *Poésies lyriques*. Ed. V. Chichmaref. 2 vols. Paris: Champion, n.d.

Heger, Henrik. "La Ballade et le Chant Royal." In *La litterature francaise aux XIVe et XVe siecles*. Ed. Daniel Poirion. Vol. 1, *Partie historique*. Grundriss der Romanischen Literaturn des Mittelalters 8. Heidelberg: Winter, 1988. Pp. 59–69.

Holenstein, André. "Assemblée d'états." In *Dictionnaire historique de la Suisse*, Ed. Marco Jorio and Christian Sonderegger. <http://www.hls–dhs–dss.ch/textes/f/F9929.php>.

Hyginus, C. Julius. *Fabulae*. Ed. and trans. Jean-Yves Boriaud. Paris: Les Belles lettres, 1997.

Jordà, Anna Alberni. "El cançoner Vega–Aguiló (BC, mss. 7 i 8): estructura i contingut." Ph.D. Dissertation: University of Barcelona, 2003. <http://www.tdx.cat/handle/10803/1679>. 4 July 2013.

Jung, Marc René. "Répertoire des poèmes d'Oton de Grandson." In *Moyen Age et Renaissance: Hommage au Professeur François Rouy*. Nice: Faculté des Lettres, Arts, et Sciences Humaines, 1995. Pp. 91–125.

Kelly, Douglas. *Medieval Imagination: Rhetoric and the Poetry of Courtly Love*. Madison: University of Wisconsin Press, 1978.

Kelly, Henry Ansgar. *Chaucer and the Cult of Saint Valentine*. Leiden: Brill, 1986.

Kibler, William W., and James I. Wimsatt. "The Development of the Pastourelle in the Fourteenth Century: An Edition of Fifteen Poems with an Analysis." *MS* 45 (1983), 22–78.

Kingsford, C.L. "Sir Otho de Grandison 1238?–1328." *Royal Historical Society Transactions*. 3rd Series, 3 (1909), 125–95.

Kosta–Théfaine, Jean-François. "Du chant d'amour au chant du désespoir, ou l'écriture d'une poétique de la tristesse dans la lyrique d'Othon de Grandson." *Romanistische Zeitschrift für Literaturgeschichte* 23 (1999), 297–310.

———. "Le *Livre Messire Ode* d'Othon de Grandson, ou l'écriture fragmentaire d'un discours amoureux." *Germanisch–Romanische Monatsschrift* 53 (2003), 355–61.

———. "De la continuité à l'innovation: le *Livre Messire Ode* d'Othon de Grandson et le *Livre du duc des vrais amans* de Christine de Pizan." *Cahiers de recherches médiévales* 11 (2004), 239–51.

———. "L'état de la recherche sur Othon de Grandson." In Kosta–Théfaine, *Othon de Grandson*. Pp. 183–94.

———, ed. *Othon de Grandson, chevalier et poète*. *Medievalia* 63. Orléans: Paradigme, 2007.

Langlois, Ernest. *Les Manuscrits du Roman de la Rose: description et classement*. Paris: Champion, 1910.

Laurie, Ian. "Les amitiés métriques: Othon de Grandson et Eustache Deschamps." In Kosta–Théfaine, *Othon de Grandson*. Pp. 123–36.

Le Franc, Martin. *Le champion des dames*. Ed. Robert Deschaux. 5 vols. Classiques français du moyen âge 127–31. Paris: Champion, 1999.

Livy. *History of Rome*. Ed. and Trans. B. O. Foster. Vol. 1. Cambridge, MA: Harvard University Press, 1919.

Massó i Torrents, Jaume. "Oto de Granson ì les balades de Lluis de Vilarasa." In *Mélanges de linguistique et de littérature offerts à M. Alfred Jeanroy*. Paris: Droz, 1928. Pp. 403–10.

Mudge, Charles R. "The Pennsylvania Chansonnier: A Critical Edition of the Ninety–Five Anonymous Ballades from Fourteenth Century." Ph.D. Dissertation: Indiana University, 1972. *DAI* 33.1A (1972), p. 282 A.

Niederhäuser, Peter. "Nidau, Rodolphe IV de." In *Dictionnaire Historique de la Suisse*. Ed. Marco Jorio and Christian Sonderegger. <http://www.hls-dhs-dss.ch/textes/f/F29244.php>. 4 July 2013.

Olson, Glending. "Towards a Poetics of the Late Medieval Courtly Lyric." In *Vernacular Poetics in the Middle Ages*. Ed. Lois Ebin Kalamazoo, MI: Medieval Institute Publications, 1984. Pp. 227–48.

Oruch, Jack B. "St. Valentine, Chaucer, and Spring in February." *Speculum* 56 (1981), 534–65.

Ovid. *Heroides and Amores*. Ed. and Trans. Grant Showerman. Second ed. rev. by G. P. Goold. Cambridge, MA: Harvard University Press, 1977.

———. *Metamorphoses*. Ed. and Trans. Frank Justus Miller. Third ed. rev. by G. P. Goold. 2 vols. Cambridge, MA: Harvard University Press, 1977.

Pagès, Amédée. "Le thème de la tristesse amoureuse en France et en Espagne du XIVe au XVe siècle." *Romania* 58 (1932), 29–43.

———. *La poésie française en Catalogne du XIIIe siècle à la fin du XVe.* Toulouse: Privat, 1936.

Phillips, Helen. "*The Complaint of Venus*: Chaucer and de Graunson." In *The Medieval Translator 4*. Ed. Roger Ellis and Ruth Evans. Binghamton, NY: Medieval & Renaissance Texts & Studies, 1994. Pp. 86–103.

Piaget, Arthur. "Oton de Granson et ses poésies." *Romania* 19 (1890), 237–59, 403–48.

———. "La *Belle dame sans merci* et ses imitations." *Romania* 33 (1904), 179–208.

Poirion, Daniel. *Le Poète et le prince: l'évolution du lyrisme courtois de Guillaume de Machaut à Charles d'Orléans.* Paris: Presses Universitaires de France, 1965.

Rey, Alain. *Dictionnaire historique de la langue française*. "Nouvelle édition." 2 vols. Paris: Robert, 1993.

Riquer, Martín de. "La canción de san Valentín del poeta Pardo." *Revista de la filología española* 39 (1955), 338–44.

Scattergood, John. "Chaucer's *Complaint of Venus* and the 'Curiosite' of Graunson." *Essays in Criticism* 44 (1994), 171–89.

Severs, J. Burke. *The Literary Relationships of Chaucer's "Clerk's Tale."* New Haven, CT: Yale University Press, 1942.

"Le Songe vert." Ed. Léopold Constans. *Romania* 33 (1904), 490–539.

Vitale–Brovarone, Alessandro, ed. "Recueil de galanteries (Torino, Archivio di Stato, J.b.IX.10)." Special Issue, *Moyen Français*, 6 (1980).

Wilkins, Nigel, ed. *One Hundred Ballades, Rondeaux and Virelais from the Late Middle Ages.* Cambridge: Cambridge University Press, 1969.

Wimsatt, James I. *Chaucer and the French Love Poets: The Literary Background of the "Book of the Duchess."* Chapel Hill, NC: University of North Carolina Press, 1968.

———. "Froissart, Chaucer, and the Pastourelles of the Pennsylvania Manuscript." *Studies in the Age of Chaucer: Proceedings* 1 (1984), 69–79.

———. "Chaucer and Deschamps' 'Natural Music'." In *The Union of Words and Music in Medieval Poetry*. Ed. Rebecca A. Baltzer, Thomas Cable, and James I. Wimsatt. Austin, TX: University of Texas Press, 1991. Pp. 132–50.

———. *Chaucer and his French Contemporaries: Natural Music in the Fourteenth Century*. Toronto: University of Toronto Press, 1991.

———. *Chaucer and the Poems of "Ch."* Revised ed. Kalamazoo, MI: Medieval Institute Publications, 2009.

Windeatt, Barry. *Chaucer's Dream Poetry: Sources and Analogues*. Woodbridge: Brewer, 1982.

Middle English Texts Series

The Floure and the Leafe, The Assembly of Ladies, The Isle of Ladies, edited by Derek Pearsall (1990)
Three Middle English Charlemagne Romances, edited by Alan Lupack (1990)
Six Ecclesiastical Satires, edited by James M. Dean (1991)
Heroic Women from the Old Testament in Middle English Verse, edited by Russell A. Peck (1991)
The Canterbury Tales: Fifteenth-Century Continuations and Additions, edited by John M. Bowers (1992)
Gavin Douglas, *The Palis of Honoure*, edited by David Parkinson (1992)
Wynnere and Wastoure and The Parlement of the Thre Ages, edited by Warren Ginsberg (1992)
The Shewings of Julian of Norwich, edited by Georgia Ronan Crampton (1994)
King Arthur's Death: The Middle English Stanzaic Morte Arthur and Alliterative Morte Arthure, edited by Larry D. Benson, revised by Edward E. Foster (1994)
Lancelot of the Laik and Sir Tristrem, edited by Alan Lupack (1994)
Sir Gawain: Eleven Romances and Tales, edited by Thomas Hahn (1995)
The Middle English Breton Lays, edited by Anne Laskaya and Eve Salisbury (1995)
Sir Perceval of Galles and Ywain and Gawain, edited by Mary Flowers Braswell (1995)
Four Middle English Romances: Sir Isumbras, Octavian, Sir Eglamour of Artois, Sir Tryamour, edited by Harriet Hudson (1996; second edition 2006)
The Poems of Laurence Minot, 1333–1352, edited by Richard H. Osberg (1996)
Medieval English Political Writings, edited by James M. Dean (1996)
The Book of Margery Kempe, edited by Lynn Staley (1996)
Amis and Amiloun, Robert of Cisyle, and Sir Amadace, edited by Edward E. Foster (1997; second edition 2007)
The Cloud of Unknowing, edited by Patrick J. Gallacher (1997)
Robin Hood and Other Outlaw Tales, edited by Stephen Knight and Thomas Ohlgren (1997; second edition 2000)
The Poems of Robert Henryson, edited by Robert L. Kindrick with the assistance of Kristie A. Bixby (1997)
Moral Love Songs and Laments, edited by Susanna Greer Fein (1998)
John Lydgate, *Troy Book Selections*, edited by Robert R. Edwards (1998)
Thomas Usk, *The Testament of Love*, edited by R. Allen Shoaf (1998)
Prose Merlin, edited by John Conlee (1998)
Middle English Marian Lyrics, edited by Karen Saupe (1998)
John Metham, *Amoryus and Cleopes*, edited by Stephen F. Page (1999)
Four Romances of England: King Horn, Havelok the Dane, Bevis of Hampton, Athelston, edited by Ronald B. Herzman, Graham Drake, and Eve Salisbury (1999)
The Assembly of Gods: Le Assemble de Dyeus, or Banquet of Gods and Goddesses, with the Discourse of Reason and Sensuality, edited by Jane Chance (1999)
Thomas Hoccleve, *The Regiment of Princes*, edited by Charles R. Blyth (1999)
John Capgrave, *The Life of Saint Katherine*, edited by Karen A. Winstead (1999)
John Gower, *Confessio Amantis*, Vol. 1, edited by Russell A. Peck; with Latin translations by Andrew Galloway (2000; second edition 2006); Vol. 2 (2003; second edition 2013); Vol. 3 (2004)
Richard the Redeless and Mum and the Sothsegger, edited by James M. Dean (2000)
Ancrene Wisse, edited by Robert Hasenfratz (2000)
Walter Hilton, *The Scale of Perfection*, edited by Thomas H. Bestul (2000)
John Lydgate, *The Siege of Thebes*, edited by Robert R. Edwards (2001)
Pearl, edited by Sarah Stanbury (2001)
The Trials and Joys of Marriage, edited by Eve Salisbury (2002)
Middle English Legends of Women Saints, edited by Sherry L. Reames, with the assistance of Martha G. Blalock and Wendy R. Larson (2003)
The Wallace: Selections, edited by Anne McKim (2003)
Richard Maidstone, *Concordia (The Reconciliation of Richard II with London)*, edited by David R. Carlson, with a verse translation by A. G. Rigg (2003)
Three Purgatory Poems: The Gast of Gy, Sir Owain, The Vision of Tundale, edited by Edward E. Foster (2004)
William Dunbar, *The Complete Works*, edited by John Conlee (2004)
Chaucerian Dream Visions and Complaints, edited by Dana M. Symons (2004)

Stanzaic Guy of Warwick, edited by Alison Wiggins (2004)
Saints' Lives in Middle English Collections, edited by E. Gordon Whatley, with Anne B. Thompson and Robert K. Upchurch (2004)
Siege of Jerusalem, edited by Michael Livingston (2004)
The Kingis Quair and Other Prison Poems, edited by Linne R. Mooney and Mary-Jo Arn (2005)
The Chaucerian Apocrypha: A Selection, edited by Kathleen Forni (2005)
John Gower, *The Minor Latin Works*, edited and translated by R. F. Yeager, with *In Praise of Peace*, edited by Michael Livingston (2005)
Sentimental and Humorous Romances: Floris and Blancheflour, Sir Degrevant, The Squire of Low Degree, The Tournament of Tottenham, and The Feast of Tottenham, edited by Erik Kooper (2006)
The Dicts and Sayings of the Philosophers, edited by John William Sutton (2006)
Everyman and Its Dutch Original, Elckerlijc, edited by Clifford Davidson, Martin W. Walsh, and Ton J. Broos (2007)
The N-Town Plays, edited by Douglas Sugano, with assistance by Victor I. Scherb (2007)
The Book of John Mandeville, edited by Tamarah Kohanski and C. David Benson (2007)
John Lydgate, *The Temple of Glas*, edited by J. Allan Mitchell (2007)
The Northern Homily Cycle, edited by Anne B. Thompson (2008)
Codex Ashmole 61: A Compilation of Popular Middle English Verse, edited by George Shuffelton (2008)
Chaucer and the Poems of "Ch," edited by James I. Wimsatt (revised edition 2009)
William Caxton, *The Game and Playe of the Chesse*, edited by Jenny Adams (2009)
John the Blind Audelay, *Poems and Carols*, edited by Susanna Fein (2009)
Two Moral Interludes: The Pride of Life and Wisdom, edited by David Klausner (2009)
John Lydgate, *Mummings and Entertainments*, edited by Claire Sponsler (2010)
Mankind, edited by Kathleen M. Ashley and Gerard NeCastro (2010)
The Castle of Perseverance, edited by David N. Klausner (2010)
Robert Henryson, *The Complete Works*, edited by David J. Parkinson (2010)
John Gower, *The French Balades*, edited and translated by R. F. Yeager (2011)
The Middle English Metrical Paraphrase of the Old Testament, edited by Michael Livingston (2011)
The York Corpus Christi Plays, edited by Clifford Davidson (2011)
Prik of Conscience, edited by James H. Morey (2012)
The Dialogue of Solomon and Marcolf: A Dual-Language Edition from Latin and Middle English Printed Editions, edited by Nancy Mason Bradbury and Scott Bradbury (2012)
Croxton Play of the Sacrament, edited by John T. Sebastian (2012)
Ten Bourdes, edited by Melissa M. Furrow (2013)
Lybeaus Desconus, edited by Eve Salisbury and James Weldon (2013)
The Complete Harley 2253 Manuscript, Vol. 2, edited and translated by Susanna Fein with David Raybin and Jan Ziolkowski (2014); Vol. 3 (2015)

Commentary Series

Haimo of Auxerre, *Commentary on the Book of Jonah*, translated with an introduction and notes by Deborah Everhart (1993)
Medieval Exegesis in Translation: Commentaries on the Book of Ruth, translated with an introduction and notes by Lesley Smith (1996)
Nicholas of Lyra's Apocalypse Commentary, translated with an introduction and notes by Philip D. W. Krey (1997)
Rabbi Ezra Ben Solomon of Gerona, *Commentary on the Song of Songs and Other Kabbalistic Commentaries*, selected, translated, and annotated by Seth Brody (1999)
John Wyclif, *On the Truth of Holy Scripture*, translated with an introduction and notes by Ian Christopher Levy (2001)
Second Thessalonians: Two Early Medieval Apocalyptic Commentaries, introduced and translated by Steven R. Cartwright and Kevin L. Hughes (2001)
The "Glossa Ordinaria" on the Song of Songs, translated with an introduction and notes by Mary Dove (2004)
The Seven Seals of the Apocalypse: Medieval Texts in Translation, translated with an introduction and notes by Francis X. Gumerlock (2009)
The "Glossa Ordinaria" on Romans, translated with an introduction and notes by Michael Scott Woodward (2011)

Documents of Practice Series

Love and Marriage in Late Medieval London, selected, translated, and introduced by Shannon McSheffrey (1995)

Sources for the History of Medicine in Late Medieval England, selected, introduced, and translated by Carole Rawcliffe (1995)

A Slice of Life: Selected Documents of Medieval English Peasant Experience, edited, translated, and with an introduction by Edwin Brezette DeWindt (1996)

Regular Life: Monastic, Canonical, and Mendicant "Rules," selected and introduced by Douglas J. McMillan and Kathryn Smith Fladenmuller (1997); second edition, selected and introduced by Daniel Marcel La Corte and Douglas J. McMillan (2004)

Women and Monasticism in Medieval Europe: Sisters and Patrons of the Cistercian Reform, selected, translated, and with an introduction by Constance H. Berman (2002)

Medieval Notaries and Their Acts: The 1327–1328 Register of Jean Holanie, introduced, edited, and translated by Kathryn L. Reyerson and Debra A. Salata (2004)

John Stone's Chronicle: Christ Church Priory, Canterbury, 1417–1472, selected, translated, and introduced by Meriel Connor (2010)

Medieval German Texts in Bilingual Editions Series

Sovereignty and Salvation in the Vernacular, 1050–1150, introduction, translations, and notes by James A. Schultz (2000)

Ava's New Testament Narratives: "When the Old Law Passed Away," introduction, translation, and notes by James A. Rushing, Jr. (2003)

History as Literature: German World Chronicles of the Thirteenth Century in Verse, introduction, translation, and notes by R. Graeme Dunphy (2003)

Thomasin von Zirclaria, *Der Welsche Gast (The Italian Guest)*, translated by Marion Gibbs and Winder McConnell (2009)

Ladies, Whores, and Holy Women: A Sourcebook in Courtly, Religious, and Urban Cultures of Late Medieval Germany, introductions, translations, and notes by Ann Marie Rasmussen and Sarah Westphal-Wihl (2010)

Varia

The Study of Chivalry: Resources and Approaches, edited by Howell Chickering and Thomas H. Seiler (1988)

Studies in the Harley Manuscript: The Scribes, Contents, and Social Contexts of British Library MS Harley 2253, edited by Susanna Fein (2000)

The Liturgy of the Medieval Church, edited by Thomas J. Heffernan and E. Ann Matter (2001; second edition 2005)

Johannes de Grocheio, *Ars musice*, edited and translated by Constant J. Mews, John N. Crossley, Catherine Jeffreys, Leigh McKinnon, and Carol J. Williams (2011)

To Order Please Contact:

Medieval Institute Publications
Western Michigan University
Kalamazoo, MI 49008-5432
Phone (269) 387-8755
FAX (269) 387-8750
http://www.wmich.edu/medieval/mip/index.html

Typeset in 10/13 New Baskerville
and Golden Cockerel Ornaments display
Manufactured by Cushing-Malloy, Inc.
Medieval Institute Publications
College of Arts and Sciences
Western Michigan University
1903 W. Michigan Avenue
Kalamazoo, MI 49008-5432
http:/ /www.wmich.edu/medieval/mip

WESTERN MICHIGAN UNIVERSITY